ON THE COVER...

Ed Ruscha's *George's Flag* canvas adumbrates multiple levels of meaning. First off, it's a pretty picture. Secondly, it invokes patriotism, Old Glory billowing in the breezes. Thirdly, it connects with Hollywood, the elongated image recalls a CinemaScope film. Finally, the background coloring of sunset maroons and yellows recalls the nineteenth-century romantic realist landscape paintings of Frederic Church, Thomas Cole, even Albert Bierstadt, and others who studied abroad and were indebted to Dutch landscape painters of the seventeenth century.

Ruscha's piece resonates, paraphrasing Warren Buffett's pronouncement that it was a mistake to bet against America for the past 237 years. At the November 2014 Christie's auction, Ruscha's *Smash* sold for a record $30.4 million, estimated at $15 million to $20 million. Sotheby's Jasper Johns' *Flag*, a 1983 painting hardly more than a foot square, made $36 million the night before. It was also a record for a Johns canvas, estimated at $15 million to $20 million in the catalog.

Master Class
FOR
Investors

Master Class

FOR

Investors

STAND ALONE TO WIN BIG

Martin Sosnoff

ATALANTA PRESS
NEW YORK

ISBN 978-0-692-37761-1
eBook ISBN 978-0-692-42093-5
All photo permissions appear on page IX

Project Manager, Della R. Mancuso, Mancuso Associates, Inc.
Designed by Mary Kornblum, CMYK Design, Inc.
Edited by Rick Ball
Graphs prepared by Network Graphics
Composition by Jeffrey Stern
Printed in the United States of America
First Edition

9 8 7 6 5 4 3 2 1

For Toni, the one and only

*«When you write down the good things you ought
to have done, and leave out the bad things
you did do, that's memoirs.»*

WILL ROGERS

Contents

continued

ILLUSTRATIONS

GRAPHS AND TABLES

My Streetwise Glossary

■ **activist** An old greenmailer now commanding more capital. Respected in boardrooms, even by the *Wall Street Journal*. Carl Icahn.

■ **Amazon.com** Either the next Pan American Airways, killed by its ambition, or a speculator's dream.

■ **balance sheet** What nobody—excepting junk bond players—cares about until a company is on the brink of bankruptcy.

■ **book value** What nobody ever cared about—except Larry Tisch and Warren Buffett.

■ **discounted cash flow** What analysts use to justify stocks that sell at outrageous valuations.

■ **downside surprise** A quarterly occurrence.

■ **EBITDA** What analysts use to justify stocks that sell at outrageous valuations.

■ **equity risk premium** Another way of valuing the market through the rearview mirror. When stocks go up, academics reason why the equity risk premium should go to zero (Dow 36,000). When stocks decline (Black Monday), everyone believes the equity risk premium was too low.

■ **executive compensation** Don't ask. Read the proxy document and vote no.

■ **Fed watching** What to do so you know what will be in their brains 12 months out.

■ **free cash flow** What analysts and some businessmen use to justify properties that sell at outrageous valuations or discounts. Free cash flow above a 6 percent yield gets my attention.

■ **greenspeak** What Treasury bond futures discounted three months in advance, although always indecipherable.

■ **guidance** What management hands out to lazy analysts. The objective is to get 100 analysts projecting earnings within a penny of each other. Management then beats the consensus by a penny. This makes the stock go up—as in Intel.

■ **index funds** A *Consumer Reports* best buy.

■ **irrational exuberance** A speculative way of life that Alan Greenspan disdained but John Maynard Keynes embraced and took advantage of as a commodities trader.

■ **long-term buy**   How analysts denote a stock that is likely to remain doggy for years and years.

■ **market technician**   Someone who writes opinions on his wife's ironing board. Also an oxymoron.

■ **metrics**   Shorthand for income statement analysis inclusive of gross margins, revenue growth, cash flow and pretax earnings. A company has good or bad metrics based on quarterly comparisons.

■ **money market fund**   The worst place to put your money maybe for five years longer.

■ **NASDAQ**   A gigantic car wash emporium that uses dirty water and normally humbles its users.

■ **neutral**   How analysts classify a stock that is nearly a disaster.

■ **private equity operators**   What savvy politicians yearn to be after leaving office.

■ **S&P 500 Index**   What almost everyone is measured against, because it's easy to beat, sometimes.

■ **sequential growth**   Quarter-over-quarter growth rather than year-over-year comparisons. Stocks that sell at 80 times earnings or more must demonstrate sequential growth of 15 percent or better. Otherwise, they dive off your screen. (No company can do this for more than a couple of years.)

■ **sombrero formation**   NASDAQ's and Greece's roller-coaster trajectory from the bubble top.

■ **stock picker's market**   Nobody has the foggiest idea what happens next. Good luck, schmuck!

■ **the takeaway**   After a lengthy and discursive session with management, analysts leave with a new spin to the earnings outlook. (It can be positive or neutral, never negative, but definitely what management wants you to take away.)

■ **the triple top**   What the market fought for 14 years and then broke out of to everyone's surprise.

■ **upside surprise**   A very rare occurrence.

■ **VIX**   A dumb indicator of sentiment options traders and market technicians follow despite its many sudden reversals.

■ **volatility**   A way of life. Also, what made George Soros super-rich.

Investment Methodology

1

Government Spending Emphasis
Federal Reserve Policy Emphasis
Analysis of Critical Economic Variables
GNP Analysis of Demand Momentum
Review of Inflation Momentum
Interest Rate Forecast
Capital Formation Environment

2

Balance of Payments Trends
Rate of Change in OPEC Surplus
Price Changes in Precious Metals
Interest Rate Review by Major Countries
Inflation Review by Major Countries
    The Dollar vs. Other Currencies
    Geopolitical Changes
    Equity Valuation Comparison

3

Current and Projected Institutional Cash
    Flows and Asset Allocation
Analysis of Institutional and Corporate Cash
    Flow and Asset Allocation
Total Value of Equities to New Issue Supply
Dollar Value to New Issues to Cash Flow
Speculation Analysis (Margin Debits, Low/
    High Price Ratio) Turnover,
    Volatility of Low Price Stocks

4

Analysis of Riskless Return to Our Required
    Attractive Return
Analysis of Intermediate Bond Yields to
    Riskless Rate
Analysis of Long-Term Bond Yields to
    Intermediate and Riskless Yields
Determination of Alternatives to T-Bills
    Relative to Yield Curve
Analysis of S&P 500 Current and Forecast
    Earnings, Yield and Rate of Return on Equity
Projected Range of Price/Earnings Multiple
    for S&P 500
Total Return Analysis Equities to Various
    Bond Sectors
Price to Book & Replacement Value Analysis
    Mix of Equities to Fixed Income

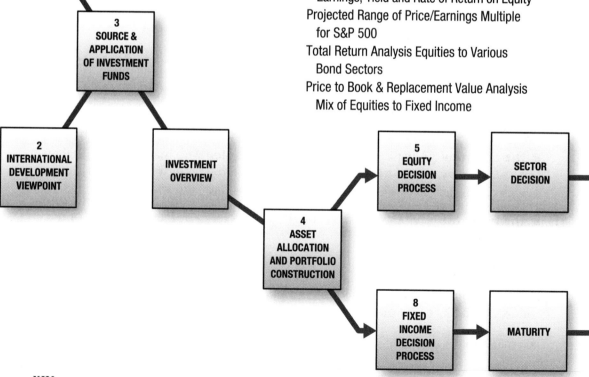

5

SECTOR DECISION
Growth Industries
Cyclical Growth Industries
Cyclical Industries
Energy and Natural Resources
Interest Sensitive Industries

SECTOR ANALYSIS
Macroeconomic Earnings Determinants
Relative Earnings Comparison
Changes in Return on Capital
Relative Value of Assets, Earnings and
    Equity Prices
Current P/E, Book Value to Historical Ranges

6

Revenue Growth
Cost Analysis
Leverage Factors
Relative Earnings Momentum
Relative ROE Momentum
Reinvestment Rate Comparisons
Net Cash Flow Trends
Relative P/E Ratio to S&P 500 Index
Investor Attitudes
Technical Review

7

Earnings Projections
Dividend Growth Projections
Relative P/E Judgment
Relative and Absolute P/E Comparison
Development of Risk/Gain Expectations
Estimate of Realizable Asset Value
Analysis of Quality of Earnings

8

Maturity Mix
Classification Mix
Government/Agency vs. Corporate
    Quality Ratings

9

Loss Limitation Review
Fundamental Changes in Perception
Valuation Change
Technical Deterioration
Senior Management Accountability

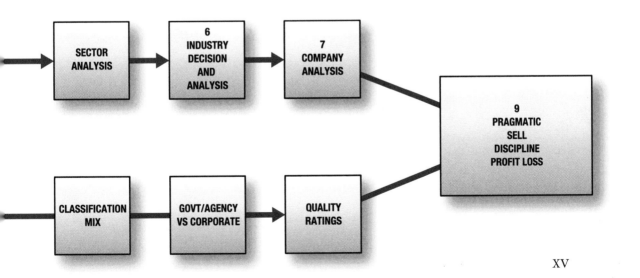

Acknowledgements

First, I need to doff my hat to those who were close to me, but now departed. Strangely, my fiction writing professor at the City College of New York thought I could be the next Paddy Chayefsky, but I wasn't. Wall Street beckoned me, Teddy Goodman succumbed.

My old, old friend Jerry Goodman, who wrote *The Money Game*, inspired my financial writing. Be funny, iconoclastic and bedrock serious as well. Jim Michaels, *Forbes'* editor in chief for decades, made me toe the line. I couldn't use Yiddish expressions. His readers in South Dakota would scratch their heads. I never listened. Bob Lenzner was my mediator with Michaels, and he kept me writing.

Nobody on The Street ever taught me much, directly, but I learned a lot by watching and doing. Mike Milken comes to mind, along with Barton Biggs and George Soros. Jerry Tsai and Larry Tisch were always chock-full of ideas, concepts and actionable stocks, both long and short. I miss the interchange at the Regency breakfast room. I used Tisch as a role model: Be tough, fearless, but ethical and fair in all your dealings.

This book was put together by a team of very professional operators, namely Della Mancuso, Mary Kornblum and Rick Ball, a great copy editor who found more dangling participles than you could shake a stick at.

For my partner of some decades, Craig Steinberg, many thanks for your unwavering supportiveness and for restraining me from jumping into the river when a stock blew up.

My personal assistant, Julie Gold, who's unflappable, typed and retyped countless chapters while perusing much fact checking and confirming research.

Lastly, but also firstly, my wife, Toni, is always there when I cry for help. Toni reads my stuff and polishes it to a high gloss after many challenges on diction, paragraph structure and chapter organization.

Bless you all!

INTRODUCTION

Tomorrow Ain't Another Day

September 11, 2001

"**Y**ou get your ass out of that meeting! Now!" My wife Toni's voice came in hysterical but muffled on my Nextel cellphone.

"I can't leave this second," I said. "We are deep into this finance committee meeting. It could take NYU into the ranks of the big three 'B' schools. Harvard, Wharton, whatever."

"Rome is burning, you idiot! Haven't you heard? Two jet planes plowed into the World Trade Center's twin towers. They're burning out of control, imploding."

"I'll leave in fifteen minutes."

"Now! Now! Get out of that building if you love me. Head uptown on foot. I'll be waiting on the plaza at 101 Park."

"I'm only on the eleventh floor."

"Have you tried jumping from the eleventh story?"

"It's not an option. I'm snapping shut my rucksack and leaving."

Six of us, with Stern School of Business dean George Daly, had figured out $43 million would do the trick. Raise faculty salaries competitive with Harvard, force early retirement and renovate several existing halls. The job was convincing the university's board of trustees to approve our retention of annual surpluses from tuition and fees, some $8 million per annum. Business schools, unlike liberal arts colleges, make money. When I asked a Chinese girl why so many Asians in New York wanted an MBA, I got a snappy answer. "Why not?"

The dean called our attention to black smoke belching and billowing irrepressibly from the upper facade of a WTC tower. "Do we want to go up on the roof and watch?" an assistant dean asked. This was said in a matter-of-fact voice for which the dean would apologize the next day in a phone conversation when the depth of the calamity had sunk in.

I walked uptown on University Place, pivoting backwards every 20 or 30 steps to gaze at the wounded tower. Office workers streamed out of buildings on both sides of lower Park Avenue, walking north briskly, hushed, but without panic. The stray cars in the street idled patiently, waiting for the waves of pedestrians to part. They waited a long time.

The market, of course, would close. Hong Kong, Tokyo and the bourses of Europe would sell off the next day, probably 5 percent, I mused. How many more panics would I endure? Never sell into panics. My only question is whether I buy aggressively on day two or just hang in. The Cuban missile crisis, Jack Kennedy's face-off with Roger Blough over steel price increases, Black Monday—you had to buy them all. It was like shoving in your table stakes and waiting for the fifth card to turn over.

Was this different? Had I made too much money in the trenches over 50 years? What more did I have to prove? The first beard on The Street in '64 was mine. When I read about the symposium on the Cuban missile crisis at Princeton University in the nineties, it surfaced that our country had been within a hair's breadth of a nuclear holocaust. The Cubans itched to launch the Russian intermediate-range missiles at our coastal cities. The Russians said *nyet*. Instead of putting all my money into IBM and Xerox that afternoon in 1962, I should have booked a plane for Toronto. Sometimes you get lucky—with shit for brains.

As I plodded methodically up Park Avenue, I remembered where I was on Pearl Harbor Day: shooting baskets in the schoolyard of P.S. 90, East Bronx. It was cold and windy. My fingers stiffened and I came up short on successive set shots. I ditched the three-man pickup game and headed home.

War for a 10-year-old was something you read about in your history textbook. The D-day Parade that flowed south down the Grand Concourse from Fordham Road to Cardinal Hayes High School was for me a straight business day, not a commemoration. I sold cat balloons, a quarter apiece, stretching the rubber and then inflating the balloon with a portable pump slung on my shoulder like a burp gun. Middle-aged veterans of World War I worked the crowd, too, aggressively pinning cloth poppies on the lapels of eligible males who had to cough up a buck, sometimes less. I pushed whiskered cat balloons on sticks into the hands of the kindergarten crowd. Selling out a gross of balloons made me 25 bucks, a small fortune in the early forties.

I never forgot this lesson. When the circus is in town, you hustle and sell peanuts. When there's speculation in the air, you buy, buy, buy and save the research for later. I terminate analysts and money managers who lose their nerve. If you have six positives to buy a stock matched by six negatives and it's too hard to make a decision, go teach Security Analysis 101 somewhere. Make yourself into a many-handed economist, but get out of my office. The prime reason to do security analysis is to forge courage to buy stocks after they've disconnected from reality on the downside.

After 45 minutes on foot, I met Toni on the plaza of 101 Park Avenue. "You are in denial," she said. "The towers have collapsed. The Pentagon is on fire; maybe the Sears Tower in Chicago is hit. God knows what's next. The least you could have done was think of me. The cellphones don't work. I can't reach the kids. Let's head for Central Park. I'll feel safer."

I hugged Toni sheepishly, apologizing for my indefensible reaction. I trace back my cold-blooded attitude towards public spectacles to my balloon days on the Grand Concourse. When the locals panic, you start buying. Whoever said money managers aren't snakes, ever ready to strike at a poor mouse trembling and frozen in its predator's hungry, beady eyes?

You do what you have to do if you want to get rich when you're young. Khrushchev ordered the Russian freighters to turn about and I bounced home across the Brooklyn Bridge feeling like a million. The mechanical tape ran six hours late that day, and I wouldn't know what I had paid for all the Xerox I gobbled up until tomorrow. At Merrill Lynch's offices, willowy girls with trim ankles chalked up on blackboards the prices for Dow Industrials that they scanned off the chattering ticker.

The U.S. Steel vs. Jack Kennedy face-off was less traumatic. Wall Street in 1961–'62 was a button-down white shirt and fedora enclave. Double-breasted suited partners in brokerage houses loathed Democrats in the White House. Kennedy obviously was anti-business. Price controls lurked around the corner. But they overlooked Joe Kennedy, who advised his son to tone down his rhetoric. The paper ticker that ran across Joe Granville's desk then lagged by four hours. I was next door over. Joe was E.F. Hutton's gabby market letter writer. Every house put out a daily letter, Teletyped to all offices. The brokers digested its contents—technical gibberish—with donuts and coffee.

Kennedy ran neck 'n' neck with Nixon in the 1960 election. I watched him, standing up in his open black Caddy convertible, waving to the crowd along lower Broadway. From my twelfth-floor Hutton office, Kennedy looked suntanned, blue-serge suited, almost collegiate. Who knew that he had jaundice? When it was Nixon's turn, Dick Fant, Hutton's research partner, dropped off a carton of multicolored confetti. I was told to scatter it out my window as Nixon passed by;

I refused. Dick Fant caught my eye but decided to let it pass. After all, he had mentored me, taught me how to stand alone once I completed my research.

Fant, a Virginian with impeccable manners, was the only boss I ever loved like a father. Two years later he would succumb to stomach cancer. We always addressed him as Mr. Fant. His last words to me from his hospital bed were "Martin, you're a fine analyst. Don't believe more than half of what anyone tells you, and don't take notes while you're interviewing the headman. You'll miss the nuances. Watch his face and listen to the inflections of his voice." It was the best advice I ever got, and I followed it religiously. So do professional poker players in every hand they stick in.

When '87's Black Monday unfolded, I was up to my ass in a hostile tender bid for Caesars World. I had owned 15 percent of Caesars for years. No practicing money manager with institutional clients had ever done a "hostile." Later, in the mid-nineties, Michael Price would be revered in the press for his proactive stance against custodial managements. I was at least five years ahead of my time and labeled "controversial," which is a euphemism for a person of uncertain heritage. The commuters from Greenwich would whisper to each other as they flapped their crispy *WSJ*s off page one. Post-Enron, the SEC began to exhort money managers to vote proxies aggressively and act like owners, not passive shareholders.

Days after Black Monday, Jerry Tsai, the first gutsy Manhattan Fund manager in the early sixties, gave a reception in the Pierre ballroom for his Street buddies. His bubbly, curly-headed bride looked like a young Beverly Sills. I remember standing next to Larry Tisch, discussing the market's risk premium. It had to rise, I said, as I thought of my four million shares of Caesars cascading down from the mid-twenties to 10 bucks. Tisch, a monosyllabic player, just nodded his head. Years later, I would learn that he was buying the market like I had in the early sixties. I stood frozen in my tracks, immobilized in my Caesars position with no checkbook ready-to-buy.

Here I was, enmeshed in a takeover filled with tense litigation, making investment bankers, lawyers and syndicate banks rich. Gaming is a regulated industry. I had a presence for years in Nevada but none in New Jersey. Some assistant professor in a New Jersey State teachers college opined that my application should be denied. Too much leverage. I wrote off $20 million in fees and expenses and went back to managing money. Grandiosity had crept into my psyche. Where was the poker-faced kid cold-bloodily stuffing buy slips into the pneumatic tube? Gone, but not forgotten. I went back to work. Gimme a yellow pad, a pencil and a telephone and I'll operate. Be a buyer and seller of paper, I thought. Keep a low profile. Read 10-Ks and 10-Qs. If you want to run a business, buy yourself a grey flannel suit and go work for General Motors or Alcoa.

During the demoralizing summer of '02, when chief financial officers put guns to their heads or marched off to courthouses in handcuffs, I started to buy hundreds of thousands of shares in single-digit stocks—Nextel, AOL Time Warner and El Paso. A hailstorm of fear pelted the market, day after day. You make serious money doing what's hard to do when you do it. Warren Buffett bought the Williams pipeline for 6.5 times cash flow and El Paso rose 40 percent in one day's trading. The asset value of its properties, net of debt, was no longer conjectural. Nextel doubled after its second-quarter results blew way past the analysts' consensus. America Online as yet struggled against page-one stories in the *New York Times* and the *Wall Street Journal*. The media love to kick around their competition. The media and short sellers were winning, but not for long.

Multibillion-dollar accounting scandals like Enron, Qwest Communications, Adelphia Communications and WorldCom surfaced weekly. General Electric, General Motors and Coca-Cola decided to expense options issuance because it would cost them just pennies per share. Microsoft, with options outstanding of 20 percent of their capitalization, stuck sullen and silent. The economy had drifted back to 1 percent GDP momentum while the consensus was at 3 percent, the normal growth pattern. GM hurriedly reinstituted zero-cost financing to keep its factories humming. Core retailers like Wal-Mart, Costco and Sears, Roebuck sagged, while Tiffany collapsed. The market was about to bet that the consumer wouldn't and couldn't carry the economy. The wealth effect! The wealth effect! Nonsense proliferated.

All this misplaced bearishness unfolded while I was island hopping in the Aegean Sea. There I was, with an immature gull huddled beside me on the harshly pebbled beach. He rested on brown-and-white outstretched wings like a downed airliner. Then his head nodded. When it touched the spent surf's edge he labored to lift it, exhausted, near death. I gazed skyward for his mother hovering to feed him a fish, but he was abandoned. My companion keened weakly, then lifted himself, then keeled over. When his hooked, yellow bill touched the water, he twisted his head sideways and I saw the sunken, dulled eye. He sank one last time, then expired in three inches of quiet water. The gull's wing and tail feathers fanned out and he bobbed like an orange peel in the gentle surf.

I gingerly picked my way over the rocky bottom into deeper water, slipped my goggles down over my eyes and swam off. Don't identify with an expiring gull unless you have to, I thought. I swam parallel to the beach with a methodical breaststroke. The Aegean Sea was cold, then invigorating and finally too cold. I came out when my toes stiffened, ready to cramp. "All oceans are polluted, no matter how beautiful they look," my eye surgeon had warned me. "Don't screw up my corneal transplant work." The yacht's tender beached beside me and I swiveled over the rubber pontoon. A fax had arrived hours ago. My old buddy Joel Leff had expired, finally, from an inoperable brain tumor. I had filled my swim time composing an obit notice for faxing to the *New York Times*:

We were young together, money managers on a high floor in the GM building gazing out at a world we longed to own. I shall miss the jaunty phrase, the Edwardian tailoring, the incisive cerebration and impeccable taste in everything. A cross between Mercutio and Tybalt, you are imprinted in my memory, so the decades-long friendship endures.

The market had punctuated our idyllic meandering in the Aegean Sea with daily declines of 2 percent, sometimes more. Closing prices on my portfolio arrived near midnight. Captain Mike would find me in the salon and hand me the fax sheet—to be digested with a double espresso and baklava. Our guests, five couples, were actors, writers, lawyers and doctors. A professional reading of *The Vagina Monologues* was under way. My personal portfolio, mainly HMOs and insurance properties like Ace, was shedding millions, but I kept a smiley face. Nothing I owned was pricey, but nothing was too cheap to pick off or average down.

"I think a few more shoes have to drop," I said to Toni.

"Maybe everything in Imelda Marcos's closet," she shot back.

Lainie Kazan, who played for peanuts in *The Vagina Monologues* on Broadway, was riffing her extended Jewish orgasm. We sat back and howled. I longed for one more glorious bull market before I went to the Great Barn in the star-studded western sky. My God, I thought, the late nineties were a sham. When you adjusted for the tons of options issuance, outrageous write-offs and crazy, optimistic actuarial assumptions on corporate pension funds, earnings just grew at their historical rate, maybe 4 percent, not the 8 percent to 9 percent all the pundits, including Alan Greenspan, had accepted.

"When the S&P 500 Index hits 750, stocks are distressed paper," I mused. Periodically surfacing, courageous value players like Larry Tisch, Sam Zell in real estate, more recently, Carl Icahn picking off Apple, weigh in; first silently, then publicly.

My ship's engines purred with a rich resonance that reminded me of an old Pan Am flying boat revving up in the bay at LaGuardia Airport. I used to bicycle out from the East Bronx to watch the lumbering flying boats take off. For a nine-year-old, there was a big world out there. It was 1942. The transistor wouldn't break out of Bell Laboratories till the late fifties, when I arrived on Wall Street. I rode my brother's 28-inch bike and had to wait for the pedals to come up to my feet. The market in the summer of '02 felt the same way. No solid connection.

"What's our game plan if they bomb Grand Central Station, Lincoln Center, Yankee Stadium—everywhere we go?" I asked Toni. The grand salon had quieted down after the reading.

She shot back at me, "It's not an 'if.' It's how soon and how often they hit us. They poison the watershed lakes; a chlorine gas cloud blows in from Jersey. Maybe they crack open the reactor at Indian Point. Always a weak link in the chain."

"If you believe all that, what are we doing in the Big Apple?"

"A good question. Why can't you work out of Poughkeepsie? Nobody cares about Poughkeepsie except Vassar. We should buy motor scooters. I'm storing three cases of Evian in the wine cellar. You need water to survive. We'll never get out of the city. I'm tipping the garage manager twenty bucks, monthly, to keep our car up front."

"In '62," I said, "during the Cuban missile showdown, even LaGuardia stayed open. You could have hopped a plane and landed in Toronto an hour later. That option's gone."

"What did you do?" Toni asked.

"I stayed at my desk. Bought the market, fully leveraged, at twenty-seven years old. It was a no-brainer. If the Russian freighter carrying missiles to Cuba didn't heave to for our navy it was academic. World War III. 'Bye-bye, Miss American Pie.' I should have waitlisted myself to Toronto, the Bahamas, anywhere but 61 Broadway. You do things when you're young that you don't do later on," I said.

"What about now?" Toni pressed on. "How do we hedge our bets now? Your biggest positions are HMOs and casualty underwriters. Total disasters if Al-Qaeda detonates a dirty bomb over New York. Thousands upon thousands of casualties. The hospitals overwhelmed. Panic in the streets."

"There's reason to run a market-neutral portfolio today," I said. "The market carries no risk premium for terrorism, actually for anything negative that could happen. We're looking at a 30 to 50 percent schmeiss in its valuation. A market back to 10 or 12 times earnings like in '82 when interest rates were 15 percent on FNMA paper and Chrysler ran out of working capital. You don't want to own AAA munies, either. Just Treasury bonds. Interest rates go to 4 percent like in the early sixties. [By August they were almost there.] If nothing happens you can't hedge by selling S&P 100 futures. Too expensive. Cost you 3 percent or 4 percent every three months to cover your ass."

"I get the picture," Toni said. "Don't we need hard assets in the safe? Diamonds, lots of Ben Franklins? I pulled our hiking boots out of the closet, rucksacks, too. Then we hop on our scooters."

"I'm with you," I said. "Head for the Canadian border. Fly to Costa Rica. They don't stamp passports there for the hop to Cuba. Dollar bills go far in Havana. We lease a house, maybe fly to Hong Kong. Get us a sampan in Harbour Grand Kowloon."

"How much can we carry with us?" Toni was into the problem.

"I figure $25,000 in fives, twenties and C-notes," I said. "We put $100,000 into 3-karat diamonds. Grade D flawless. Maybe three or four stones. Carry the toy poodles with us. Tyrone and Mary cache the gems in their leather collars."

"You better not be putting me on," Toni said. "The world has changed… for the next hundred years. You've finally learned to keep your cellphone on and recharge it before you go to bed."

"But I'm not ready to run a market-neutral portfolio with our money. I can short drug stocks and airlines against my hospital and HMO positions. Brokers are great shorts against our insurance holdings. The public ain't coming back… maybe for years 'n' years. You can't believe in America 365 days a year any longer. Schwab just announced another layoff."

The market is in denial, I thought, not me. The average tech house with position on the board—Intel, Dell and Microsoft—sold at 30 times forward 12-month earnings projections. Six months ago they sold at 40 to 50 times forward estimates. Tyco was supposed to be another GE. (Later, its headman, Dennis Kozlowski, was packed off to the slammer.) The market took a third off GE, IBM and AIG. Now they are selling at 15 to 20 times forward numbers and nobody believes in the numbers. Pension fund profits had melted down. Actuarial assumptions needed to be lowered substantively later this year and next. Most of GM's earnings would be earmarked for its pension fund deficit and health care costs for retirees. The great tech houses might have to expense up to 25 percent of their earnings on existing option programs. That can of worms rested outside their front door.

One by one, analysts were beginning to read and comment on 10-Ks, 10-Qs and proxy statements to cipher prospective dilution. Microsoft had options on 900 million outstanding shares on a 5.4 billion share base. For years, Intel, Dell, Microsoft and others sold put options on hundreds of millions of shares that were now in the money. They would be buying back very expensive stock. Dell would be tapping all its earnings in fiscal '03 to cover over $2 billion put options at $45 a share with its stock at $24. Microsoft spends billions buying back shares, annually, to keep down dilution. The transfer of wealth from shareholders to management and its employees someday had to end. The betrayal of capitalism by Enron, Tyco, Dynegy and its ilk did raise the consciousness of money managers, shareholders, the SEC, Congress, even the FASB and the NYSE—all our institutions that had failed us along with the FBI, the FAA and the CIA.

Cisco, IBM, Intel, Citigroup, AIG, GE, Microsoft, Dell—in other words half the market cap of the S&P 500 Index—should carry a complexity discount, even a duplicity discount, for years to come. The footnotes in annual reports, 10-K's and proxy statements have become pivotal analytical documents. But analysts still ignore the enormous variance between GAAP (Generally Accepted Accounting Principles) and non-GAAP earnings, which exclude options dilution.

After the 2000 tech bubble, it was open season on the 25 largest-cap properties in the S&P 500 Index. Price-earnings ratios stood crushed by as much as 30 percent since yearend '01—without any serious earnings upsets. The mid-cap tech sector had sold at 40 to 50 times projected earnings, but now at 30 times. Many still sold at 10 times book value. The best you could say then about benchmark properties like Applied Materials, Nokia, Veritas Software and Cisco was that the metric of market value to revenues had come down from 10 and over to mid-single digits. In the heady days of the Internet, Yahoo sold at 100 times revenues. Analysts rationalized this outrageous metric by resorting to elaborate discounted cash flow modeling. The problem with the market is not terrorism, or accounting mufti-pufti, I thought, but overvaluation.

If you believed, as I did, that 2015 corporate earnings were likely to compound near 5 percent, with good dividend growth and 30-year Treasuries ranging no higher than 4 percent, the S&P 500 was likely to sell at 15 times earnings or better for years to come. This is bull market stuff. Gone are the days of $500-billion market capitalizations for Microsoft and GE. Apple is number one, at over $700 billion. Only when you go below the $100-billion market caps do you find the median multiplier below 15 times earnings. For 2014, there was major upside in the defense sector, hospitals, HMOs, many regional banks and fire and casualty underwriters. They all carried one common denominator: a low price-earnings ratio. My rule of thumb is to own underappreciated or controversial properties at one times their growth rate. Apple and Facebook qualify.

Let's not blame geopolitical upsets and terrorism for manic-depressive markets.

Overvaluation and corporate greed got out of hand in 2007. Warren Buffett got it right. His salary is nominal, nobody gets options, and he buys companies for cash, if possible. Do a good job and here's your cash bonus. We will never get back to that old-fashioned construct, so the market will be the indirect arbiter of what's fair. If you use up half or all your annual earnings for stock buybacks to neutralize options issuance, shareholders finally will wake up and sell. Hopefully, pirate capitalism is on its last legs. So far I'm wrong. Software houses like Salesforce.com take too much away from shareholders for themselves. Their share count compounds at 5 percent.

Investors with a sense of history know that the rate of return on equities can be negative even for a 10-year span. The historic rate of return on equities comes in at 6.1 percent, with an equity risk premium of 2.4 percent and the inflation-adjusted rate of return on 10-year Treasuries at 3.7 percent. Even the Greenspan valuation model is deeply flawed. In the absence of rising valuation levels, real returns are systemically lower than earnings yields throughout financial history. Calling the market cheap when Treasuries are yielding 4 percent has no meaning if AAA corporates are closer to 6 percent. The first sign of GDP resurgence will tighten this spread, overnight.

For me, it's always sombrero time, but as a fully invested skeptic I hope my sense of valuation bails me out. A sombrero chart formation is normally a profile of a moribund property. It was WorldCom, US Airways, even American Airlines. Chartists chant Kaddish when they uncover sombreros, but there may be easily mined gold therein. After their roller-coaster rides in 2008–'09 you coulda bought Citigroup and Bank of America for a song. Same goes for US Airways, MGIC Investment and Sirius XM Radio.

JDS Uniphase was the quintessential sombrero chart of the nineties. Like plastics in the postwar era, optoelectronics was the catchphrase in tech mania. What saved JDSU from falling off the chart into bankruptcy was a cash hoard of $1 billion. At its peak, JDSU sold at 100 times revenues. Actually, NASDAQ itself, same years, traced a giant sombrero, a fitting metaphor for The Street's and everyone's irrational exuberance, a polite phrase for stupidity.

I do keep my sixties pocket slide rule on the desk as a reminder that numbers finally govern, not words. Courage is a seldom remarked trait of a successful money manager who gets his numbers right and calls in his buy or sell orders, going against the grain of sentiment, what everyone thinks they know. Judy's prancing companions on the yellow brick road had it right: You need a heart, brain and courage.

On 9/11, like the Tin Man, I coulda used a heart, but it had nothing to do with investing and everything to do with staying alive.

From the pre-meltdown Internet insanity near 1,600 on the S&P 500, the index traced a fat W formation. It touched down under 800 during this mini-recession late in 2002. Then the market took a 45-degree upward slope until yearend 2007. The financial meltdown of 2008 to early 2009 set back the averages momentarily below 700. Then we made the right side of the W, taking out the old 2000 high late in 2013.

Net, net of the whole thing, the market acted like a roller coaster over 14 years with ample good reasons for its jitterbugging. If you seriously violated conventional valuation discipline, chances are you got washed out with little wherewithal for a comeback.

PART I

The Art of Money Management

JEAN-MICHEL BASQUIAT, UNTITLED, 1982

ONE

The Market Is Never Efficient

*N*obody believes me when I tell them how I sold newspapers in front of Yankee Stadium when I was barely six years old. It's true. My brother George, three years my elder, introduced me to Fats, the genial newsstand dealer who would give us 10 *New York Suns* and *Journal-Americans*. These were the afternoon papers that front-paged box scores and Aqueduct's racing results.

In the 1930s baseball was an afternoon game, starting at 3:00 p.m. The "break" when the crowd emptied out of the stands came early evening, and you needed something to read as you strap-hanged on the shoulder-high loops that dangled in the subway cars that took you to Times Square or more distant station stops.

I made a penny on a 3-cent newspaper. George, bigger and more visible to the "break" crowd, would sell 20 or so papers and was Fats's favorite. "Paper, paper here! Latest box scores." George's voice carried better than mine. Fifty years later, Mike Milken would paraphrase what I had learned as a street kid. "You gotta give them what they want when they want it." It was his way of coaxing out a block of stock when he had the other side of the trade. A good trader goes for both sides, buyer and seller. Milken understood leverage; at 6 years old, I had no clue. In the seventies, Mike explained to me his MAD ratio. When the market value of a stock is greater than the market value of its debt, the company is financeable, nowhere near insolvency.

By the time I was 10 or 11, I had graduated to bigger and better things at the stadium. The Sosnoffs, a family of five, lived in a three-room walk-up apartment on Sherman Avenue, bordered by Grant and Sheridan east and west, a 10-minute walk to the stadium. Summers, I'd show up every morning for a turnstile boy's job. Ticket-takers in red caps tore stubs in half and I'd turn the stile. It had a counter, so you didn't want it to spin out of control. I got 50 cents for this job and by the second inning was released to sit in any unreserved seat in the outfield.

To this day I can recite the Yankees' 1939 starting lineup. I remember Lou Gehrig in pre-game practice throwing a sky-high ball to himself while gabbing with Bill Dickey, the Yankees' statuesque catcher, at home plate. Gehrig would backhand the descending baseball at his hip without glancing up more than a split second, not breaking his patter with Dickey, a good listener. The crowd caught every nuance and loved it. Talent is everything in money management, too, and it shows at an early age, either with or without full credentials. Yes, I have an MBA and a very low number as a chartered financial analyst, but I can't put my finger on any formal training that was a revelation or shining light. Money management is an existential act requiring enormous courage, stamina and skill, everything Lou Gehrig—the first "iron man"—radiated, showing off at home plate with the impassive Bill Dickey, his straight man.

Academics, of course, get it all wrong. Their talk about random walks, efficient markets and risk premiums leaves me cold. Fortunately for them, the stock market is an overflowing treasure chest of ongoing statistics. Countless assistant professors who must publish or perish concoct papers riddled with integral calculus equations that appear quarterly in the *Financial Analysts Journal*, which I stopped reading about 20 years ago because of such gibberish.

While I was working for my MBA my advisor touted me off calculus unless I was going for an economist. "Nobody uses much integral calculus on Wall Street, kid," he said. "It's who's doing what to whom in the backseat of the car. What's ahead for the next twelve months is what you live by." This was the second best advice I ever got.

Warren Buffett, in one of his 30-page *tours d'horizon* in Berkshire Hathaway's annual report in the early nineties, disposed of the "efficient market" in one sentence, referring to Black Monday, when the market dropped 22 percent overnight, and came near to imploding, obviously inefficient. Academics have written dozens of papers rationalizing this event, but they surely ring hollow.

Don't trash all the academics. At a graduation ceremony at Bard College I had the pleasure of introducing James Tobin, the economist who birthed his Q ratio. At lunch, I was telling Tobin how much I admired the elegance and simplicity of his insight. Briefly, the Q ratio deals with the capital stock or infrastructure of the country and compares it to the market value of corporate equity. When the market value of the Big Board is less than the replacement cost of corporate hard assets, you can rest secure the market is undervalued. Much of the eighties, this was true. It spawned Mike Milken, hostile takeovers and the great leveraged buyout (LBO) scene that crested with the Kohlberg Kravis Roberts LBO of RJR Nabisco.

The Q ratio now stands well over par, actually over twice par, which is why you now see more discriminating LBOs. Today, you can carry your finance traunch with BB debentures yielding just 5 percent. In the eighties, credit cost you 9 percent. Market bulls pooh-pooh Tobin as quaint and obsolete. How do you figure in Coca-Cola's trademark, an ethical drug house's patents or any serious intellectual property like cloud computing software? This is valid, but Tobin is right, because his insight is based on how businesses are priced—fairly valued, overvalued or undervalued over successive cycles. It's a long-cycle reading that you file away but never discard from your apperceptive mass.

Never govern yourself by a dividend discount model, either, because its moving parts are too changeable—dividend payout ratios, earnings growth, inflation and interest rates. Believe me, a dividend discount model is far less relevant than Tobin's Q ratio. Everyone punches in too high a growth rate for earnings. Try 5 percent rather than 6 percent, a big difference. Markets are only efficient over decades. When the Dow Jones average sinks 100 points, my wife invariably asks me what happened—why? My answer never wavers: "I have no idea." I wince when listeners take seriously some CNBC commentator who dutifully reports the day's doings with no interpretive commentary.

What does it mean if the Dow is down 100 points but NASDAQ is up and the Standard and Poor's 500 Index is flat? Did two or three stocks in the Dow drop 5 points? The divisor is over 6 now, so that's 30 points in the average if one high-priced stock drops $5. With the Dow over 18,000, a 100-point move is random chicken feed. While "Christmasing" at the El San Juan Resort and Casino in Puerto Rico on the eve of the millennium, a 26-year-old analyst at PaineWebber batted out a Qualcomm paragraph on the First Call system most of us then subscribed to on our computer screens. Now it's Bloomberg we use. Analysts had been behind the pitch all year, underestimating Qualcomm's earnings power. The PaineWebber kid tried to preempt Wall Street operators, who traditionally take off Christmas week. He reasoned that Qualcomm's royalty income stream from its CDMA wireless telephony patents should be capitalized at 150 times forward 12-month earnings.

My ears perked up like a papillon. Qualcomm had gone around the clock 10 times for us, and I decided to peel off some while they wanted it at $800 before its four-for-one split. Qualcomm by mid-June 2000 had traded down to $60, post-split, a drop of 70 percent. My only mistake was not giving them all I owned. Over the years I have done better phasing into and out of stocks, gradually. In the Qualcomm case the "break" lasted about two hours and it was net, net of the whole story, finished business.

The "old" Gilded Age lasted some 40 years, from 1870 to the eve of World War I. Then the politicians threw it all away with arms races and interlocking alliances. Edison's electric light, the elevator, telephones and automobiles changed the face of the country and how people lived and worked as much as the railroad and Fulton's steamboat. The "new" Gilded Age lasted until yearend 2000. Everyone believed in the magic of technology—the Internet, wireless telephony, ever more powerful computers and breakthrough drugs for heart disease, arthritis, hypertension and cancer. Valuations streamed off the tops of pages until earnings deconstructed. The capital goods boom ran out of gas. The conundrum is that everyone is locked into the stock market now more than ever before. Historically, the market's valuation is still as rich as it's ever been, but the excesses largely were purged in 2008–'09. The national pastime is not just baseball. The Big Board and NASDAQ get their due share of airtime.

The predicament for money managers in our new Gilded Age that started spring of 2009 is how to deal with a market that contains pockets of serious overvaluation, like Internet properties, parts of biotechnology and cloud computing. Ignoring the wide disparity in GAAP vs. non-GAAP earnings is a serious evasion by analysts and money managers. It's a clear road to Hoboken, pushing spaghetti in a hole-in-the-wall dive.

The last week in July 2000, the market sliced about 25 percent off the valuation of benchmark properties like Nokia, Texas Instruments and Applied Materials. End-of-cycle jitters for semiconductors and wireless handsets filled the air. Early in 2001 they took Cisco out to be shot. Same for Twitter, spring of 2014, and Microsoft late January 2015.

Black Monday stands, but the market did top out on August 26, 1987, and fell steadily for weeks. Academics don't mention this. Interest rates were rising, the economy peaking, and macro stats wobbly: weak dollar, rising trade deficit and a Congress that thought insider trading was the gut economic issue of the decade. They were fighting last year's war, as they would in 2013–'14. Consider, the Japanese minister of trade wagged his finger at us and said we were soft, undisciplined and uncompetitive. He pontificated just as Japan's bubble was about to reach its maximum circumference, in the eighties. Two decades later Nippon still had not gotten over their overinvestment in capital goods, real estate and buried, unreported bank rot.

Aside from the aberration of Black Monday, the Internet bubble of 2000 and the 2008–'09 bank meltdown, we have been living mainly in a new Gilded Age.

Paul Volcker gets 80 percent of the credit, Bernanke, 20 percent. Volcker plunged the country into a gut-wrenching recession in 1981–82. Interest rates on FNMA 5-year notes soared to 15 percent. Home builders mailed Volcker crosses made out of two-by-fours; Chrysler was bailed out by the Treasury. It was cheaper than paying unemployment insurance. Same went in 2008–'09 with General Motors. The S&P 500 Index touched down at 100, yielding 5.6 percent, valued under 10 times depressed earnings. It's Warren Buffett's recurrent dream. Post–Black Monday, I remember, Larry Tisch was an avid buyer of equities, probably his last bullish gut play until oil supertankers sold for scrap value, afloat or mothballed.

The country changed for the better after Volcker's 1982 *lavage rapide*. Labor givebacks began. Jimmy Hoffa's ghost could no longer threaten to paralyze the country's interstate commerce. Membership in the UAW peaked, and General Motors closed down their second-floor cafeteria in the GM building on Fifth Avenue, a profligate utilization of high-priced square footage.

Jack Welch of General Electric was the first big honcho to wise up. He threw capital at automation, reducing the labor content of his goods. GE's labor rolls burned down to 300,000 from 500,000. Then Welch played gin rummy with his divisions. Anything that wasn't number one or two competitively in its field was discarded. Unskilled laborers no longer made $15 an hour. They worked for the minimum wage. Jimmy Hoffa disappeared. Jack Welch was first to employ his prime credit rating to leverage GE's balance sheet and move into the financial services sector, now half the company's earnings but about to be spun off. Welch still is imitated. His most recent disciple was C. Michael Armstrong of AT&T, whose move into cable television and wireless telephony was dramatic but five years too late.

A century's worth of market stats show even if you come in at the top of a cycle, if you remain invested for at least a decade, your rate of return can exceed Treasury bills and bonds. An entire industry—financial counseling for individuals—is based on this premise. In 1999, the book *Dow 36,000* suggested the risk premium for equities was too high. There shouldn't be any risk premium, because stocks outperform bonds and have dividends that grow. The authors insanely capitalized future earnings of the S&P 500 at 100. This is seven times what the index sold for in mid-2014. The Dow Jones index dropped under 10,000 early in 2001, fulsome with volatility, which often spells overvaluation. During 2009 it based at 6,649, but by yearend '14 it breeched 18,000. Stocks normally twice as volatile as bonds suggest an equity risk premium of zero is foolishly optimistic except when interest rates are minimal and the perception is they can rest there for years to come.

This may be happening as I write this piece. Worth repetition. This may be happening as I write this. Nobody takes Alibaba, Gilead Sciences, even Actavis away from me. If wrong, I'll be pushing the spaghetti in Hoboken.

The late Joe Wilson, headman at Xerox in the late fifties and sixties, when Xerox was Xerox, had no tolerance for lazy security analysts. The magic of xerography then was comparable with the early scalability of, say, Facebook, Twitter and Google. Because it was one of the few technology games in town, along with Fairchild Camera and Syntex, Xerox was besieged with requests for interviews. The chief financial officer, courtly Kent Damon, solved this problem by getting his chief to hold a quarterly analysts' meeting. Wilson, alone, ran it like a presidential press conference.

Unlike today, when the art of teleconferencing is a highly stylized ballet where analysts are spoon-fed "guidance" by management, Wilson wouldn't tolerate dumb questions or anything as crass as asking how the next quarter was shaping up. You asked about research priorities, competitive forces, production ramp-ups, but you could never pin him down on numbers. Wilson was right. He believed analysts must build their own models of earning power. He had no interest in micromanaging the earnings consensus to the fine-tuning that the Coca-Colas and Intels of the world do today. Of 100 analysts following Coca-Cola, the consensus rarely varies more than a penny or two.

The object wasn't to get an earnings consensus within a penny from 30 name analysts and then exceed it by a penny, quarter after quarter. Xerox continually surprised itself and Wall Street with the scalability of xerography in offices and then in desktop portables. The country was copy hungry. Nobody had personal computers or printers. Secretaries stood liberated from rolling four-page carbon booklets into their IBM Selectrics, a messy process when you made typing errors.

My encounter with Xerox as a newly introduced product (the 914 office copier) preceded my experience with Xerox the stock. Ralph Reis, my neighbor in the next cubbyhole on E.F. Hutton's research floor, was a Rochester boy with a chemical engineering degree from MIT. Close to Eastman Kodak and Xerox when it had a Haloid in front of Xerox, he prevailed upon Kent Damon to direct that one of the first 914 copiers to hit Wall Street late in 1959 be installed at E.F. Hutton, our workplace. The 914 was metered, and within hours we noted secretaries flocking to the copying room from distant floors at 61 Broadway. The 914 spit out clean copies on white paper stock at a rate of six to seven per minute, an unheard-of phenomenon.

At day's end, Ralph would check the meter, go back to his semi-logarithmic paper and plot Xerox's revenue momentum, using the Hutton experience as typical. The counter started to mount in an arithmetic progression the next few weeks, but then the game ended. The overhead partner, an anachronism in a tailored double-breasted suit, left over from '29, locked down the machine. At a nickel a copy, its expense was a troubling item to him.

Reis was in despair. How could he extrapolate Xerox's numbers if administrative heads were about to choke off copy making in its infancy? Haloid-Xerox, as a stock still traded over the counter, tempted us, but it was volatile. Nobody, particularly analysts, had any capital to speak of. Even $15,000 in salary was serious money. Ralph and I had emptied our checkbooks, and we stood frozen in the headlights.

"This is a disaster," Ralph moaned.

"I'm not so sure," I said.

"Why not?"

"Did you catch all those secretaries feeding the machine?" I asked.

"Xerography is too expensive," Ralph answered. "They've got to cut the costs per copy real fast."

"They'll figure it out," I said. "Remember, the learning curve on the 914 is still low. Damon told us that."

"It's bearish," Ralph moaned.

"No, no," I cried. "I've got it. Shutting down the machine is the most bullish scenario you could hope for. Go back to your log paper and extrapolate enormous usage. Every office in the country! The stock's going to the moon." I pounded the table and broke a yellow pencil in my fist while I was crushing ice cubes in my mouth. Ralph's eyes lit up. Smart, hungry analysts recognize basic insights, early on.

Xerox, of course, did go to the moon over the next 20 years, until Canon and Kodak gave them a run for the market. Ralph held on tenaciously, never tiring of the follow-up work necessary to keep abreast of an unfolding story. I tired after a couple of years but made a lot of money. Ralph held on and got very rich, but let's hope he got out in time.

Nothing is forever; the number of growth stocks that maintain their primacy decade over decade can be counted on one or two hands. Buffett held on to Coca-Cola and Gillette long after they lost their edge. Not even Microsoft, with 90 percent gross margins, was safe and secure in desktop computing. Xerox now is an also-ran conglomerate, valued at 10 times earnings like a tired industrial, which is what it is, not a leading-edge technology play.

For me, the Xerox experience was seminal. Yes, I've done my share of analyst modeling, but I tend lately to discard extrapolations and look for rock-hard insights. To this day, I retain my old pocket-sized slide rule in my pencil holder on my desk. My young analysts finger it like a relic from the crucifixion cross of Jesus. The slide rule is there to remind me to work the numbers after the first outburst of rational exuberance.

The public's undisciplined trading of stocks off Internet chatter is a loser's game. You are a second derivative. What's a second derivative? Well, when your hometown sprayed the trees with DDT to kill the mosquitoes, the DDT killed all the town's cats and then you were overrun with rats. The cats were the second derivative of the DDT. If you can't link DDT with cats and rats, don't play in my game.

George Soros understood linkage better than most of us. The consensus, he knew, is always wrong. It misses the pivotal variable in each phase of the unfolding financial market cycle. Then it congeals into another consensus once it recognizes the rats are multiplying, but fails to understand how the Pied Piper is going to corner the rats and exterminate them. In the Xerox case, I was a maniacal demon, watching secretaries flock to the machine from distant floors. Then I did the work and bet a bunch.

Anything lifestyle changing, even cigars, can shape hockey-stick earnings trajectories for at least a few years. Better you cotton on early, before analysts' extrapolations get out of hand. Call this a disciplined deduction.

TWO

The Other 99 Percent
Ain't Winning

*L*emme tell you about the Sosnoff family's precious possession during the Great Depression. It was a scratched-up, black, upright, no-name piano. Our family of five hung around it and sang in unison, my mother sight-reading borrowed sheet music: "South of the Border (Down Mexico Way)," "Alexander's Ragtime Band," "And the Angels Sing."

Our piano was deadly flat on bass notes and sharp on treble keys, but so what? It functioned fine for the Sosnoffs. We lived in the East Bronx, three flights up—a walk-up tenement, one among hundreds.

Once school let out late in June, my parents gave up our apartment. The family summered in a tar-papered shack at Croton-on-Hudson. We overlooked Indian Point Park, then a sandy beach the color and consistency of brown sugar.

I'm talking late thirties, early forties. Nuclear power generation wasn't even a concept then. We owned so few cumbersome possessions that the New York Central Railroad allowed us to board with all our clothes and baseball bats. My mother lugged on board her 30-pound Underwood typewriter.

But what to do with our piano? Well…I and my two older brothers, Gene and George, were in charge of moving this beloved monster down to a neighbor's apartment on the ground floor, its home for the summer. The poor took care of each other during the Depression, a seldom remarked sidelight. The corner candy store took our phone messages. Phones were beyond our means until 1946.

Over the years, the three brothers evolved into a handy mover team for non-Steinway instruments. There was actually a moving-van enterprise named The Four Brothers at that time. We'd upend this object, tip it back and shove a dolly underneath to receive our baby. Amid fulsome cursing and much sweat equity, maybe an hour finished the job.

In early September, the return trip for our piano, up three flights, took several hours. Very dangerous if the dolly slipped out. Somehow we managed not to self-destruct. It was unthinkable to turn our piano loose like a mangy dog, never to be seen again.

When I was nine, my father walked me over to a second-story music school on 125th Street, three blocks south of his tailor shop. There, Pop bought me my choice of a nickel-plated alto saxophone, priced at $35. He paid for my sax a buck a week and contracted for weekly music lessons at 25 cents the half hour. Above the music school, on the third floor, a tap dance studio's class rapped out its rhythms, all of us striving upward in a dismal economic setting. Economists labeled it the Great Depression. For us it was just Hard Times.

Around this time, New York's greatest mayor, Fiorello La Guardia, somehow scrounged the money to create four special high schools, including the Bronx High School of Science and the High School of Music & Art, which I later attended. No Music & Art, I would have graduated from a young punk into a hood. There was no such concept as a teenager then.

Music, the theater—all the arts—were a must-do in our family. My elder brother Gene took me to the old Metropolitan Opera House, where standing-room admission was one buck in the late forties. You could sit in the third balcony of Broadway's theaters for $1.10. *Life with Father* played, and Ethel Merman was belting out "Anything You Can Do, I Can Do Better" in *Annie Get Your Gun*. Today on Broadway and at the Lincoln Center, good seats in the house are pegged at $195. Plays with big stars price premium seats around $500.

While I was writing this piece, the *Wall Street Journal* reported Steinway Industries had accepted a private equity bid of $438 million, over one times sales. Steinways now retail new anywhere from $57,000 to $142,000. Average income of buyers tops $300,000.

We just bought a Steinway Model M, circa 1916, mahogany, $45,000 reconstructed. My annual income is unprovable. At the National Museum of American Illustration, a labor of love by Judy and Laurence Cutler in Newport, Rhode Island, I noted a painting by Hamilton King, *Lady at the Piano*.

This was transformed into a 1900 illustration by the Victoria Greeting Card Company. A tall drink of water gowned in floor-length velvet and lace, a coiffed Gibson Girl hairdo, legs outstretched languorously. The subject touches the keys with her fingertips. Beautiful women at pianos resonate.

In my late teens, I made sideman in a name dance band with a five-man sax section. I had traded in my nickel-plated sax for a sweet-toned Selmer, who actually acquired Steinway in 1995. I didn't blink at the $200 price tag because I had to have a Selmer to survive in the music world.

What in the world do pianos and saxophones signify for financial markets? Actually, plenty. Objects and services that enrich your emotional life hold their primacy just so long as quality remains impeccably high. Steinways handcrafted a hundred years ago adumbrate ethereal tonality, pads soft to the touch, still highly competitive with new models.

When I scan my portfolio daily, each position must spell out quality goods. I'm disinterested in commodity plays unless they're giving 'em away, when bordering on insolvency, like the coal industry currently. I long for properties with great cancer drugs, like Gilead Sciences, hot General Motors pickup trucks or non–gas guzzling Boeing jet aircraft. Primacy in media content and distribution get my attention: Walt Disney, Comcast, 21st Century Fox and News Corp.

Like upwardly mobile families who believed in the humanities, staying power counts for stocks, too. My list embraces Gilead, Celgene, Biogen Idec, Google, Boeing, JPMorgan Chase, Citigroup (finally) and News Corp. They're over-weighted and overloved by me—hopefully for the next five years. I'd include Microsoft and Facebook, too.

I associate the Great Depression with my father's tailor shop in Harlem. As a 10-year-old I had no idea I was poor, belonging to the underclass. After all, my parents were too proud to go on "relief," the equivalent of today's food stamp safety net. I had a lively throwing arm from third base, a big deal in the school yard.

Pop's presser, Mac, bathed in steam from the hissing pressing machine, used to mumble, "I'm too poor to live and too poor to die." Playing the daily numbers kept him in place. Pop would buy a 25-pound bag of potatoes off a wagon for a quarter and we'd eat them with sour cream, day in, day out.

This sweltering setting is a recurrent memory for me, now sensitive to the widening gap between very rich, the comfortable and subsistence poor. My two black Mercedes S550 sedans parked in the driveway are feisty trophies. When the revolution comes, forking over the keys with no arguments is not an issue for me.

There were 46 million recipients on food stamps in 2014, finally peaking, with the individual stipend around $144 monthly. A coterie of young Republican con-gressmen actively scheme to whittle this number down closer to zero. Hopefully, they'll lose. I am sensitive to safety nets. In my early twenties, I came back from the Korean War in 1954, and my unemployment insurance, $25 weekly for 20 weeks, soon ran out. After fighting with the 1st Cavalry Division's 7th Regiment,

I no longer felt like John Wayne, riding back to the stable after giving the Indians hell. I had no civilian work records, just an AB.

The higher the market presses, the more I remember about what it's like to be dirt poor, flat broke. Of late, there's a huge buildup in genteel poverty, namely college graduates whose student loans tot up to a trillion bucks, over $25,000 apiece. For graduate students and medical school attendees, the burden swells up to $250,000 per capita after years of hard slogging.

Meanwhile, tuition inflation at private colleges and universities compounds irrepressibly near 5 percent annually. The academic community in fact is the fifth column, undermining the country's future growth rate. It's going to be a while before newly graduated debtors qualify for home mortgages, even new car financing.

Legislation on student loans is a mini-disaster for college men and women. It calls for a floating rate tied to 10-year Treasuries plus 2.05 percent. If 10-year paper holds at 2.5 percent, borrowing costs next June would fix at 4.55 percent. The catch-22 is that the long-term trendline for 10-year Treasuries approximates 5 percent.

Prospective borrowing costs a few years out could range between 6 percent and 7 percent. This is a heavy cross to shoulder. For graduate students, add another percentage point. In short, our country is failing its younger generation, who so far take all this sitting down. Where are the protest marches?

In my day, college tuition ran around $600. You'd work summers and earn your keep. Currently, the bill at a small, tidy college runs around $45,000 per annum, including room and board. It's impossible to earn your own way unless you're dealing in molly. Unemployment in 2014 for college graduates held at 4 percent, double the 2 percent norm.

The Street's simple-minded focus on monthly unemployment percentages doesn't do justice to the seriousness of the plight of the country's growing underclass. Consider that unemployment for 16- to 19-year-olds runs at 25 percent, not the 15 percent long-term trendline. For 25- to 34-year-olds, normally 5 percent joblessness now sticks at 8 percent.

For decades, the rate of growth in the labor force ranged between 1 percent and 2 percent. On a 150-million base, the country therefore needs to add nearly two million new jobs per annum just to keep unemployment rolls from bulging. Payroll data in the financial sector and state and local governments is likely to remain flat for years to come, and these two factors account for a sizable 18 million jobs. Tax receipts for New York State finally turned positive in late 2013, running at a 5 percent surplus in 2014. But none of this surplus is earmarked for additions to employment rolls.

The construction industry lost two million jobs from peak to trough, 2007–'09.

There's growth in the food service sector, but these low-paying jobs use part-timers who get no health care or pension benefits. This is a 10-million totality making new highs, but it has no meaning.

Payrolls in the manufacturing sector sadly spelled out the demise of our competitive mettle compared with low labor-cost zones in South America and the Far East. U.S. manufacturing employment peaked in the late seventies at close to 20 million. The biggest decline came in the past decade. We're basing out below 12 million workers. So far, the Administration acts like a toothless tiger on this issue.

As a percentage of non-agricultural employees, manufacturing is under 10 percent, compared to its early postwar peak of 33 percent. This degree of erosion stopped me in my tracks. The plight of the skilled working population in terms of earnings power is insidious: 2 percent annualized growth, down from 4 percent in the nineties.

The days of 8 percent wage bumps in the seventies are gone but not forgotten. Ask the Teamsters and UAW, who forged such sweetheart contracts with automakers and others. We ceded market share to Japanese and German manufacturers. Never again. Total employment less government workers holds below the 2007 peak despite all the wealth re-created by the Federal Reserve Board. The only employment chart that's in new high ground is temporary help.

What does all this portend for the country, for GDP growth, personal consumption expenditures, home building and interest rates? Does tax policy refocus on the top 0.1 percent in upcoming elections? Probably, but only in a cosmetic way. The rich, even the middle class, just had their net worth restored by Ben Bernanke. Ben kept telling everyone who'd listen that low interest rates would rest in place for the foreseeable future, at least two years. Janet Yellen also talks the talk.

Here is the deep basic: At the end of 2013, the net worth of households and nonprofits reached into new high ground at $80.7 trillion, a gain of $9.8 trillion for the year, up 14 percent. Equities rose $5.6 trillion and real estate $2.3 trillion. The top 1 percent had a very good year, while the top 0.1 percent bought $24 million vintage Ferrari cars and Jeff Koons's *Balloon Dog (Orange)*.

Household debt lifted only 5.4 percent at yearend. State and local government debt declined at an annual rate of 4.9 percent in the fourth quarter. New York State just forecasted tax receipts rising at a rate of over 5 percent this year. When I look at margin debt on the Big Board, it approximated just a couple of days trading volume.

Shoeshine boys haven't releveraged themselves since their washout in the Great Crash. Pension funds rest approximately 10 percentage points too low historically in terms of asset allocation in stocks. The public also retains too much cash earning zilch. I see maybe $2 trillion of open-to-buy for equities in the next few years. This is serious money, considering the Big Board's valuation at $15 trillion.

Late in 2013, stock pros finally believed Bernanke meant what he said, and "risk on" pervaded the air. That personal consumption spending is below consumer debt is a critical reading. The consumer can carry GDP above a 3 percent growth rate in the next few years by reducing savings. Then, capital goods spending kicks in and keeps GDP rolling. If oil sticks near $70 a barrel, add 1 percent to personal consumption expenditures and GDP which could run near 4 percent during 2015.

But I worry. Average weekly hours worked and overtime hours bounced off recession lows but stick below the mid-nineties peak. Employment in the health care sector shows strong growth, but these are low-paying jobs. The inflation in medical costs, over 10 percent per annum, does impact consumer spending, particularly retail sales of soft and hard goods. Wal-Mart blamed lackluster sales on the reduction in allocation of food stamps.

Labor's take of the GDP is depressing, at new lows for the entire postwar period (*Figure 1*). Employee compensation is below the lows in the 1950s. All this while profits of nonfinancial corporations forged to new highs early in 2014. Is it any wonder that there is pressure for raising the minimum wage level to $10 an hour? Supplements to wages and salaries, mainly health care, peaked in the early nineties and are headed down, too.

This is the stuff bread riots and revolutions are made from unless politicians raise transfer payments or change the tax structure to benefit wage earners. Just the opposite is happening. Pressure from the corporate sector to lower their tax rate is building. But tax rates have been trending down for decades from a trendline of 40 percent in the mid-sixties. How many investors know this? How many labor union leaders have processed all these ratios? Congressmen, too (*Figure 2, page 18*).

European auto sales erosion is a reminder of what hurts in a zero-growth economic setting. Auto sales there peaked early in 2007 at 12 million units, but we're down to 8.5 million, with no recovery in sight, early in 2014.

My simple read is that the country—namely our politicians—is failing the younger generation, forcing deferral of personal consumption spending for years and years. Young doctors working at hospitals never will earn much more than $120,000 annually. I'm not sure what a law degree or MBA gets you in a relatively stagnant economic setting, but probably not much more.

COMPENSATION OF EMPLOYEES
as a Percent of Gross Domestic Product

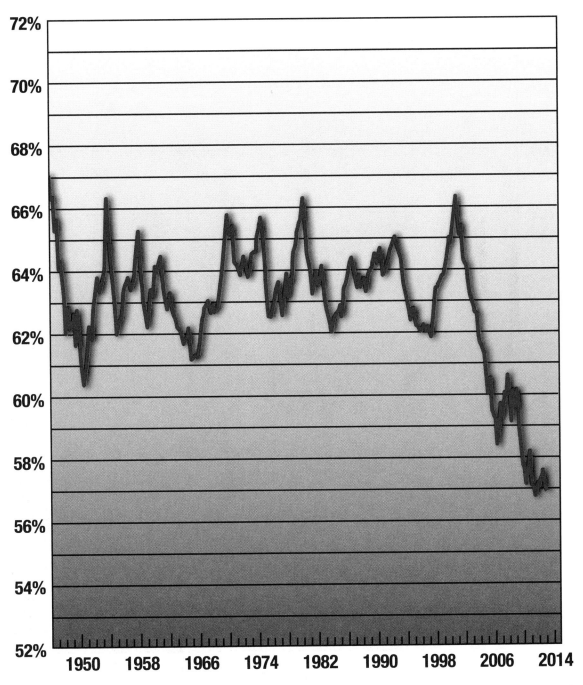

Figure 1

Source: Safian Investment Research

TAX RATE FOR U.S. NONFINANCIAL CORPORATIONS

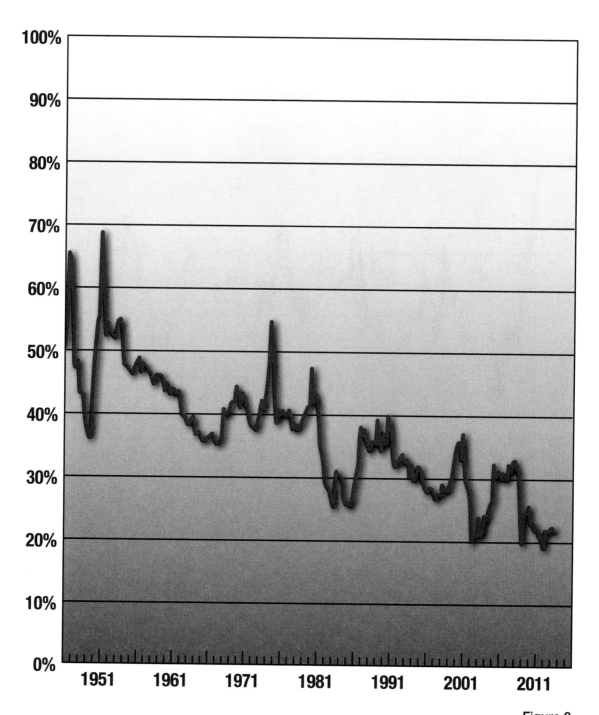

Figure 2

Source: Safian Investment Research

The bull market in vintage racing cars recently gained an eye-opening data point: A 1958 Ferrari 335S that had been bailed out of a U.S. Customs warehouse in New York for $1,000 in 1963 was sold for $21.5 million in a private transaction to an Austrian collector, Andreas Mohringer.

Eerily, the top 0.1 percent widens its lead over all other subsets. Operators like Steve Cohen, Leon Black and Steve Wynn bid up contemporary and modern art to heady levels. Edvard Munch's iconic *The Scream* was knocked down to Leon Black at $120 million. Steve Cohen countered with a winning bid over $100 million for Giacometti's *Chariot* at the November 2014 evening auction at Sotheby's. Yachts for the very rich wax sleeker, longer and faster moving. Jeff Koons was retained to decorate a yacht's exterior. It takes a crew of three just to keep the windows bright and shiny.

Many hedge fund operators missed knocking the cover off the baseball during 2013 and 2014, but the S&P 500 Index had a vintage year in 2013, up 32 percent. Meanwhile, tens of thousands of Detroit's retirees may lose some equity in pension and health care funds. Where's their safety net? JPMorgan Chase increased its litigation reserves all year to cover excesses in lending and underwriting. The final settlements bill looks like $30 billion all in. But its earnings power is irrepressible, even with flattish net interest margins. Jamie Dimon took home nearly $20 million in 2013 compensation, more in 2014.

Inequality flourishes everywhere. The gap between winners and losers among the top 25 largest capitalizations grows wider, with negative numbers embracing ExxonMobil, Google, General Electric, Chevron, Verizon, IBM and AT&T.

Because the country faces deep-seated issues of joblessness, lopsided income distribution and a defanged Oval Office, I can't extrapolate more than moderate recovery in GDP. Low rates of interest should hold for years to come. Historically speaking, mortgage rates even at 4.5 percent remain a great bargain. The Big Board's largesse prevails, and I'll battle not to feel too guilty about it.

Sadly, the Occupy Wall Street crowd was vociferous but shouldered no ideology or specific agenda, so their protests petered out. They shoulda at least dug down into the Labor Department's unemployment stats, or perused a bunch of corporate proxy statements to comprehend the scope of corporate management's methodical rapacity.

The SEC thinks insider trading is a big deal, but it's not the deep-set issue. Ask the other 99 percent who feel the country let them down. All Attorney General Holder accomplished was penalizing shareholders by tens of billions, $30 billion alone for JPMorgan Chase's transgressions. Managements weren't fined personally, collared and sent to the slammer. Their take-home pay shows sizable year-to-year growth in most cases.

Academic economists point out that there's been a downsizing of the middle class over the past 25 years or so. The middle 60 percent of the population in the United States has lost income share to the benefit of the richest top fifth. Plutocrats like the Koch brothers campaign to change the country, plumping for laissez-faire, less government and an end to environmental legislation. I'd do the same if I owned major interests in petrochemicals complexes.

We need more upgrading in the country. Outsized incentive compensation, as in Gilead Sciences and Salesforce.com, sets a bad example of corporate elitism—nested in 85-page proxy statements blessed by compensation consultants like Gilead's Frederic W. Cook & Co. I wonder if more than a hundred investors read this document methodically. Maybe I'm the lonesome reader.

If you define the middle class as those households with income between the 20th and 80th percentiles—the middle 60—the United States has the highest income inequality in the developed world, with Nordic countries the least. We show some upward movement in middle-class households. Nobody would argue that a secure middle class isn't vital for a country's growth and stability.

Many middle-class families remain financially vulnerable because of low net worth accumulation. Conspicuous consumption by the top 1 percent, even the 0.1 percent, imposes psychological burdens on middle-class families, who feel deprived, unable to afford comfortable housing, snappy automobiles and exciting vacation spots. Ben Bernanke certainly understood that a secure middle class is vital for economic growth.

But increased spending at the top level of income distribution imposes not only psychological costs on families in the middle; it also raises the cost of achieving goals that most middle-class families used to regard as basic. Home ownership is a prime example. Hardly appreciated is that middle-class families are financially vulnerable because of minimal net worth—which is primarily in their homes. One has to go above 150 percent of median income to enter the top 20 percent.

Contrastingly, the wealthy can be defined as people who don't need to work. Usually their wealth exceeds 30 times mean middle-class income. This assumes a realistic real after-tax income flow of 3.3 percent (*Figure 3*).

Over the past 30 years or so, the middle class lost income share to the top 20 percent. Additionally, income inequality increased sharply over the past generation. This coincides with loss of manufacturing jobs to the rest of the world. Income growth for American households in the middle was very slow. I leave aside the question of whether income inequality is good for economic growth, because it's impossible to prove, just a working hypothesis.

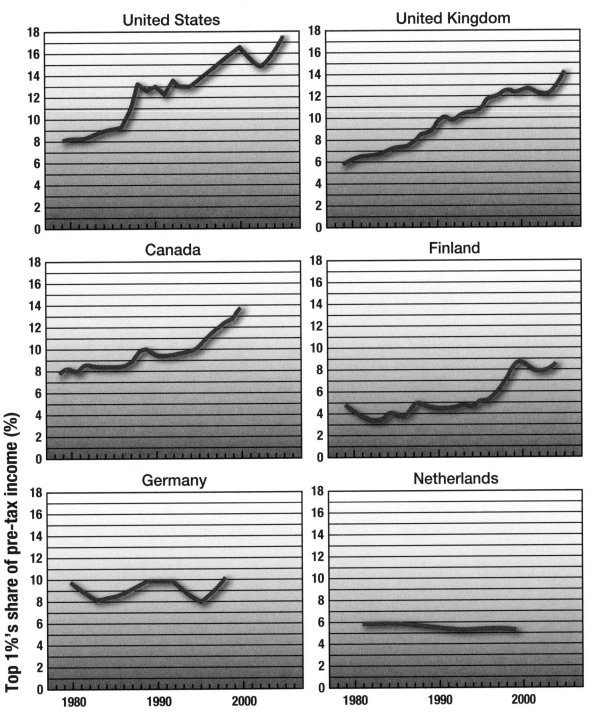

TRENDS IN TOP-HEAVY INCOME INEQUALITY
Six Countries, Late 1970s to Mid-2000s

Top 1%'s share of pre-tax income (%)

United States

United Kingdom

Canada

Finland

Germany

Netherlands

Figure 3

Source: *Income Inequality*, Gornick and Jäntti

Certainly, Louis XVI, Czar Nicholas II, even Cleopatra believed in income inequality. Far easier to prove is that rising top-heavy income inequality tends to reduce middle-class income growth. Even Obama's Administration won't touch the issue of abolishing hedge funds' and private equity's ability to treat income as carried interest, taxed at (lower) capital gains rates. There is more advocacy for a corporate tax cut, although the current rate is well below rates in the sixties and seventies. Meantime, the middle class sees their fortunes near stagnation, while the poor are subjected to relative if not absolute deprivation. Net redistribution of wealth, world-wide, is put at less than 1 percent by the Luxembourg Income Study.

Financial assets hold at a minimal level for the middle class. Equity is typically in their homes, as two-thirds are homeowners and 75 percent of their wealth is tied up in real estate, with average debt of $25,000 versus $75,000 in home equity. Hot real-estate neighborhoods like Williamsburg, Brooklyn, are the exception. Families who bought 20-foot-wide townhouses there for $15,000 in 1946 now turn them over for $2 million and move on to Florida. Real estate taxes average around $6,000, never grossed up to reflect current valuation. No politician in Greater New York would touch this issue with a 10-foot pole. Most surveys of income distribution exclude capital gains, so in a bubble environment for equities, income inequality is misunderstood. Inequality is very understated.

If I were a graduating medical student with a $200,000 tab for schooling, I'd conclude life is unfair. Gilead, Salesforce.com, Occidental Petroleum? I could have used dozens of other examples. They all coast home free, under the radar of what's appropriate and positive for the long-term health of the country. Student loans, over a trillion, are tied to an adjustable rate of interest that can escalate to 8 percent, a heavy cross to bear. Wall Street analysts refuse to deal with the widening gap between GAAP and non-GAAP reported earnings, particularly for tech houses, where the difference is mainly excessive stock grants to management.

Everyone focuses on the revenue growth rate, which I find a dangerous concept in valuation.

THREE

Roids on the Cabuie

My first job as a money manager, back in 1964, was working for Jack Kaplan, then 75 but still hearty and opinionated. I was charged with being his eyes and ears, a bird dog, but not his brains. Whenever Jack caught a cold he played the Cowardly Lion, thirsting to bang out his inventory of stocks. I had spent weeks analyzing American Express after Tino De Angelis filled his storage tanks with water and siphoned off the salad oil for which AmEx was extending credit. Tino was trading in commodities and flamed out. Buffett was accumulating AmEx, too. He still holds his position, with an unrealized gain in the billions. One day when I was out of town, Jack traded out of AmEx for a short-term gain. I confronted my boss, whose bulbous nose was cherry red and runny.

"Gus Levy called and asked for some gross, so I kicked it out," Jack mumbled.

"Why didn't you bang out some of your crap like United Fruit and New York Central? That's dead paper."

I pointed at him and he didn't like it. Jack had a violent temper. He could rant and rave nonstop for 10 minutes, crescendoing into physicality. His office was filled with half a dozen borax chairs, and he flung one against the wall, screaming how dare I second-guess him. The chairs were imitation birch, with faux Moroccan-leather seats.

I wouldn't play Leporello to his Don Giovanni, so I grabbed a chair and flung it against the opposite wall. These were 125th Street and Lenox Avenue chairs, expendable. I'd learned to stand tall for my bedrock conclusions. Jack respected gumption. I lasted a year, which was a long hire for him. He was worth $100 million then, a lot of money in the sixties. His wealth derived from Cuban molasses and Welch's Grape Juice. I was worth $100,000, which was a lot of money for a 30-year-old paying $200 a month rent. My takeaway from Jack was worth a fortune, truly. The rich often churn their stock market money capriciously. My odd notion that the wealthier you are, the more research you do proved a romantic fallacy. Jack, about Napoleon's stature, liked to trade because it made him a big man on Wall Street. Gus Levy at Goldman Sachs knew how to stroke him and roll up commissions. It turned me cold, more cerebral, even methodical.

During the mid-sixties, after Boeing ramped up its 707 jet, airlines turned into growth stocks. Money brokers then financed convertible debentures on 10 percent margin. I cashed in Eastern Air Lines paper at $400, and Boeing, United Aircraft and United Airlines convertibles all hit double par for me. I had enough capital to start my own money management firm and haven't worked for anyone since.

The stock options market in the early seventies embraced a coterie of market makers with minimal capital. Many had graduated from OTC trading desks. They understood and could calculate volatility, perhaps not so precisely as the Black-Scholes model that decades later garnered a Nobel Prize in economics, but well enough to get by and not misprice quotes on the puts and calls they traded. I wasn't smart enough to short NASDAQ at its peak in 2000. The late Leon Levy, an old friend, shorted NASDAQ and went long on the euro, one of the few simple but great spreads that rode the peak of the NASDAQ sombrero down to its right side's wide brim. If you have to think about a great concept, even a short, for more than 15 minutes, it's probably not a good idea (*Figure 4*).

Shorting growth stocks during the '73–'74 recession was as rewarding as shorting NASDAQ at the top early in 2000, when this index peaked at 5,000. NASDAQ bottomed in the spring of 2003 close to 1,000, thereby creating its giant 5-year sombrero formation. Momentum players like Janus became the Morgan Guaranty patsies 25 years later, comparably wiping out at least 50 percent of their clients' capital. "Geez! We should have seen it coming" was the chief investment officer's mea culpa at Morgan in 1974.

My '73–'74 caper in the options market had comparable percentage gains to Leon's but on a much smaller scale. Leon logged nine-figure money. It took just one phone call to his Bear Stearns trader. I had to hondle with a bunch of market makers, day in, day out. Word spread that everything I sold naked crumbled to sawdust. My number-one trader at Salomon Brothers, "Symphony Sid," shepherded my options orders on board-listed paper through the Chicago Board of Trade. The "Roids" stood for Polaroid and the "Cabuie" for the Chicago Board Options Exchange. He was Symphony Sid because of his running patter on trades, minute by minute. Can you imagine?

Writing call options, covered and uncovered, is a humbling experience because you can be right months later but lose your *gatkes* short term, particularly if you write one-month options—my game. Your rhythm must be as exquisite as a great

NASDAQ "SOMBRERO"
Weekly High/Low Price & 40-Week Moving Average

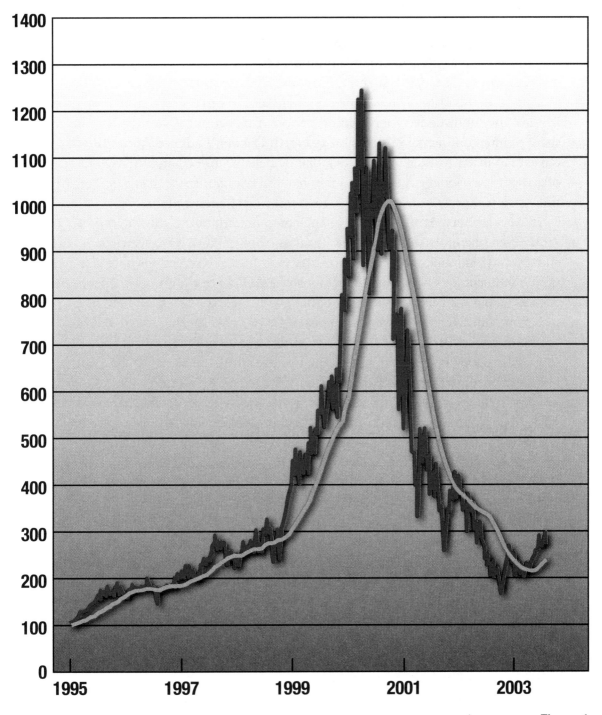

Figure 4

Source: Safian Investment Research

ballerina. A crappy stock rallies just before the naked calls you wrote are set to expire and you drop a multiple of what you received for writing this paper. This has KO'd me so many times that I have learned to loathe the third Friday in each month, which is expiration-date time. What I do is jump in and write options on the succeeding month, sometimes a multiple of what I had previously written. The market owes me, I say, sub silentio. Nobody pays attention!

You do all this not only to sharpen trading skills, but to protect short-term profits until they anniversary your holding period. Taxes count. I've already built my share of intercontinental missile silos in North Dakota. I admire Warren Buffett's tenacity to marry forever a good stock that he believes in. Yet, an objective analysis of growth stock longevity suggests just a handful reign for more than a decade. My time span is shorter—three to five years—and I carry a few regrets.

I love washouts. At the bottom of the communications cycle in the summer of 2002, everyone understood that the business plans of AOL Time Warner, AT&T and Qwest Communications made no sense. Accounting conventions proved downright fraudulent for Qwest and flimflammish for AOL. Their high yield paper found no bids, along with airlines and fiber optics purveyors. Not only was there negative cash flow, but fixed assets were schmeissed to 10 cents on the dollar. Banks and insurance underwriters took huge hits on their inventory of high yield paper.

Cellular phone operators didn't escape this bloodbath. Cable franchises were tarnished, too. All of them were overleveraged, with debt to cash flow ranging up to seven or eight to one, like Cablevision. Three to one is the respectable leverage yardstick today. Nobody was cash flow positive, and capital spending to build out networks was accelerating, not diminishing—not a pretty picture! The three cellular properties that traded—Nextel Communications, Sprint PCS and AWE (AT&T Wireless)—sold at two to three dollars a share and nobody cared. The headman at WorldCom, Bernie What's-his-name, was sent to the slammer, long term, for kiting his numbers.

I cared. I remembered James Thurber's classic piece about when he was a ROTC cadet. His company was in the throes of close-order drill, and the commands from his colonel rattled off like a machine gun: "Right flank march! Left flank march! To the rear march!" Then the colonel said, "Right turn march," which is a helluva different command. The entire company marched off in a flanking movement and Thurber found himself alone in a right turn. The colonel screamed out, "You're all wrong and this man is right!" So much for close-order drill and crowd behavior; wherever you encounter it, head for the exit.

At first, cellular properties had sold like Internet stocks. They weren't valued on cash flow but on pops, which was as ridiculous as eyeballs. If a cellular operator's network covered a population of 20 million it was valued on the prospect of increasing its market saturation from 5 percent to 50 percent. Then, you discounted prospective cash flow 10 years out and came up with a spic-'n'-span buy recommendation. Not reality. Just mindless ciphering.

Nextel peaked at $79 but by mid-2002 was tarred as a near basket case at two bucks. Its balance sheet was weighted down by $15 billion in debt, with an equity market value of $3 billion. The rating agencies, Moody's and Standard & Poor's, put Nextel on credit watch for a downgrade from a C rating. Anything below C is reserved for an impending bankruptcy. Nextel had huge capex embedded in its business plan, and negative cash flow. Its ratio of debt to cash flow stood at 7 to 1, and the 9⅜ debentures in the spring of 2002 traded at 50 cents on the dollar, comparable with Continental Airlines at its nadir. There were no bids of any size—except mine. Motorola, a 10 percent owner of Nextel's equity and a major supplier, had much to worry over. Craig McCaw, a pioneer in cellular telephony, saw his net worth melt away by several billions and he was leveraged elsewhere with boats, homes and Internet investments. Motorola and Craig McCaw sold huge tranches of their holdings prematurely, early in '03.

What did I see? Analysts were mild to stubbornly negative on Nextel. Too much leverage, too ambitious a business plan, impending industry rate competition, a cobbled-together network, archaic billing systems that cried out for centralization, plus a spectrum technology that was appraised as inferior to CDMA, which could accommodate high-speed data, the coming growth footprint.

I saw an operator who was gaining market share, adding 450,000 subscribers quarterly. They had push-to-talk, a two-way communication capability that nobody else would have for years to come, and a detailed plan to centralize billing. I discounted rate competition near term. *The only reason to do serious security analysis is to steel yourself to march off in one direction, alone.* Our business model assumed Nextel would continue to grow its subscriber base with rates stable. It assumed some economies of scale and that its network could sustain growing minutes of usage even at peak periods during the day. (When the northeastern electrical grid failed, Nextel's backup system failed like everyone else's on August 14.)

Our model adumbrated a company that would turn cash flow neutral in two to three quarters and then cross over to free cash flow territory, a billion in 2003 and $1.5 billion or more two years out. By early 2003 everyone on The Street had disregarded pops and even EBITDA as valuation yardsticks. Free cash flow was the metric that counted. (It still does.) Mid-2002, on a billion share base, Nextel at $3 was selling at three times projected free cash flow six quarters out. With

10-year Treasuries yielding 4 percent, a free cash flow multiple of 20 times seemed appropriate. Media properties like Viacom were there. My model chanted loud and clear. Give Nextel a multiple of 10 times free cash flow and the stock could see $12 four quarters out and high teens to $20 sometime in 2004. (It reached $18 mid-June '03.)

I dove in for our clients and a million shares for myself, along with $10 million face value of the debentures selling at $60. From $3, Nextel doubled in three months. The analysts began to reconfigure some of their numbers, but gingerly. Recommendations slithered up from sell to neutral. There was still too much debt on the balance sheet. Bad debt from deadbeat subscribers was a serious issue according to JPMorgan, and rate competition was still lurking in the shadows, they said. Verizon and AT&T Wireless sported unassailable balance sheets. All of Nextel's competitors were working on push-to-talk features. Verizon's model would debut in September '03. Nextel's monopoly would end shortly, which would erode its subscriber base. So they said.

The wall of worry proved a mirage. Nextel cantered along in a measured rhythm. Management got busy buying up $3 billion of its debt and preferred issues with cash on the balance sheet and equity-for-debt swaps. Its ratios of financial strength were building, quarterly. By the first quarter of '03, even the credit agencies begrudgingly upgraded Nextel from a basket case to a prospective credit rating upgrade. I calculated that Nextel already was better than a BB bond and rapidly approaching investment grade. The stock traded 20 million shares daily, ticking at $12, the bonds, above par. Craig McCaw had sold stock at $7, Motorola, half its position at $10. Nextel sank back a point or two but just for a few days. There were incessant negative comments coming out of JPMorgan, while Goldman Sachs was neutral to mildly negative.

I talked with the analysts following Nextel. Many were old long-lines telephone analysts, uncomfortable with the cellular sector, afraid of its leverage, rapid change and intensive competition for incremental subscribers. They chose not to stick out their necks even though viscerally they sensed the company was viable. It was now fashionable on Wall Street to reduce the proliferation of "buy" recommendations that had debased research during the Internet years. Analysts had turned "risk averse" at the bottom, particularly for commodity-based enterprises like Nextel.

When Nextel crossed $12 and traded as high as $15, I got busy. It had hit my projected near-term valuation. The textbooks say you're supposed to rebalance when your stock hits its model's valuation unless you're willing to upgrade your model for higher growth. I wasn't willing, as yet, but I did see $20 a share as a possibility one year out if the economy's rpm's picked up. But during the spring of 2003 the economy was stalled out on the eve of the invasion of Iraq. I decided to sell one-month options on my position and roll them forward, month after month, to protect my profits. After all, Nextel could sink back a couple of points. Who was I to call a turn in the economy? Academic economists were projecting a long and deep recession. The consumer was tapped out and needed to rebuild his savings pool, they pontificated.

Because Nextel was volatile paper, its one-month option premium was outsized, near 10 percent of the stock's price. A one-month call with the stock at $12 sold for over a dollar. The stock that I had bought at $3 nine months ago was yielding me 35 percent on my cost for the options I sold. I wrote thousands of covered calls, and then I decided to overwrite, naked on thousands more. Nextel would sink 25 percent and I would protect all my unrealized gain, I mused. The optimum outcome would be for Nextel to trade in a narrow range so all the calls I wrote would expire worthless. I saw myself making a million dollars monthly on my options-writing gambit if the stock just held its own, traded in a narrow channel.

Nothing on Wall Street ever comes wrapped up like Xmas. Some months, the stock stabilized, but then Nextel spurted from $12 to $15 and I had to cover at a huge loss. I loathed that third-Friday expiration date. Nextel turned squirrelly—it would rally obscenely in the morning of that third Friday and I'd cover thousands of options; then the stock would close down on the day, with an intraday range of 50 to 70 cents. I nicknamed Nextel Mr. Wiggly, a penis whose longitude was indeterminable moment to moment.

Thus, I botched my options-writing gambit, selling more options when Nextel dipped and covering when Mr. Wiggly spurted. The market was teaching me new lessons. Don't overwrite. Sell options on strength and cover on weakness. You could never fine-tune your timing. The trend of the market counted, as did spot news on the cellular sector and Nextel's competitors. Comments by analysts and management's appearance at brokerage-house conferences might trigger overreactions up- or downside. Motorola's and McCaw's sales made a splash, too.

Fundamentally, Nextel's quarterly financial reports, all upbeat, better than analysts' consensus, called the tune. By May of '03, Nextel ticked comfortably at $15, which touched off new analyst downgrades at JPMorgan, Goldman Sachs and Bear Stearns. Analysts who hated the stock at $3, then $7, later $12 and now $15 got in their licks. Nextel was fully priced even on their belated upgraded metrics of cash flow, earnings and free cash flow. Verizon was ready with its push-to-talk phone, and Nextel's spectrum would sponge up billions to upgrade in 2005. Finally, its data capability was too slow and they would lose subscribers. Just wait 'n' see. Their insane cleaver rested on the table.

I grew accustomed to such a noise level. As long as Nextel climbed this wall of worry, the stock had blue sky ahead. When The Street finally caved in and learned to love Nextel, it would be time to sell. My viscera said that day might never arrive. Mr. Wiggly would never, ever, reach its old high of $79 when analysts waxed foolishly irrational, but its buoyancy was nearly assured by their risk-averse reservations and cooled ardor. The most potent metric of any stock's trajectory is beating analysts' expectations, quarter after quarter. It works without fail.

By mid-June '03 the S&P 500 Index was flirting with 1,000, up from 800 since late March. Sprint PCS was getting good response to color-picture phones with their "2 months free" promotion. Motorola, Nextel's supplier, wouldn't have a picture phone available for at least a year. Could Nextel lose some subscribers? Maybe, yes. When you're older, maybe wiser, you don't overreact to news like this by banging out a block of stock. It would take more to shake me out, but I did sell thousands of July 15 calls at a buck.

The next day, Nextel popped up over a buck and I was losing money. I hated shooting myself in the foot, so I bought 200,000 shares of PCS around $5. This was a big room-for-improvement story, which was just what our new, frothy market was all about. An analyst at SG Cowen had just downgraded PCS from buy to hold and upgraded Nextel to buy. I felt better, but not about to fall in love with this ragamuffin, PCS. Too much debt on the balance sheet, skimpy free cash flow. Where had I heard that story before? Nextel popped another point over two days, trading near $18. I bought three hundred thousand shares. Something I never expected to do. At least it would partially offset any incremental losses on my options inventory. Investing is an existential process where one action leads to another. Table stakes pot-limit poker comes to mind, unfortunately.

For any stock under research, you build a detailed earnings model. Anyone can do this, but the trick is to ferret out the critical variables for valuing a property. There are so many metrics that analysts pull out of a hat to justify recommendations that you gotta be sensitive to what the overriding metric should be, depending upon where you are in an economic cycle and in the life cycle of the property you're fluoroscoping. During 2002, for Nextel, it was the ratio of EBITDA to enterprise value, but it would change a year later for me as Nextel turned cash flow positive.

The new metric, free cash flow, suggested that the stock at $14 had legs, maybe to $21. Nextel needed to keep a lid on capital spending and not fall prey to rate competition. Both were good bets in an accelerating economy. On my free cash flow projections, PCS and AWE were even cheaper than Nextel—if they made their numbers in 2005. Finally, the focus would revert to the metric of new subscriber additions. Albeit 10 percent top-line revenue growth, nobody would improve on their numbers, and The Street would award the group a big yawn—like copper and oatmeal, they'd spout.

Nextel's June '03 quarterly report blew holes through all analysts' estimates. Within 24 hours even the disbelievers were rationalizing the value of the stock at $20. Nextel's bond rating was bumped up to BB—with a positive trend by the rating agencies that preferred to lag behind the financial facts by a year or more. Based on my projected coverage of interest charges, Nextel was already investment-grade paper, BBB.

Within 12 months, Nextel had levitated from a perceived basket case to a most respected competitor with outstanding metrics. My updated model showed prospective free cash flow in 2004 approaching $2 a share, which would push the stock into the high twenties. I took a deep breath and exhaled slowly. My options-writing frenzy, a foolish interlude, was history. High-octane investing is a seamless loop requiring total focus, akin to Grand Prix racing. Fortunately, I didn't need to get measured for a racing car seat. I could lose my ass, but not my life.

I ended up transferring my Nextel position to my foundation at $33 a share. Years later, Sprint bought Nextel at a premium price.

FOUR

Is Your Portfolio 1961 Château Latour?

*A*t our 2014 Memorial Day dinner *chez moi*, my good friends Arthur and Kathy brought along a single bottle of '61 Château Latour. Now, 1961 was a great year; the Latour still holds its fruit, with no residue of tannin and a beautiful nose, sort of tobacco-like and cedary. This can be a three-dimensional experience, but don't spend $2,500 or more, what Latour '61 auctions off at nowadays.

I grilled Arthur on their bottle. A friend had presented this gem 30 years ago, but he'd stored it upright in his closet since then.

"You're a moron, Arthur," I told him. "This wine can't possibly be good. It's pure vinegar by now. You've committed fratricide, infanticide, even moneycide."

"I forgot I had it," Arthur gulped.

"This wine died 20 years ago, abandoned in your closet, probably at 80 degrees with no humidity." I showed him the disintegrated dried-out cork and then decanted his bottle. Surprise! When I sniffed, sniffed, sniffed, the bouquet came through as pure cedar closet with the hint of a Siglo VI Havana.

"This is impossible," I said. "The wine may have survived your stupidity." I poured a dash in my wine glass, swirled it around and sipped. The wine was a survivor, a hundred-to-one shot in the Kentucky Derby from post 20, gamely holding off the closing favorite, "The Closet," at the finish line.

"Luck of the Irish," I told Kathy, a shiksa from the Texas Panhandle. "This is one for the record books. I'll consult my wine library to see if there's a precedent for this miracle."

First, I scanned Robert Parker's opus *Bordeaux.* Parker agreed with me—or better, I agreed with Parker: "A remarkably viscous, huge, intense wine that is one of the biggest and richest wines I have ever tasted from Latour….A phenomenal bouquet of walnuts, cassis and cedar inundates the nose….The 1961 Latour has the potential to last a hundred years. Anticipated maturity 2000–2050."

Finally, I grasped why Arthur and his shiksa couldn't destroy their lone treasure held in bondage in a stuffy closet. It was too muscular to smother, even in its stale dungeon.

Next, I turned to Michael Broadbent's *Vintage Wine*. Broadbent and Parker have my respect above all other wine meisters. Broadbent is a weather freak who points out that the 1945 and 1961 Bordeaux vintage were subjected to frosts and heavy rains, respectively, thereby reducing crops to small, thick-skinned grapes producing deeply colored, concentrated and tannic vintages. Broadbent, in my dated 2002 edition, last tasted this beauty in September 2000. He noted, "It will go on."

"So, Arthur. Learn something from your carelessness. You probably took 40 years off the life of your '61 Latour bottle, but got away with it. Don't do it again."

My lesson is something else. Never be too dogmatic and definitive about wine or even financial markets. In the worst of times, survivors pop up. Resiliency is one of the dominant themes in developed countries. I'm still not sure about Greece, but the U.S. won't sink into the mud for more than a handful of years. I looked at my portfolio and asked myself, is it possibly comparable with a 1961 bottle of Latour carelessly stored in a hostile setting? Could it last 100 years?

In the junk bond sector, my decision normally is to avoid duration risk, with few exceptions. Average duration is seven years. I assume all my callable preferred stocks will be called sooner or later at $25, but they are mainly bank preferreds bought at the bottom of the market in April of 2009, in single digits. Yearend 2014, they yield 6 percent, selling near par $25.

I've learned a painful lesson. The Bank of America preferred was bought at the same time I bought the common stock, both at $7.50. Five years later, 2015, the preferred trades over $25, but the common seems stalled out around $17. The bank stayed in business, so the preferred traded up to its call price, but the common stock still lacks an earnings story. Still waiting. Bank of America's mortgage portfolio is a long-term workout and they'll be sued until the Twelfth of Never. Litigation reserves even for JPMorgan Chase are measured in multibillion-dollar tranches, destined to be fully tapped through 2016, at best.

In my junk bond portfolio, two positions doubled: Continental Airlines and Florida Power & Light's hybrid issue, which converts in seven years to yield LIBOR plus some 333 basis points. The airline position was analogous to a shaky bank preferred. Bought at the bottom of the cycle, the only variable was its survival. Continental's income statement showed it was cash flow neutral even in the recession setting, a good indicator.

The FPL Capital Management investment was a curious anomaly. Institutional investors turned up their noses on hybrid bonds, hesitant to take the interest rate risk if LIBOR remained minimal. I checked a long-term chart on LIBOR and drew a trendline through the 3 percent level. This was good enough to postulate this bond would yield 6.5 percent in its sunset years. Trading at $111, there are no offerings today.

In 2009 you could inventory at par bonds like Valero, Altria, Lubrizol and Rio Tinto, all carrying 9 percent coupons. This BB paper now trades around $130, yielding to maturity 4 percent. The country remains yield starved. You need to go down to single B–rated paper with a 10-year duration to obtain a 5.5 percent return. My B paper was the best asset class during 2014, bar none, worldwide, as good as the S&P 500 Index. You don't need a three-day seminar to figure it out or worry about how many iPads and iPhones Apple ships.

Unlike wine, the trajectory towards maturity for growth stocks normally lasts no more than five years. Ten at most. Maturity for a first-growth vintage wine is 25 years or so, but then it plateaus for a couple more decades. Inventorying wine is a one-decision endeavor. Sadly, one-decision investing is forever a life-threatening construct. Morgan Guaranty Trust in 1973–'74 flamed out on growth stocks that stopped growing. I'd rather own an airline selling in single digits with promising turnaround prospects than Salesforce.com at 30 times 2017's EBITDA. "Price quality is everything!"

Like investing, the only way you learn about wine is by doing, or tasting. There is no better classroom than a dining room full of opinionated followers of the grape. A horizontal tasting, where you sample a broad cross section of first and second growths of the same year's vintage, is most instructive.

A couple of hundred of us gathered at the Four Seasons restaurant years ago for a tasting of the '86 Bordeaux. The Four Seasons then was run impeccably by Paul Kovi and Tom Margittai. Designed initially as an automobile showroom in the Seagram Building, its airy amplitude was a refreshing change from the holes-in-the-wall on Manhattan's side streets, where you dined a nose away from the bordering table's cigarette smoke.

The Four Seasons radiates Belle Epoque panache. Everyone is treated with deference and *égalité*. The proprietors of Château Margaux, a Greek family living in France, the Mentzelopouloses, were guests of honor at the tasting. André Mentzelopoulos bought Margaux in '79 for about $18 million after the French government refused to allow a first-growth château to pass into foreign ownership. National Distillers notched the premium bid but lost out. Today, you couldn't touch this property for $300 million.

The early line on the '86s, as stated by Robert Parker, a keenly read wine critic who writes a bimonthly called *The Wine Advocate*, was that they are as good as the '82s. The '82s were expected to turn out on a level with the '61s or '59s, which is saying a lot, but 30 years later they've peaked and are losing fruit.

If Parker is wrong on the '86s, his star will diminish like a market letter writer who predicts a 1,000-point bull move and strikes out. Because of the loaded tannin in the '86s, the wines didn't mature for 20 years. My take currently is "very good but not exceptional," excepting the Haut-Brion. Everyone must consult his own mortality table before investing therein. You don't want your grandchildren chugalugging this stuff with Whoppers.

Even the wine merchants at our table took notes. The white Pavillon Blanc du Château Margaux ushered in the reds, 17 wines in all. It had a distinctive white Bordeaux character and a mouth-filling aftertaste. I jotted a note to buy a couple of cases. This before we had made our way up to the first-growth blockbusters, recently bottled, existing as wine futures at your better purveyors.

The '86s were babies, their eyes still closed up. You got a sense of the wine's structure and fruit but were overwhelmed with the harsh tannins, the product of a hot summer, nearly a drought in Bordeaux. Those châteaux that delayed picking until mid-October were blessed with hot sunny days that ripened the Cabernet Sauvignon grapes to perfect intensity. Château Margaux falls in this category, along with Mouton Rothschild.

All of us had this info before tasting these 1986 first growths. Parker has rated Mouton at 100 and Margaux at 99, with Haut-Brion at 92 and Petrus at 90. Rating an immature wine 100 is the equivalent of paying 100 times earnings for Twitter because you had a dream they were going to make a fortune from advertising revenues on smartphones.

Our table discounted Parker's ratings. The Haut-Brion was the winner, with a big mouth and full bouquet. Yes! The biggest worry was its forward development—that it would poop out by 2006. (Not so!) The Mouton Rothschild came in second, with an overpowering aftertaste. Latour was closed and Petrus bland. Château Cheval Blanc showed good structure; Ausone was just plain closed and light bodied. The Margaux had its typical *goût de terre*, the taste of the earth. Château Lafite Rothschild ranked with the Margaux, Mouton and Haut-Brion.

The most interesting part of the evening, aside from the tasting, was the commentary from a guy who makes the Château Margaux wine, Paul Pontallier, a youngish estate director with a good command of English. Pontallier defined his mission as divining what the grapes want to express along with the soil, the climates and the ages of the vines. "Above all, a good winemaker needs patience to define a great vintage."

I muttered to the arb on my right, "He talks like a portfolio manager." A good money manager deals successfully with as many variables as a first-growth wine-maker. (Referring to my dinner notes, I see I spelled *patience* "patence." This after 17 wines.)

Instead of the age of the vines, we deal with the economic cycle's durabil-ity. Fluctuating interest rates and Federal Reserve Board policy emphasis match the rain and when-to-pick variables. Corporate earnings power is the intensity of the grapes engendered by the sun's rays. The stock market technicians are the Robert Parkers of the world, who rate wine with numbers. Wine merchants equate with high-powered institutional brokerage houses.

The chatter on Wall Street matches wine trade hyperbole for Bordeaux. So far, the wine trade has proclaimed 10 "vintages of the century": '45, '61, '64, '70, '75 and '82, possibly '90, and recently 2000, 2009 and 2010. The '82s were trumpeted before the grapes reached the fermenting vats, because they were laden with sugar. Parker was their earliest booster.

There were few bulls yearend 2012 when the market began its 21-month spurt to 2,000. Market letter writers and investment strategists hung bearish. But the market didn't care that Goldman Sachs had 14 reasons for optimism and pessi-mism. The public has hundreds of billions in money market funds, but the market doesn't give a damn their interest rate borders zero.

Twenty years from now we'll know whether the 2010 Mouton Rothschild is a perfect 100, Margaux a 99. Maybe I'm right about Haut-Brion. Until I see more wine merchant exuberance on The Street, I intend to stay fully invested in 2015.

Sadly, unlike vintners, retailers and banana plantation bosses, money managers can't cite inclement weather for subpar performance. I'm not keen on Berkshire Hathaway's 10 largest holdings, as I don't see IBM, ExxonMobil and Wal-Mart as likely outperformers mid-decade, but they're big slices of corporate America. I'd compare them to vintage wines that have peaked but are likely to plateau for a decade or longer.

It is notable that 50 percent of Buffett's portfolio rests in the financial sector. No pharmaceuticals or basic industrials show up, but he does own all of Burlington Northern and Santa Fe Railroad. Not even Icahn Associates is so extremely con-centrated. Apple is a $7 billion holding out of $33 billion invested. For Buffett, Apple is like the sweater girl everyone yearns to touch, but fears a loaded mouse-trap nestles in her bra.

FIVE

The Inner Game of Investing

GEORGE BELLOWS, *JACK DEMPSEY AND FIRPO*, 1924
Collection—Whitney Museum of American Art

George Bellows, whom I consider one of a dozen great painters of the 20th century, didn't depict swans paddling majestically in Central Park. One iconic canvas shows Luis Firpo knocking Jack Dempsey through the ropes in a no-holds-barred backroom boxing bout, one of a series on the inner seams of old New York. Here's Bellows's points:

- Try everything that can be done.

- Try it every possible way.
- Be deliberate.
- Be spontaneous.
- Be thoughtful and painstaking.
- Be abandoned and impulsive.
- There is nothing I do not want to know that has to do with life or art.
- Revolt against authority and mainstream society.

You can't invest like John McEnroe used to play tennis. Lose your temper and you'll pay dearly. Buying at tops, selling at bottoms, discarding winners and staying with losers are emotional gin rummy kinds of decisions that turn out badly. Bernard Baruch summed it up when an anxious player handed him his portfolio and asked for advice. Baruch wouldn't even look at the list. He just said, "Sell it down to your sleeping level." Not only do you need to purge emotional reactions to losses, but to successful plays as well.

Never judge yourself as a good or bad investor. Your ego stays out of the business. There are no good stocks or bad stocks. When a stock you buy turns south, ask yourself whether your entry point was timely or not. If anxiety is fear of the future, concentrate on bringing action or reaction back to present time. The serious investor is ever sensitive to macro events and how they play out in industry sectors and subsectors such as oil drillers. I'm always thinking about what's ahead for the next six months, maybe 12, but no more.

Like a professional singer or musician, I like to tune up with scales and arpeggios. It gets me concentrated on the here and now and takes about 30 minutes of pre-opening "practice." What I'm trying to do is program myself to be a winner rather than play defensive ball. Our traders canvas The Street for me. I know which houses are upgrading or downgrading stocks, changing earnings projections or publishing "think pieces" on the market, the economy, specific stock sectors or big capitalization stocks that we follow. If the analysts or pundits are serious professionals, I'll ask for a printout and get it in minutes. By 8:30 a.m. our traders have caught up on the rest of the world's overnight statistics. I know where the European bourses and the Nikkei averages have ticked, the price change in gold and oil, which currencies have rippled out of alignment. Many Department of Commerce monthly series statistical releases are published at 8:30, too: consumer prices, unemployment, retail sales and changes in inventories. The bond market opens at 9:00 and takes its cue from these numbers, which the *WSJ* fashions into stories for its next-day edition.

By the time you've read the papers, the news is already discounted in the marketplace. Similarly, earnings releases and news on mergers, acquisitions and takeovers normally print on the tickers intraday. The news from the Capitol on the progress of specific legislative initiatives like health care, defense spending and budget issues is early on leaks and comparably stale by the time you read it in your paper of record. I assume anything I read is at least two days old and The Street's players, both traders and money managers, have digested it before the public sees it in print.

Nobody should spend more than 15 minutes on any newspaper. I digest the *Wall Street Journal*, the *Financial Times* and the *New York Times*, including its sports section, in 30 minutes, over breakfast. The *Times* tells me about wars, national disasters and infighting in the Capitol. I find the *Financial Times* columnists less Establishment-oriented. Their focus is the continent. When something is rotten at Daimler Benz, they bring the story sharply into focus.

Before I open the *WSJ*, I scan the table of contents for stories of prospective investment significance or pieces that can embellish our scope on running policy initiatives like health care and the budget. On March 24, 2001, the *New York Times* published a front-page story that the Republicans were considering a $60-billion up-front tax cut. Because I believed the country needed upwards of $300 billion in stimulus, I concluded nobody in the Capitol was tuned in to the seriousness of the impending recession. It kept me from putting cash reserves to work with the market in a free-fall mode.

In the *WSJ*, turn to the box on "Most Active Issues," a list of 15 NYSE stocks. Sometimes there's a discernible pattern that you store in your bank of apperceptive mass. Sector rotation within the market and specific industry groups falling in or out of favor are intermediate-term trends that you must process. I watch this list like I would a pinball machine lighting up and buzzing as the steel balls bounce off the rubbers.

For me, the most revealing daily stock table is the "new high" list. The *WSJ* and the *Times* publish this box in the smallest type size known to the Western world; the *Times* makes this crucial data practically invisible to the naked eye. By March of 2001 the new-high list was all but obliterated, suggesting the market's breadth was narrowly based. You attack and dissect this list by carrying forward a couple of deep basics. Most of your money needs to work in sectors that are acting better than the market. Your stocks should be big capitalization properties with excellent liquidity and no serious financial risk.

The daily new-high list tells me which buses are leaving the station and compels me to reassess our major sector weightings. When a big-cap stock, over $100 billion, hits the list without me, I begin screaming for the full story in 24 hours or less with charts, tables, 10-Ks, analysts' reports, whatever it takes to make a decision, thumbs up or thumbs down.

To add scope and emphasis to the daily new-high snapshot, we track big capitalization stocks with outstanding monthly and year-to-date performance. These shooting stars confirm where the flow of new money is headed. You begin to see clear-cut patterns of sector strength and you sort out stocks for analytical coverage you normally pass on. Despite fully publicized cutbacks in defense spending, several avionics and missile contractors soared during the nineties. General Dynamics, Northrop Grumman, Martin Marietta and Lockheed Martin were worth a quick study for their underlying asset values, cost containment and successful downsizing, plus rising earnings. These stocks doubled over 18 months and still sold near 12 times earnings later in 2000, very reasonable. Over the next decade they fulfilled their promise. Lockheed sells at 15 times earnings, while Boeing emerged with an enormous backlog of aircraft. Mid-decade, the analysis shifted to profit margin enhancement and free cash flow generation. Boeing is one of the few stocks I can safely say I'm in for the next three to five years.

After all the snapshots are digested, you switch to a wide-angle lens for the annual reports and 10-Ks, which frequently revise all that's gone on. Yearend write-offs, changes in accounting conventions for research, health care, pensions, depreciation and inventories are common even for hallowed names like IBM, General Motors and Procter & Gamble. Aside from outright fraud and embezzlement, I find 95 out of 100 annual reports worthless.

I lug home dozens. By midnight, I'm fast asleep, the carpet littered with the blue-suited carcasses of corporate chairmen, their messages in stilted corporatese, moribund and mute. The frequency of 4-color photography and the size of the books vary directly with stock prices. It will take two Black Mondays, back-to-back, to squash annuals down to a sane 24-page production. Wal-Mart does it in 20 pages. Their numbers speak louder than words on recycled paper.

Securities analysts, like Talmudic scholars, start at the back, where the footnotes to the financials are printed in small type. When the headman's message opens with "Results for your company were mixed," you know your company is up to its waist in quicksand. An entire subsector of the public relations industry does nothing but design and write four-color jobs for hundreds of companies. Their diction and artwork are readily interchangeable.

If you read a dozen 1989 and 1990 annual reports of banks and S&Ls, you would never have known their loan portfolios were crumbling into dust. The same goes for yearend 2007. Not even a hint of the fiasco in mortgage paper. This is the "One-Horse Shay" kind of poetic license as typified by Dun & Bradstreet. Everything is growth, growth, growth, except every three or four years there's an enormous restructuring write-off. Everyone charges off billions for "restructuring initiatives." Wall Street analysts love write-offs because then they can go back to extrapolating growth for the next cycle. Everyone ignores the fact that the write-off engulfed and devoured years of previously reported earnings and net worth. Even IBM was guilty.

Few annuals tell you what's ahead for the new year. The documents chronicle the past without interpreting the dialectics of change. The distortion is comparable to looking through a rearview mirror. After x-ing out the glossy photos, I look for nuances of change in the corporate mindset. Sometimes it's reassuring to find management is as tough as ever about getting its stock to dance. The GE report is perennially a masterpiece, an agglomeration of no-nonsense info on every sector of its business, written by their general managers. Jack Welch told you up front how he was positioning GE for the next decade.

Searching through the IBM wreckage in the early nineties, I uncovered one last damning piece of evidence. The shareholders list rested intact! IBM still boasted three-quarters of a million owners despite its year-to-year $25 billion shrinkage in market value. Inertia among investors, both institutional and individual, can never be underestimated. It suggests the public's image of IBM hadn't changed in 10 years—before Apple, Compaq, Dell and Sun Microsystems pecked 'em to death. I placed the IBM book cover-up on my work table as a reminder that money management is a continuous process of reality testing. A management that can't write a candid and organized report to shareholders is a company you don't want to own at any price—until they change.

IBM finally changed. John Akers took early retirement and an outsider, Lou Gerstner, came in and cleaned the stables. Years later, a sailing buddy of Tom Watson, IBM's founder, explained it to him in two sentences. For years they had the business all to themselves. Watson built up six layers of management and could never react fast enough to change. The 2000 IBM annual was a great read, full of info on how management was positioning its company for the years ahead. Intel and Cisco needed to reinvent themselves by 2014, but nowhere could you find management pronouncing adequately on research priorities, capital investment and divestitures.

During the early sixties as a securities analyst I had to disabuse the tailored partners I reported to on stocks they loved to recommend. Many lived in the past, their perception of the management and competitive mettle of companies like GM, International Paper and International Harvester sadly unfocused. In the nineties this myopia was even more dangerous, considering the dimming future of Eastman Kodak, Xerox, Procter & Gamble, Motorola, Kellogg, Sears, Allstate and dozens more that were held in high esteem for too long. I pore over hundreds of annuals and maybe a handful hit pay dirt as actionable research ideas. Like a homicide detective interrogating a suspect, you listen to what is said or unsaid, read the body language, and squint at the small-print evidence. Finally, the symbolism emerges—they're either winners or losers. First read the footnotes in the back. Then, look at the disparity between GAAP and non-GAAP earnings. If it's more than 10 percent, chances are the company is being run for management and key employees. Note year-over-year share dilution. For Twitter it's 8 percent. Salesforce.com is another egregious offender.

For the do-it-yourself investor, *accept my point of view that you can only invest wisely if you have sifted all the available facts in any situation. When you develop a macroeconomic point of view that diverges from the consensus, implement it aggressively. Assume that if you've hit the mark, the consensus will fall into line within six months.* But actively monitor your working hypothesis. It has to be reconfirmed with unfolding statistical data. Don't be stubborn. If the facts don't fit your conclusion, fold your hand. When the facts reconfirm your position, buy more. Finally, you plan an exit strategy based on a model of valuation that relates stock prices to their return on capital over a full cycle. Financial information at the margin unfolds daily. Process it dispassionately. Ninety-five percent of what you hear and read is noise, to be discarded as garbage. Maybe 5 percent of overnight news requires a follow-up to see whether it modifies your point of view on how the future will unfold for the world, the country, or specific industries or companies. Close reading of quarterly corporate reports is a must.

The reason for due diligence is to muster courage to act without inhibition, particularly when markets are hysterically ebullient or in a panic mode. You do the security analysis, then buy the properties you believe in when they are in free fall. I did this with Citigroup, Bank of America, MGIC, Sirius XM Radio, Goldman Sachs, Gilead Sciences, Boeing and Las Vegas Sands. Conversely, I couldn't buy into the technology rout in March of 2001, unable to benchmark properties like Cisco, Intel and EMC. There was more than an inventory glut. Capital spending had dried up their customers.

When you know an industry and all the players involved who manage the primary properties, as the sector segues into its cycle you shed lingering reservations and swing for the fences. I did this in the gaming industry in the eighties when

Vegas was still underbuilt but beginning to turn into a family destination resort. A great player of craps watched me for an hour and then chided me for playing defensively. You're supposed to play to win, taking the full odds behind the line whenever you can. My feeble excuse was that I was out of my element. Wall Street is where I'd learned to be fearless, to separate the real from the unreal, to leverage institutional stupidity and time my buying into panics just when dawn was about to break.

I did this better when I was younger and had much less to lose. When Roger Blough of U.S. Steel faced off with President Kennedy over raising steel prices, The Street panicked, anticipating price controls. But Jack Kennedy was counseled by his father, Joe Kennedy, a seasoned corporate player, who advised his son to cool his jets. I bought Xerox, fully margined, in '62 and it worked.

Historical memory either distorts the present or focuses it brilliantly. I had to terminate a very bright fiftyish technology analyst because his image of Motorola, IBM and Texas Instruments was formed a decade ago. He was late tuning in to changes at the margin, particularly for Motorola, whose primacy in cellular technology was stripped away by Nokia. Later, he missed Apple and preferred Yahoo over Google. If historical memory helps you comprehend the here and now it's a plus, otherwise throw it in the wastebasket. I've been known to take entire corporate files a foot thick and dump them as impediments to perception.

Historical memory is more useful as a valuation tool in appraising the entire market rather than specific stocks and sectors. During 1999–2000, I steered clear of all the dot-coms as impossible to model with the exception of AOL, which we bought early on. The context was a 5 percent yield on 10-year Treasuries and corporate earnings power touching down around $50 a share from $56.51 in 2000, but rebounding late in 2002 to the mid-fifties level. Since Congress didn't enact a massive tax cut, the recession would elongate and the U-shape of the economy would broaden. The S&P 500 Index could go lower, maybe to 1,000. But at least I had a working hypothesis that kept me from freezing up by anticipating the future.

Comparable dynamics got me back into the market during the opening of 2009. The TARP devised by Tim Geithner and Ben Bernanke bailed out Citigroup, General Motors, AIG, Bank of America, Fannie Mae and Freddie Mac. Stocks had touched down at 10 times earnings, yielding over 5 percent. Historically this is deep valuation territory that sucks in value players like Buffett.

Unlike many of my generation, I've eschewed short selling because it screws up my head and makes me anxious. I do write covered calls against long positions when the market feels toppy. Sometimes, I'll box positions by selling calls and using the proceeds to buy puts. Again, all this activity is aimed at quieting the mind to reconcentrate on maximizing bull market plays.

In America, at least in the long run, optimism pays. The stock market has out-performed all other assets despite its Blackish Mondays. Staying invested is more fruitful than moving into and out of markets, particularly if you're running billions. I've learned not to forecast too definitively on interest rates and the valuation structure of the market. It's better to seek out companies, businesses, industries and management that you believe are going into phase and stay with them for five years, sometimes longer.

Finally, never fall in love with a stock that goes up and makes you feel smart, like the old Xerox. You'll regret it. If you need more love and admiration, buy a dog. My wife, Toni, and I live with 10 poodles. Six standards and four toys. We breed and exhibit same. If you want a puppy, give us a call. There's a wait list at $3,500. Twenty-five years ago the going rate was $300, and no wait list. You just had to pass an intensive interview.

SIX

How to Make a Billion (in 25 to 50 Years)

*S*ometime in the mid-sixties, I telephoned my father, who had retired to Key West after operating a tailor shop in Harlem for over 30 years.

"Pop, I'm a millionaire," I said excitedly.

"Bah! Martin, I don't believe you," he said.

"But it's true, Pop."

"Nonsense, Martin," he said. "If you were a millionaire you'd have racehorses and a yacht like J. P. Morgan."

"Pop, I don't like boats, and the track doesn't interest me. My playpen is the Big Board."

In 1960, maybe a handful of Jewish boys from the East Bronx worked as analysts on Wall Street. There were Italian traders and margin clerks, while aged "men of color" wearing grey smocks ironed partners' *Wall Street Journal*s early mornings before they arrived at work. My father's Russian peasant persona dictated that once you had a job or ran a store, you married it for life. Early on, I used Pop as a negative role model and never looked back. The historian Frederick Jackson Turner's "frontier thesis" was ingrained in my psyche.

Milton Kirschbaum, one of my hedge fund partners, late sixties, wrote down on his passport that he was a professional speculator. Milt had emerged from the pits in the Chicago Board of Trade. He'd claim that, end of cycle in grain markets, the same handful of guys ended up with all the money.

When people ask me what I do, I don't tell them I'm a money manager. I say, "I'm a securities analyst, a generalist. I fluoroscope anything and everything."

Over 40 years ago, Secretariat won the Belmont Stakes, going away, by 31 lengths. His world record of 2:24 for 12 furlongs on the dirt still stands. The stock market contains no big capitalization properties in Secretariat's class. Apple started its run from the low thirties, peaking out at $700, then shuffled back into the pack but came on gamely. Google's still a contender, up 1,300 percent since going public nine years ago, but 2014 was a negative year.

Biotech properties tripled in a couple of years. Throw in Gilead Sciences, Celgene, Biogen Idec and Regeneron, too. Bank properties like Citigroup came back from the ashes of 2009—a buck a share then, before its reverse split of 1 for 10. But banks are banks, not uncontended franchises with airtight operating momentum.

The market ain't Secretariat, either. Over the past four decades it compounded at 7.8 percent, after emerging out of a vicious recession in 1973–'74. How many operators bluster out of their stall at 6:00 a.m., rise up on hind legs, forelegs pawing at the blue sky?

"Come on down, Red," his exercise rider would chide Secretariat. "Come on down." Mike Milken came close to Secretariat during the eighties. By 9:00 a.m. he'd already taken three successive breakfasts with wannabe honchos and banking clients. Mike lugged around two lawyer briefcases filled with his "deal" material.

The market pulled away from all the boring, edgy pundits who saw nothing but downside at yearend 2013. The Fed's bond buying cutback didn't scare the bond crowd one bit. Facebook's gutsy $19 billion buy of the Internet messaging property WhatsApp didn't panic its holders. I expected Facebook to drop 7 percent or 8 percent overnight, the size of implicit deal dilution for a company charging users a buck, annually.

Facebook, and now Alibaba, may contain a heart as big as Secretariat's. (When the vets autopsied him, they found a heart nearly sized like a watermelon.) Actually, my Saturday at a recent Belmont Stakes race didn't run true to form. The short-odds favorites, Orb and Oxbow, finished out of the money. Nobody in my crowd of horsemen and owners held tickets on Palace Malice, the winner. Nothing but red faces.

What a fit metaphor for our Big Board, where favorites like Microsoft faded badly and few stocks run true to form for more than a couple of years. The time for this mile-and-a-half Belmont was 2.30.77, nearly seven seconds slower than Secretariat's record run. Evidently, the gene pool in horses is too big to reproduce this reddish chestnut colt's quality, even after 40 years of intensive breeding.

During Secretariat's reign in 1973, the market faltered badly, sucked into quicksand by one horrendous recession induced by real estate overspeculation. We recovered in 1975, but wage inflation, induced by General Motors and others, did us in by 1982.

Then, Paul Volcker decided to rid the country of its inflationary excesses. And so he did. The market touched down at book value, and yielded over 5 percent, sold under 10 times earnings. Take this base into consideration when calculating the S&P 500 Index's compound annual rate of return.

Seabiscuit prevailed during the Great Depression, a great come-from-behind horse, an inspiration for the $2 bettor. But this feisty runner was no metaphor for the unemployment rolls. I didn't like what I read about the late-2008 anti-stimulus dissenters at the FRB and U.S. Treasury after they bailed out Bear Stearns but pushed Lehman Brothers into bankruptcy. Don't ever expect our government to do the right thing, implicitly, by betting on the winning horse. European central bankers remain spineless, pressing monetary policy but knowing only fiscal stimulus, lower taxes and infrastructure spending can create jobs and consumer demand.

Early sixties, anyone worth a million was in the top 0.1 percent, not the top 1 percent category. Net worth of $100 million was rarefied, super-wealthy, comparable with $10 billion today. The great fortunes made by technology honchos and conglomerateurs were yet to come, a 1980s phenomenon. Microsoft went public in the eighties. In the early sixties few people even knew hedge funds existed. A fund with $20 million made you a big operator.

Today, there're dozens of private partnerships with $20 billion or more in open-to-buy. Late fifties and early sixties, good operators scored with Polaroid, Xerox, Syntex and Fairchild Camera—all big capitalization growthies, easily analyzed. Currently, well-heeled operators of private capital focus on what they believe are inefficiently priced properties with huge operating leverage. Many picks are small capitalization stocks, under $5 billion in market capitalization. Sotheby's, MGIC and Sirius XM Radio come to mind.

Carl Icahn was an exception with his $4-billion gut play in Apple. Few hedge fund operators even owned Google, up 54 percent in 2013, and 1,300 percent since going public less than 10 years before. In Greenlight Capital's top 10, Apple comprised 13 percent of its portfolio, preceded by Micron Technology at 15 percent. These two positions comprised 28 percent of its top 10, followed by SunEdison and Marvell Technology, the fourth position, making it 39 percent. Concentration is a two-edged sword, an indicator of a money manager's moxie and thrust to outperform. All 10 holdings are controversial. Greenlight knows how to stand alone, so label this courage.

Greenlight Capital

Top 10 Holdings as of September 30, 2014

Security	Weighting	Market Value ($ billions)
Micron Technology	15.1%	1044.0
Apple	13.3%	924.1
SunEdison	5.8%	401.7
Marvell Technology	5.1%	355.7
Aetna	3.5%	243.7
IAC/InterActiveCorp	2.9%	197.4
Lam Research	2.9%	197.2
Cigna	2.7%	188.1
Citizens	2.7%	187.4
Consol Energy	2.7%	184.6
	56.7%	3923.9

Although I've made serious money in small-cap properties, I never invested big gobs of capital therein. I prefer uncovering big-cap properties with minimal financial risk but with prospectively huge operating leverage. In the mid-seventies I owned 15 percent of the New York Times Company. The Sulzbergers finally had hired a professional manager to run the company but not the newsroom. Walter Mattson came through, and the *Times*'s operating margins approached parity with the *Washington Post* and Gannett and then topped out and I sold out. It declined for the next 30 years. Buying the *Boston Globe* for $3 billion was the peak for big-city newspaper franchises and came near to destroying NYT's balance sheet equilibrium.

The outside investor is disadvantaged in uncovering management leverage, but it can be the pivotal variable, such as Lou Gerstner taking the reins at IBM when it floundered. Hopefully, the recent merger of American Airlines and US Airways, where US Airways' managers supersede AA's, will bear fruit. Aside from Jamie Dimon, who carried JPMorgan Chase through the bank meltdown in 2008, the headmen at Citigroup, Bank of America, Merrill Lynch and American International Group were shown the door, replaced by cost cutters if not bean counters.

Microsoft, early in 2014, tapped its new maximum leader—an insider, Satya Nadella. I have no edge on his evaluation. But anyone's better than Steve Ballmer, who ran the company for too long, over a decade. Microsoft's leadership struck out or was late on all major new developments in its business—cloud computing, smartphones and Internet vending. They pissed away tens of billions on bad acquisitions and investments like Barnes & Noble's electronic reader initiative. Microsoft's Xbox may be viable but from inception has lost many billions. As an investment, Microsoft is a reallocation of assets and R&D story, but too tough to call, selling near the market's earnings multiplier of 16 times earnings.

I breezed through the tenth-floor exhibition space at Sotheby's, viewing auction lots in the upcoming sales of Impressionist, modern and contemporary art. Anthony Grant, my cicerone, informed me that there are at least a hundred prospective buyers of iconic pieces that sell for upwards of $25 million. As a serious collector of contemporary art, I found the ground soggier than Wall Street.

JEAN-MICHEL BASQUIAT, UNTITLED, 1982
Private Collection

I thought maybe a couple of dozen big players, but Anthony, Sotheby's contemporary art expert, takes the pulses of big hitters, daily, and knows better. Warhol, Jackson Pollock, Barnett Newman, Giacometti, Richter, Basquiat, Franz Kline, Rothko, Clyfford Still, Lichtenstein, Jasper Johns, Jeff Koons—the list does grow longer.

My frustration is, I coulda bought all these iconic properties in the eighties for under $100,000 per canvas. But I didn't. I sold Warhol and Richter prematurely to buy other artists. This was unlike my stock picking and money management. You stay with a good-acting stock for its full cycle, maybe five to 10 years.

Basquiat's best work, done in 1982, now goes for $25 million and up. It then sold for $2,500 apiece. Mark Rothkos went for $1,200 in 1954, now $75 million. So, a $10,000 investment then is now pegged easily over $100 million. Art investors can learn something from Warren Buffett. When you like something and it's confirmed in the marketplace, marry it for life rather than sell and lament over taxable income.

But once I tire of a work on my walls, I bang it out and substitute something new. This kind of behavior has cost me, big-time. Collectors I know are capable of buying 20 to 30 pieces by the same artist, storing them in a warehouse for 10 to 20 years and then, if they guessed right, feeding 'em out into the auction market.

In 1990, I turned down Richter's canvases at the Anthony d'Offay Gallery. I thought they were too pretty. Normally, when Toni, my wife, and I like an artist's production we accumulate four or five pieces. A $500,000 investment in Richter in 1990 would be worth $250 million in 2014's roiling art scene.

If you refer to your compound interest table you'll find these are better returns than Warren Buffett logged over 50 years of investing. Year by year, Warren had to apply himself intensively, while sipping his Diet Cokes. The art buyer needs to apply himself for a couple of hours, maybe buy an artist's catalogue raisonné, thumb through the pages, read his biography and then raise a paddle at Sotheby's or Christie's evening sales.

My 2014 yearend reading of the art market, using *Art & Auction*'s calculations for the top 50 artists in demand over the past decade, shows nearly a 400 percent rate of return. My experience over the same period is comparable. The S&P 500 Index dating from 2003 shows just 50 percent growth. If I had reversed the ratio of art investments to equity holdings in 2003, I'd be sitting on Easy Street today. This assumes I sold nothing in the interim, an unlikely occurrence.

But the contemporary art indices based on auction prices don't do justice to the tremendous moves within subcategories. For example, a Christopher Wool word painting available at $250,000 less than 10 years ago made over $24 million in 2013.

As a money manager, confined within the construct of straight fees, with no incentives, the best I can do is buy a stock at $1, sell it for $2 and take a 1 percent management fee. I'm no Steve Cohen or Carl Icahn. I did leverage myself once by a billion dollars in the eighties to make an unsolicited bid for Caesars World, but I lost that battle and decided never again to be so concentrated.

Learn to love leverage and employ margin when it's cheap, since 2009. I carry a huge high-yield bond portfolio and concentrated but liquid equity holdings.

All my stocks trade millions of shares daily on the Big Board. I could bang 'em out in 15 minutes if necessary on minimal down ticks. I'm talking about Gilead Sciences, Citigroup, Bank of America, Kinder Morgan, Actavis, Alibaba and Apple.

For billionaire wannabes, there is always the old-fashioned way of entrepreneurial success as in Bill Gates, Sam Walton, Rupert Murdoch, Steve Wynn, Craig McCaw and Ron Perelman. This is the older generation of workaholics. Many tapped Milken's capacity to raise bond money for their deals during the eighties. Venture capitalists backed Google's founders Sergey Brin and Larry Page as well as Facebook's Mark Zuckerberg and Steve Jobs in Apple's formative years. Sequoia's $8 million investment in WhatsApp is worth billions a few years later.

Michael Bloomberg, founder of Bloomberg L.P. after he left Salomon Brothers, filled the space of online financial data better than his competition and deserves all his successes. I discount many of the Russian oligarchs, beneficiaries of Boris Yeltsin's giveaways of natural resources in return for political backing. They were just there at the right time as Russia imploded.

To make even hundreds of millions you need to cobble together decades of great years. Reciprocally, you can't afford any big down years. Warren Buffett is your model here. Don't ever buy a property that can't come back. Xerox, Polaroid and Eastman Kodak come to mind. IBM stumbled and needed an outsider, Lou Gerstner, to make its comeback.

Lehman Brothers went down for the count of 10, while Citigroup and Merrill Lynch saw the wolf on their doorstep, as did General Motors and AIG. Banks were grossly overleveraged at the peak of the cycle for financial assets, 2007. Their committees on risk management were feeble and lied to by head traders. The prime case was the London Whale caper at JPMorgan Chase. Bad trades somehow get stashed into desk drawers.

There is one more way to reach 10 figures, but it's odious, consumes your work life and is certainly amoral, bureaucratic and a long grind. Fight your way onto the executive floor of a major corporation, hire a compensation advisor who knows what can be accomplished legally, and appoint your friends as patsies to directorships where they will approve the rape of your corporation at the expense of passive shareholders.

Ray Irani, headman at Occidental Petroleum, got away with the outrageous compensation package that made his fortune over decades. He was recently unseated by activist institutional investors, but it took decades. Even in later years

Irani's package ran as high as $70 million in 2010, down to $45 million for 2013.

Financial sector honchos like Sandy Weill walked away with a billion generated by options grants from deal activity that in the long run proved deeply flawed. The concept of building a financial department store covering operations in brokerage, insurance, real estate and banking came apart at the seams in 2008. Headmen at Citigroup, AIG, Merrill Lynch and Bank of America couldn't get their hands around risk management and overleveraged balance sheets.

A more insidious construct disturbs me. You find it among almost all operators in the technology sector. Namely, key-employee share-based compensation runs between 10 percent and 15 percent of total earnings, in some cases much more, year after year. Normally, shareholders receive minimal dividends, although this is changing at some of the big houses like Cisco, IBM, Microsoft and Intel.

Whenever I see a variance of 10 percent to 15 percent between GAAP and non-GAAP accounting, I print out the company's proxy statement. Normally, it's 60 or more pages of boilerplate, but it can't hide executive compensation from all sources. Actually, I don't have a problem with headman compensation up to $20 million per annum if we're talking about a leading-edge world operator like Qualcomm.

Dr. Paul Jacobs's 2012 compensation at Qualcomm, including all incentives, totted up to $19.6 million. This is a delicately evolving house, largely tied to wireless technology. You either get research priorities right or competition leaves you in the dust. Think Nokia vs. Apple. This ain't oil futures determining your annual earnings. But Qualcomm's share count still edged up, year over year, despite buybacks.

At least this isn't Richard Fuld, headman at Lehman Brothers, who creamed off 1 percent of earnings, some $40 million in 2008 just before Lehman flamed out. When I look at the bushels of options and stock grants issued by tech houses, inclusive of Cisco, it's obvious management and its key employees come first and shareholders last.

Sadly, the big money in our country is coined by the top one tenth of 1 percent—the 99.9th percentile. Being in the top 1 percent of earners is no longer a big deal; you're just comfortable, not exactly filthy rich. Barring entrepreneurial genius coupled with 12-hour workdays, passive players need to use leverage, preferably other people's money. Let's leave aside hedge fund operators and private equity houses. The 20 percent override on profits construct makes you very rich once you build your fund to over $16 billion. We're talking an easy $200 million "take" in a good year taxed at the capital gains rate. So far, no politician dares to touch this giveaway.

Short of entrepreneurial genius, options leverage and raking off 20 percent of the profits from running a multibillion-dollar private equity fund, the individual investor must put together a long string of felicitous investing and skirt big mistakes. Employment of enormous leverage in commodities trading, currencies or gold is forever treacherous for non-professional players. Your pants can be taken down with the snap of fingers. I'm still working actively on the problem, mainly looking for operating profit margin leverage in small-cap, mid-cap and large-cap properties.

Let's assume you're not a professional investor but do understand economics and the stock market and are capable of spotting major trends with serious investment impact. I'll assume you follow the financial press, even read some trade press publications and log on to Bloomberg News and CNBC on your tablet display. Not that all this "keeping up" adds much, but at least you're in sync with the market's daily fluctuations and noise level.

You do need a chart service, not a stock market chartist's music sheets but monthly financial charts that go back decades. They track interest rates, inflation, stock market valuation, unemployment, corporate tax rates, pretax operating profit margins, investor sentiment, industry capacity utilization, cash flow of corporations and their capital spending as well as government spending. I could go on and on, but the objective is to understand historical norms, how the country and major corporations work, how they turn dysfunctional and finally reach bottom valuation.

All this grunt work gets you nowhere. For example, nobody is ever right even on forecasting GDP. But your keeping up with the numbers earns you the right to call inflection points and take a contrarian point of view. Going back over 50 years, during the Cuban missile crisis the market panicked before the Russian tanker hauling more medium-range missiles to Cuba heaved to upon confronting our naval vessel's signal. The NYSE broad tape then was a Rube Goldberg electromechanical assembly that ran six hours late by mid-afternoon (*Figure 5, page 54*).

I put in my orders to buy obvious iconic properties like Polaroid, Xerox and Eastman Kodak and then walked home across the Brooklyn Bridge, sure I had done the right thing. I think there was a 50 percent margin requirement then, but I had overbought and next day I was admonished by the head margin clerk. My account would carry a 100 percent margin requirement level for 30 days. If I were a good boy, they'd restore my margin capacity.

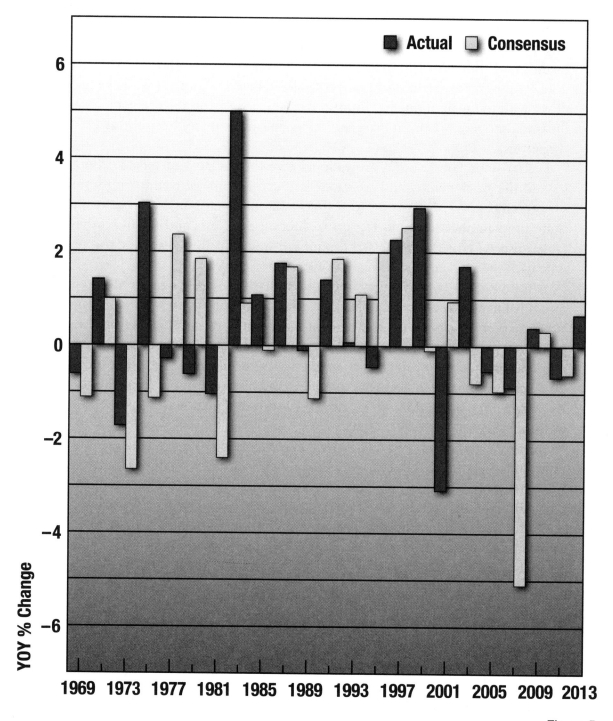

U.S. REAL GDP GROWTH: ACTUAL VS. CONSENSUS
YOY%, 1969–2013

Figure 5

Source: Bernstein Research

I did take an objective interest in Cuba. Thirty years later I learned that Castro was screaming at the Russians in Cuba to launch the missiles targeted on our mainland but the Russians refused. The world came within an ace of obliteration. I got lucky, but I had programmed myself to win, concentrated on the here and now in space and time. If I had bet this way on the eve of World War I, that the major powers would finally turn rational, I would have lost everything.

I loved old Wall Street. In 1961, Wall Street was a small village with research in its infancy. There were few serious analysts covering budding technology houses, ethical drug properties, even new financial sectors like the savings and loans in California.

Scrounging every possibility to add buying power, I found myself a money broker who dealt in convertible bonds, which didn't come under the Federal Reserve Board's margin edict. On 10 points of capital you could buy a convertible bond trading at par.

I was lucky, because I had just come back from a field trip to Boeing in Renton, Washington. They issued me a bicycle and told me to pedal anywhere on the plant's floor and talk to whomever. Boeing had just introduced its 707, which spanned the Atlantic and Pacific nonstop. The jet age took off. I bought converts in United Airlines, Boeing, Eastern Air Lines and United Aircraft. They doubled and tripled. Friends in UAL's controllers' office sent me monthly traffic numbers, which exploded into 25 percent to 30 percent readings. Never seen again.

Meanwhile, I got to know Herbert Allen at Allen & Company. We were both interested in gaming casinos and he was involved with the Freeport Casino in the Grand Bahamas. In those days it was easy for a young analyst to call up a partner in another brokerage house, ask for a meeting and discuss specifics on their investment banking relationships.

As an aside, Herbert Allen told me to look into his brother Charlie's Syntex venture. They were working on a birth control pill using extracts of a plant grown in Central America. I did my work, bought a bunch of six-month calls on Syntex and cleaned up.

I was a hardworking 27-year-old analyst when the jet age arrived, and semiconductor R&D was prolific. Bob Noyce, running Fairchild Camera, was very forthcoming. But any outsider could have subscribed to the weekly *Electronic News* and garnered serious tidbits on notable developments with investment impact. I breakfasted, lunched and dinnered, five days a week. By 11:00 p.m. my socks were soaked in perspiration. You do what you gotta do!

Available today to all are the financial prospectuses of all new issues—Twitter, Facebook, Alibaba, et al. There's sufficient data therein to at least determine that the company going public is substantive and worth following. Admittedly, its valuation is chancy. Anyone coulda bought gobs of Facebook in the mid-twenties.

All you had to believe was they would make a smooth transition from computer advertising to the smartphone. This was an easy double over 6 months.

Every thoughtful individual investor may not have my information retrieval capacity, but he can make calls on tsunami-like events such as the Cuban face-off, Black Monday, the Lehman bankruptcy and the 2008–'09 meltdown by relating the market's panic lows to historic valuation yardsticks.

Obvious in all this is the assumption that it ain't the end of the world as we know it. Normally, at market inflection points, pundits freeze, too timid and flummoxed to make the courageous call that the market has finally bottomed or at least is fair value. The Federal Reserve Board came close to freezing up in 2008–'09. Buffett believed in taking measured risk and was his own FRB to corporate America. He banked Goldman Sachs, Bank of America and others. Later, he cashed in billions in profits on outstanding warrants.

Nobody offered Martin Sosnoff warrants. I had to buy the underlying stock in Citigroup and Bank of America, which in early '09 traded for their option value, ranging from a buck to $5 a share. Playing with your own money, you learn to allocate maybe 10 percent of capital to crapshoots, companies top-heavy with debt and facing insolvency in less than two years if their business tanks. You look for operating leverage as in airlines, banks, insurance underwriters, even natural resources, operators in coal, iron ore and copper.

Assess their debt issues as well. Bank of America's preferred stock appreciated more than the common stock from the 2009 bottom of $5. Continental Airlines' debenture issue sold in the mid-fifties with under three years' maturity, an 18 percent yield to maturity. All you had to do was predicate that the airline wouldn't end up in receivership. I cashed in at par.

At yearend 2014, Microsoft, with $10 billion in free cash flow, meaningful dividend payout capacity and a solid enterprise computing division, I reasoned, could sell at the market's valuation a few years out. It got my money as a low-intensity recovery play.

From all this come several precepts—arguable, but proved sound for me in the battle for investment survival, if not primacy:

- Growth stocks sport finite lives—five to 10 years.
- Nothing is forever. Close out big mistakes and forget them. You learn nothing from sins of commission.
- There's no monopoly on brains.
- Growth stock investing is the "in" place to be; the frontier beckons pioneers. Keep a "Go West" attitude.
- Discipline! If Twitter is too hard to model or pricey, pass it by.

- Understand all the macros. Politics has led economics ever since the Egyptian pharaohs stored wheat. The Russians ached to bury Disneyland, but they failed. Khrushchev's GDP couldn't keep up with ours so they imploded.
- The NASDAQ 100 is the purest index to measure yourself against as a player. Even if you're a muni holder it uncovers how much you left on the table or didn't leave there.

In the interests of full disclosure, January 2015, I'm citing my portfolio compared with Buffett's listing. Unlike Buffett, I'm underweighted in financials. I, too, hold mainly big capitalization securities with maximum liquidity. My portfolio morphed during 2014 and can be found in this book's concluding chapter. Almost 60 percent of my portfolio is concentrated in biotechnology, namely Gilead Sciences, Actavis and Biogen Idec. Gilead tripled during 2013. My average position is $10 million or more, with emphasis on the Internet, financials, biotechnology and energy. The 10 biggest yearend 2014 holdings follow:

Sosnoff	Berkshire Hathaway
Gilead Sciences	Wells Fargo
Citigroup	Coca-Cola
Micron Technology	American Express
Actavis	IBM
Energy Transfer Equity	Procter & Gamble
Enterprise Products Partners	ExxonMobil (sold)
Biogen Idec	Wal-Mart
Bank of America	U.S. Bancorp
Boeing	DirecTV
Delta Air Lines	DaVita HealthCare

Nothing defensive about me. Dividend-paying capacity is irrelevant except for master limited partnerships. In a buoyant market my portfolio should levitate 25 percent or more, but it's not geared to go to the moon. It did rise 52 percent in 2013, and 15 percent in 2014. Compound your money even at 10 percent and it doubles in seven years. I hope to double the S&P 500's annualized performance, but I rate myself against the NASDAQ 100.

My downside risk is greater than Buffett's, but not dangerously so. What's eerie about Buffett's construct is over 60 percent of his portfolio is concentrated in four holdings. I'd grant you that overall his holdings are more defensive than mine, but properties like Coca-Cola, IBM, Wal-Mart, ExxonMobil and Procter & Gamble in 2013–'14 showed decelerating top-line growth, and earnings sloughed off. Not one is capable of easily reinventing its construct. Buffett already has proved he's untouchable. The symbolism of his top 10 is: "I've done it over 60 years and can afford to coast now with typical GDP kind of properties absent sizable valuation risk. You go make $25 billion on your own."

The pivotal precept is never to leave yourself open to be buried in a bear market. Don't be masochistic, riding a property down to zero. Enron comes to mind. Every cream puff scores in a bull setting unless heavy in electric utilities and American Telephone. Not my cup of tea.

SEVEN

The Value Investor's Dilemma

You can't just own value stocks because they're cheap, what we call a value trap. Growth stocks like IBM, Intel, Hewlett-Packard and Microsoft turned into value stocks because they lost their technological primacy.

Many value properties go through all the motions of a major corporation, but cycle over cycle generate minimal free cash flow because earnings are reinvested in the business at low rates of return. When a recession hits, earnings fall off a cliff and the company rethinks its initiatives. The rake's progress is value destruction. Currently, the materials sector is a prime case of excess capex and acquisitions at the cyclical peak. Several coal operators could collapse into insolvency by 2016.

Successful value investors need to be early in the cycle for each of the properties they choose to play. Cummins entered its engine cyclical recovery in 2010, and I bought it because my belief was the heavy truck engine cycle could last at least several years. Cummins was gaining market share cycle over cycle, so you couldn't be left at the post if you called the upturn timely.

When my old buddy Joe Rosenberg joined Larry Tisch at Loews in the late sixties, they argued over whether Joe could give his office a fresh coat of paint. Tisch never lost his frugal mindset. When it was a seller's market for media properties, he sold CBS and later bought Diamond Offshore Drilling when it was a buyer's market for oil drillers selling at 10 times earnings. It helps if the properties you invest in are misunderstood by the analytical community.

Aside from showing frugality, value players make non-dilutive acquisitions at cyclical turning points, use debt leverage fearlessly, pay themselves modest salaries and token dividends and periodically buy back stock from the public. This leads to outrageously high rates of return on equity, whether it be insurance, banking, retailing, hotels, broadcasting or the industrial sector.

There are many great professionally managed corporations run for shareholders. They include some of the biggest, like Berkshire Hathaway, ExxonMobil, PepsiCo, Coca-Cola, Merck and Disney. Of late, I'd include Apple, Alibaba and Facebook.

My biggest test for management is their rate of return achieved on incrementally invested capital, the reinvestment rate. Net free cash flow is what they strive for, the clay they ache to sink their fingers into and shape, each according to his dream and game plan. I shy away from custodial management with no net free cash flow to reinvest, like utilities.

The crossover from passive investor, like me, to Wall Street operator takes an emotional commitment and brass balls. You can't play the Cowardly Lion. It's John Waynesville or bite the dust. Years ago, when I asked Rupert Murdoch if he would sell me five to ten million shares of News Corporation when it was trading around $4 a share in Australia, he looked at me as if I were totally insane. "I'm never going below 50 percent control," he said, in his flat, matter-of-fact Australian accent. (Later, he did.)

The capacity of a great operator to continually surprise his shareholders is the biggest thrill I get out of managing money. By the millennium, News Corp. was a major player in film production (Fox), satellite broadcasting and television programming, with huge residuals in syndicated shows. Its market capitalization zoomed to over $40 billion, now $80 billion. The New York Times Company, in business 150 years, sports a market capitalization of $2.5 billion. Good newspapermen, but horrible businessmen.

Sam Walton, a piece of Americana now gone, summed it up. Sam's symbolism was just plain folks delivering the best for less—"You come in and see us, you hear?" The corporate office of Wal-Mart sat in Bentonville, Arkansas—not 500 Park Avenue or the World Financial Center with its arboretum of willowy palms. A warehousey structure that whispers "Discount City" is the company's metaphor and billboard.

When I think of Sears closing its stores for a couple of days to write down its merchandise, I have to laugh. How are they going to duplicate a corporate culture where employees are associates and advertising expense is less than half its competitors' outlays? Wal-Mart point-of-sale and inventory-control systems were early on state-of-the-art, and it showed up in high inventory turnover. Unfortunately, they are far behind Amazon for Internet fulfillment. Before Sam made a warehouse visit he'd pull out the roster chart and memorize everyone's name. This is what you do when your family owns 39 percent of the company. Sears is a basket case now, while Wal-Mart went to the moon and soldiers on.

Walton's achievement is that he took a prosaic business like discount retailing and turned it into a smoothly oiled powerhouse. He delivered for less to his heartland customers. Sears delivered 50 years ago, but they lost it after Julius Rosenwald retired. It sold then at 30 times earnings. Walton paid himself $325,000 a year, which is a hell of a lot less than most General Motors vice presidents. Tisch took $100,000. The total compensation of Wal-Mart's 16 executive officers was less than Saul Steinberg took out of Reliance Group before it plunged into receivership. Frugality pervades even Wal-Mart's annual report: no fancy photography, 20 pages on recycled paper. I pass on Wal-Mart now as a stock. Their footprint is just too big and growth is harder to come by.

Think of all the crap financial publications put us through, cataloguing the filthy rich. Only a handful of Wall Streeters made it by investing their own money. The secret words are "other people's money." This holds for the great real estate and LBO fortunes that used bank debt and limited partner's capital. If you want to make a billion, the easiest route is to borrow a billion. Just convince the banks and investment bankers that you're the jockey they should bet on. Very few of the super-rich founded their own companies. Some notable exceptions: Jeff Bezos of Amazon, Bill Gates of Microsoft and Ray Kroc of McDonald's, now gone. Include Sam Walton of Wal-Mart, Ernest and Julio Gallo and Messrs. Hewlett and Packard, as well as Murdoch, Steve Jobs and Larry Ellison of Oracle. For them, wealth was an abstraction of entrepreneurial energy.

For passive investors, singling out entrepreneurial geniuses who have identical agendas with their shareholders is difficult but not impossible. You start with annual reports, hopefully plain-talking documents radiating energy and results. Frugality counts, but even more significant is the capacity for surprising you. Share buybacks of more than 10 percent catch my eye. Audacious acquisitions that are non-dilutive get triggered near the bottom of industry cycles. Buffett's purchase of Burlington Northern and Tisch's buy of a major fire and casualty underwriter, CNA, was duplicated a year later by Sandy Weill of Primerica.

Sandy bought a big tranche of Travelers below book value and followed with the cash purchase of American Express's brokerage business, Shearson, also a non-dilutive deal, and then, finally, Citicorp, a merger of equals which proved too big to get your hands around. You need to figure out when to get off the bus.

Try to separate what's pejorative for Wall Street from what's real waste and hurtful to our economic well-being. GM and IBM each pissed away at least $25 billion in shareholder equity during the eighties. Both closed sizable plants they had just recently finished paying for. These two enterprises at their peak employed over a million, boasted impeccable balance sheets and paid out half their earnings to shareholders.

It took a $25-billion write-off in 1992 for GM to issue its annual report simply in black and white on recycled paper. They even kept it under 50 pages. The demise of GM and IBM anguished hundreds of thousands of families much more than all the heartburn dished out by dot-com blowups a decade later, when code-writing computer nerds dropped off the screen.

At the core of any successful investment is the leverage inherent in entrepreneurial management. Donald Trump actually reversed this schema by leveraging the public with junk bonds to bail himself out of moribund casino investments that turned sour years ago. Columnist Michael Thomas aptly pegged Trump as "the Prince of Swine." The passive investor needs street smarts to pick and choose his jockeys early on. Beware of grandiosity. Jokingly, Ted Turner once told me that if he could raise the capital he'd buy the Atlantic and Pacific Oceans. Later, he vied for CBS but lost out.

Value investing is not just buying stocks that sell at a lower price-earnings ratio than the market or a discount to book value. There has to be an energizing force. Early 2015, viable value themes in the market abounded: autos, department stores, defense contractors, domestic oils, tech houses like Apple and Micron, cellular operators like T-Mobile. GM could be a rising-share-of-market story. And, of course, the big banks are leveraged to rising interest rates.

Following the '82 recession, price-to-book value produced exceptional returns but proved useless after the recovery. Since the late eighties, smart value investors shifted to cash flow–based models and threw in share buybacks as critical variables. The ratio of enterprise value to EBITDA and price-to-revenue models also showed value added.

The most telling variable for me is price to free cash flow. When the free cash flow yield rests above 6 percent, I get interested. Apple is a prime case, but there are many more in the media sector, like Comcast, 21st Century Fox and Walt Disney. Boeing remains a prime candidate. My projection is free cash flow explodes to near $15 a share in 2017, a yield of over 10 percent.

Because most financial stocks, specifically banks and brokerage houses, are perennially leveraged to their capital base, I use hard book value as a benchmark. You buy brokerage houses near book value and sell them around 1.5 times book. The last great opportunity was the financial panic of 2008–'09. But even now, these properties sell at book and 10 times forward 12-months' earnings, a 30 percent discount to Wells Fargo. They awaited a steeper yield curve to become market leaders.

Our house is characterized by consultants as a large-capitalization core equity investor with the accent on growth. It's true, but any property that we think is misperceived and that has huge free cash flow gets our money. The stock must have one more thing—rising earnings, or at least the expectation of a turnaround in the numbers.

High levels of capital spending and a rapidly rising share base, often because of deal mania, are telltale signs of a management racing out of control. Too much of this took place in the telecommunications sector. Vodafone, WorldCom, JDS Uniphase and all the dot-coms were good examples in the growth sector. Currently, Facebook, Salesforce.com, Twitter, even Google and Apple are overpaying on notched-in deals.

Curiously, as NASDAQ fell below 2,000 in March 2001, we started applying some of the same yardsticks to growth stocks. For former growth icons like Cisco, EMC, Hewlett-Packard, Oracle and Intel we used price to revenues as a yardstick. The tremendous reversion to the mean for Cisco, now at six times revenues, makes you ponder whether Cisco is broken forever or a comeback kid.

My most successful investments in 2000–01 were in tobacco, HMOs and insurance, as the players bled in the dot-com fiasco. Stocks like Ace and XL, bought near book value at the beginning of the cycle for fire and casualty, and reinsurance underwriters come to mind. HMOs were tarnished by years of federal and state regulation as well as analyst fears that medical cost ratios couldn't be contained, but rising rates prevailed. UnitedHealth and WellPoint rose 40 percent, mid-'13 to mid-'14. I missed 'em. Anytime you find a company at one times its growth rate and you like the management and its business, you jump in whether it's perceived as a growth stock or value paper. WellPoint and UNH had converged. They could be bought by all money managers without causing style drift (*Figure 6, page 64*).

Ironically, practically all of technology has reverted back to the value sector, barring Internet houses and cloud computer operators. Start with Microsoft, with a market capitalization at $400 billion, and work your way down to Hewlett-Packard, Cisco, Intel, Micron Technology, even IBM, but not Texas Instruments after its big move. The pivotal issue is, can these properties renew themselves or at least maintain sufficient earnings to diversify, buy back stock and pay out sizable dividends? Hewlett-Packard and Microsoft I deem investable. Micron Technology, selling below 10 times forward earnings, carries a built-in fear content that Samsung might overexpand in memory chips and drive down component pricing. I'm taking that risk, and so far it's a home run. Delta Air Lines got my money, too.

GM was my sentimental favorite. Absorbing daily front-page rabbit punches from the financial and consumer press for going on two months, the stock didn't give an inch. Reasons? Too cheap, and their monthly selling rate for cars and trucks exceeded consensus. If GM's share of market ever tops up a point, say from 18 percent to 19 percent, the stock would sprout wings. At $40, up 20 percent, it would sell at 3.5 times enterprise value, which is what a newsstand goes for.

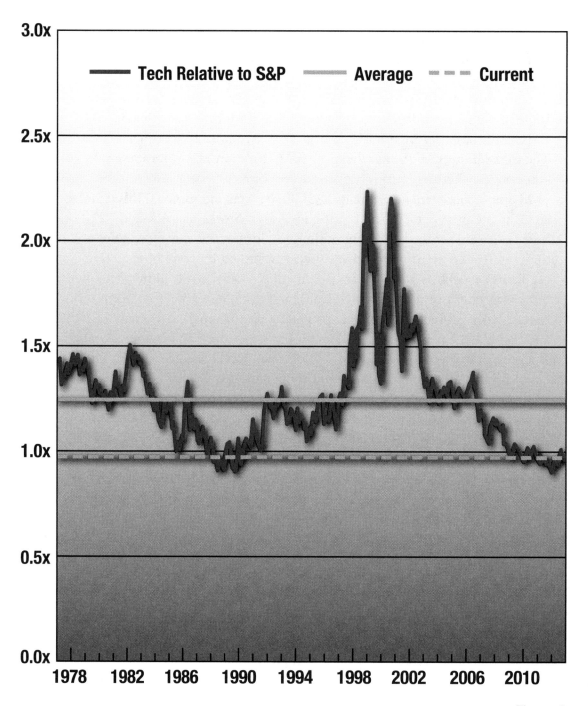

LARGE CAP TECHNOLOGY PRICE TO EARNINGS RELATIVE TO THE S&P 500

Figure 6
Source: Bernstein Research

You gotta be early. Wait too long to dot i's and cross t's and most of the move is history. Like Buffett, I'm overweighted in the financial sector. My crash helmet stays buckled, but the history of interest rates is on my side. They're headed up in 2015–'16. If not, I never shoulda bought these marble-pillared monsters—who proved capable of mass destruction.

EIGHT

The Market Is a Three-Ring Circus

Look at the Big Board not as a single arena but as part of a three-ring circus. The main ring is the S&P 500. It is flanked by the Dow Jones Industrials and NASDAQ. Think of the three rings full of circus horses traveling at different speeds. They gallop in the NASDAQ ring, trot in the Dow Jones side ring but cantor in the main ring.

Professionals who run big blocks of money devoted to large capitalization stocks are monitored by how well they do relative to the Standard & Poor's Index of 500 stocks. This is a capitalization-weighted index where a handful of stocks like Apple, ExxonMobil, Cisco, General Electric and Microsoft control how the index performs. GE, Intel, Microsoft and Cisco were 4 percent positions in the index around 2000, so if you didn't own them, and they rocketed up, you were likely to underperform competition and have some explaining to do. Cisco was a 1 percent position in the index in '98, but by midyear 2000 it had grown to 3.5 percent. Many of us had underweighted Cisco, which was growing earnings 50 percent per annum. Some of us are allergic to stocks at 80 times earnings. We were finally right. Cisco by April 2001 was just 1 percent of the S&P 500, along with Coca-Cola. Yearend 2014, their weightings had settled down to 0.7 percent for Cisco and 0.9 percent for Coke, their day in the sun gone but not forgotten.

For years, money managers underweighted Coca-Cola, GE and Microsoft and had trouble keeping up with the S&P 500, particularly in '98. Then Coca-Cola, which approximated $500 billion in market valuation, broke down, followed soon after by Microsoft. Microsoft was number one at yearend '99, a $500-billion market capitalization. Many more money managers underperformed the index in '99 because they had underweighted properties that always seemed too pricey. Yearend 2014, Microsoft was a 2.1 percent weighting, market cap $400 billion, a mediocre stock over 15 years but a great performer, up 28 percent for 2014.

You have to bore into the S&P 500 to understand where the motive power rests. Is it large-capitalization growth stocks creating the excitement, or are prosaic industrials like General Motors, DuPont and Dow Chemical doing the work? How do different sectors of the market move relative to each other? If the macroeconomic forecast is for a slowdown, chances are countercyclical stocks like drugs will outperform industrials and technology. This migration started at midyear 2000 when the NASDAQ Index, dominated by technology plays, dropped 10 percent one week in July. The tech bubble had imploded. Utilities rose 26 percent in 2014 because yield-starved investors piled in.

Not only do you need to understand which sectors of the S&P 500 Index are dominant at various points in an economic cycle, but you must anticipate how the S&P 500 will perform relative to NASDAQ, the Dow Jones Industrials and the Russell Growth Index, based on sentiment, where the earnings leverage is building and when it's likely to peak.

If you're a money manager playing catch-up in a bull market, you'd jump onto horses in the NASDAQ ring and shed nags in the Dow Jones circle. Some money managers are momentum players. They only ride the fastest horses with the flashiest bridles and saddles. In 2000, how else could you explain Yahoo at 220 times earnings and JDS Uniphase at 150 times earnings?

Although an entire industry of counseling firms is focused on analyzing the performance of money managers for their institutional clients, anyone can fluoroscope a money manager in two minutes. Get the six-month report of any mutual fund. It denotes its 10 largest holdings and breaks the portfolio down into sectors, comparing its weighting with the sectors of the S&P 500 Index.

The telltale giveaway is the "10 largest holdings" category. If it's not at least 30 percent of the fund's assets, the money manager is either a coward, very bearish or a closet indexer. Good reasons not to invest with him. Conversely, if the 10 largest holdings are 40 percent to 50 percent of the fund's assets, the money manager is either crazy, a genius, wildly bullish or about to go down in flames if he's wrong. Warren Buffett more or less has a 10-stock portfolio, but with low volatility. Most mutual funds carry 100 or more positions. Several funds are closet indexers. They mimic the index, with a few flourishes here and there. You'll do better in an index fund with a minimal management fee.

Often, sector weighting more than stock selection determines investment performance. Technology was 33 percent of the S&P 500 pre–bubble peak. If you stood underweighted in technology while it zipped up, you floated dead in the water. Late 2014, tech held a 19 percent weighting. Health care, the third largest sector, about 13 percent currently, midyear 2000 topped out at 17 percent. Underweighted in health care? Terrific, but where were you in '93 when health care took off after the Clinton initiative for a national health-care system was defeated? Warren Buffett missed technology and health care, almost 50 percent of the market. This worked just so long as Coca-Cola bubbled up, but when Coke fizzed out, Buffett underperformed badly in '99. Ignore index weightings at your own peril (*Figure 7*).

It's important that there be no non sequiturs in your index weightings. If your call on the economy is for a recession, you'd better not own industrials. Be overweighted in drugs. Energy was 6 percent of the index after oil prices weakened and petrochemical quotes slipped. Now it's almost 11 percent. If you believed banks' ever-rising loan losses had peaked, you'd overweight banks in the financial sector, but maybe you should overweight fire and casualty stocks, which are countercyclical. Looking inside each sector to denote when it's in cycle is critical to performance. Drug stocks can do well while HMOs and hospital paper tanks, which is what happened in '97 and '98 then reversed in 2000 and again during 2014.

Brokerage house stocks pre–2000 bubble were a function of NASDAQ. The new-issues market and investment banking profit centers were driven by NASDAQ's buoyancy. So, while Merrill Lynch and Morgan Stanley were financial sector stocks, they were captive surrogates of deal activity as the Ciscos and Yahoos galloped in the NASDAQ ring. When NASDAQ swooned, it took brokers down with it.

Looking at the rising price for a barrel of oil during 2013 until late '14, we decided that the ultimate leverage was in oil service operators like Schlumberger and Halliburton. That oil would hold above $100 a barrel was our working hypothesis. Then we modeled each investment property to make sure that we weren't overpaying, that the group didn't discount more than the first year of what we expected to be at least a 3-year cycle. When WTI oil quotes broke sharply below $100 a barrel late summer, we banged 'em out.

At the bottom of the market in '91, technology was only 6 percent of the index, but it peaked at 33 percent late in 2000. Although technology earnings compounded at an exceptional rate (high twenties), two-thirds of the sector performance came from rising price-earnings ratios. In early '98 we bought Sun Microsystems and Oracle at 20 times earnings. By mid-2000 they both sold at more than 60 times forward 12-months' earnings projections, because they were dominant players in the Internet infrastructure sector. The 20 times valuation was correct. Earnings collapsed early in 2001.

S&P 500 SECTOR WEIGHTINGS

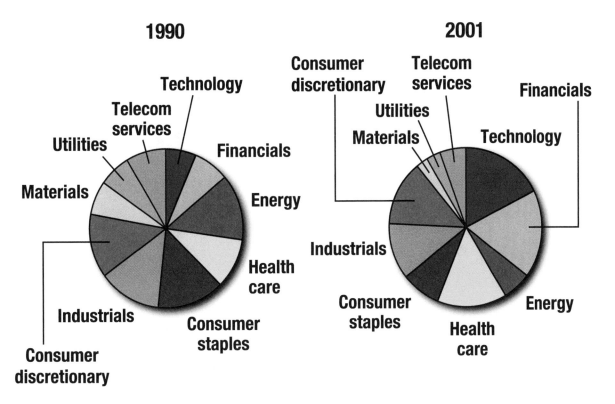

1990

2001

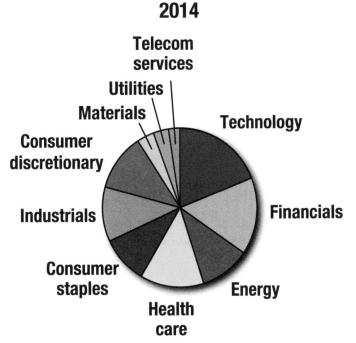

2014

Figure 7

Source: Poors

Top 25 Stocks in the S&P 500 Index (as of March 31, 2001)

Rank in S&P 500	Company Name	Percent of S&P	Market Value (Billions)
1	General Electric	4.1	415.8
2	Microsoft	2.8	291.0
3	ExxonMobil	2.7	280.7
4	Pfizer	2.5	258.6
5	Citigroup	2.2	225.9
6	Wal-Mart	2.2	225.6
7	AIG	1.8	186.4
8	Intel	1.7	176.8
9	Merck	1.7	175.1
10	IBM	1.6	167.6
11	SBC	1.5	151.1
12	Verizon	1.3	133.2
13	Johnson & Johnson	1.2	121.6
14	Royal Dutch Petroleum	1.2	118.9
15	Bristol-Myers Squibb	1.1	116.3
16	Cisco	1.1	114.5
17	Coca-Cola	1.1	112.2
18	Philip Morris	1.0	105.0
19	Home Depot	1.0	100.1
20	AOL Time Warner	0.9	93.7
21	Bank of America	0.9	88.3
22	JPMorgan Chase	0.8	86.6
23	Eli Lilly	0.8	86.3
24	Wells Fargo	0.8	84.8
25	Oracle	0.8	83.8
	Total	38.8	

Fast-forwarding to 2014, the top 25 names in the index showed markedly disparate performance, suggesting a stock picker's game. Nobody believed the index carried wind at its back. Apple recovered, but Google trailed. Microsoft rose 20 percent. Berkshire Hathaway, a play on Buffett's 50 percent weighting in financials, rose 20 percent. Wells Fargo, up 20 percent, was a grossly overweighted position there. JPMorgan and Citigroup underperformed. Amazon dropped a snappy 20 percent and Schlumberger gave back its gain. The top 25 names in the S&P 500 mainly sell at modest price-earnings ratios, with the exception of Facebook. When market pundits wring their hands over valuation of the S&P 500, they ignore this qualification of non-pricey valuation among many of the top 25 names.

Top 25 Stocks in the S&P 500 Index (as of December 5, 2014)

Rank in S&P 500	Company Name	Percent of S&P	Market Value (Billions)
1	Apple	3.7	677.3
2	Microsoft	2.2	402.6
3	ExxonMobil	2.2	399.6
4	Johnson & Johnson	1.6	301.1
5	Berkshire Hathaway	1.5	369.8
6	Wells Fargo	1.4	282.7
7	General Electric	1.4	262.0
8	Procter & Gamble	1.3	244.8
9	JPMorgan Chase	1.3	229.4
10	Chevron	1.2	212.3
11	Verizon	1.1	202.4
12	Pfizer	1.1	199.5
13	Intel	1.0	181.1
14	Bank of America	1.0	181.0
15	AT&T	1.0	175.9
16	Merck	1.0	173.7
17	Coca-Cola	0.9	190.5
18	Citigroup	0.9	167.2
19	Google Class A	0.8	368.1
20	Google Class C	0.8	364.5
21	Facebook	0.8	207.4
22	IBM	0.8	162.4
23	Walt Disney	0.8	158.1
24	Gilead Sciences	0.8	153.6
25	PepsiCo	0.8	146.3
	Total	31.4	

Consider the reshuffling of industrial standings. Apple went to the top of the class from nowhere; Google, too. GE faltered but ExxonMobil held on. Pfizer faded and so did Merck. Citigroup, with a market capitalization of $225 billion in 2001, needed a major blood transfusion from the Federal Reserve Bank and now carries a valuation of just $167 billion.

Down in the middle of the list, price-earnings ratios are much lower, but nobody marries GM or Dow Chemical for life. It's where stock picking makes a difference. Using the level of the S&P 500 as a forecasting tool is diminished even more by the changes in the composition of the index over the past decade. Microsoft first went public in 1986. By 1999 it had mushroomed into the number-one spot, sporting a $500-billion market capitalization. During 2014, staid, understandable properties like Union Pacific, Walgreens, Eli Lilly, Hewlett-Packard, Amgen, EOG Resources, Duke Energy, Simon Property Group, Caterpillar, Actavis and Allergan rose in high double digits.

One should never feel secure that owning big-capitalization properties protects you from downside volatility. The market lopped 40 percent off names like Microsoft, Coca-Cola and Qualcomm in a couple of months back in 2001. When Eli Lilly lost an appeals court case on patent rights on Prozac, the market sliced $30 billion off its $100-billion market cap—overnight.

Money managers are much more sensitized to changes in earnings power metrics for stocks and stock groups than historic overvaluation or undervaluation. Stock groups tend to overshoot or undershoot valuation as sentiment waxes and wanes. Frequently, the art of money management is anticipating changes in sentiment and moving in or out early. Technology and energy sectors dominated earnings momentum in the S&P 500 during 2000. But within these two sectors, oil stocks were lackluster. However, the leveraged oil service sector (drilling rigs) boomed as their earnings cycle bottomed out with oil futures ticking over $25 a barrel. There were few surprises in drug stocks' earnings except for Merck. The market corrected this oversight in a day. The HMOs, detested by The Street, came through with good medical cost ratios, and stocks like WellPoint, Oxford and UnitedHealth Group rose 50 percent off their lows. In the face of serious short selling, Gilead rose over 40 percent in the first nine months of 2014. Analysts used a discounted cash flow valuation model when they shoulda employed a straight current earnings multiplier.

Everyone knows that over a long cycle—five to 10 years—the valuation of the S&P 500 is governed not just by earnings growth but also by Treasury bond rates and inflation. Rising bond yields over a year or two will top out any bull market, even with rising earnings. In the first five years of the nineties the S&P 500 compounded at 5.5 percent, in tandem with earnings growth of 5.4 percent. In the back half of the nineties earnings accelerated to 10 percent, but the market grew at a 26 percent rate. Ten-year bond yields started the decade at 7.8 percent and ended there in '94. By '99, 10-year Treasuries hovered near 6 percent and stayed there through 2000. The S&P 500 Index doubled from 15 times earnings to a 30 multiple. Part of the bull move related to changes in composition of the index, but let's face facts, the market had the wind at its back in terms of benevolent macros.

All of 2013–'14, the Fed worried about deflation and high unemployment. Historically, the market sells at a mid-teens price-earnings ratio in such a setting, and that's what we got. The pivotal variables in 2015 are GDP momentum, corporate operating profit margins and FRB policy, notoriously troublesome but add factors to project successfully. A trading market ensues if housing starts and industrial production remain dormant.

When macroeconomic forces are a big yawn, the market cottons on to story stocks and wild analyst extrapolations of earnings and price-earnings ratios. The way money managers exploit this setting is by searching out subsectors of the S&P 500 and overweighting them unmercifully. The Chinese generals threw hundreds of thousands of troops at the defending marines in the Chosin Reservoir sector. We slaughtered them with superior firepower, artillery and fighter bombers from aircraft carriers. The courage of the marines in Korea, man to man, was awesome, as were the Chinese infantrymen who just kept coming on but had no technology backing them up. Courage is a seldom remarked personality trait for money managers. I'm not talking about mindless overspeculation but the capacity to implement a well-researched hypothesis using a Chinese general's massing of his troops and dispatching them into the forward battle line in cold blood.

Money management is an existential act. You are what you do, not what you think. You can always martial 10 good reasons to buy a stock or overweight a sector. Likewise, you can find 10 reasons to go the other way.

Our deep basic call that NASDAQ was too treacherous by mid-2000 led to a strategy of anti-NASDAQ sector weightings. Overweighting in health care, energy and financial services fulfilled this hypothesis. Our problem with the consumer staples sector was that we couldn't find attractive earnings stories. Procter & Gamble, McDonald's and growth retailers like Gap showed poor metrics. We held modest positions in Kimberly-Clark, Tiffany, Wal-Mart, Costco and Lowe's.

In 2013–'14, we fleshed out the consumer discretionary sector, conceptually based on the convergence of the communications, media and Internet sectors. This included cable broadcasters, wireless purveyors and telecommunications giants like Verizon, Comcast, Walt Disney and 21st Century Fox, as well as Facebook and Alibaba.

The information highway turned out to be a fruitful concept early on. Later, competitive forces intensified with the capacity of Wall Street to underwrite enormous equity and junk bond offerings for telecommunications managements who thirsted to expand their footprints nationally and internationally. We expected a five-year media and telecommunications cycle, but market forces compressed it into 24 months. Health care, a low weighting at yearend '99, absorbed our exodus from a grossly overweighted "concept play" in technology that peaked at 25 percent of our assets under management. Pushing big blocks of money around from sector to sector is the name of the game. When stocks levitate, analysts ratchet up target prices. When they fall back on valuation metrics like 10-year discounted cash flow projections, run for the exit. It's over.

Notable in the S&P 500 are the minor weightings in utilities and telecommunications. In total they are a 5 percent sector. If you double-weighted them right before the onset of recession, you would do exceptionally well. The biggest risk is they are dead in the water when the economy's improving and interest rates levitate.

Big increases in sector and specific-stock weighting normally come from earnings growth or lack of same. This applies to technology, financials and industrials. Late fifties and sixties, Polaroid became a dominant position in the Dreyfus Fund and made their performance shine. Decade over decade, energy is a lessening percentage because of its cyclicality. The variable in technology weight is usually valuation, which is extreme both up and down. Tech was a much smaller sector in 1990 than it is today. Same goes for financials. Utilities and materials show big shrinkage from 1990, again based on valuation and minimal earnings enhancement. All other sectors show minimal change. Looking ahead, tech is reasonably priced, along with industrials. If interest rates elevate, the financial sector is destined to outperform, while utilities and consumer staples turn back into dead money. I'm betting this happens.

Without a working hypothesis, you'll flail miserably, jumping from one ring to another, probably late on all your moves.

NINE

True 'n' False
American Beauty Roses

Was a Pepsi two cents during the mid-thirties Depression? I know a nickel from the jingle "Twice as much for a nickel, too," but that sounds early forties. Then you could buy cigarettes, loose, for a penny each. New York's bodegas preserve such package breakdowns.

My father pulled in maybe five bucks a day in his sweatshop on Convent Avenue, Harlem, competing with the Spotless chain, whose flyers offered to dry-clean your suit for 29 cents, later 39 cents. A tailor shop in August was warmer than Chinese laundries then, maybe 110 degrees, with its pressing machine gurgling steam. I remember the stack of long-necked Pepsi bottles on Pop's sewing table. Cola and his pipe got him through a 12-hour day. My job was riding the C train down to 125th Street with his dinner in an old pot cheese canister. Afterwards, Pop would walk me next door for a soda before I grabbed the subway back to our pre–air conditioned East Bronx rabbit hutch. (Still there.)

PepsiCo's headquarters in Purchase, New York, overlooks acres of velvety lawn dotted with museum-class contemporary sculpture. It is, today, just as much a potato chip purveyor as a soda water bottler. Coca-Cola, its nemesis, diversified less felicitously with Columbia Pictures and frozen orange juice. The Atlanta operator still holds worldwide primacy as a soft drink purveyor, but per capita consumption of cola drinks has peaked and Coke was late getting into vitamin water, even plain water. Stateside, PepsiCo and Coca-Cola battle for market share points. They put away 7Up and lesser bottlers, outspending them unmercifully and spectacularly with assists from Michael Jackson, Madonna and a busload of 19-year-old dancers. Do Coca-Cola bottlers still run plant tours for grade school kids? They gave us promotional pencils in the thirties. Even then, they understood: Grab 'em young, you hang on to them for life. American Express mailed my daughter a green card when she was a college freshman. Her liquid assets consisted of a pair of Rossi's and a 10-speed bike, maybe a dozen 8-track music cartridges.

Budweiser, the powerhouse beer distributor out of Anheuser-Busch, moved into snacks years ago with its Eagle brand and then folded it. High-quality goods, but the Busch family couldn't dent PepsiCo's Frito-Lay tonnage. It rolls on and on, with 10,000 multi-stop delivery trucks blanketing the country. Maui chips, the class act, don't travel, and Cape Cod kettle-cooked crunchies are much too pricey for guys in underwear watching the Yankees sweep in another three-hit shutout, Tanaka on the mound. Bud kept gaining market share in beer and ratcheted up prices periodically, in a 2 percent per capita growth industry. It added up to double-digit earnings momentum, which analysts readily accepted. I passed on the beverage sector.

For me, Kellogg's and Quaker Oats, now part of PepsiCo, were false growth stocks. PepsiCo, Anheuser-Busch and Coca-Cola were nearly the real thing. Kellogg's looked like a great growthie, with per capita consumption of wheat- and oat-based cereals steady in a roughage-conscious anticholesterol aerobics world. Kellogg's wanted so badly to stay a mid to high-teens growthie that management kept bumping prices, some years over 10 percent. The analysts say a bowl of ready-to-eat cereal is an uneventful 19 cents. Nobody cares.

I care. Raise prices 10 percent per annum and it's a double in seven years. Per capita consumption of cereal is flattish, and price bumps must be less frequent. Philip Morris learned this with Marlboros. RJR Nabisco pressed Oreo prices so hard it lost market share to store-brand cookies. Kohlberg Kravis Roberts pulled their equity offering of Nabisco when Wall Street gagged on the underwriting price point. Finally, Nabisco was sucked up by Philip Morris.

Whatever happened to Mission Orange, Dad's root beer? Why didn't Dr Pepper's celery soda take off? They existed as cellar curiosities. Philip Morris sold its 7Up acquisition. They couldn't figure out how to beat up on the colas. This billion-dollar mistake was overshadowed by the Marlboro Man's horse. Their Miller beer struck out as a distant and not too profitable runner-up to Bud, and Post's Grape-Nuts got outslugged by the Battle Creek champion, Kellogg's.

My file on growth stock investing dates back to the late fifties. Semiconductors, airlines, color television and birth control pills came in, and railroads, utilities and oil turned into wallflowers, but not Hertz and American Express. Then, American Electric Power, Pennsylvania Railroad and Peabody Coal were dubbed socially acceptable growth stocks. The Boeing 707 jet took care of railroads, and nuclear power tarnished AEP. Low residual prices for oil and gas gave steam coal a run for its money, and they still remain cheap boiler-fuel substitutes. West Virginia turned Republican against the Gore environmental initiatives, and Obama doesn't campaign there. Coal is a dodo.

In the early seventies, elite equities, as measured by the financial press, included DuPont, Kodak, Mobil and Xerox. When Xerox bought a Wall Street brokerage house, its early-on guiding light, Joe Wilson, had to groan in his grave. Today, all these goods sell below the average market valuation, unable to renew themselves, or no longer exist. No Polaroid. Xerox bowed out of its insurance subsidiary, Crum & Forster, a billion-dollar mistake. By yearend 2000, Xerox touched down at $4 a share after a credit downgrade to junk status on its debentures. Fifteen years later it's still near seller. As late as '85, Texas Commerce Bancshares made the short list of best-managed corporations. Soon after, it drowned from oil field and real estate loan cramps and was merged into Chemical Bank. Continental Illinois, a '78 star, fell to earth buying syndicated oil field loans with phantom asset coverage during our 2008 meltdown. Countrywide, Washington Mutual, Lehman, even Merrill Lynch ceased to exist or were merged out by the U.S. Treasury and FRB.

How would you have liked to compete with Cisco, Wal-Mart, Philip Morris, Amazon, Home Depot, Toyota, PepsiCo, Coca-Cola and Apple? Well, ask Wendy's, 7Up, IBM, the New York Herald Tribune, JCPenney, Sears, American Brands, Lionel and Toys "R" Us. Some of the last-named companies are out of business, merged out, marginal or wobbling along. If I gave you the capital base and the staffing, your entry dues would be years and years of deficits. The first-named group made their reps and delivered the goods, day in, day out, to a loyal clientele. They don't play patsy while you're learning the business, but hopefully keep renewing themselves with productivity gains, testing new formats and new products. Some, like Coca-Cola, got stodgy. They could have had Snapple, bottled water and Gatorade early on.

Wall Street supplies the ciphering that defines growth stocks in statistical jargon. Years ago, when nobody employed much leverage, we used a high return on equity as the basic yardstick. If IBM showed a 25 percent return, year in, year out, it was a growth stock when most corporations with multibillion-dollar capitalizations averaged just 12 percent. Genuine growth stocks sport high reinvestment rates and grow revenues 10 percent or more annually. They retain earnings and reinvest them wisely. Warren Buffett's a growth stock just so long as he outperforms the stock market. When he slipped in '99, the high premium over book value eroded some. His investment record over the past five years is mediocre.

A growthie, the real thing, not only fights off challenges from teenage gorillas with overflowing testosterone, but overcomes macroeconomic static. Inflationary or deflationary cycles phase in and out. There are currency realignments, cross-border wage differentials, competitive new product introductions or copycatting, as well as competition from quasi-governmental corporations—a long list. Countries like Japan, France, the UK, Germany and South Korea subsidize competition in aircraft assembly, steel, aluminum fabrication and telecommunications. Boeing would get killed in a worldwide depression, but it outsells Airbus Industries, the European consortium. Fokker, the Dutch aircraft builder, packed it in decades ago.

In the sixties, Wall Street was enthralled with the "razor blade" concept of growth investing. We bid up stocks like Gillette, United Aircraft (jet engines), Beech-Nut (gum), FRAM (oil filters), Genuine Parts (auto replacement parts) and Champion Spark Plug. Few repetitive usage stocks stood the test of time, racked by competition and stagnant product innovation. For a while, General Electric outdid United Aircraft in jet engine technology, and UA ended up buying a wire-and-cable producer at the peak of its cycle. Gillette, number one in stainless steel razor blades, diversified into men's toiletries and batteries to no avail. Rechargeable batteries is now the killer app.

Motorola moved rapidly into cellular communications with state-of-the-art lightweight portable handsets, an adjunct to its telecommunications equipment business. It purveyed infrastructure systems worldwide to cellular phone franchises. Cellular phone profits rose in the nineties but couldn't overcome the cyclical influence of its semiconductors sector. This led analysts and money managers to reassess Motorola. Finally, cellular phones and services fell apart. The market trashed Motorola; same for Nokia, who gained market share worldwide and was the low-cost producer until Apple and Samsung fielded smartphones, where Nokia was a late entry.

Security analysts, like specialists in dendrochronology (the science of reading tree trunk rings), project growth rates by ciphering precise historical data. Unfortunately, a growth stock, like a tree, battles continuously with its physical environment and competitive forces. When I built a swimming pool, a 300-year-old olive tree nearby succumbed within a year. Were its roots contaminated by my children's play, splashing chlorine-laden water?

There are just a handful of growth stocks made with 18-karat gold. Tiffany is apt here. They fulfill basic needs better and longer than the competition. Walt Disney passed on, but his company moved into sports broadcasting, theme parks and blockbuster movies. Nobody has buried Disney World yet. Las Vegas, with theme resorts and family destination hotels peaking, renewed itself, diversifying in Macao and Singapore. Wynn and Las Vegas Sands are great free cash flow stories, probably good for the next five years, but near-term pricey on enterprise valuation.

At Sotheby's in Monaco, decades ago, a 1934 Mercedes-Benz 500K Special Roadster was auctioned for 17.8 million francs, close to $3 million. This model was acclaimed the most beautiful automobile of the year at the 1935 International Motor Show in Berlin. It is a gorgeous two-seater convertible with a sweeping fender line. Why isn't Daimler Benz a great stock? Well, BMW is giving 'em a run for market share. Rolls-Royce engines power jet aircraft because the company can't scale up car demand much more in Beverly Hills.

I asked my favorite antique car dealer on the Côte d'Azur why such craziness in auction prices. One antique Ferrari sold for $38 million in 2014. All my artist friends there had warehoused Ferraris. They eschew paper assets. This conversation took place during a worldwide recession 20 years ago.

"Well," he said, "a 1934 Mercedes coupe is a thing of beauty. Very rare."

"But you can't hang it on the wall," I said.

"You can build a garage for it," Jean-Jacques said.

"Where is the Ferrari you put on the order books?" I asked.

"Of my model they made 300 pieces. There was a three-year waiting list and the price was up to $300,000; now it's $200,000. The chances are I must take delivery. I can no longer sell my place on line for a profit."

Yearend 1972, growth stocks peaked at 2.7 times the market's valuation. Each succeeding market cycle witnessed declining relative prices for growthies until the late nineties. In the summer of '93 they bottomed near parity with the market index, a 15-year low. The next stop, late nineties, the market pegged valuation for Coca-Cola, Wal-Mart and Microsoft at 1.5 times. Low interest rates and dormant inflation invariably create rising growth-stock valuations. But, as Merck faltered below a 10 percent growth rate mid-'93, the market took it down to 13 times estimated 1994 earning power, below the market's valuation. Conceptually, big capitalization equities like Merck were sources of cash for money managers when NASDAQ took off for its '98–'99 spring to 5,000. When Alan Greenspan dropped the fed funds rate 50 basis points early in January of 2001, NASDAQ rallied almost 15 percent overnight and drug stocks declined sharply. Everyone managing money got busy discounting the next economic expansion.

Now at mid-decade, money managers challenge valuation of traditional growth stocks. Aside from Internet properties and biotech houses, the golden oldies like Coca-Cola, PepsiCo, Merck, Pfizer, Cisco and Microsoft sell either at a small premium to the market or at discounts. Most everyone, including me, is skeptical that their franchises are intact or that R&D is sufficiently productive. This goes for Intel, EMC, Oracle and Hewlett-Packard. I paid no more than 10 times earnings for the last-named group.

Disbelief in Growth Surfaces in 2013–'14

Company	Estimated Premium or Discount to Stock Market Valuation, May 2014
Google	10%
Apple	-10%
Merck	zero
Eli Lilly	zero
Bristol-Myers Squibb	zero
PepsiCo	+15%
Hewlett-Packard	-35%
Proctor & Gamble	zero
Coca-Cola	10%
Intel	-10%
Microsoft	-10%
McDonald's	zero
Cisco	-20%
Oracle	-15%

Source: Author's estimates

Why so many bargains today? First, earnings surprises. No company in this list is exempt from hiccups, so there is much residual disbelief. Gross margins for technology companies trace a downward slope, with the exception of Intel. The decompression in valuations between growthies early nineties and 20 years earlier was the thematic strand of the early nineties, critical to our call that growthmanship would reemerge in 1994 as the best construct until overvaluation set in, possibly at two times the market's valuation, years later. Thus, the Internet bubble in 1999–2000 and then its utter collapse.

The market traded at 18.4 times earnings during 1972, not radically different than 2000, when it exceeded 20 times. Yearend 2014 we're at 17 times. Premiums for growth ranged up to four times the Standard & Poor's Index—but not for long. The '73–'74 recession and worldwide competitive forces collapsed earnings for Polaroid, Xerox, Avon Products and Eastman Kodak. They never came back. Thirty years ago, Wal-Mart was a small regional discount house and Microsoft was still a private company.

Morgan Guaranty Trust stood as the Green Bay Packers of the investment management world throughout the sixties and early seventies. It took the bear market of '73–'74 to uncover their hubris. These were sober, dark-suited Harvard MBAs who believed in America 365 days of the year. They nearly destroyed their temple of investment with an overpriced inventory of obsolete companies. The perishability of their largest holdings is the final caveat. Nothing is forever, not even for a decade. Companies must renew themselves in each cycle or trail off into mediocrity, just as RCA and International Telephone did in communications and consumer electronics and Xerox did in printing. The life of a growth stock averages five years.

Morgan Guaranty's Portfolio
Largest Holdings at Yearend 1972

Company	Price-Earnings Ratio	Premium over Market Index
IBM	37.4	100%
Eastman Kodak	48.2	165%
Avon Products	65.1	253%
Sears, Roebuck	29.5	60%
Xerox	48.9	166%
Procter & Gamble	32.0	73%
Walt Disney	81.5	343%
Polaroid	90.7	393%
Schlumberger	57.2	211%

Once Wall Street falls out of love with an industry, it's broken, and purgatory can last five years or more. Computer industry analysts missed the call on IBM's earnings power for five straight years, underestimating competitive pressures on gross profit margins. Intel, with world primacy in semiconductor technology, sells below the valuation of Caterpillar and John Deere because almost everyone, including Intel's management, finds it impossible to model desktop computer demand for its integrated circuits even one quarter ahead.

Growth cycles normally run for three or four years of outperformance. Then cyclicals take over for a year or two. Growthies came back big in '94 and kept going throughout the decade. There were good reasons. Note the chart on profit margins (*Figure 8, page 82*). They went through the roof in the latter part of the decade. Managements substituted stock options for big salaries, wrote off intellectual property when they made acquisitions and bought back stock with free cash flow. Analysts chose to disregard all this accounting largesse. An unprecedented cycle in capital spending for technology fueled revenue growth—until it stopped working in 2001.

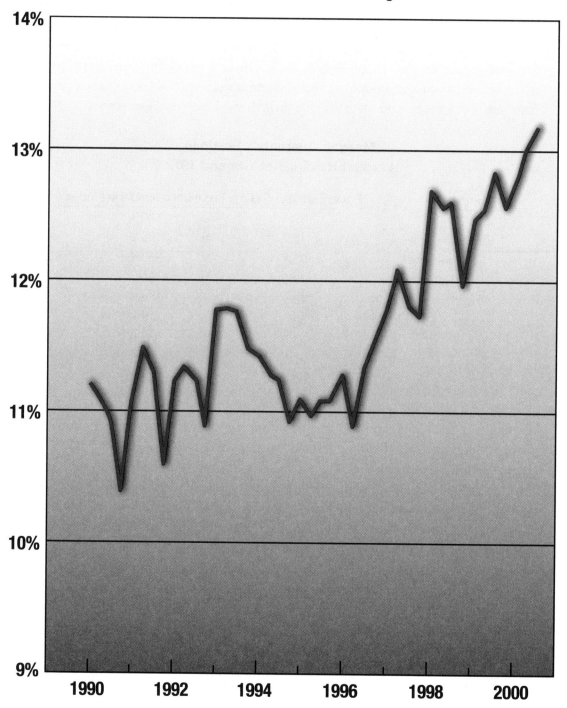

PROFIT MARGIN 1990–2000
Traditional Growth Average

Figure 8
Source: Safian Investment Research

The beneficiaries of exponential computer power and miniaturization are no longer the black-box assemblers like Hewlett-Packard or integrated-circuit pioneers like Intel. Gross margins show slippage when inventories rise. Rather, it's the packagers of entertainment, information and telecommunications who leverage technology. The names are household words: Comcast, Google, Apple, Netflix, Twitter, 21st Century Fox and Facebook. The Internet and cellular telephony spawned a whole new class of super-growth stocks whose compound growth rates reached 50 percent or more and defied gravity at least for a couple of years. This was unprecedented in financial history, but recalled Polaroid's run in the fifties and sixties.

In the sixties, when growthies sold at 60 times earnings, Wall Street said it was scarcity value. Not enough of 'em to go around. This was bull market rationalization patter. Very dangerous. The current overheated action at Sotheby's and Christie's suggests the rich wax different than you or me. They pay crazy prices for canvases of 19-year-old French and Italian models—Renoir and Modigliani picked their beauties out of the marketplace in Paris as much for their bodies as for their painterly qualities. Billionaire octogenarian Walter Annenberg indulged himself in Picasso canvases after he had sold *TV Guide* at a growth-stock price to Rupert Murdoch. Same goes for David Geffen and Eli Broad, both great collectors of contemporary art with their own made-to-order museums in Los Angeles.

There were many collectors around in the sixties, like Yasuda, the Japanese insurance underwriter that bought van Gogh's *Sunflowers* for umpteen millions. For them, prestige was more important than shareholders' capital. There is no way you can "run the numbers" and pay over $300 million for Château Margaux, but plenty of crazies ached for such trophies. The Rothschilds, after all, are known more for Château Lafite and Mouton Rothschild than for their postwar investments in copper mines and banks. (The French government took their bank away from them.) Château Latour changed hands in the summer of '93 at $121 million, approximately 30 times earnings, and still a trophy premium. The British conglomerate Allied-Lyons sold this "ultimate brand" because they needed the cash. They had dropped $220 million in foreign currency trading. François Pinault, the French buyer, beat out AXA and Chanel. Pinault wisely admitted the Latour buy had nothing to do with business. Allied-Lyons booked a loss on Latour, which at its bubble peak was valued at $200 million. Vanity investing can work. Give Pinault's contemporary art museums in Paris and Venice a look-see; he's a fearless collector and controls Christie's.

At Gulf & Western, Martin Davis lived in Charlie Bluhdorn's shadow for decades. How should the market have cranked that into its computer console? The takeout or "full value" price of a contested acquisition is determined as much by projections of narcissistic grandiosity as what banks will lend you to do a deal on the coverage of fixed charges. Davis was willing to destroy Gulf & Western's near-term earnings power to fulfill his dream of becoming a dominant world player in entertainment. He changed the company's name to Paramount.

When AT&T touched down at $18 by yearend 2000 the market disregarded earnings power and construed the property on a sum-of-the-parts valuation. Two weeks later the stock was $24. The franchise value of its cellular properties accounted for much of the estimated $35-a-share target valuation, where it rests now. It pays to know what properties are valued at by avid buyers lurking in the bushes, like Valeant's hostile bid for Allergan. It ticked at $80 a share in 2013 and $220 a year later.

Aside from personal liquidity, the price of anything in the world finally boils down to interest rates and the "cost of carry." Trump could carry the Plaza just so long as his net worth, along with his flow of funds statement, looked good to the banks. The takeout price of a growth stock counts up to much less when interest rates are 14 percent, not 7 percent, or even 3 percent. This is why all stocks—but deal stocks, particularly—do well in a soft interest-rate setting. Acquirers employ much more leverage, sometimes 400 percent above the Big Board's 50 percent margin. Hambrecht & Quist successfully underwrote the Robert Mondavi Winery in Napa Valley not because its reserve Cabernet Sauvignon and Chardonnay carried the company. The second-tier Woodbridge wine, $8 a bottle, mass marketed, forged its respectable earnings history.

For many businesses, particularly media, a rising acquisition price was the critical variable, not current earnings. Cable broadcasting is a good example. It was true not just of Time Warner but also of Turner Broadcasting, CBS, News Corporation and DirecTV. The residual value of Paramount's, Disney's and Warner's film libraries ran into billions and became a bankable asset with Citicorp and its brethren.

A gold mine is a gold mine only so long as the price of gold is buoyant. When quotes turn south, the mine turns into a pitiful hole in the ground with inflationary costs of operation. The same goes for copper, coal, iron ore, silver, aluminum, steel, paper, petrochemicals and oil. These are undifferentiated commodities with low profiles of per capita consumption and roller-coaster price charts. You gotta buy 'em when commodity prices are in the doghouse, like Jimmy Goldsmith did with Newmont Mining, and sell 'em when charts are still zippy. Even De Beers, a near monopoly, is subject to cyclical demand variance in diamonds.

The perfect growth stock is a simple business that fulfills a universal need. Management is entrepreneurial and thinks like a shareholder. There is product pricing flexibility and customer loyalty. The corporation earns its money in cash, reinvests it wisely and hoses the competition. Try Apple. Growth operators don't blame disappointing results on the weather, like retailers and banana-tree growers (Chiquita finally filed for bankruptcy early in 2001, claiming it was shut out of the European market. Hurricane blowdowns were a recurring phenomenon.) Growthies are locked onto secular trends that outstrip population and GNP momentum. The consumption of music and films exceeds that of milk, and cellular phone traffic grows faster than the bleach in your washing machine. Procter & Gamble in '93 wrote off $1.5 billion, closing down 20 factories and decimating its employment rolls. It's still "restructuring" 20 years later under successive headmen.

After owning the *New York Times* for years, I sold it out when operating profit margins peaked. Profitability at the *Times* in the early eighties was less than half Dow Jones's or Gannett's margins. From its record high in '86, over the next five years the *Times* declined 50 percent. This is cyclical growth, another kind of animal. A great growth-stock candidate should leverage its earnings through margin improvement as well as revenue growth. It's taken the *Times* decades to find its stride again after foolish Internet investments and the near bankruptcy buy of the *Boston Globe* at the peak of newspaper valuation. Meanwhile, Rupert Murdoch took News Corporation to the moon: 21st Century Fox boasts a market valuation near $80 billion, while NYT languishes at $2.5 billion.

With all the integrated circuitry in our cars, cellular phones, talking dolls and laptop computers, why did it take so long to tackle the civilized world's toilet flushing system? Have you ever looked into the water chest and watched the wobbly steel ball rise as the water rushes back when the rubber stopper falls into its slot? Someone does it better now, but the replacement cycle for toilets is slow moving.

Growth stock analysis remains a fuzzy business. Trainloads of analysts and money managers search out and evaluate prospective growthies. Like the New York Yankees, the lineup on the Big Board changes, month to month, year over year. New players come up to the big show and .220 hitters are "sent down." Few stars shine for more than a decade. If a growthie lasts as long as the tenure of the average National Football League starter, 3½ years, it's rare and probably too overpriced to be worth a look. Everyone likes to hold 'em as long as they can, because we all know how hard it is to latch on to another Derek Jeter. A sought-after characteristic for a growthie is to sail calmly through a down economic cycle.

There are examples of wonderful start-ups that grew into multibillion-dollar businesses, but they shouldn't be lumped with growth stocks. Sneakers once were called tennis shoes. You bought them in Woolworth's for three bucks, a commodity that came in one choice, oatmeal-colored canvas with thin white laces. Today, sneakers look like overdesigned ski boots, with pockets, air-cushioned heels and insignia.

Reebok, Nike and the rest of them went to South Korea and contracted production. You could have three meetings in a hotel room in Seoul and nail down sneaker production. There is ease of entry, marginal product differentiation and a limited secular growth pattern. After you fill up your closet with these buttery yum-yums, you're finished until there are holes in the soles or your toes stick out. Stocks like Nike may top out despite all their net free cash flow, share buybacks and great marketing skills.

Nike is basically an advertising agency specializing in athletic footwear and sportswear. You can't administer prices forever or lock out competition. Gross margins peak and you start diversifying with cash flow, a precarious confluence of forces. Catch a Nike very early or stay away; its valuation may collapse to 10 times earnings before long—as happened to Compaq, Hewlett-Packard and Dell Computer when revenues topped out.

Another kind of false growthie is more substantive, because you make money owning it, but it's tricky stuff. The overriding theme is good management that puts shareholders first. Kroger and Safeway were good models, but I stayed away because top-line growth was just a couple percentage points. Most of the earnings growth came from assimilating acquisitions until finally they're all gone. I own CVS Health, the drug house retailer and distributer, because I think they're mid-cycle in their footprint.

Managements like Citigroup for decades made dilutive acquisitions of other banks, credit card purveyors, brokers and small loan houses that fit their grand design as a worldwide player in financial services. Some grand designs absorb a decade of repositioning expenses and often prove astigmatically disastrous, like JPMorgan's purchase of Washington Mutual and Bank of America's overpaying for Countrywide. Ask oil companies who bought retailers like Montgomery Ward, gas gatherers like Texas Oil and gas or steel makers. There is a road sign in Monaco for the Merrill Lynch office. A positioned franchise rates consideration, but the upstart Schwab harnessed technology to its client network early on. Schwab as an asset gatherer gets my money. Even its money market assets survived the 2008 meltdown.

Growth stocks are independent, masculine entities purveying impeccably packaged products most of us want to consume. Apple, for example. We don't care much about pricing and come back for product upgrades. The passive investor gets rich only if he comprehends the hidden agendas to satisfy Wall Street's need for 15 percent earnings momentum. The market pays for high unit growth and some pricing power—not just price leverage as in cornflakes, Pampers, Marlboros and Mach3, 4 or 5 razor blades.

The compound growth rate for a dozen or so tech houses reached unprecedented levels in the late nineties, over 50 percent. All of a sudden Cisco rose to the biggest market capitalization in the S&P 500, peaking at $500 billion before correcting to $350 billion at yearend 2000, now $140 billion. Coca-Cola was way down the list after giving GE a run for top dog. Philip Morris in 2000 was the biggest gainer among the top 25 stocks in the S&P 500, but it still sold for 10 times earnings.

The world remains hungry for bandwidth to transmit data and handle eyeballs on the Internet. Thus Google, Facebook and Apple, even Amazon. Internet purveyors like Amazon needed data storage capacity for its millions of new customers. Cable television operators still move into telephony, film production, interactive shopping and video on demand. A core group of tech houses emerged as the Levi Strauss purveyors of blue jeans to gold miners staking out their claims. Many names are all too familiar today: Yahoo, Qualcomm, EMC, Cisco, Sun Microsystems and Intel come to mind. Ma Bell started to embrace TV broadcasting and wireless telephony late in the game. MCI WorldCom saw the need for data transmission but had no footprint in wireless. It then flamed out on crass accounting that proved fictitious and criminal.

Analysts and fund managers periodically get caught up in the euphoric rationalization of valuation. At its peak in 2000, Yahoo sold at 100 times revenues and Cisco near 100 times forward earnings power. JDS Uniphase sold for more until the market cut it down. Optics was the magic word for expanding data transmission exponentially in the existing fiberglass networks. Stocks like Yahoo and Amazon corrected 90 percent from their highs during 2000. But Amazon at $16 still sold at three times revenues, an unprofitable business model with 20 percent gross margins. Fifteen years later, little has changed. Wal-Mart, with an impeccable business model, sold at one times sales. As capital spending flattened out, many of these tech growthies reverted to cyclical growth, even industrial status.

An aside on accounting excess is called for. Tech houses keep payrolls low by issuing options. It started with Microsoft in 1986, but by 1998 properties like Qualcomm, with a lock on much of the intellectual property in CDMA wireless technology, had massive dilution from options issuance. The same for Cisco. Not only do options keep payrolls understated, but you get a tax credit on the dollar amount of issuance, thereby increasing cash flow. Cisco carried acquisitions to the limit. Buy a sister tech house and immediately write off its intellectual property, thereby reducing R&D expenditures but adding future revenues to your existing base. If your stock sells at 100 times earnings you can overpay for everything. The worst offender, currently, is Salesforce.com, whose options issuance amounts to 40 percent of revenues, thereby entailing major shareholder dilution, year after year.

There are many understandable properties with hegemony and great business models that have withstood the test of many cycles. You can start with Wal-Mart and Home Depot; both were under 30 times earnings in April of 2001, now 18 times. Actually, my favorite retail franchise is Tiffany, whose worldwide reach keeps stretching. Lowe's is to Home Depot as Costco is to Wal-Mart—a strong second but no undervaluation spread. In technology, if I had to buy some properties now for the next three years, I would embrace Google, Apple, Micron Technology and Microsoft. Gilead Sciences and Biogen Idec cover you in biotechnology, Charles Schwab in financials, Comcast and 21st Century Fox in media. Halliburton and Schlumberger are my oil service plays, not the producers. I've just covered about 75 percent of the S&P 500's sectors.

These are my American Beauty roses. Actually, the really gorgeous long-stemmed beauties are grown in Equador and flown in daily to New York. The deepest ruby reds are named Black Magic. They take your breath away just like a great growth stock. And like roses, growth stocks wither. The telltale sign is a decelerating revenue line, which is followed by a decline in the return on equity. The short, happy lives of growth stocks don't surprise me. Consider: The average holding period for a stock in a growth mutual fund is under 18 months and shortening. It's a fast track for most of us, who risk getting chewed up like maiden two-year-olds in a claiming race. Buffett is the only exception; his holding periods embrace decades.

Over successive cycles, I've learned discipline:

- Never pay more than two times the growth rate for anything.
- If a stock is compounding earnings at 25 percent, the price-earnings ratio shouldn't top 50.
- You make the most money buying properties at one times their growth rate.
- To accomplish this, you gotta be early or buy when there's panic in the air.
- Nobody said courage doesn't count.

In December of 2000, Microsoft touched down at $40, one-third of its '99 peak. The market was saying Microsoft had lost it! "Another IBM." A month later MSFT hit $61. Yes, NASDAQ had rallied, but no 50 percent. Microsoft's December quarterly earnings statement was instructive. With 85 percent gross margins they had enormous discretion over spending for R&D and marketing. Both these expense lines flattened out, so they made their guidance numbers. Today, Microsoft's gross margin is under 65 percent. Coca-Cola couldn't do this. The igniting factor for Microsoft as a stock was the healthy revenue line for server software. This still counted in 2014. The market's not stupid for very long. Without a shot at a healthy revenue line you're rated as an also-ran. Cloud computing software has to take off for Microsoft to be a stock during 2015–'16.

Growth vs. Value Annual Performance

Year	S&P 500 Value Index (%)	S&P 500 Growth Index (%)	Difference (%)
2001	-11.7	-12.7	-1.0
2002	-20.9	-23.6	-2.7
2003	31.8	25.7	-6.1
2004	15.7	6.1	-9.6
2005	5.8	4.0	-1.8
2006	20.8	11.0	-9.8
2007	2.0	9.1	7.1
2008	-39.2	-34.9	4.3
2009	21.2	31.6	10.4
2010	15.1	15.1	0.0
2011	-0.5	4.7	5.1
2012	17.7	14.6	-3.1
2013	32.0	32.8	0.8
2014	12.4	14.9	2.5
Annualized Performance 2001–2014	5.2	5.2	0

Source: Poors

Measurement of growth vs. value investing shows they're neck 'n' neck, but note big variances over three- to five-year periods. The tech collapse in 2001 ensured value would outperform growth for several years. Growth and value managers live in walled-off worlds. Counseling firms warn clients when managers deviate from mandated style. In their book this is a capital offense.

Net, net of the whole thing, to excel, growth and value managers need viable properties with above-average returns on capital. The name of the game is making money, not growth or value investing. Big risk in value investing is, you freeze up with dead paper in your portfolio because you think it's too cheap to discard. Then the wolf scratches at your door with a bankruptcy notice. Emotionally, I'd like to soar to the moon with growthies, but when properties like banks, airlines and insurance underwriters tick down to their option value (a buck or two), I'm ready to pounce. By the spring of 2009, the entire stock market sold at book value and 10 times earnings. I licked my chops, plunged into frigid water and never looked back.

PART II
Putting the Numbers
in Focus

RICHARD LONG, *A SNOWBALL TRACK*, 1964

TEN

Can Quants Replace Conceptual Investing?

RICHARD LONG, *A SNOWBALL TRACK*, 1964
Private Collection

I need to touch things I invest in, whether they be horses, cars, sculpture or companies. Touching is not just about hands, but eyes, ears and mind. If you listened to Donald Trump's embroideries, you knew the end of the cycle in collectibles and LBOs was at hand in '89.

Richard Long has made his art out of trekking here and there. He calls it "working in circles." You identify solely with the traces of his passing—a shadow, his footprints, the line on a map, the line of arrows marking the direction of the wind as it buffets his body on the trail. With Long you pass through rain, sun, mud and snow, wind and water and rock formations. Long says, "My work is about real stones, real time, real actions. I use the world as I find it."

Years ago, I assigned our computer programmers the task of reviewing postwar market cycles and coming up with a schema that would outperform the market. I hoped our quants could develop portfolios that outperformed us. The fallout in ideas—industry groups and specific stocks—could help us implement outsized concepts with lead time on the market.

Money management, like Richard Long, works with ratios and proportion, measurement and perception. One of Richard Long's early works was this photo of a snowball and its track. The path became a central image in his work. A path can take you for a walk (Black Monday), or it can be one you choose for its rapid change, like NASDAQ. Boiled down, what I do is manufacture money—or sometimes destroy it with my stupidities. Like Long, I get my energy from being on the road, watching the world go past me. As Long says: "Wind can blow in all different directions for different reasons to do with the shape of the land. I very much like the idea that in a subtle way the wind line was also reflecting the shape of the land."

Our programmers stand untrained in security analysis and portfolio management. They are mathematicians who never leave their windowless offices to interview managements or talk with market technicians, politicians and economists. They don't read the *Wall Street Journal* or any other financial publication. Neither do they read corporate annual reports or extrapolate statistical releases from our government on the health of the national economy. They hover around the air-conditioned room that housed our Hewlett-Packard Spectrum 600, subsequently updated to six servers and 50 computers.

I talk to Katie, our senior programmer, once a quarter, right after she hands in her updated portfolio. Katie's model uses an equivalent universe of stocks. Neither of us has an edge. Because Katie runs a paper portfolio, she doesn't get charged for buying and selling, except commissions. Our portfolio, in billions, entails costs for entering and exiting, which can reach a couple of percent when the market is unaccommodating. Even so, Katie's portfolio usually outshines us. There is one glaring exception. When the economic cycle reverses, *the model underperforms the market for a couple of quarters before the computer picks up the new inflection point*. The underperformance of the paper portfolio is a leading indicator of cyclical economic phasing and industry group rotation. It happened in 1990 with the oil war and the relapse in corporate earning power during 1992, and again at yearend 2000 in the tech bubble. Same goes for 2008–'09 when the financial crisis hit the country.

There is a certain tongue-in-cheek attitude when Katie and I meet. What goes unsaid is the computer program's capacity often to beat our brains out by selecting and weighting macroeconomic indicators and statistics of the business cycle better than our analysts. What the model says is that the fortunes of most industry groups are foretold by what's going on in sectors of the economy that seem on the surface totally unrelated to a specific industry. In other words, Katie thinks I'm a moron.

I keep telling Katie that such things as housing stats have nothing to do with automobile sales. That using housing stats to predict automobile sales is a derivative of a derivative. Katie says, "Maybe so, but it works." The correlation is high, but not in 2014, with buoyant auto sales and depressed home starts. Both housing and automobiles have to do with trends in consumer credit and interest rates, maybe consumer confidence. The computer couldn't deal with the concept of pent-up demand. So I won this round.

One year, the model's overweighting in energy stocks rested on the high correlation between energy stock prices and the country's net exports. This is abstract stuff. To rationalize energy stocks with our export volume, one has to leap to the conclusion that if our exports are growing, the rest of the world is growing faster; therefore, oil demand and consumption are rising rapidly. In 2001 we discarded this insight and increased our weighting in oil service operators. Same-o in 2014. Our exports remained depressed. Oil service properties like Schlumberger and Halliburton boomed because the reserves-to-production ratio was too light. This was pure security analysis. Oil drilling budgets finally were rising at a 20 percent clip because of underspending in previous years. The computer doesn't pick up micro industry changes as they're happening.

When Iran and Iraq stopped fighting, spot oil prices collapsed. When Iraq overran Kuwait, prices soared. The model doesn't pick up wars and revolutions. You have to do that part yourself or wait six months for the computer to catch up with reality. When OPEC cut production by 1.5 million barrels a day in January of 2001, oil service stocks bottomed. With the civil war between Sunni and Shia sects boiling over in June 2014, oil futures rose a snappy 5 percent, practically overnight.

The model has been consistently overweighted in growth stocks, including computers and semiconductors. Here there was no discernible pattern except above-average earnings growth, but nothing is forever. Starting in the summer of '88, technology stocks underperformed for five years, indicating a slowdown in the industrial sector of the economy, later confirmed by GNP statistics. Same in 2013 and '14. Gross margins fell in the computer sector, but the model portfolio lagged this perception of too many computer companies fighting for market share. Early 2014, technology was a buy, as capital spending bottomed out throughout the industrial heartland.

Early nineties, the model also picked up gold stocks, which correlate with the producer price index and have a negative correlation with consumer credit delinquency rates. When oil prices collapsed, gold broke down to $340 an ounce. When oil boomed, gold snapped back to $410. *The computer couldn't sniff out Middle East geopolitics or declining inflation.* Gold prices relapsed to the $340 level but then recovered back over the $400 mark because the players no longer feared central banks selling off gold on the open market. When this fear resurfaced in the late nineties, gold collapsed to $260. There's so much overcapacity in basic industry, worldwide, that gold is an on-and-off geopolitical play. With the FRB pining for inflation 2013–'14, gold looked obsolete as an investment vehicle.

In the cyclical sector, the model again picks up net exports, earnings growth and a negative correlation with the Consumer Price Index. Since many cyclical companies—steel, aluminum, chemicals—are worldwide operators, it is understandable that low inflation, growing worldwide demand and a net export condition paint a benevolent background for cyclical earnings power and worldwide economic momentum. But the computer couldn't fathom the end of Marxism in the Soviet Union. This led to the Russians dumping aluminum, copper and nickel on the London Metal Exchange and depressing quotes to five-year lows. Nobody's perfect. With electric power costs running off the page in 2001 and oil-based feedstock prices squeezing the Dows and DuPonts, basic industrials needed worldwide GDP accelerating markedly for an earnings story. Worldwide becalmed GDP was death for the materials sector past few years, with coal operators facing insolvency and iron ore quotes way below cost of production, mid-2014 into 2015.

The interest-sensitive sector, largely banks, insurance underwriters and construction-related companies, again responds to the net export conditions of the country. Interestingly, bond yields are not a factor in predicting their relative attraction. Earnings growth, again, is a critical factor, as is the negative correlation with the consumer and producer price indices. If you think the world's going to grow handily in a reasonable inflationary environment, banks should do well. The computer didn't detect the coming meltdown in financial assets, 2008–'09.

From the bottom of the economic cycle in '82 till the autumn of '88, the model outperformed the market averages. Some negative divergence began in the summer of '88 and ran through 1990, suggesting a change in trend among broad economic indicators. This was very helpful. We shifted out of an overweighting in the cyclicals and concentrated more of our invested assets in non-cyclical earnings power—the foods, tobaccos and ethical drug houses. We repeated this migration late in '98 and then switched back to early-on cyclical growth in media, technology and retailing at yearend 2000, and again in 2009. Ben Bernanke's insight on stimulus was my leading indicator. I refused to meet with Katie so she couldn't screw up my head.

During the fourth quarter of '88, megamergers erupted in foods and tobacco. Pillsbury and Kraft Foods were bought out at 50 percent premiums above market value. R.J. Reynolds Tobacco was $56 before Kohlberg Kravis Roberts bid $108, topping management's offer. The battle for brand name surfaced as a worldwide phenomenon. PepsiCo bought Quaker Oats for its Gatorade in 2000. Sony bought CBS Records, and the Japanese paid a billion-dollar premium for the InterContinental Hotels chain from Grand Metropolitan, an English conglomerate. Everyone overpaid for these properties. Growth stock valuations peaked by yearend '91, preceding the death of the Marlboro Man at 51 from lung cancer. LBOs peaked in 1989. The computer didn't pick up the surge in Tobin's Q ratio from under par to 150 percent.

Sanely, the bedrock of the model is the extremely high predictive power of corporate earnings. If a company's earnings are growing faster than the market's aggregate earnings, the stock attracts attention and outperforms. The model uses trailing 12-month earnings per share divided by the Standard & Poor's Index of 12-month trailing results. Because the model disregards price-earnings ratios, you run the risk that if you own a lot of high-priced growth stocks and the earnings foul up—as they did in 1973, 1993, 2000 and 2008–'09—you self-destruct like the Marlboro Man. Polaroid went from 50 times earnings to a 10 times valuation when its results faltered, and then bankruptcy. The same downside volatility in 2001 hit the generic sector of medium-sized or emerging growth stocks. There was a faddish concentration of money in Internet names. We diverged from the model as our core investment process found valuation absurdly high. For valuation, we use forward 12-month earnings projections.

The pivotal concept is: Stocks that go up contain a growth story attached to their backs. They can't outperform unless they're growing faster than the market and faster than analysts' projections. Qualcomm was the number-one performer in

1999 because all the techies were swinging late and underestimating Qualcomm's numbers. At its peak, it sold at 100 times earnings. Currently it's 18 times earnings. As Will Rogers used to say, "If it don't go up, don't buy it." The art of money management is buying earnings momentum stories at least six months before they're picked up by 30 sell-side analysts. Nobody tells you how to do this, because it's visceral and based on macro calls on worldwide economic momentum, comparative interest rates and currency parities. Lifestyle changes like color TV, instant color film, cellular telephony and the Internet come along every decade, going back to the fifties. Cellular providers projected market saturation at 8 percent in the nineties, not the 100 percent-plus we have today.

The model uses an 800-stock universe. Then, correlation coefficients are computed for eight macroeconomic indices and relative earnings comparisons made for each stock. There are just nine factors (eight indices plus earnings), which are statistically significant for each stock. On average, 3.5 factors of a possible nine end up as usable for a specific company. Then weightings are derived for each of the "statistically significant" factors. These weightings are based on the previously computed correlation coefficients and cross-correlations among the indices and relative earnings. This means a lot of back-testing validates the specific factors like net exports, the Consumer Price Index and installment credit. The model then comes up with a ranking of stocks from most attractive to least attractive for the next quarter.

The idea of going to the moon with a handful of stocks should be reserved for a handful of genius money managers. I need a portfolio of 30 stocks to feel comfortable. The portfolio the computer spits out is never everything you expect to see or what your research analysts are covering closely. You do begin to see a confluence of stocks in specific industry sectors. These patterns force you to consider rotating money into new sectors or concentrating more assets in one sector or another, usually the sector you wish to hate the most, like gold, copper, and defense contractors. I excluded gold and copper in the slowing economy of 2013 but bit on Lockheed, a nice winner. At yearend 2000 our weighting in technology was 35 percent of assets, but shortly thereafter the unwinding process began. The pivotal variable was overvaluation as well as the peaking of information technology spending.

The armchair investor can walk away with a few deep basics. Buy a server and hire a couple of computer programmers. They can duplicate what we did. Short of giving in to the quants, you develop an appreciation for the influence exerted by seminal economic forces on stock prices. You can do this from your armchair next to the fireplace. Is the euro going to outperform the dollar? Maybe not. My call in late 2014. Then you look at all the multinationals like Coca-Cola with more than half their sales in Europe and say no way, José.

Since 1981, our model proved economic indices have led stock prices more often than earnings momentum, although earnings momentum was the critical sustaining variable late in '89 and all of 1990, most of the late nineties, 2000 and 2001 and finally 2009. This suggests players are becoming more and more sophisticated, relying on more abstract concepts than linking arms with the prettiest girl walking down Fifth Avenue. When Alan Greenspan cut the federal funds rate 50 basis points early in January 2001, NASDAQ rallied 15 percent in a couple of hours. The market got busy discounting the next economic recovery even while tech houses were pre-reporting bad earnings numbers. Drug stocks sagged, as did the entire non-durables growth sector. I keep asking myself where the next macro perception is going to be fixated six to 12 months ahead.

If you have the "feel" of a cycle—inflationary or non-inflationary, slow growth or rapid growth—you must place more chips in specific sectors of the market. You buy handfuls of stocks that cluster in the preferred sectors and stay with them until the macroeconomics reverse. When the big picture changes, you change, early on. Nothing is forever. Five years, often yes, sometimes no. The last great growth cycle ran from post–Black Monday, early '88, through 1991. Four years on, two years off is often the pattern. When the economy slowed in '94, growth took off again. Post–2000, the growth model changed from NASDAQ pyrotechnics because of its extreme overvaluation. With the exception of biotechnology, nobody wants to pay more than two times the growth rate for anything. The technology index yearend 2014 sold at no premium to the market, waiting for capital spending to kick in, finally. I'm betting this is a 2015 phenomenon.

The model helps because it takes much subjective bias out of big-picture forecasting. The near unanimity of the financial community on big calls is almost always too late or too early. On Wall Street everyone reads the same source material, talks to the designated spokesperson in the corporate and government sectors and takes lunch in the eating clubs where everyone still dresses in dark suits. No wonder the economic forecasts are nearly uniform.

If you can project, six months in advance, trends in consumer credit, net exports, housing permits, long-term Treasury bond yields, producer and consumer prices, delinquent consumer loans and unemployment levels, you are an online computer's equal, easily its better half. Good hunting, but don't expect to be right more than 50 percent of the time. You gotta know when to pull the plug on your computer, too, and stand alone as a gut player.

ELEVEN

My Charts Worth 10,000 Words

*J*ust as a doctor making rounds reads patient charts to focus on vital signs, investors need charts to develop a sense of financial history, how one cycle compares with another and how each cycle adumbrates its own specific future. A relevant chart works as an illumination, suggesting a course of action in securities markets, both bonds and equities. Charts are helpful in developing a strong, even unwavering point of view. If a picture is worth a thousand words, a relevant chart's worth 10,000 words, at least.

Without a working hypothesis, you are just a sandpiper buffeted in a windstorm with no sense of direction or capacity to find your rightful place on the beach. Charts are to navigate by. Like Polaris, the North Star, they keep you focused. The more gales to endure, the more charts you need to interpret the maelstrom.

There are critical macro forces that a money manager must respect and process if he's running billions. Because? You need lead time, at least six months, before a change in trend becomes obvious and part of The Street's daily noise level. The list is so long. Are corporate profits about to top out? Is inflation going to accelerate or remain quiescent? Are we in a growth-stock cycle or is value more attractive? Where are interest rates heading? Is Federal Reserve Board policy about to become more or less restrictive?

What about fiscal policy? Is it a drag on the economy or about to become stimulative because the budget surplus is too big a share of GDP? Corporate profits? Are they taking too big a share of national income? If so, could there be a public outcry, finally, that leads to changes in tax rates for corporations and the wealthy? Where does the middle class come out, and what are the implications for personal consumption expenditures? I think of health-care cost escalation as the fifth column in the middle class's personal consumption expenditures. It could double in seven years.

Macro research puts the big picture in focus. Then everything else falls into place: growth vs. value, sector overweighting and underweighting, and finally, individual stock selection. The charts herein are rarely published in the *Wall Street*

Journal or the consumer press. Economists update and comment on many of these trends but they sprout multiple hands. There is always hedging—on the one hand and on the other hand. Aggressive money managers are more like submarine captains than economists. They man the periscope, focus on what's in front of them and then bark orders. "We're in a growth-stock cycle! Fire the torpedoes, all of 'em! Get me the story on Apple and Amazon!"

A word on Alan Greenspan. He was great at stepping in early in the autumn of '98 and of course the morning after Black Monday. I have great reservations about whether Greenspan read the nineties as well as he read the mid-to-late eighties. Not only did Greenspan underestimate tremendous gains in productivity because of the unprecedented capital goods spending boom, he also completely ignored the ominous fiscal drag that took place during the Clinton Administration. Republicans controlled the Congress and few spending bills except for defense made it through the legislative process. The Federal Reserve Board probably contributed to the rate of inflation in the country by raising interest rates unnecessarily. There were approximately 50 changes in the discount rate between Greenspan's ascendancy in '87 and his retirement in 2006. If nothing else, they plastered Alan on the front page. The reason we wallowed in a budget surplus when Clinton was president is a combination of a divided Congress and a scintillating stock market that by the mid-nineties was throwing off substantive capital gains tax receipts, over $80 billion in fiscal 2000. (Politicians didn't mention this.) Meanwhile, the public kept spending, reducing its savings rate to next to zero. Nobody anticipated this macro variable or caught its inflection point.

By the autumn of 2000, retail sales in the country hit a stone wall. Same-store sales hardly grew. The exceptions were few—Wal-Mart and Costco—and even they experienced some contraction in growth. Stocks like Gap, Saks, Home Depot, Federated Department Stores and K-Mart were cut in half or worse. Apple Computer hit a speed bump and, of course, Xerox practically self-destructed and admitted publicly that its business model no longer fit the printing and copying market. Cisco's management didn't wake up until March of 2001. The capital goods cycle, particularly information technology, had fueled the tech boom. It was over, but nobody rang the bell. Cisco had to junk $2.5 billion in inventory, an enormous sum even for them.

Start with my favorite chart for the present cycle from 2008 on: Industry capacity utilization rates (*Figure 9*). Don't let it put you to sleep, as yet. It's number one because it kept me bullish for 10 years, and maybe for five more. I never worried about interest rates for a minute, nor about inflation. Just so long as corporate profits remained buoyant, I didn't need to worry much about overvaluation in the market, either. Under 80 percent rate of utilization is synonymous with recession

CAPACITY UTILIZATION
Total Industry

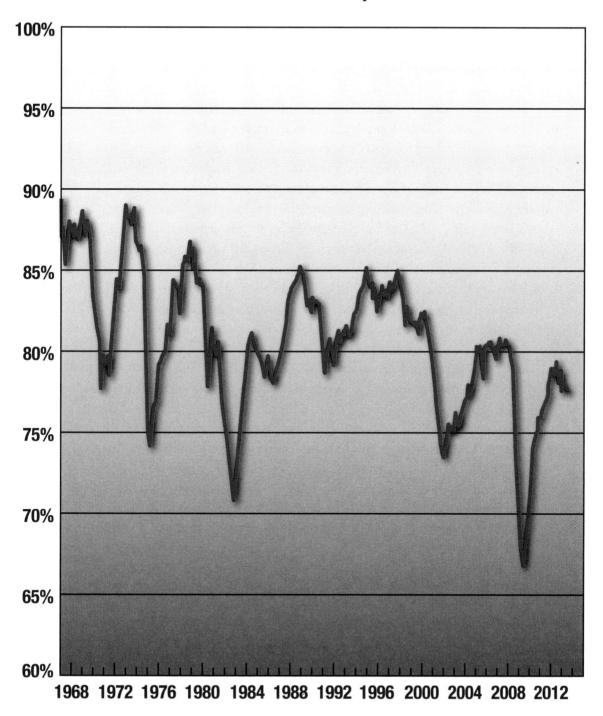

Figure 9

Source: Safian Investment Research

as compared with previous cycles. It keeps the FRB on hold and underscores the inherent leverage in manufacturing. During 2013–'14 I had overweighted prime industrial properties like Boeing, Honeywell, United Technologies and Precision Castparts. Without steeply rising capacity utilization, labor unions hold no leverage and inflation remains quiescent, the FRB a sleeping tiger.

Why has capacity utilization remained so low for so long? Check out the following chart on capital spending (*Figure 10*). It practically ran off the page from the mid-nineties until 2000. Corporations took on gobs of debt to expand capacity. Borrowing costs stayed low. At one point, AAA corporate bonds traded just 25 basis points above 10-year Treasuries, a great bargain for corporate borrowers. Towards yearend 2000, it raised the issue of an economic contraction, albeit mild. The consumer had all the Nike sneakers he needed in his locker at the club. Spreads began to widen during 2000 as defaults reached a level not seen even in the Mike Milken days of high-yield excesses. Defaults were cropping up among retailers, telecommunications properties and Internet operators. The Street was beginning to question Amazon's business model and cash flow assumptions. The negative financing gap between capital spending and cash flow had widened. This couldn't go on. Corporate profits flattened out late in 2000. This chart is not going to run off the page, after all, and it foreshadowed the recession of 2001–'02.

Currently, corporations swim in liquidity. There is no financing gap, but a cash flow surplus. This suggests more share buybacks, acquisitions for cash and rising dividends, exactly what we've got—good for several more years. Good for the market and good for Wall Street houses and operators. Note that the negative financing gap in 2000 and 2007 was a good leading indicator of end-of-cycle growth. End of 2014, stocks like Allergan and Actavis got fat on deal activity.

I like this chart on stock valuation, if only as an antidote to tons of bearish sentiment that brewed during 2013–'14 (*Figure 11, page 104*). What it says is, the average stock in the S&P 500 Index is selling at 16 times earnings, and that's within its long-term valuation construct. Confirming this mid-teens price-earnings ratio is low inflation. Anywhere under 3 percent, stocks invariably sell above 15 times earnings unless we're in deep recession territory. Mid-decade, this wouldn't be the correct call, because corporate profit margins hold up in an environment of low interest rates and contained wage expense. Punditry, through much of 2014, ran decidedly negative. Even the FRB called attention to excesses in Internet properties and biotech houses. Alan Greenspan weighed in on the side of a sizable market correction, too. By September the market had levitated 9 percent and peaked close to 2,100 by yearend. Pundits turned bullish on 2015, pointing to the market's "reasonable" price-earnings ratio.

CASH FLOW MINUS CAPITAL SPENDING

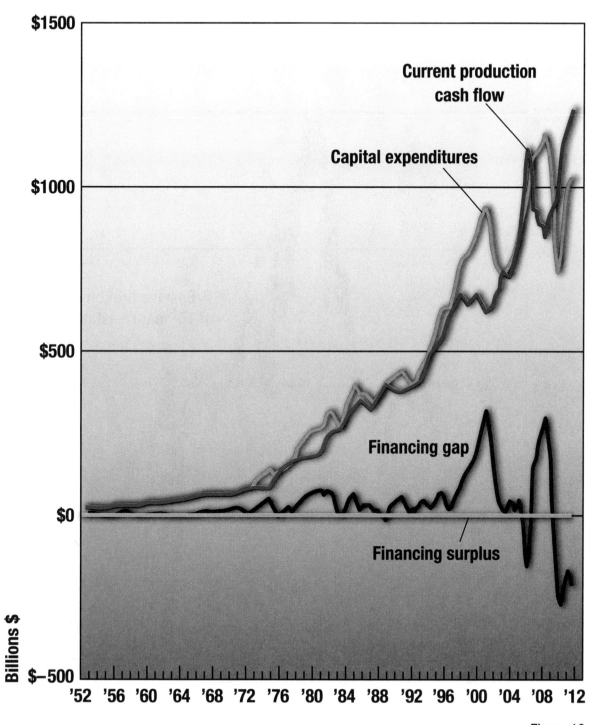

Figure 10

Source: Safian Investment Research

PRICE-EARNINGS RATIO — S&P 500 INDEX
1985–2014

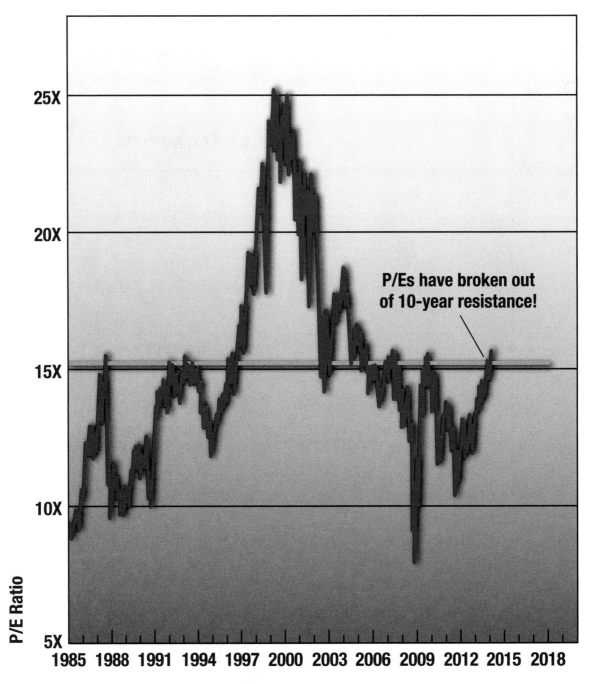

Figure 11

Source: Cornerstone Macro

The market's feverish quality is captured in NASDAQ volatility, finally retracing its Internet bubble peak, end of 2014. At its bottom in 2002, it lost almost 80 percent. Because many large tech houses like Apple, Microsoft, Intel, Facebook and Cisco disdain the New York Stock Exchange, valuation of Internet and cloud computing houses has pushed NASDAQ weighting to almost 50 percent of the NYSE.

The Big Board is close to being overshadowed by NASDAQ, adjusted for trading volume. On its introduction of the new smartphone and watch on September 9, 2014, Apple traded 19 million shares. On its big beat fourth-quarter report it traded over 40 million shares. NASDAQ, in the public's consciousness, is the center ring rather than a side ring. It foretells unmerciful volatility for the market both ways until absurdly valued properties like Twitter, Salesforce.com and LinkedIn play themselves out. NASDAQ at the peak of the Internet bubble traded at 140 percent of Big Board volume. It rose 21 percent towards yearend 2014, 50 percent more than the S&P 500 Index. In 2014, I took the other side and bought tech properties selling at 10 times earnings—Hewlett-Packard, Microsoft, Micron and Cisco, but not Intel and Oracle, whose fundamentals were more conjectural (*Figure 12, page 106*).

The next visual on operating profit margins actually contains scant forecasting weight, already in new high ground and likely to hold there through 2015. Its course is tied to GDP momentum. Finally, wage expense and interest rates may come into play. My guess is 2016 is its inflection point, when it will be showing some reversion to the mean (*Figure 13 page 107*).

History counts. Next bar graph confirms a mid-teens price-earnings ratio just so long as real 30-year Treasuries stay below a 4 percent yield, what we had during 2014. Two years ahead I'd expect to see 2 percent inflation and long-term Treasuries yielding 4.5 percent, not 2.9 percent. A real yield near 2.5 percent keeps the market's valuation comfortably around 16 times earnings. An actionable chart, just so long as you get the variables of inflation, earnings, and nominal interest rates confirmed (*Figure 14, page 108*).

This matrix on market valuation is what pundits employ to confirm optimistic calls, at least over a 12-month period. A do-it-yourself matrix, it combines an earnings call with the price-earnings multiple you think the market should reach. For 2015, I'd use a P/E ratio of 16 and earnings for the S&P 500 Index at $130 a share. This gets me above 2,100 for the market, maybe 5 percent higher than 2014's yearend level. Call this a workable hypothesis, but with no room for disappointments.

NASDAQ 100 STOCK INDEX
1994–2014

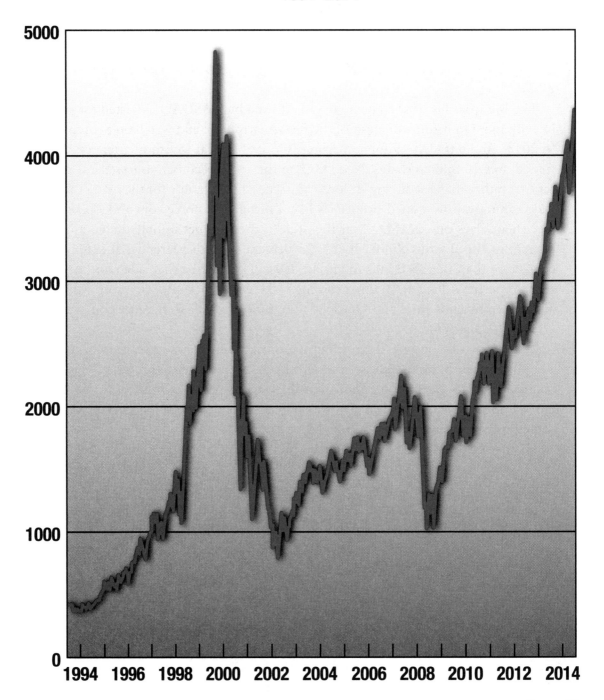

Figure 12

Source: Bloomberg

S&P 500 OPERATING MARGINS (QUARTERLY)

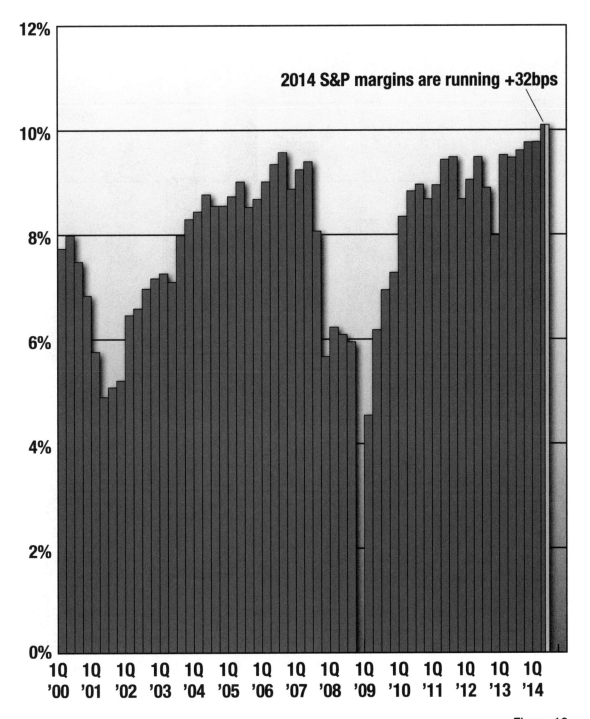

2014 S&P margins are running +32bps

Figure 13

Source: Evercore ISI

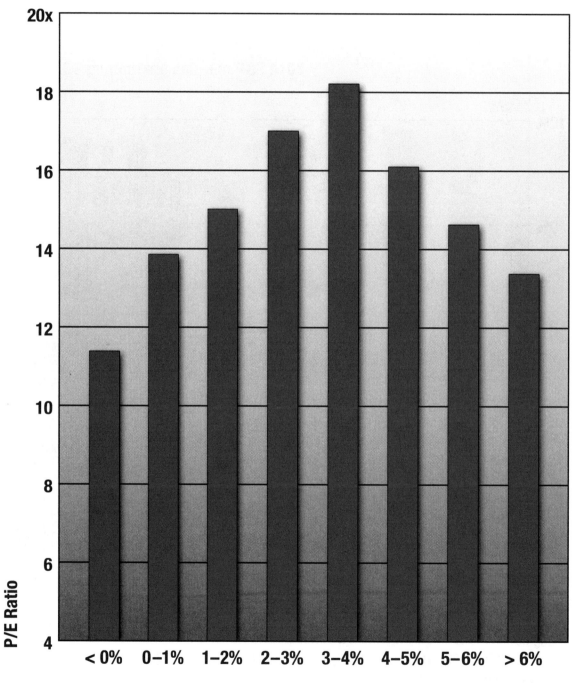

P/E RATIO VS. LONG-TERM TREASURY YIELD SINCE 1930
Real Long-Term Treasury Yield

Figure 14

Source: Thomson Reuters & Morgan Stanley

MARKET VALUATION AS OF JANUARY 2015
S&P 500 Closing Value 2000

PE	$115	$117.50	$120	$122.50	$125	$127.50	$130
				EPS			
15.0	1725	1763	1800	1838	1875	1913	1950
15.5	1783	1821	1860	1899	1938	1976	2015
16.0	1840	1880	1920	1960	2000	2040	2080
16.5	1898	1939	1980	2021	2063	2104	2145
17.0	1955	1998	2040	2083	2125	2168	2210
17.5	2013	2056	2100	2144	2188	2231	2275
18.0	2070	2115	2160	2205	2250	2295	2340

Liquidity has never been better for corporations, going back to the fifties. Sooner or later all this is expressed in deals, rising dividends and accelerating share buybacks. We're already there, but it could intensify in 2015–'16 (*Figure 15, page 110*).

Based on previous cycles, it could take five years for wages to regain previous levels, a very benign environment for corporate profit margins. The guys in work boots are being shortchanged. Labor costs have fallen below the early 1950s (*Figure 16, page 111*).

A spread of 200 or so basis points between low-grade corporate debentures and 10-year Treasuries proclaims generalized yield starvation for investors. Additionally, spreads contract when GDP accelerates, which is what this graph says. I dunno. What's good is that tight spreads can last for several years. That I do believe. BB corporates rose over 14 percent during 2014, the best return for all U.S. asset categories excepting the NASDAQ 100 (*Figure 17, page 112*).

All these charts taken together formed my belief that profit margins hold on firm ground in an environment of low interest rates, minimal inflation and modest wage escalation. GDP runs at a normalized rate of 3 percent or better. On paper, everything comes out neat, but the endgame is anything but a bed of roses. Because of the fadeaway in oil futures, Federal Reserve tightening is pushed out maybe to 2016.

Back of mind is the concept of "necessary fallibility." Charts can't isolate inflection points. You can miss these by years. Consider: Black Monday, 9/11, the Cuban missile crisis, even Paul Volcker's resolve to rid the country of its inflationary bias at all costs. It took 15 percent interest rates to do so. None of these events was readily predictable from chart readings or anything else. Sometimes, it's a vague, queasy feeling around your belly button that's the best leading indicator of big trouble ahead. I've learned to respect this feeling and act upon it, entitled from voluminous data processed over the years. Axiomatically, politics leads economics.

FINANCIAL RATIOS OF NONFINANCIAL CORPORATIONS

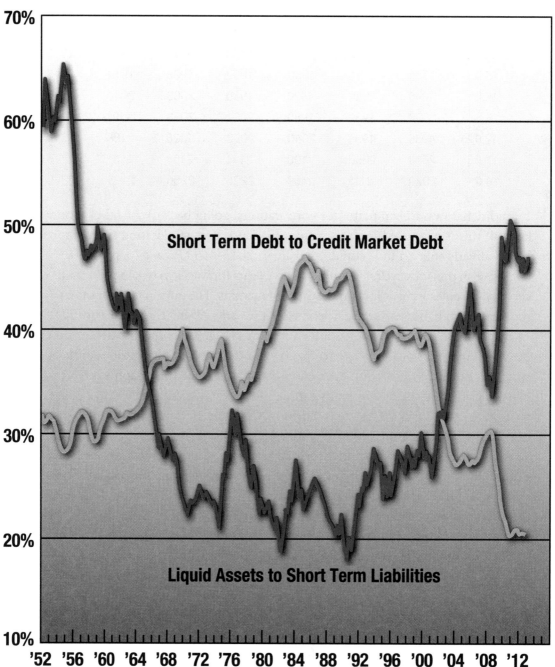

Figure 15

Source: Safian Investment Research

WAGES AS A PERCENT OF GDP
FOR NONFINANCIAL CORPORATE BUSINESS

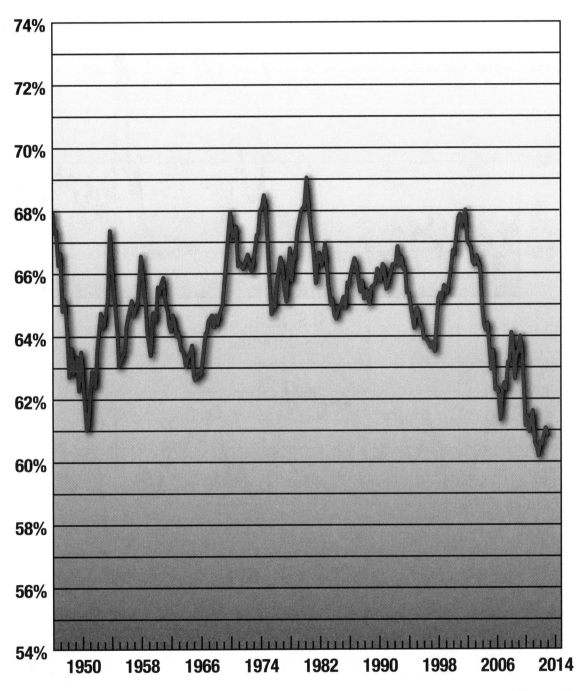

Figure 16

Source: Safian Investment Research

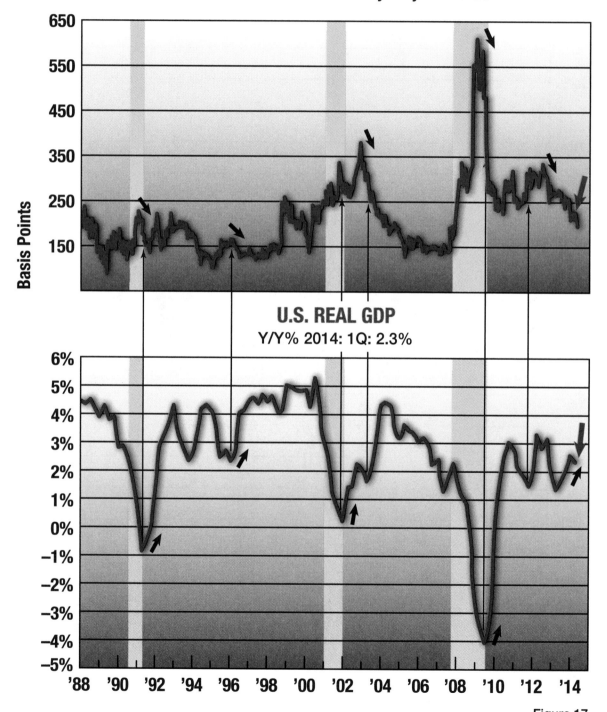

BAA BOND YIELD (MOODY'S)
Minus 10-Year U.S. Treasury May 7: 217 BP

U.S. REAL GDP
Y/Y% 2014: 1Q: 2.3%

Figure 17

Source: Cornerstone Macro

One leading indicator that I ignored showed extreme backwardation, oil trading in the low eighties a few years out. If you believed this reading you'd have banged out all your oil and gas properties on the basis that the players in oil futures are professionals and know what they're doing. Because oil futures contracts don't have much depth to them in terms of a sizable open interest, I ignored this indicator. Futures quotes did break sharply autumn of 2014, with WTI down from $115 to below $60 by February 2015. Rig operators like Transocean dropped over 60 percent. Even a "polite" property like Schlumberger lost 30 percent from its high over a couple of months. For me, this was a costly lesson.

Professional investors, energy managements and keen observers of supply and demand like Daniel Yergin, head of Cambridge Energy Research Associates, first saw mid-decade supply and demand closer to equilibrium at $100 a barrel for WTI oil. Saudi decontrol of the spigots, with oil demand plummeting, was the pivotal variable. They decided not to cut production despite sloppy demand late 2014. With the dollar strong, they decided to hold share of market rather than cut back unilaterally. Who knew? Backup is their fiscal budget can manage deficits because of dollar reserves approximating $700 million. But dollar reserves carry their solvency. Futures charts indicated oil pricing nearing incremental cost of production everywhere but the Mideast. Prospective production outages never surfaced in Iraq, Nigeria, Syria, Libya, even Iran with the blockade prevailing. With non-OPEC supply growing, the world was awash in oil at yearend '14. Interestingly, the futures chart forecasted that $80 a barrel was the right price for oil, looking out a couple of years, but this was professionals' guesstimates (*Figure 18, page 114*).

The ultimate leading indicator is the published notes from the Federal Reserve Board's Federal Open Market Committee. They still tell us to expect money market rates holding close to zero for the foreseeable future (mid-2015). Only much lower unemployment stats could trigger a change in policy. Home buyers currently can finance 30-year mortgages, non-amortizable the first 10 years, near 4 percent. Historically speaking, this is a bargain rate of interest. So, low mortgage rates signal housing's recovery. The Fed's outlook on GDP momentum, unemployment and inflation anticipates a sluggish, tensionless economic setting, which is what we've already endured (*Figure 19, page 115*).

I'd expect home buying to turn buoyant in years to come, just on low cost of carry alone. You can expand aggregate purchasing power on low borrowing costs and low energy prices to embrace automobiles. Consumer spending ratios to disposable income trend higher with lower savings rates. All powerful drivers of GDP. What emerges from such ciphering is a healthy economic setting with no excesses creeping into the system, at least for 2015. Nobody can see more than a year ahead. Economists and the FRB dream of catching inflection points but rarely get it right.

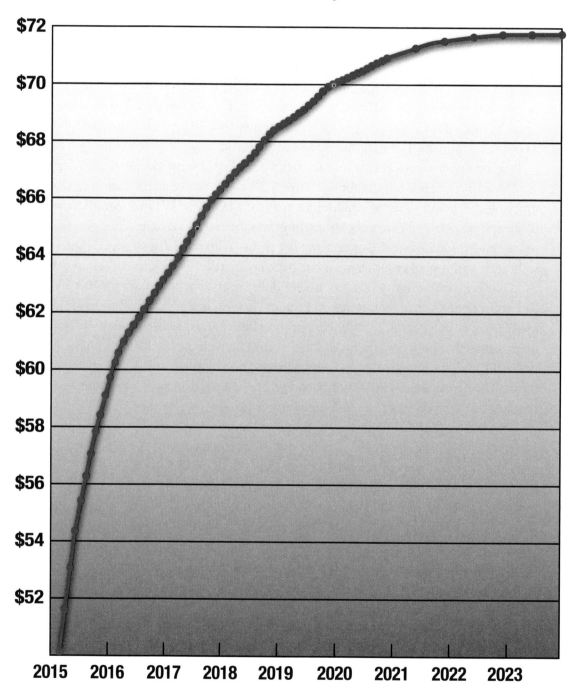

OIL FUTURES 2015–2022
as of February 2015

Figure 18
Source: Bloomberg

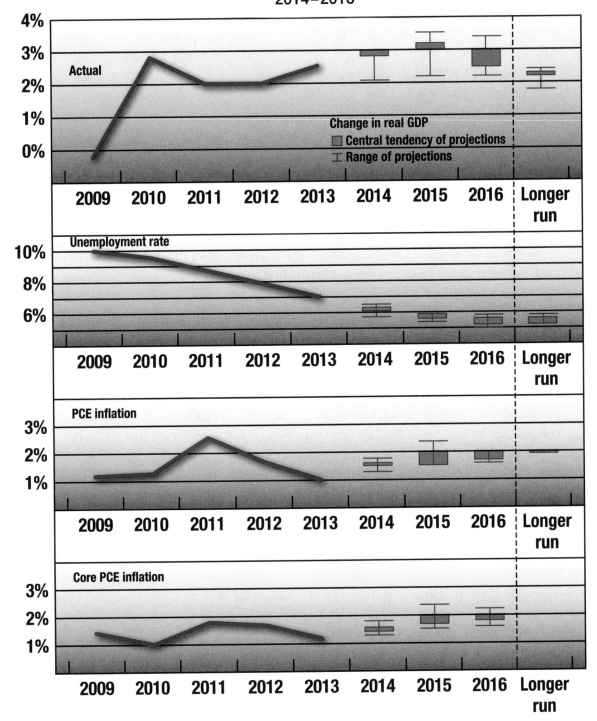

CENTRAL TENDENCIES AND RANGES OF ECONOMIC PROJECTIONS
2014–2016

Change in real GDP
■ Central tendency of projections
⊥ Range of projections

Figure 19

Source: Federal Open Market Committee

The ultimate irony on leading indicators is they don't always work when you expect them to kick in. Corporate liquidity hasn't worked in forecasting the pickup in capex. It's always around the corner, excepting the auto sector, but observers worry this is premature. Nothing's black or white. All these suckers cry out for interpretation within their historical context (*Figure 20*).

Days of simple capital goods and inventory recessions passed in the early sixties when industrial production peaked at 30 percent of the economy. We're below 15 percent now, but nobody cares. Facebook is three times the size of General Motors' market capitalization. Apple holds the number-one slot in the S&P 500 Index previously held by ExxonMobil, around forever but finding it more costly to replace its oil reserves. Note the plunges in the motor vehicles sector during the deep recession in the early eighties and 2008–'09.

The big surprise throughout 2014 was that the high yield index of BB bonds and preferreds levitated, putting away many equity and fixed income indices. Not only was index buoyancy reflective of institutional and individual investors' yield starvation, but it was a confirming indicator of prolonged corporate health. Coverage of interest expense, even on a pretax basis rather than EBITDA, turned more comfortable. Apple successfully floated $12 billion in corporate bonds, little more than the U.S. Treasury pays on its debt (*Figure 21, page 118*).

The high-yield market believed the Fed's benign 2015 forecast, as yield spread compression with 10-year Treasuries was continuous, heading towards 150 basis points over 10-year Treasuries yielding 2.2 percent. Spreads can stay low for several years. The fed funds rate, 25 basis points, may last into 2016. But if you drew a trendline over a 30-year interval, I would use 4 percent. Nobody sees this coming or is factoring a normalized fed funds rate into their bond yield forecasts. When it comes, the bond crowd traditionally panics and compresses a major sell-off into a couple of months (*Figure 22, page 119*).

Stocks do much better than bonds after the Fed's initial bump in rates. Maybe it's because the FRB telescopes its intentions early on. Even if fed funds rise to 2 percent by mid-2015—not my call—this level would be well below historic norms. The same goes for 10-year and 30-year Treasuries. If 30-year paper rose 150 basis points to 4.5 percent mid-2015, it shouldn't impact price-earnings ratios. Rather, it would confirm the business cycle remains intact.

MOTOR VEHICLES AND PARTS INDUSTRIAL PRODUCTION

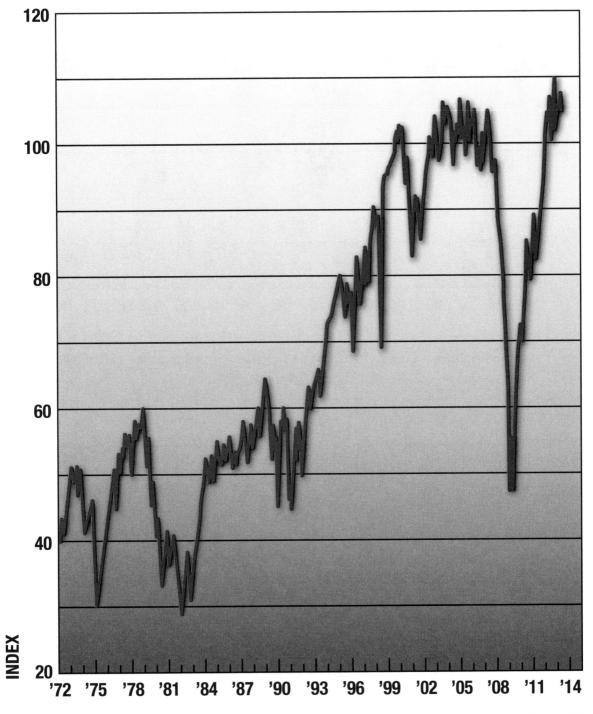

Figure 20

Source: Safian Investment Research

THIRTY YEARS OF U.S. FED FUNDS RATES

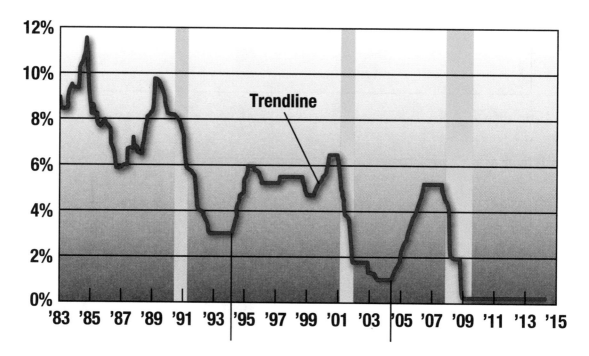

BAA Bond Yield (Moody's) minus 10-Year U.S. Treasury

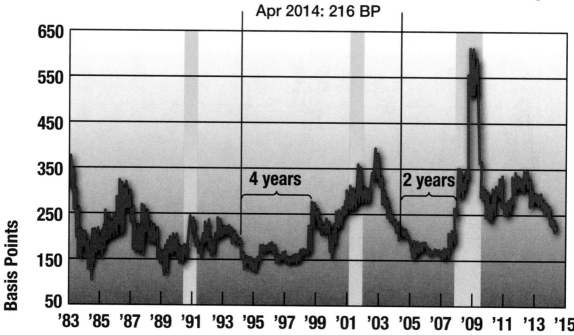

Figure 21

Source: Cornerstone Macro

JUNK BOND YIELD (MERRILL LYNCH)
MINUS U.S. 5-YEAR TREASURY

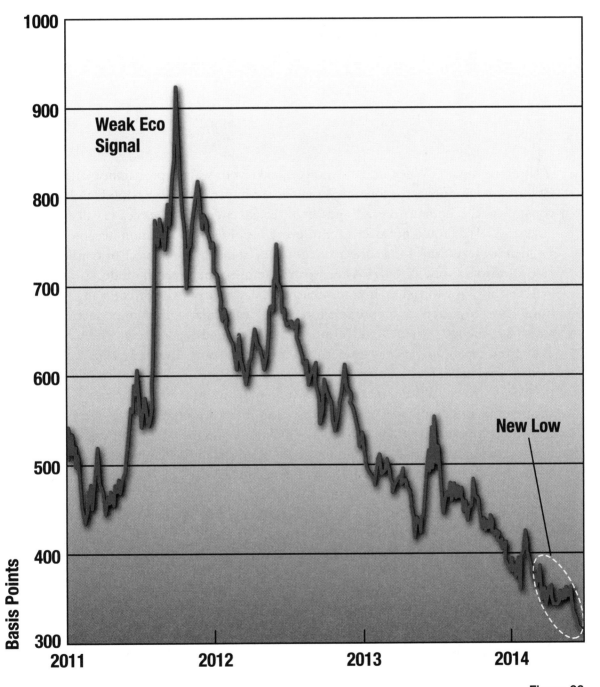

Figure 22

Source: Cornerstone Macro

TWELVE

How to Leverage Institutional Myopia

Alan Greenspan: "When in the dark, you make your way by probability. The relationships among macroeconomic variables are imperfectly understood, and as a consequence, economic forecasting is an uncertain endeavor....Forecasts will often go astray....We should not overreact to every bit of new information because the frequent observations for a variety of economic statistics are subject to considerable transitory 'noise.'" This is Greenspan in semi-opaque speech mode.

Not only have I lived each year intensively, day by day (The Street is my life), but I have forgotten or suppressed too much. Particularly, how imperfectly we anticipate change. When Black Monday cast its jagged shadow over the world, aside from Japan, major bourses declined more than ours. Everyone believed we would export a big recession. Instead, consumers kept buying and the country and the world grew far above forecast. Players hold more information at their fingertips than ever before, but few of us can make it sing. Black Monday was triggered by a bad monthly balance of trade statistic, $17 billion. It was the peak number, but the market couldn't fathom it. By the summer of '91 the trade deficit had dwindled to $4 billion, even less in some months. Our trade deficit early in 2001 was running at a $130-billion annual rate, but nobody cared.

I hope you are thinking of all the econometric models fashioned by huge beasts of computers in air-conditioned rooms. You now know they go astray when they miss a new variable. There is no Wizard of Oz with a computer-based world model behind the forecast, processing unexpected changes in national monetary policy, currency parities, oil prices and balance of trade numbers. Finally, the numbers aren't published until the spring of the year in question, so they're obsolete even before seeing the light.

The Iran-Iraq cease-fire touched off a collapse in crude oil prices, from $18 a barrel to $12 practically overnight. It forced economists to reduce their inflation forecasts and trade deficit numbers for the U.S. Vice versa when Iraq overran Kuwait two years later in 1990. Oil popped from $17 a barrel to $28 in days, and then collapsed back to $20. In 2001, OPEC discipline held oil prices above $25 for longer than anyone dared forecast. By 2014, when ISIS invaded Iraq, the market was a bit wiser. Oil quotes ticked up just a couple of bucks, over $100. Iraq invades Kuwait, Brazil and Russia default on their interest payments, a president is shot or drought hits the soybean belt. Long-Term Capital Management missed the Russian default in October '98 and self-destructed. Volatility in oil futures is a given.

When I came down to Wall Street in the late 1950s, investment research was in its primitive state. The partners called their analysts statisticians. Old ciphers left over from the 1920s pored over the dusty annual financial handbooks of Moody's, Standard & Poor's and Best's. Wall Street confined itself, humbly, to analyzing aged numbers. This has changed, but examination of the last 25 years' financial markets is still humbling.

The valuation structure of the market takes time to change—normally years. In the 1960s stocks sold at multiples averaging close to 20 times earnings, because interest rates snaked along at 4 percent. Inflation was not an issue until Lyndon Johnson escalated the Vietnam War. It took the market several years to wise up. When interest rates zipped up to 7 percent, valuations dove into the low teens.

The last hurrah for the market was 1972, until the late-nineties dot-com hysteria. Stocks sold at 18 times earnings and growth stocks soared off the page. Then the recession of 1973–74 destroyed growthmanship for many years. The head of investments at Morgan Guaranty Trust summed it up in plain white-shoe diction: "Geez! We should have seen that." Price-earnings ratios fell into single digits and averaged under 10 for the next decade. All you guys who came into the business since the bottom in 1982 or even 1990, wake up!

After 1982, inflation marked time at 4 percent more or less until 2008's bank meltdown. But the Fed panicked in early '84 when the economy was booming and Treasury notes yielded 13.5 percent. In the pre–Black Monday cycle, the valuation structure of the stock market didn't take off until interest rates broke below 10 percent in the third quarter of 1985. When interest rates touched down at 7.2 percent in March of '87, the market had reached 20 times latest 12-month earnings. By the summer of '88, interest rates rose to 9.5 percent, and the market sold down to 10 times estimated 1989 results.

Hussein's oil war led Wall Street to forecast a 1991 recession, and the market backed off 400 snappy points from its 3,000 high. This hovering level of

3,000-plus late in the spring of '93 contained an implicit forecast of resurging corporate earnings during '93–94. It proved out as a conservative assumption. Currency parities showed comparable volatility. The dollar fell 10 percent during the spring of '92 and rose 15 percent the opening months of '93. All this suggests that congenital astigmatism of financial market participants is broadly based. The post–World War II recession that never happened is the best example of absurdly wrong groupthink.

Linear extrapolation—what economists do—is the worst kind of group forecasting. It assumes the present trend lasts and lasts. It never catches turning points. Instead of concentrating on whether conditions are changing for the better or worse relative to expectations, it concentrates on the generality—things are good or bad. If IBM's earnings are growing at 15 percent a year, but the forecast is 17 percent, IBM is a disaster in the eyes of money managers, but remains a rapidly growing industrial if you paint with a broader brush.

Anticipating change at the margin is part of the art of money management. How can you tell when a stock is a screaming buy or an outright sale? On Wall Street there are two broad categories of money managers. They are either value players or growth-stock buyers. The armchair investor without an intimate knowledge of a specific industry sector and the leading companies vying for primacy has to rely on outside advice or use his common sense. *Never discount anecdotal evidence or what your eyes tell you.*

Economists tell you the rate of savings in the country is very low and that eventually consumer demand will slough off. But no economist dares forecast exactly when it will happen. He hides in the consensus, with few exceptions. I liked Steve Roach of Morgan Stanley for standing up with a synchronous worldwide recession call in March of 2001. At Goldman Sachs, its London economist Gavyn Davies at least alluded to the rising possibility of recession. Meanwhile, Abby Cohen, Goldman's New York–based stock market diagnostician, was calling for the S&P 500 Index to reach 1,650 late in 2001. She saw S&P 500 earnings reaching $60 a share as late as mid-March, while corporation after corporation was pre-announcing earnings levels far below previous months' "guidance" to analysts.

Aside from the inertia of forecasts, understanding how the investor herd tries to avoid risk and the stigma of loss is crucial to "stand-alone" investment action. Remember the Jack Benny skit when the holdup man tells the comedian "Your money or your life, mister." There is a pregnant pause and then the audience catches on. The pause lengthens and lengthens and the laughter crescendos when Jack says, "I'm thinking it over."

Jack was violating the psychophysical determinants of choice in risky and riskless contexts. This is a fancy way of saying what Daniel Bernoulli said in 1738. Bernoulli was explaining why people are averse to risk and why risk aversion decreases with increasing wealth. Ask yourself, which offer you would accept: An 85 percent chance to win $100 with a 15 percent chance to win nothing or a sure win of $80? If you chose the $80, you have shortchanged yourself in terms of mathematical probability. The 85 percent chance to win $100 is worth $85. Bernoulli was right to conclude that individuals do not evaluate prospects by the expectation of their monetary outcome but by the expectation of how the outcome is going to make them feel. The TV quiz show *Who Wants to Be a Millionaire* proved this, weekly. A whole new school of behavioral economists focuses on how consumers act under pressure.

Conversely, the institutional market's incapacity to differentiate risk is often reflected in yield differentials between corporate bonds and Treasury notes, where the spreads don't represent realistic risk appraisal. Yield spreads between government bonds and corporate bonds can vary as little as 25 basis points, a meaningless differential for an individual investor but significant in the eyes of a pension fund or corporate treasurer. This phenomenon surfaced during '93 and again in 2000 and 2014. There was little upside in the corporate sector, but yield spreads stubbornly narrowed. The same goes for banks that fund risky credit money one point over prime for the sake of growing their loan portfolios. This is how they dropped a trillion dollars in Latin America and then again in mortgage-backed paper, 2007.

Going against the socially accepted macro-forecast is so fundamental it has its own name—contrarian investing. I prefer the French expression *à rebours*, "against the grain." The contrary forecast assumes the consensus is always wrong. What isn't widely understood is how shabbily the consensus forecast is constructed and its telling short-term impact on financial markets. After Black Monday, interest rates collapsed, based on the consensus view of impending recession. The Federal Reserve Board changed horses in midstream, from tightening to easing credit. By springtime, it went back to tightening, and interest rates rose from 8½ percent to 9½ percent. Prevailing conclusions in the country switched in a few months from recession around the corner and a feeble dollar to an overheating scenario with galloping inflation and a strong currency. Both proved erroneous.

The International Monetary Fund, in studying its baseline economic forecasts for the world, discovered their forecasting errors were so great as to make them practically useless for suggesting policy initiatives. Staff economists blamed a world rich in economic and geopolitical upheaval—oil, for example—for missed turning points. For the past 15 years, their year-ahead forecasts for the seven major industrial powers missed GNP growth by 1 percent. Considering baseline GDP growth averages 3 percent or less, we are talking about a 33 percent error gap. The error was being too optimistic and disregarding policy initiatives of specific countries. They totally failed to predict the worldwide slowdowns of '91–'92 and 2008–'09. Economists are not tuned in to politicians. Forecasting errors widen as we approach balance of trade and currency categories. Understandably, forecasting errors are universally shared between international and national agencies. Desk officers talk to each other and, summertime, meet at the same conferences in Paris and Venice. Comparable perks, comparable mindsets.

The naïveté of international agency forecasting is underscored by the basic assumption that "present policies" remain unchanged, including constant exchange rates and oil prices. To avoid the embarrassment of causing market movements in specific countries, forecasting must be neutral. So why forecast at all? Only to provide a consistency check on governmental policy. If you assume the country is growing at 3 percent per annum until the end of time, you can estimate your tax receipts and plan a budget. This isn't forecasting at all, but rather a convention employed in economic scenario building and fiscal management. Sooner or later, everyone gets into trouble with huge budget shortfalls.

The record of the International Monetary Fund, by their admission, is little better than a guess when it comes to balance of payments trends. The OECD Economic Outlook numbers aren't any better on a country-by-country basis. The patterns of error, not surprisingly, are commonplace and recurring.

Everyone missed the call on the 1982 worldwide recession because it was the product of the Group of 7's major economic power monetarists, led by Paul Volcker at our Federal Reserve Board. The central bankers indulged in a séance of mutual emulation as to who could raise interest rates fastest and mostest. Thousands of economists saw this happening but underestimated the staying power of central banks. Nobody forgot this episode, and in pre–Black Monday '87, when Treasury Secretary Baker started to argue publicly with his counterpart in West Germany over relaxing the reins, financial markets overreacted, fearing contradictory policy developments among OECD countries.

What's so revealing is that, looking at the record of our GDP momentum quarter by quarter for the last 35 years, you never get trendline growth (around 3 percent) more than 18 percent of the time. If you exclude quarters with negative growth, our economy grows at a 4.6 percent rate, not 3 percent. GNP has grown at a 6 percent rate more frequently than an average rate. It took just three quarters for GDP to go from over 6 percent in the second quarter of 2000 to near zero in

March of 2001. It helps to keep this in mind when you see the overreactions of financial markets to quarterly reports from the Department of Commerce. Year after year, economic forecasts of GDP fluctuate around the 3 percent level, safe but inaccurate.

True to form, the National Association for Business Economics' late–September '14 median forecast from 46 economists called for 3.1 percent GDP growth for the fourth quarter and slightly short of 3 percent during 2015. The FRB projection is between 2.6 percent and 3 percent. I was at 3.5 percent to 4 percent. These PR releases are published by the financial press with little or no commentary as to relevance. They do add to the noise level of the market, but hold no value added. Quarterly updates can be sizable, as the economist crowd rushes to catch up with the numbers.

Just like the enormous volatility of currencies, changes in interest rates normally are large and can be long-lived. The passive forecast on interest rates is one of little or no change. What we have currently. Cycle over cycle, interest rates increase in volatility. There's nothing in the cards except financial markets' deregulation, which causes more volatility by allowing participants to bid freely for their sources of funds to make loans. The Blue-Chip consensus has missed its inflation forecast more years than not by over one percentage point. Since inflation has averaged 3 percent, the forecasting error can average 33 percent or more.

The way to look at forecasts is to assume they're politically induced or conventionally trendline. Economists should be viewed as a flock of shorebirds stationed on the beach, invariably facing into the wind. For me, the force of inertia, from the scope of the world's dialectics down to national momentum, is an overwhelming part of the noise level in a money manager's life. Aside from monthly reports of the Institute for Supply Management, which at least give you an accurate feel for month-to-month industrial momentum, you are operating in no-man's land. Greenspan quietly tuned in to these numbers when he cut the fed funds rate 50 basis points January 3, 2001, not waiting for the scheduled forward FRB meeting date later in the month.

When everyone is bearish on stocks or bonds, assume everyone has been overexposed anecdotally and buried in articles exuding gloom and doom. The financial press publishes the OECD, World Bank and incumbent Administration's numbers with scanty critical commentary. Security analysts understandably use such trendline forecasts, extrapolating earnings for specific industries and companies. Earnings estimates are equally wide of the mark, even for major entities like IBM, General Motors, Coca-Cola, Citigroup, even Google. Whenever our micro-forecast comes near the consensus, I shudder. When our analysts' earnings estimates mirror the consensus, I know there is no money to be made in that paper. Alas, too efficiently priced. Anytime the bullish consensus gets down under 40 percent, you can assume most everyone has sold down to the sleeping level. Good news, usually forthcoming, creates a humungous rally. It never fails.

I discount most generally accepted indicators of sentiment. They include the Conference Board's barometer reading of consumer sentiment and of course the scores of eggheaded Blue-Chip economists. They're a cross section of forecasters at banks, industrial corporations, think tanks and brokerage houses. Likewise, I find the ratio of puts to calls and the percentage of market letter writers who are bullish or bearish, worthless. Why should a hundred guys cranking out market letters be given any weight unless three years of tax returns reveal applied Street smarts?

The level of cash in the hands of aggressive equity mutual funds and the amount of margin debt can be very misleading numbers, too. Margin debt has to be discounted by the level of free credit balances at brokerage houses and then related to the total value of the market. What's indicative at mutual funds is the monthly level of net sales, because you can be sure that positive cash flow is soon to be pumped onto the Big Board.

I like to get right down to ground zero by tracking what analysts are projecting for the top 50 or 100 companies measured by their market capitalizations. If the earnings revision trends towards the downside, you know everyone is cautious-to-scared and vice versa. Similarly, I track the ebb and flow of earnings projections for the Standard and Poor's Index by The Street's research pundits. I go one step further. I know many of the players, so I call and make sure they mean what they say and are not just filling up space. Second-quarter 2014 earnings releases showed analysts grossly underestimated earnings for leading properties like Google, Facebook and Gilead Sciences.

Analysts normally fear to step out too far ahead of their consensus. They rarely publish exactly what they think on either the low or high side. Trend and direction are much more important than pinpointing earnings for the market, specific industries and individual corporations. Financial journalists at the *Wall Street Journal* and the *New York Times* quote all these players, weeks, even months after their pronouncements. The reader absorbs stale news that has long ago percolated through the markets and was far off base. For the research-based money manager, anticipating the momentum of earnings growth rates at variance with the institutional consensus is critical for early movement of big blocks of money into and out of broad sectors of growth and cyclical industries.

Outsiders should look for anomalies. The sun doesn't rise and set on Wall Street. Black Monday proved the country was intact even if The Street's circuit breakers had burned out. That day, I called J. Irwin Miller, headman at Cummins Engine in Columbus, Indiana. "Everyone's sleeping soundly," he reported. "Consider—our home prices never budged." When you have the conviction to stand alone—go for it! During the summer of '93 the inexorable strength of the yen relative to the dollar allowed me to creep into the brains of Alan Greenspan and President Clinton. The policy of benign neglect of the dollar suggested the Fed didn't fear any spike in inflation and wouldn't tighten monetary policy. Stay fully invested. A reversal in yen-dollar parity could be the prime leading indicator of rising interest rates and would make me think twice about staying the course. Late nineties, the telltale sign of a non-inflationary environment was the capacity utilization level of industrials. It was very low, never more than 82 percent. It kept me in long-duration bonds and stocks free of anxiety. Nobody in the financial press ever referred to this phenomenon. It wasn't "news." Capacity utilization 15 years later rests under 80 percent. Labor still has no leverage and inflation is dormant. My junk bonds outperformed equities during 2014.

Was Alan Greenspan drowning in his own pomposity by mid-2000? I sensed that unconsciously the adulation of Washington had gotten to him. Too many small changes in the fed funds rate. Greenspan was playing to the grandstand, more so with George W. Bush in the Oval Office. The country wouldn't come out of its recession so fast. Neither Republicans nor Democrats dared to deal with the need for a huge upfront tax cut, maybe $400 billion in 2001 pushed down to the payroll level. From a money manager's point of view, it was too soon, in the spring of 2001, to discount the next recovery. Not because of what was happening, but because too little was likely to happen. The hard fact actually was a soft conclusion. Same goes for 2015.

Look at the institutional myopia non-professionals could have easily bet against:

1987: Black Monday Blues. "The country will lapse into recession. Buy bonds. Sell equities." Wrong! The right perception: "The sun doesn't rise and set over Wall Street. It's a big country. Buy the biggest and best properties." This conclusion would have carried you through 1991 at full throttle.

1990: The Banking Crisis Is upon Us. "Real estate won't come back for five to 10 years. We are entering a decade of asset divestment if not depression. Fannie Mae is an overleveraged disaster." Fannie Mae and the banks at least tripled from their 1990 lows by yearend '92 and outperformed during '93, too. Fannie and Freddie remained engines of growth throughout the decade. Both sold at one times their growth rate, approximately 15 times earnings in March 2001.

1993: Bill Clinton's a Disaster for Equities. "His tax program leads to sluggish growth for the country and disappointing industrial earnings power." My working hypothesis was: The "tax the rich" program could slow economic growth, but interest rates work lower and stimulate investment and spending for big-ticket items like homes and cars. "The public remains risk averse so stocks are expensive." This was 180 degrees wrong. Low interest rates supported high valuation for equities. The public flocked into mutual funds like never before.

October 1998. "The Russians' default on their debt will create a worldwide meltdown in credit markets. Brokerage houses and banks face huge losses on bond paper and derivatives." But you could buy Merrill Lynch and Morgan Stanley near book value. Three years later they traded between two and three times book. Lehman was supposed to fold. Technology stocks took off on a 24-month tear that raised average valuation from 18 times earnings to over 50.

Yearend 2000. "The market should trade between 1,450 and 1,550 based on corporate earnings growing at least 8 percent to 10 percent. Technology, 30 percent of the S&P 500, must be fully weighted in portfolios. A proactive Fed and Bush's tax cuts should keep GDP growing at least 3 percent." By March 2001, this "consensus" forecast was in total disrepute. NASDAQ had collapsed, corporate earnings looked lower, not higher, and the market traded near 1,100. By some definitions the Big Board was in bear market territory, having declined 20 percent from its peak earlier in 2000. Abby Cohen's was the only unqualified bullish forecast left standing by mid-March 2001. Even she tentatively alluded to the possibility that she might change her Goldilocks scenario, the S&P 500 earning $60 a share and reaching 1,650 by yearend. The S&P 500 Index didn't reach to 1,650 for more than 12 years.

The IMF's senior economist, Prakash Loungani, points out that during the nineties only two of the 60 recessions in his sample of countries were predicted a year in advance by the consensus. In two-thirds of the cases, recessions stayed unpredicted in April of the year in which the recession took place. The consensus expected 3 percent GDP growth in the year of the recession itself, and this wasn't corrected until October of the same year.

2008–'09. Until the U.S. Treasury and FRB decided to save Citigroup, economists and market pundits called for another Great Recession. The market touched down at book value and yielded over 5 percent, selling at 10 times depressed earnings power. Nobody blew a whistle and said, "Buy!" even after the U.S. Treasury saved Citigroup, AIG and General Motors.

When you begin to hear stray voices mumbling there's a 10 percent chance of a recession, assume it's 50 percent. When you see 50 percent in print, probably you're in the eye of the maelstrom. When everyone confirms we're in a recession, it's probably close to over and you should implement a conservative buying agenda and be prepared to average down or up some 10 percent. Barton Biggs decades ago used to say about Far Eastern markets, "When the locals are panicking, I jump in!"

TWO DAYS BOTH WAYS

STONE STONE

STICK MUD

LEAF PUDDLE

MUD STRAW

LEAF MOSS

MUD LEAF

STALK STALK

STONE BERRIES

HEDGEHOG SKIN FERN

BIRD DROPPING HORSE CHESTNUT

PUDDLE BIRD DROPPING

STICK STICK

STONE STICK

PLUM PLUM

BEECHNUTS BARK

MOSS BEECHNUTS

MUD LEAF

MUD PUDDLE

BRACKEN CROW'S WING

BERRIES BERRIES

STONE STONE

STICK STICK

PAMPAS GRASS APPLE

STICK STONE

MUD MUD

STRAW BIRD DROPPING

LEAF BERRIES

MUD STRAW

STONE MUD

CABBAGE MUD

STONE LEAF

THINGS AND MARKS
AT THE START AND AT EVERY MILE
ALONG A TWO DAY WALK
OUT AND BACK ON THE SAME ROAD

SOUTHWARDS BRISTOL TO GLASTONBURY
NORTHWARDS GLASTONBURY TO BRISTOL

1990

THIRTEEN

Numbers Louder than Words

*V*ariety and density mark this Richard Long wall piece beyond the reach of photography if the viewer makes an effort to picture the words (opposite page: *Two Days Both Ways*, 1990). Just as this is visual art using words, a serious reader of corporate statistics must emerge with a word picture made from the montage of numbers exhibited over a five-year period. Parsing successive financials of any corporate property, one can construct syntactically a conclusion as terse and bedrock as a Shakespearean sonnet.

There is a variation, where words do overcome images. Andres Serrano's ethereal wall piece of the crucified Jesus is titled *Piss Christ*. When exhibited at venues, it drew blue-in-the-face reactions from many—including Senator Al D'Amato—and incited vandalism and death threats. The piece was "clearly blasphemous" and had to be withdrawn. The image itself, however, radiated a benign serenity. Its theme was free speech, but nobody saw it in that way.

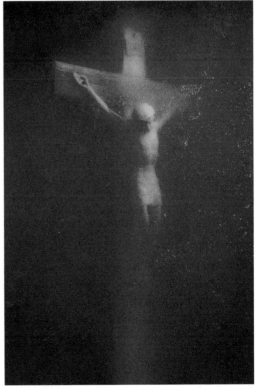

As late as August 2014, Serrano's 1987 photograph prompted protests. At the Fesch museum in Ajaccio, Corsica, 50 protesters stood outside the Palais Fesch holding placards demanding its removal. The museum's directors stood fast. Serrano created an edition of 10, one of which hangs on my hallway entrance wall. It goes unremarked to this day. The photo is a blurry, soft, red-tinted image of the crucifixion, an unremarked beauty.

ANDRES SERRANO, *PISS CHRIST*, 1987
Collection—Martin Sosnoff

Unfortunately, few financial reports highlight relevant statistics or ratios unless they are outstandingly supportive of management initiatives. There is no single stat or financial ratio that unlocks the enigma of a faceless financial statement. Oftentimes, results presented are misleading cipherings blessed by auditors who have ignored reality for their fees. Banks, S&Ls and annuity underwriters carried sunken assets coming home to roost in 2008. Regulators and the Federal Reserve Board, not their auditors, called them onto the carpet. The reader needs to rearrange, disregard or zoom in on certain numbers, depending upon what you are looking for.

If the non-professional investor lacks specific competence to play financials like a Chopin étude, he'd better be able to make visceral conclusions on the money. Merck, Intel and Microsoft research is productive. General Motors is catching up to Toyota. (Look at the pictures.) Citicorp was a reckless bank, but not Citigroup. The Time Warner management finally is working for shareholders. Polaroid didn't field any new toys and would fail. Coca-Cola and ExxonMobil are run more for shareholders, year after year. Not Salesforce.com, LinkedIn and Twitter. Look at their internal stock giveaways.

You start out with a working hypothesis and then try to prove it. The dividend is safe; R&D is productive; industry primacy is weakening; the asset value of the enterprise is overstated or undervalued. Management must raise more equity, thereby diluting shareholders as in banks. Operating margins are going down, but that's good because the company is gaining market share (Wal-Mart). Gross margins are down, but that's bad because the company is outgunned by competition (IBM, Dell and Pfizer).

Wall Street spends much of its time figuring out the next quarter's earnings without dealing with fundamental issues of management motivation, sterile research or worldwide competitive forces crunching market share and operating profit margins. Rarely do analysts tear apart balance sheets, at times more revealing than income statements. Wall Street focuses on a company's current year, compares it with year-ago numbers and then forecasts the next 12 months' results. Much more revealing is the analysis of a full cycle. Examples are plentiful.

From the mid-eighties, IBM continually disappointed its followers. Screening out rhetoric, all you had to do was compare earnings with the gross plant and property account. Earnings stagnated, while the gross plant account doubled by $25 billion. IBM had doubled its size, spent tens of billions and got no incremental return on investment. This abysmal performance more than anything else reflected the competitive forces and management's failure to field new products fast enough to preserve its dominant market share. It took an outsider, Lou Gerstner, to set things right in the nineties. Currently, you could say the same, more or less, for Intel, Hewlett-Packard, Cisco and Microsoft, all betting to renew themselves. When they sell at 10 to 12 times earnings, you dust them off periodically and take a look-see.

Conversely, several great successes are underpinned by massive and productive research and development, but Merck, Pfizer, Bristol-Myers Squibb and Eli Lilly turned fallow. Duopolistic positions in hypertension drugs, cardiovascular drug therapy, painkillers and cholesterol control belonged to Merck for many years. No accident. Merck spent approximately 13 percent of a rapidly rising revenue base on R&D, but then they lost it. No new blockbusters. Comparable initiatives led to Intel's dominance of the microprocessor market for small computers. Biotech houses like Biogen Idec and Gilead Sciences fielded major new drugs with great efficacy in liver cancer and multiple sclerosis treatment.

For all, the ramping up of R&D is the common denominator. If sales rose 40 percent, so did R&D. Operating profit margins are preserved, but there's no pressure to show all the profits. This is long-cycle stuff. Wall Street rarely factors back into earnings at least part of enormous discretionary R&D and marketing expenditures. Microsoft always looked expensive to valuation players, while Ford and GM on the surface seemed too cheap to pass up. Microsoft's gross margins held up while GM's earnings disappeared in 2008–'09.

When a high tech operator's gross margins begin to slip, sell it. The slippage in Cisco's gross margins, even a decade ago, was most revealing. Inventories ballooned as well. This was a telltale sign that management had misread the fundamentals of its business. Cisco's stock traded in the sixties while the numbers spelled trouble. Months later, the stock traded below $14. They were still downsizing mid-2014, terminating an additional 6,000 employees. Only its boodle of over $50 billion in cash on a market capitalization of $125 billion kept the stock afloat.

Bill Gates summed it up in his plain-talking '91 annual report (40 pages): "The story of our company starts with a vision: Someday we'll see a computer on every desk and in every home." A decade later, he was close, with 50 million computers outstanding in the U.S. More than a billion people around the world were computer literate. Then, another decade later, Apple and Samsung tablets ended Microsoft's primacy of desktop computing. They poured money into computer games, cloud computing and storage, but lost primacy to Amazon.

Levi Strauss sold jeans to the Klondike gold prospectors but later needed to become a sportswear house to survive. Years ago, Microsoft stood as the Coca-Cola and Levi Strauss of the computer industry, not undiscovered but under-owned by institutional investors. Microsoft's market capitalization shot up from $8 billion to $18 billion in the early nineties. Then it sprinted to $500 billion by yearend '99. The guys in black T-shirts headquartered in Silicon Valley put away many of the blue suits in Detroit, although not necessarily forever: By 2014 GM came back, along with Ford. Apple is now *numero uno* in the S&P 500 Index. ExxonMobil, number two, below $400 billion, isn't even close and they've been in business since 1882, Rockefeller's old Standard Oil of New Jersey.

The inertia of shareholders who back tired horses is seldom noted but nonetheless remarkable. American Telephone's, IBM's and GM's shareholders counted in the millions, while Coca-Cola had near 150,000, Microsoft fewer. IBM and GM disappointed for decades, while Microsoft doubled and doubled. All this while household names like Hewlett-Packard, Eastman Kodak and Intel soared and then flamed into the ground.

Years before Ford and GM floundered, a cursory scan of their balance sheets and cash flow statements would have uncovered a rising probability of trouble. Capital spending relative to previous years was rising. It suggested the ongoing press to upgrade assembly plants and field world-class cars, matching Honda and Toyota. The cash flow statement is the pivotal financial exhibit for capital-intensive properties. Ford barely managed through the financial meltdown of 2008–'09. GM required $50 billion in U.S. Treasury financial aid.

Bankruptcies among airlines dotted the financial landscape throughout the nineties and during 2008–'10. Pan Am, Eastern, American, America West, Continental, Braniff and Midway bit the dust, followed by TWA. USAir was an almost. When the Iraqis invaded Kuwait, international traffic stalled to a standstill and these carriers ran through their working capital within months. An overleveraged balance sheet was the common denominator. Few in management owned more than token amounts of stock. So, little reason not to gamble with leased aircraft and new route applications. Delta destroyed its pristine balance sheet with hundreds of millions in losses from the acquired European route structure of Pan Am.

Ironically, from the 2008–'09 crisis emerged a solidly structured Delta and American; both turned cash flow positive in 2014, even buying back stock and paying meaningful cash dividends, a first for the industry. I bet a bunch on the conceptual basis of a rationalized industry in terms of fare structure, fuel-efficient fleets and less-than-cutthroat competition from low-priced carriers.

For every industry there is an optimum balance sheet construct. The more cyclical your operations, the more equity you need. America West, a highly motivated, efficient, nonunion carrier, tried to do too much on route structure expansion.

American Airlines and United carried equity positions approximating their debt, while America West sported a debt-equity ratio of nine to one, higher if you adjusted for leased aircraft. Even Delta, AMR and UAL remained grossly leveraged carriers when you factored in leased aircraft liabilities. Shortly after applying for Pacific and European routes and bidding for the Trump Shuttle, America West succumbed into bankruptcy. Management's big eyes and its foolish balance sheet construct were red alert lights. They would've needed five big years back-to-back to purify their balance sheet. The economic cycle, alas, is unforgivingly short for airlines.

For every have not, there's a have. A covey of multinational giants like Cisco, Microsoft, Gilead, Apple and Google sport unassailable balance sheets. Their cash flow statements brim with enormous sums of discretionary capital available for share buybacks, acquisitions and higher dividends. When all three courses are even-handedly pursued, you can conclude these are managements working for share-holders, totally focused on increasing the market value of their stock. ExxonMobil, Walt Disney and Coca-Cola also fit this mold. ExxonMobil is one of very few oil managements who after the mid-eighties decided it wasn't capable of successful diversification into technology and started to buy in its equity. Schlumberger, after its disastrous acquisition of Fairchild Camera, tried again early in 2001 with a dilu-tive deal for Sema Group for over $5 billion. The market didn't like it.

ExxonMobil's brethren busied themselves buying up uranium, copper, coal and gold mines and diversifying further into petrochemicals, with mediocre to disas-trous results. This followed a rash of billion-dollar mistakes during the seventies, when Mobil bought Montgomery Ward, which ended in receivership. The source and application of funds statement is the pivotal numbers exhibit for oil operators, along with their oil-reserve life measured in years. ExxonMobil spends much more to keep its reserve-to-production ratio constant, a major negative today.

How do you know when a management is out of control? A snappy review of its debt structure over successive years may be enough. If the ratio of debt to equity is rising and earnings are flat to down, the summary conclusion is that management won't or can't live within its income and maybe is sticking to some grandiose master plan for market primacy. It could be a steel operator striving to upgrade antiquated blast furnaces or a bank management going on an acquisition binge, like Bank of America buying Merrill Lynch even while its bad loans mounted. Polaroid was a classic example of a deteriorating business plan totally destroying shareholder value.

In these situations the investor listens to management's five-year plan and then quietly checks out. You can't win until a new mindset takes over. By 2000 it happened even in banking, when two proud giants, Citicorp and Salomon Smith Barney, merged as equals and reduced headcount. It took the specter of disaster for John Reed to modify his master plan for dominating the world's financial markets. Shortly thereafter, Sandy Weill eased him into early retirement at Citi. Successive heads at Yahoo wisely stepped aside. Yahoo badly needed a new business plan, and they needed new blood to execute same. So far, nobody has succeeded in growing the advertising revenue base. Google prevails.

The "bruised ego" scenario is a twist on the return-to-respectability play. I'm all ears. Here, a high-metabolic operator loses the game of musical chairs in the boardroom and goes elsewhere to run another company. Sandy Weill, who was sidetracked by American Express's headman, Jim Robinson, took Jerry Tsai out of his Primerica holding. Jerry was tired and ached to sail his newly designed yacht on the Côte d'Azur. Aside from the analysis of the basic businesses of this financial conglomerate, you had to trace the upstreaming of the subsidiaries' earnings to the parent (Sandy). Only then could you project the debt-carrying capacity of the corporation, the probability of Sandy making a major acquisition without destroying the credit ratings of subsidiaries like Commercial Credit.

Safe leveraging under a sound and frugal operator can lead to an accelerating growth rate, which is what makes a stock dance. Sandy made successive strategic acquisitions: Shearson, Travelers Insurance and finally Citicorp. From a second-string loan office operation to a world-class player in financial services in five years. Not bad. Easily predictable, but in the end, unmanageable. IBM today is still on track to leverage its balance sheet and shrink share count meaningfully. Apple is a new face in this game, egged on by Carl Icahn's noise level.

Not all leverage is bad. In August 2014, Kinder Morgan announced a transformational transaction that consolidated its regional oil pipeline properties, ending their status as master limited partnerships. Morgan made his fortune ($10 billion) after leaving Enron and buying their pipeline assets. His intention was to reduce the cost of capital for future acquisitions of outstanding MLPs. Their cash flow would support the parent's fixed costs of capital and leave something over for increasing the dividend-paying capacity of the parent company.

The midstream energy sector is very capital intensive, covering regional pipeline expansion along with storage facilities and natural gas production. Scale, asset diversity and stability of cash flow position Kinder Morgan as a core infrastructure property. I stopped ciphering and bought the stock. Not only was valuation reasonable, along with a 5 percent expected 2015 yield, but any investor in the world would have to consider owning KM! It had scale, a $90-billion market capitalization, an above-average yield likely to grow 10 percent per annum and earnings growth of 10 percent, assuming a studied rollup of public MLPs. Income-oriented investors, growth players and value investors could all converge on this paper.

I waded in and hoped to live happily ever after, but my portfolio of MLPs dropped 5 percent to 10 percent when oil futures collapsed near yearend. I still saw rosy prospects for management attracting major tranches of capital from offshore money pools seeking above-average yields on their equity and fixed income commitments. Plus, rolling up MLPs wouldn't be so costly. Kinder Morgan moved contrapuntally to its MLP brethren early in 2015.

Every decade harbors its "the king is naked" surprises. Management excesses are covered up until criminal events beyond accounting control take over. Enron and WorldCom fitted this mold. I remember looking at their income statements and saying to myself, "They look too pretty." In the eighties, failure of the Continental Bank in Chicago surfaced when oil fell to $9 a barrel and its oil-patch loans proved under-collateralized, even fictitious. In the sixties, American Express survived its client's "Salad Oil Swindle." But AmEx's blue-card business was growing 30 percent per annum. Government Employees Insurance was once weeks away from receivership in 1972 but survived with the concurrence of regulators when it relented on too-aggressive underwriting. Its core franchise of policyholders remained intact and Geico came back. Buffett was an early player.

Our capacity to construe Equitable Insurance as a potent asset gatherer of variable annuities and not a real-estate disaster led to a great recovery play. Early in 2001, the SEC finally challenged Lucent's accounting conventions, but you could have picked up their trouble in rising inventories and slowing inventory turnover, same as Cisco. In the financial meltdown, the mortgage-backed securities flimflam caught most major bank managements asleep. Countrywide Credit, the worst offender, was bought out at a premium price by Bank of America, later causing tens of billions in write-offs and fines. Did management do its homework?

During the mortgage-backed securities meltdown of 2008, both Fannie Mae and Freddie Mac claimed they were solvent, but they were leveraged 100 to 1 and had guaranteed trillions in mortgage paper for a couple of basis points. It took $200 billion to bail them out.

Salomon Brothers was a great case of a dominant company whose raised-finger culture foretold trouble. John Gutfreund was Salomon, and Salomon was Gutfreund. It's why The Street never paid much of a premium over book value. Subliminally, we understood Solly got carried away trading bonds—its eyes too big, its head traders known affectionately as swinging dicks, each a profit center, some in eight figures. You couldn't pick this up reading an annual report. But you could see wild swings of hundreds of millions in trading profits, quarter after quarter. Even Buffett, a shareholder, got sucked into this snake pit, but came in later and rationalized operations. Solly's ultimate rogue play was illegally cornering the Treasury bond auctions in the spring of '91. Gutfreund's boys had blown one cigar ring too many in the faces of competitors and the U.S. Treasury. Organizations like Solly, and later Lehman, bought billions in T-bonds on 1 percent margin and financed same below money market rates. Ten million buys a billion-dollar position with a positive carry, but you gotta be right or you're gone.

After all the reading and ciphering, I wouldn't dream of discounting anecdotal evidence on the role of the chief executive in shaping the future of his company. No matter how the numbers dance, I refuse to invest in a company whose head-man I disapprove of. Maybe it's his lifestyle or how he treats people inside and outside the business. In the long run, character and personality govern stats. Mike Milken, a great family man, didn't smoke, drink (not even coffee) or swear. And yet, his fanatical ambition toppled him from a position far superior to Gutfreund's. Larry Tisch, long gone, was my favorite frugal operator, with 100 percent integrity. The headman at Dish Network, Charlie Ergen, is famous for his corporate frugality: Everyone flies coach, and some even double up in hotel rooms. I won't invest in tech houses like Salesforce.com and LinkedIn because they're run for insiders, with enormous dilution of the shareholder base.

Sometimes it pays to stop your ciphering and reading. You walk around, look, and listen to what isn't being said. When I showed our Hungarian guide in Budapest the book on Richard Long's exhibition at the Hayward Gallery in London, she flipped through the pages and cried ever so softly into her tissue. Didn't have to explain her years of intellectual deprivation. It was exactly midnight, so the state-run restaurant where we dined cut off its lights. I signed the AmEx check by candlelight while teenage waiters stacked chairs. There was a 90-degree heat wave in Budapest, and the streets teemed with locals in bathing suits. Their Russian-designed apartments were unsleepable hotboxes. We walked through the park surrounding the parliament building, which was in a state of continuous sandblasting to shed the grime deposited by the two-stroke Ladas everyone drove. What the eggheads at the American think tanks missed was the political symbolism of pollution in the Marxist world. Anyone walking in Budapest would have sniffed it out. The state was poisoning its citizenry. It foretold Chernobyl and the implosion of the Soviet Union.

Next day, back in Nice, a couple on a black Kawasaki 1000 zipped by us, gunning through an 18-inch opening across the white divider line. The *femme*, riding postilion, hugged her *mec*, breasts pressed against his shoulder blades. Her white T-shirt billowed in the wake of their *moto*. I glanced down at her high-backed sneakers as they pulled away; the laces rested untied. I was back in my western-ized Europe, thank God. A decade later, sneaker manufacturers designed laceless sneakers but kept the lace holes intact.

It's the iconography of smart money, I thought. You spot 18-inch lanes through the minefields and bank through the turns, relaxed, with boots unlaced just as long as your reflexes tick. You're always pressing the numbers to dance. *Good money managers know how to stand alone after they do the work.* I think of all the number crunching we did on Fannie Mae in 1982. When it was all done, the pivotal vari-able was the conclusion that management had held to a conservative lending con-struct in their loan-to-value ratios on mortgages. Wall Street was convinced Fannie would self-destruct when real estate values turned south. Actually, their loan loss reserve appropriations were never exceeded, even quarterly, by charge-offs.

By the mid-nineties FNM sold at three times book value and was considered one of the few unassailable financial services franchises. Wrong! They screwed up in 2007–'08 guaranteeing trillions in mortgages destined for foreclosure. And all this for a couple of basis points. AIG's stupidity was comparably disastrous. They guaranteed credit default swaps for a couple of basis points. A handful of traders in their London offices sank the parent in New York.

In Fannie and Freddie, The Street had missed management's personal profit motivation in leveraging the balance sheet. More earnings, higher profit partic-ipation and stock grants. When I asked a board member who understood the portfolio of credit default swaps, the answer was only two: the chairman and his chief investment officer.

When you buy a business that's public cheaper than its private value, you know you're on pretty firm ground. This is where I invoke Tobin's Q ratio. Fixed assets should be valued near replacement cost—no big premium entailed. The unwritten rule on new issue underwriting was that deals are supposed to be priced 10 percent under comparable public properties, but the rule no longer is followed. When Merrill Lynch brought Sam Zell's REIT public, it was oversubscribed almost four to one. Pricing accommodated the public's hysteria. The stock came at a huge premium to estimated asset value. I love Sam, but I passed on the deal. There are always telltale ratios that make me prick up my ears. Any company that announces a share buyback of more than 10 percent gets a look-see. Our computer spits out names where the reinvestment rate is rising or holding at 20 percent. (The reinvestment rate is what you earn on profits plowed back into your business.)

Conversely, declining reinvestment rates, like IBM's and Intel's, turned me off.

In my shop, nobody writes up buy or sell ideas in words. We all use numbers to convey meaning. Projections of top-line revenues, profit margins, product pricing, operating rates and capacity additions lead to earnings projections. Then we translate growth projections into valuation numbers. A rapidly growing company will sell above 20 times earnings if its growth rate holds up. Because cyclical companies like autos show low rates of return on net worth, they should sell at low ratios of enterprise value. In 2013 these ratios got too low and we bought GM at 2.5 times enterprise value, about 10 percent of what a pricey tech house sells for. Once an airline, copper producer or automaker sells at more than 1.5 times book value, it's a sale candidate unless you love the business for another three years.

Good investment ideas are simple and should take no more than five minutes to understand, provided you have someone reliable modeling the numbers. Our investment in Facebook came after comparing it with other Internet operators like Twitter, Google and Amazon. We looked at the variance between GAAP and non-GAAP earnings to confirm management wasn't running their company solely for insiders. Whenever I see stock-based compensation running over 10 percent of revenues, I pass. Twitter's valuation ran off the page. A couple of months later the stock faded badly, from low seventies into the thirties. Facebook corrected just 10 percent. We invested hundreds of millions in bank stocks at the bottom of their cycle in 1990, and again in 2009, based on our assessment they had dropped to net asset value per share going forward, after giving them haircuts of 40 percent on commercial real estate portfolios. This turned into a bedrock assessment. All the numbers fit easily on one page.

FOURTEEN

Decadence and Debasement in Security Analysis

*M*y memory bank of Venice stretches over 60 years, starting in the early fifties when I thumbed through Frommer's *Europe on 5 Dollars a Day* for a budget-priced room on a side alley off the Piazza San Marco. Decades later, on a soft summer's night in 1974, Nixon devalued the dollar and the S&P 500 Index touched down at 100. Everyone in '74 ended up strolling into San Marco, after dark, enticed by Florian's and its rival cafés. They purveyed viscous espresso, pastel-colored gelati and Viennese waltzes. Their accordion players, fiddlers and wide-vibrato tenors resonated in this awesome spaciousness with a mellifluence singular to San Marco.

Times have changed. Only a handful of tourists in 2014's summer crowded around the musicians' stands, while acres of empty chairs blessed the four quadrants of the piazza. The cathedral awaited its parishioners. Economists label this forlorn condition of overpriced goods and no takers as stagflation. For me, stagflation is the dirtiest egghead word in the Western world. You can't make money in equities. Period. All the great small restaurants in the alleyways of Venice are thinking of closing. Only day-tripping tourists off the tour boats crowd the square during the day.

OK, you say, so Italy is a stagnant, overpriced country. I say the acres of empty chairs hit me hard, after logging decades of Venetian memories. My mind raced on inexorably. Europe would need more than another season to come back—after the Germans relented and lowered their interest rates so everyone else could come down to zero. But no politician dared raise the issue of deficit financing to get their economy going. At home, New York's top 1 percent tore out their hair when they had to roll over three-year CDs yielding 1 percent.

If you keep mumbling to yourself, "Geez! I should've seen that one coming," the ball has thudded into the catcher's mitt and you're out on strikes. It could be IBM, General Motors, the euro, gold or Japanese bank stocks. You'd better know the stories, the players' consensus and the symbolism of what's in the air—NASDAQ speculative froth or San Marco depression or a weak euro, finally.

Once your theme is in place, fill in the names. You are now in the realm of stock picking, where thousands of analysts spend their time without much value added. GM and IBM may eventually go out of business or be merged out like American Motors, but now they meet their payrolls and have access to capital markets. All of Wall Street's research on IBM and GM is focused on predicting earnings over the next 12 months and relating it to the current stock price. Boatloads of analysts fail miserably, year after year, because they fumble the reduction step at the stove. GM didn't make competitive cars economically for decades and lost share of market. IBM's overhead was swollen over a Watson generation to twice its competitors' cost structure. Period. *If you can't be reductive, don't play.*

Security analysis is a fool's game, because you are always on the outside looking in. Big companies don't let analysts see much more than the Serbs showed the Red Cross in Sarajevo. My fieldwork is to get to know managements, particularly when they are under pressure. I met with every bank president in New York in the autumn of 1990 to confirm they had no fix for their bad real estate loans, but that the Federal Reserve Board would give 'em time before the accounting had to catch up with market clearing prices. That's how you gain enough nerve to play the blackness-before-dawn routine. It was like Soros looking into the eyes of the Italian prime minister on the eve of lira devaluation and sensing panic.

It pays to watch how savvy businessmen invest their stock market money. Kirk Kerkorian bought almost 10 percent of Chrysler's capitalization, over 28 million shares, under $10 on the eve of C's '92 new model introductions. Chrysler had an iffy balance sheet and a negative analyst consensus. Too tough to call, they mumbled; if the Grand Cherokee flops, C's gone. By yearend, Chrysler ticked at $36. The same analysts who had predicted the turnaround in GM that never happened were recommending Chrysler on a $4-a-share earnings projection. Chrysler had reentered the analysts' universe and finally got some coverage after appreciating 250 percent.

Days before the millennium, while most money managers were sunning themselves on the beaches of the Caribbean, a 26-year-old analyst broke into electronic print with a forecast on Qualcomm that put it at $1,000, a double over 12 months, justifying a valuation at 175 times earnings power in 2001. He got his 15 minutes of fame. Qualcomm sprinted over 100 points in a few hours and I banged out my position.

The technology sector was making a farce out of a once staid profession—security analysis. Ben Graham is gone, maybe outmoded, along with Larry Tisch, Warren Buffett and a host of value investors left in the dust during this market cycle where dot-coms, biotechnology and Internet infrastructure purveyors have gone to the moon and back. These sectors still remain outside the perceptive mass of many old and wise investors.

It's easy to blame the Internet and the proliferation of business news broadcasts for moving the locus of the investment horizon from long-term to instant gratification, the noise level of a crowded craps table. The rot runs deeper. On the individual level, young analysts thirst for instant stardom. They are encouraged to seek high profiles by brokerage house management because it's good for business. At the corporate level, outsized options grants have created an insidious level of contact with analysts who are manipulated into a groupthink mode.

Qualcomm is actually an interesting case study on Wall Street research. To a man, analysts grossly underestimated Qualcomm's earnings power years ago. The company was perceived as a wireless phone producer with a small royalty income stream on the side. In fact, Qualcomm's handset business was irrelevant. It was there as a driver for semiconductor chip sets that enriched its CDMA royalty stream. Finally, it was properly perceived as a semiconductor house with a growing royalty stream from its 3G and 4G patents that are significant and growing. Qualcomm is a worldwide play on the proliferation of wireless smartphones. Where was this 26-year-old while Qualcomm advanced around the clock a dozen times? Currently, everyone tries to figure out when smartphone sales peak. Some of us believe it's around the corner, 2016 at the latest.

Security analysis is no longer security analysis. It's show business. Jim Cramer, a former hedge fund operator, will go down in history as the only money manager who made more money talking and writing than managing money. Cramer has something to say, at least twice daily, on his TheStreet.com website. His chatty, wise-guy style is what Internet journalism is all about.

In the Internet and biotechnology sectors, most stocks had no discernible earnings power for years. To overcome any queasiness in valuation, analysts took refuge in 10-year discounted cash flow models. What they don't tell you is that by tweaking discount rate assumptions, terminal price-earnings ratios, interest rate and growth assumptions, you can rationalize Amazon going to the moon and back in one day. If that doesn't work, you can recommend Amazon on its revenue run rate and then project a Wal-Mart–like operating profit margin five years out.

For Salesforce.com, analysts can only justify its valuation using a multiple of revenue metrics, currently 7.5 times. All other metrics make it look surrealistically, wildly overpriced. The career path for analysts has changed markedly since the '95 Netscape IPO, which was a seminal event in valuation for Internet infrastructure properties. The enabling word that unlocked valuation constraints based on earnings was "metrics." *Any company that could write a business model showing enormous scale in revenue run rates was bankable.* Earnings suddenly turned irrelevant if the hockey-stick revenue chart prevailed. Even in its formative years, Amazon was bankable, raising billions in bond money and equity on this premise.

The accent on metrics is now pervasive not just in technology but telecommunications, media and biotechnology, too—sectors embracing a good chunk of the S&P 500 Index, north of 40 percent. Any industry missing good metrics turns saleable. How else can you explain the compression in valuation for retailing, supermarkets and much of the non-durables sector embracing high-profile stocks like Coca-Cola and Procter & Gamble?

Analysts' research flashes on computer screens long before written pages reach clients. The informational retrieval capacity on your Bloomberg is all-embracing: Follow-ups on earnings reports, management conferences and commentary on what competitor analysts are saying are part of The Street's daily noise level. Analysts are fodder for all the business news programs, which chatter away, some 12 hours daily. Business news sounds like Walter Winchell's staccato bursts of trivia in the forties. "Good evening, Mr. and Mrs. North and South America and all the ships at sea..."

Pre-tech bubble, Henry Blodget of Merrill Lynch, Mary Meeker of Morgan Stanley and Jack Grubman of Salomon Smith Barney all blurred the line between security analysis and investment banking, which are supposed to be ethically separated by a Chinese Wall in terms of stock recommendations. Not so. High-profile analysts lasso investment banking clients. Then they hawk their clients' stocks 30 days after an initial public offering, frequently just condensing the legal verbiage of a prospectus that they helped write.

The content of research reports hasn't changed much in 40 years. Everyone concentrates on what's ahead for the next 12 months and relates a specific stock's valuation to a broad index like the Standard and Poor's 500. What's changed is analysts pop up on my Bloomberg screen ad nauseam with valuation updates, rationalizing every 10 percent gain in a stock's trajectory. Stocks never become sale candidates, just turn average in attractiveness. When a company moves into receivership, the stock isn't unattractive, but unavailable for analysis.

The grey-flannelled "statistician," as analysts were called in post–Great Crash Wall Street, is gone. These deskbound anachronisms riffled through Moody's and

Standard and Poor's handbooks. They rarely ventured out of their offices to do fieldwork. There were few distinguished analysts in the fifties and sixties, excepting Donaldson, Lufkin & Jenrette, but everyone prized his integrity, laboring for months before issuing a research report that depicted a company's special competence and projected a growth rate tied to its industry dynamics. Nobody would pull a stock price valuation out of a hat to justify his recommendation. Nobody pursued "This is to this as that is to that" analysis. You didn't justify a stock at 50 times earnings by comparing it to a property at 100 times earnings. This kind of "convergence" thinking is what got Long-Term Capital Management into serious trouble as well as the bulls on Amazon who pointed to its low multiple of revenues compared with Yahoo. For over a decade, Amazon had gross margins of 20 percent, which didn't even cover its marketing expense line.

Until the late fifties, when the first burst of technology captivated Wall Street, few analysts did serious fieldwork. Later, Donaldson, Lufkin & Jenrette, in the early sixties, unleashed a series of 50-page papers on little-understood properties like Dun & Bradstreet and A. C. Nielsen. Research reports rarely were shared with competing houses even after Xerox's 914 copier swept the country. Top analysts' salaries in the mid-sixties were $25,000 and few of us job hopped, except to money management openings.

My mentor, Dick Fant, research director at E.F. Hutton, forced me to interview management without taking notes. The point was to keep up a conversational flow and watch facial expressions. You couldn't do this without a thorough immersion in the subject's business. In meetings with management it was gauche to ask about earnings. You concentrated on the drivers of revenues and made your own calculations. Today, through elaborate rituals of conference calls and investor relations spokespeople, corporations signal their comfort level with Street projections. Many analysts are merely reporters who rarely step out of the earnings consensus. On Coca-Cola, for example, at its peak, dozens of analysts were within a penny of each other until the slowdown abroad trashed their projections late in '98 and the stock crumbled.

The Street did show its crazy side in the sixties, but it was never so extreme. Motorola, Xerox and Fairchild Camera sold at 40 times earnings. So did United Airlines—but they had real earnings. The Street fell in love with teaching machines, bowling pinsetters, vending machines and paperback books, and then wised up. But color television, birth control pills and jet aircraft were breakthroughs that changed our lives. Without Boeing's 707 there would be no Disneyland, and Honolulu would have stayed a sleepy one-hotel town (the Royal Hawaiian).

We should thank Paul Volcker for forcing the last big recession on the country in 1982. It purged inflationary expectations and made Greenspan's job a snap. Volcker gets credit for the second Gilded Age, which started in the summer of '82 when the S&P 500 Index touched down at 100—and peaked at 1,400, 18 years later. For a while, technology sold as if this Gilded Age would last 40 years like the first one, which ended on the eve of World War I. This past business cycle lasted 10 years and succumbed to old age. Capital spending peaked and the consumer topped out riddled with debt (*Figure 23, page 147*).

By mid-2000, Henry Blodget and Mary Meeker were lunching on crow. After flogging the Amazons of their universe during '98 and '99, they had drawn in their recommendations from strong buys to neutral holds and long-term buys. In Street argot this is equivalent to "bang 'em out before they bang you." Their changes in heart came only after their list of buys had been schmeissed in half by the market. I am sure we will look back on today's security analysts as trained circus dogs who jumped through hoops of fire and showed no fear. The control word that got them to jump was "metrics." It, too, will be permanently retired, like Mickey Mantle's jersey.

The lubricious role of the multinational corporations in "managing" analysts' expectations flowered redundantly after the Netscape IPO in '95. By mid-2000 it had reached a level of absurdity, silently acknowledged on The Street but unre-marked. The symbolic relationship between analysts and management was forged on the anvil of all-embracing stock option programs. Tech houses like Intel, Microsoft and Cisco sported dozens of executives with net worth ranging into the tens of billions. At yearend 2000, Cisco's outstanding options totaled almost one billion, at an average exercise price of $24 a share.

In an insidiously sweeping gesture, Intel goes to great lengths in its quarterly earnings releases to control its analyst consensus, successful in keeping the range of earnings projections within a narrow band. More often than not, its detailed forecast of the upcoming quarter's metrics runs wide of the mark, both up and down. The June 2014 "guidance" was very optimistic, surprising even manage-ment. Revenue projections, gross margin assumptions, general and administrative expenses and R&D spending were laid out inclusive of projected capital gains and tax rate. Management then shifted to the balance sheet to cover capital spend-ing, depreciation and goodwill amortization. The deep basic was, small computer volume finally recovered. Nobody saw this coming, so the stock took off on a 50 percent run-up.

INTERNET SUBSECTOR PERFORMANCE AS OF JULY 2000*

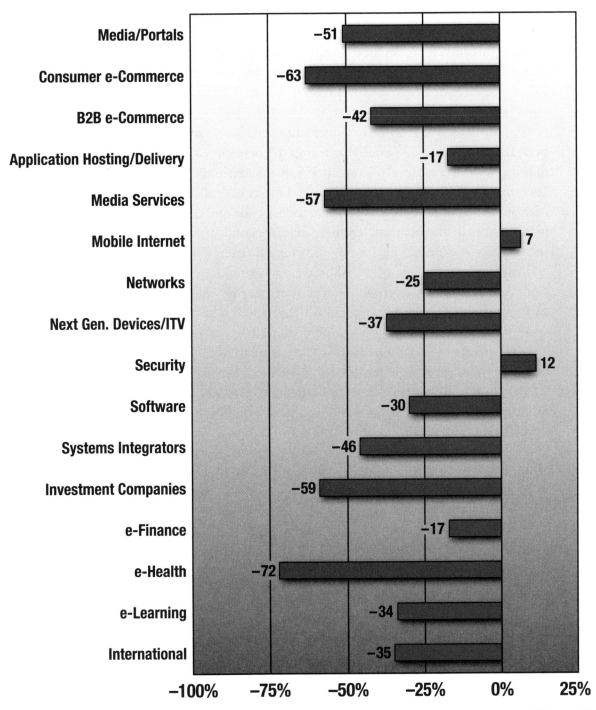

Figure 23

*By April of 2001, average category losses reached 80% to 90%
Source: FactSet, Goldman Sachs

Such prepackaged care and feeding of analysts is typical of big-cap stocks like Cisco, Coca-Cola and IBM, but nobody goes into as much detail as Intel. A growth stock that beats its guidance by a penny a share goes up. If you come in a penny light, all hell breaks loose. Analysts now spend much of their time between quarterly reports trying to figure out whether successive guidance calls are going to spin positive or negative. Intel rose more than 10 percent overnight when its latest quarterly guidance was laid out.

The last thing a tech house management wants is a negative surprise in their numbers. It would take their stock down over 10 percent, overnight. Through a carefully modulated noise level of conferences, management builds The Street's earnings consensus, month by month. Investor relations executives man their telephones. Managements speak at brokerage house industry forums, quarterly. Conference calls, within hours of the quarterly earnings release, connect all the dots. Management then signals its expectations for the upcoming quarter. I'm not amused.

In an expansive cycle nobody should be surprised that most tech houses exceed their "consensus" by a penny, quarter after quarter. Occasionally, there are mishaps. Business is so surprisingly good that there is a "blow-out" quarter. The stock normally responds with a 5 percent to 10 percent spurt, like Amazon on '14 yearend earnings. Infrequently, there is a quarterly shortfall. Analysts then feel betrayed. Management is termed "lacking in credibility." Their stock is trashed and languishes for a year or more until the management "rebuild" of its consensus. Stocks like Computer Associates, BMC Software and even National Semiconductor were doghouse dwellers. Lately, IBM could no longer control its numbers. Even Coca-Cola and Pfizer lost the luster of consistency or credibility. In February of 2001, Cisco pulled in its guidance and touched off a NASDAQ mini-panic.

Intel's quarterly report is instructive. It does all of The Street's numbers work except project quarterly revenues, but they will allude to this, signaling either capacity restraint limits or changes in the booked-to-billed ratio. Analysts have been reduced to kindergarten status. All they have to do is connect the dots. See the horsey pulling the cart.

I'm not saying there are no dissenting voices, but they are few and far between. Some 95 percent of the research that makes my desk, at least a foot high, daily, is homogeneous in language and conclusion. Let's catch Goldman Sachs, which puts out a telephone book of Internet research monthly. This is Michael Parekh waxing hot years ago on Yahoo, probably the best of breed: "We believe that Yahoo, with a 2000 P/E to growth ratio of 5.7 is attractive...relative to the other leading profitable large-cap Internet companies which have a median P/E to growth ratio of 7.6."

What Parekh was saying is that if Yahoo grows earnings nicely, it is a bargain at 236 times 2001's projected earnings. This bargain valuation is a function of other properties selling at 400 times forward 12-month projections. In short, "this is to this as that is to that" analysis skirts the question of intrinsic valuation. When Henry Blodget was asked how much of his own money he had invested in Internet plays, the response was a sheepish 1 percent.

It's hard not to conclude that analysts following the Amazon, Yahoo, eBay, Priceline.com, Twitter and Facebook axis are doing anything more than rationalizing valuation constructs that are as ephemeral as daisies. But they just can't say so. Why? It's not good for their houses, with another dozen new offerings lined up to go public. It's not just tech, either. Goldman Sachs underwrote a cigar maker at the top of its cycle, too, with the requisite stock recommendation out 30 days later. When's the last time you saw a guy puffing on a Havana?

Because corporate news is transmitted 99 percent effectively to everyone, enterprising analysts have taken to forming focus groups, conducting surveys on capital spending and consumer preferences. Anything to get lead time on trend changes. Forty years ago I used to survey shellac producers to get an edge on changes in industrial production momentum. Shellac was poured on grinding wheels, which were used in shaping metal. It was my favorite leading indicator when there was no new economy, only old-fashioned industrials like U.S. Steel and General Motors.

The nineties opened with equity commitments by individuals and institutions at historically low ratios. Pretty much what we had 2013–'14. Conceptually, this is the stuff bull markets are spun of. We had our bull market in the nineties. The millennium opened with the public's purse fully committed to stocks as never before, measured by their liquid assets and annual income level. Valuation for stocks was stretched by young analysts who had no personal experience of previous cycles, when growth stocks sold at 20 times earnings, not 20 times revenues. The middle-class investor holds most of his wealth in his home. My non–Wall Street friends couldn't even pronounce Milken's name properly in the late eighties. They called him "Milliken." Michael would have preferred to remain anonymous, as he did during the seventies (*Figure 24, page 150*).

I search for enormous disparities in the perception of earnings projections for big capitalization properties like Facebook, Google, Apple, Gilead Sciences and Qualcomm. A polarity of opinion does keep a stock from discounting the hereafter, because of latent uncertainty. I relish the entrancing "lady or the tiger" conundrum. There is no such thing as an "efficient mart stocket." It only appears efficient to those without perception.

HOUSEHOLD EQUITIES SHARE OF FINANCIAL ASSETS

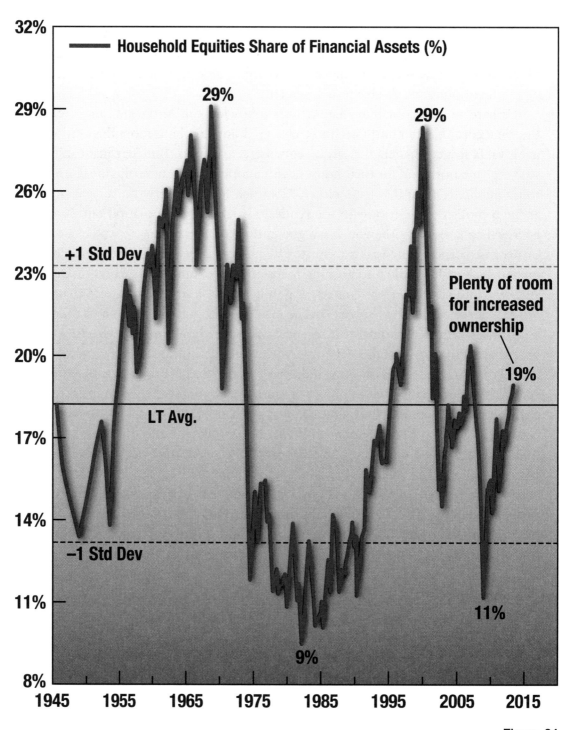

Figure 24

Source: Federal Reserve Board

In securities markets, more and more, tiny differences in input cause enormous changes in stock prices. A change of one-tenth of 1 percent in unemployment sets off a 140 pointer on the downside. The focus on our monthly trade numbers can reach Super Bowl proportions, as it did pre–Black Monday. In the mathematical study of chaos this is known as "sensitive dependence on initial conditions," or "the butterfly effect": A butterfly stirring the air in Peking signals storm systems next month in New York. Early in April 2001, when our spy plane made a forced landing on Chinese soil, the market sank over 3 percent, an overreaction.

It was not forever so. Early sixties, I'd spend three months writing a research report on a company or industry. No computers, just slide rules, adding machines and green semi-logarithmic paper as tools. Stocks traded four million shares a day and everybody thought a long time before buying or selling. I miss those days. Am I forgetting President Kennedy's face-off with Roger Blough on U.S. Steel pricing bumps? Or the Cuban missile crisis of 1962? Not exactly, but Apple traded 190 million shares, some $19 billion in market worth, one day in September 2014.

The passive investor needs to filter out Wall Street's noise level not just on big-picture stuff but on the consensus for industries and companies, too. There is an enormous "wimp factor" among Street practitioners. Economists, of course, hide in "on the one hand, on the other hand" hedging. As I have said, the economy for them is always likely to grow 3 percent next year. Similarly, most security analysts are afraid to put in writing what they really believe. Analysts are always looking over their shoulder at what their competitors are saying. There are elaborate statistical services that monitor monthly quarterly earnings estimates of all the players. No analyst cares to risk his reputation by damning IBM or Yahoo in print. Off the record, they may be candidly bearish. Conversely, analysts are invariably timid about raising projections more than nickels or dimes. They can continually underestimate earnings power—by dollars—for major financial houses like Goldman Sachs. Technology analysts for years missed by a yard on IBM, Intel and Texas Instruments.

Entrepreneurs are securities analysts, too, or at least employ a few. What makes them financiers is they're richer than most guys massaging laptop computers. They do see properties in different configurations. If a place on Boeing's order book for 747s cost you $130 million and you already own a fleet of comparable-model aircraft at under a hundred mil, you're an asset play and bankable. While analysts ciphered over seat-mile costs and tried (vainly) to forecast revenues, the Basses, Murdochs and Kluges of the world totted up asset values and cash flow. They saw it in Disney (the forever-fresh film library). John Kluge saw it in broadcasting and cellular phones (future cash flow). Warren Buffett saw it in the off-balance sheet value of Coca-Cola's worldwide distribution network.

Today, more and more analysts use the entrepreneurial EBITD rather than earnings to value stocks they follow. EBITD is earnings before interest, taxes and depreciation. EBITD is the magic word, the open sesame, what the past 25 years were all about. It is what takeover artists and Milken focused on. It made steady mundane businesses like cable television valuation stars. But EBITD in the hands of an analyst is a dangerous valuation convention. Unless there is free cash flow in a corporation's metrics, I stay away. All the EBITD isn't worth much if management just goes through the motions of staying in business with mindless capital spending and low rates of return on invested capital. Using EBITD for calculating interest expense coverage also is too facile for companies with huge undeferrable capital spending. My preferred metric is pretax earnings coverage.

Net, net, never assume the guy at the other end of a research report or telephone line is smarter than you.

FIFTEEN

How to Rate Your Own Performance and Everyone Else's

*I replaced the postulates of rational expectations and efficient markets
with my own principles of fallibility and reflexivity.*

GEORGE SOROS

*P*ublic standards of measurement forever cry out for review and redress. Consider Paul Cézanne's paintings: Submitted annually to the jury of the Salon des Artistes Français in Paris, they were refused 20 consecutive times. All these tardily recognized Impressionists, Manet and Renoir included, ended up for public viewing in the Salon des Refusés, which the emperor Napoleon III proclaimed in 1863 as a compromise, but this safety valve lapsed into desuetude within a few years.

Solitary and institutional investors need to appreciate what's out there that is inherently violent, volatile and near incomprehensibility. For example, the Shanghai Composite Index peaked in the spring of 2011 at 3,067, hit a low of 1,849 in June 2013 and would need to recapture more than 50 percent from its current level to take out its old high. I'd leave this index for self-rating by some guys behind unmarked doors in Hong Kong or Singapore.

No single index captures all compelling motive forces that reflect how good or bad investors fared over an investment cycle, what they missed and what they exploited efficiently. Consider that the Russell 2000 small-cap index, up from its low near 400 in 2009, soared 200 percent by yearend 2013. Its correction from the 2007 pre-bubble high totted up to 50 percent. The Value Line Index fared even better from its recession-'09 low, gaining near 300 percent, but it, too, lost over 50 percent from the pre-bubble high.

The S&P 500 Index, more staid but comprehensive in terms of total market capitalization, embracing major corporations, more than doubled from its spring '09 low through November '14. By comparison, 10-year Treasuries peaked at a yield over 5 percent pre-bubble, ended 2013 at 2.9 percent, and ticked at 2.2 percent late in

153

2014. These notes are not a stable repository for capital.

Digging down into the Russell 2000 index by market capitalization, starting at $5.3 billion and ending with number 25 at $3.8 billion, I recognized only three of the 25 names in the listing—Yelp, Rite Aid and Brunswick. Clearly, I'm not an active player in small-cap names, normally, but I did take fliers on analyzable properties like MGIC, Sirius XM Radio and US Airways.

The Russell 1000, a capitalization-weighted index of 1,000 stocks, pretty much duplicates the S&P 500 Index, at least for the first 500 names. Because I rarely invest in property below a $10-billion capitalization, I exclude this index from close inspection. But the Russell 2000 does easily capture what small-cap stocks are doing.

If you're a growth stock operator, the Russell 1000 Growth Index approaches the NASDAQ Composite but nowhere near in its concentration. The top 3 names—Apple, Microsoft and Google—comprise 11 percent of the index. In the NASDAQ Composite these three names comprise 19 percent of the total. Technology is a 44 percent weighting here vs. 26.5 percent in Russell's 1000 Growth list.

After reviewing all extant measurement tools, NASDAQ 100 closely mirrors what I try to do—latch onto Google, Apple and Amazon early on, while discarding Microsoft, IBM and Intel when they phased into staid maturity. This index captured my big play years ago in biotechnology, namely Gilead Sciences. It's a live-dangerously-or-die kind of construct. Energy is absent and industrials just a token 3.5 percent. No Schlumberger? For shame!

NASDAQ 100 Index
(as of 12/4/14)

Sector	Weighting	Top 10 by Index Weight	Weighting
Basic Materials	0.34%	Apple	13.31%
Consumer Goods	4.04%	Microsoft	7.87%
Consumer Services	19.36%	Google	7.05%
Health Care	14.74%	Facebook	4.21%
Industrials	3.26%	Intel	3.59%
Technology	57.42%	Gilead Sciences	3.11%
Telecommunications	0.84%	Comcast	2.86%
		Amazon	2.86%
		Cisco Systems	2.77%
		Amgen	2.54%

Consider the top 10 names, aside from Gilead, Comcast and Facebook; all are tech houses, but with markedly different special competences. All the more reason to deal with Apple, a 12 percent position in this index.

Passive investors who can't delegate or do requisite securities analysis to evaluate nuances in specific properties should try index futures or an exchange-traded fund, but only when they sense speculation is in the air and not overdone. Once The Street starts rationalizing price-earnings multipliers of 50 or more on results three to five years out, say bye-bye.

Why shouldn't institutional clients demand that their money managers be rated by some percentage of the NASDAQ 100 as well as the S&P 500? After all, money managers should be tasked to capture outstanding sector moves, particularly technology and the Internet, which are inherently earnings leveraged.

Technology comprises the lion's share, over 50 percent, followed by consumer services and health care, together another 36 percent. Everything else is irrelevant, namely industrials, telecommunications and consumer goods. Materials, at 0.28 percent, aren't for NASDAQ.

The top five weightings herein—Apple, Google, Microsoft, Amazon and Intel—tot up to 36 percent of the NASDAQ 100. Facebook makes this index at a 4 percent weight. So NASDAQ's capacity to incorporate recent new issues is laudable. Twitter, for example, is already a $50-billion market capitalization. I'd expect it to make NASDAQ later this year.

What I like here is that half the top 10 weightings correspond to positions I hold—but all investors need to consider Apple, Google, Amazon, Gilead Sciences and Facebook. Gilead, under a 3 percent weight, for me is closer to 30 percent. But this extreme overweighting is counterbalanced by the entire health care sector's weight at 13.3 percent. My biotech property turned into extreme concentration from market appreciation.

NASDAQ's top 10 holdings comprise 50 percent of the index, so it's a proxy for growth stock investing. ExxonMobil, numero dos in the S&P 500 Index, doesn't exist herein. Additionally, you won't find the financial sector's inclusion. Rating myself a confirmed growth stock investor, I track performance relative to NASDAQ, also. For 2013, the composite index appreciated 40 percent, with the S&P 500 Index up 32 percent, a notable 25 percent variance. Anyone who thinks of himself as a professional operator in big capitalization stocks should rate himself against the NASDAQ 100. This index is a leading-to-coincident indicator, highlighting the level of speculation in the air, and whether it's overdone.

The price-earnings ratio of Internet houses during the 1999–2000 bubble zipped into the clouds, followed by their comeuppance. Tech stocks are still recovering from this episode. Presently, sober reality prevails in the heart of the NASDAQ 100. Exceptions are Amazon, a 4.5 percent weighting, and Facebook, under 3 percent. Apple and Google comprise 20 percent of the index, reasonably priced goods.

I don't like to assume foreign exchange risk, which easily can wipe out your gains in stock prices. Neither do I trust the accounting conventions of all offshore companies or securities regulation standards, country by country. Foreign banks and insurance underwriters were inscrutable for decades because of their manipulation of balance sheet reserves against assets held, particularly apt for Japanese properties. Fifty years ago, Shelby Cullom Davis was the go-to guy for elucidation in Tokio Marine and Fire Insurance. Shelby spent much of his workday following the insurance industry, worldwide.

Offshore indices themselves are worth following, if only to understand the ebb and flow of multinational investor confidence. FTSE, the emerging markets index, is notable for its relatively high weighting in banks, energy and telecommunications, together comprising 42 percent of the index. Technology is a relatively small 8.5 percent. This index grossly underperforms world indices and was a good leading indicator of the blowup in Argentina, Brazil, India and elsewhere. Its modest comeback during 2014 eludes me, but reflects the worldwide recovery in bank stocks. Growth stock investors should avoid FTSE. Only when you believe countries like China, Brazil, India, Russia, Taiwan and South Africa can claim legitimate boom status, with few excesses in lending and overspeculation in real estate, should you take a flier on FTSE. Financial services make up 29 percent of this index, with health care at 1.7 percent. Too racy even for me!

You can capture how the universe fares with the MSCI World Index. Its sector weightings look more like ours: financials at 21 percent, and then 48 percent spread evenly among tech houses, industrials, health care and consumer discretionary names. In total, Apple, Google, ExxonMobil and Microsoft account for just 4 percent of MSCI, vs. 13 percent for the S&P 500. In good years, this index normally trails the S&P 500, which left it in the dust in 2013. This is an index easy to game by overweighting some sectors and underweighting others. It rose 20 percent last year, badly trailing all of our domestic indices. The gain in 2014 was a modest 6 percent.

MSCI Index as of November 30, 2014

Sector	Weighting	Top 10 by Index Weight	Weighting
Financials	20.89%	Apple	1.64%
Consumer Discretionary	12.23%	ExxonMobil	1.10%
Industrials	11.94%	Microsoft	0.92%
Information Technology	12.85%	Johnson & Johnson	0.75%
Health Care	11.65%	General Electric	0.67%
Consumer Staples	8.85%	Wells Fargo	0.66%
Energy	9.33%	Nestlé	0.64%
Materials	6.02%	Chevron	0.63%
Telecom Services	3.06%	Procter & Gamble	0.58%
Utilities	3.19%	JPMorgan Chase	0.58%

Short of performing a major area study of have-not countries like Ireland, Greece, Portugal, Iceland, even Hungary and Pakistan, I'd pass. If based in Hong Kong I'd be a player in Japan, South Korea and China, but only if I could scope their political honchos, learn whether they stand up for sound political leadership and hands-on central bank controls that make sense.

For 20 years, Japan didn't meet this minimal standard. China and South Korea proved savvy, but these are export-oriented economies that must please their trading partners. The rest of the world must grow enough to buy their goods. I like the unstated symbiotic relationship between China and us. We buy their goods at everyday low prices and they recirculate their trade surpluses into Treasury bills and notes. This is better than the gold standard, which penalized debtor countries. Conventionally, it took away their gold, forcing them to raise interest rates sky-high to hold capital from moving offshore.

Personally, I rate myself against the NASDAQ 100 for its super-growth characteristics and against Value Line because it's a straight arithmetic index that captures results for small- and mid-cap properties as well. Value Line, rather than the Big Board, is a great leading indicator for tops and bottoms.

I'm not sure how clients benchmark their hedge fund investments, but it most definitely shouldn't be the S&P 500 Index. When you sort out 13F filings to the SEC on major invested positions, these capital pools reveal a locus of small- to mid-cap properties. Carl Icahn is the exception, with his outsized investment in Apple.

Hardly anywhere do I see big-cap tech houses positioned—no Google, Microsoft, et al—which is why these operators woefully underperformed during 2013.

Private capital strategic positions rarely exceed 10 percent of assets, and do go down to small-cap properties like Sotheby's—a $3.4-billion market capitalization—Sirius XM Radio and MGIC. Aggressive stock market operators look for mispriced equities, mainly underresearched by Wall Street's analysts. Ironically, they are imitating Warren Buffett's modus operandi of 50 years ago, when he got involved with Geico, American Express and the *Washington Post*.

Aggressive capital pools should be benchmarked by NASDAQ 100, Russell 2000, or NASDAQ Composite, perhaps split evenly among the three. If so, 2013 was even more disappointing for these operators. The term "hedge fund" is no longer descriptive of how this disparate grouping invests. Actually, their only commonality is a demanding fee structure.

Omega Advisors Top 10 Holdings
as of September 30, 2014

Security	Weighting	Market Value ($ billions)
American International Group	4.2%	283.5
Citigroup	4.0%	267.4
Sirius XM Radio	3.0%	201.2
Chimera Investment	2.9%	196.2
Sandridge Energy	2.9%	195.1
Dish Network	2.8%	191.9
Atlas Energy	2.7%	179.8
eBay	2.7%	178.6
Navient	2.6%	174.2
HCA Holdings	2.6%	172.2
	30.4%	2,040.1

Omega Advisors, run by Lee Cooperman, is typical. Lee's 10 largest holdings comprise approximately 35 percent of invested capital. American International Group was a big winner, but Citigroup a laggard.

The Dow Jones Industrial Average, albeit a dinosaur, still is paid daily lip service by television and radio news broadcasters. "The market rose or declined 100 points," they report. Rarely is this change related to a percentage. After all, the S&P 500 Index ticked at 2,000, while the Dow sits over 17,000, so a 100-point variance on the Dow is pocket change.

Sadly, the Dow remains in the public consciousness, not the S&P 500 Index or NASDAQ 100. The ludicrous conceit of weighing Dow stocks by market price rather than market capitalization leads to enormous distortions that render this index useless. Consider that the top five weights in the index comprise a third of the index's valuation. They are Visa, IBM, Goldman Sachs, 3M, and Boeing.

Not a fair rendering of the U.S. stock market. Where is Apple, *numero uno* in terms of its market capitalization, approximating $700 billion? Finally, it has made the Dow Jones as of April 2015. You don't see Google here, either. Microsoft is a 1.45 percent S&P 500 Index weighting, way down on the Dow, as is Coca-Cola and General Electric. Makes no sense.

If Apple, pre-split, and Google were Dow Jones components, their high price points would account for 25 percent and 50 percent of the index, respectively, a ridiculous outcome. Throw in Berkshire Hathaway's split stock and you'd easily cross 100 percent.

The Dow is also deeply flawed in terms of sector weightings, heavily represented by industrials like 3M, Boeing, United Technologies and Caterpillar. It's too heavy in financials, very light in technology and health care. If Visa were supplanted by MasterCard, a bigger market capitalization and higher-priced stock, it would tot up to a 25 percent index weighting.

In the good old days when the heartland of America was U.S. Steel, Dow Chemical, General Motors, Kennecott Copper, Union Carbide and International Harvester, this index made some sense. Technology didn't exist. IBM's big product was its Selectric typewriter. International Harvester is long gone. Where are Facebook and Twitter? Their market caps exceed DuPont's and Caterpillar's.

The financial world has changed dramatically, but Dow Jones hasn't kept up, and the S&P 500 Index seems years behind the realities of what's going on in Internet properties coming of age in foreshortened time spans of a couple of years. Let's retire the Dow as a curiosity, a museum piece of what America was like in the 1950s. Wall Street was a small village then, and trading volume measured maybe 3 million shares daily.

In summary, *individual investors, not just institutional operators, should rate themselves against an index that closely mimics how they play the game.* Institutional investors normally use the S&P 500 Index as the benchmark for large-capitalization equity investment. Breaking down investments into growth and value classes, Russell's Growth and Value indices are usable benchmarks, too. But money managers as well as their clients still are too passive, readily accepting the S&P 500 Index as the be-all and end-all measurement standard.

Dow Jones Industrial Average
as of December 5, 2014

Company	Index Weighting	Market Value ($ billions)
Visa	9.42%	163.69
Goldman Sachs	6.99%	87.99
IBM	5.84%	161.58
3M	5.80%	103.99
Boeing	4.73%	94.26
United Technologies	3.98%	101.46
Chevron	3.96%	209.59
Johnson & Johnson	3.88%	303.73
Travelers	3.76%	34.86
UnitedHealth Group	3.59%	96.30
Home Depot	3.56%	131.31
Nike	3.55%	85.57
Caterpillar	3.53%	59.80
McDonald's	3.44%	93.73
ExxonMobil	3.35%	397.28
Walt Disney	3.35%	158.99
American Express	3.31%	95.86
Procter & Gamble	3.23%	244.22
WalMart	3.01%	271.13
E. I. du Pont de Nemours	2.61%	66.20
JPMorgan Chase	2.24%	234.38
Merck	2.20%	175.30
Verizon Communications	1.74%	201.72
Microsoft	1.73%	399.12
Coca-Cola	1.56%	190.67
Intel	1.35%	182.13
AT&T	1.21%	176.05
Pfizer	1.14%	201.56
Cisco Systems	0.98%	140.62
General Electric	0.93%	261.20

And then we encounter Warren Buffett's Berkshire Hathaway portfolio, which has very little to do with active money management. There's a hidden meaning therein. It's Warren's methodology of putting Berkshire's liquidity to work before he passes on, so he won't be missed, or better still, attain immortality.

This process began a few years ago with the acquisition of the remaining stock in the Burlington Northern rail property. Warren was buying a slice of GDP along with a play on the export coal market to China, which turned stillborn. This gambit was followed by initial positions in IBM and ExxonMobil as well as Wal-Mart. None of these positions is working out, but they did chew up some $20 billion in excess liquidity.

Huge legacy holdings in Coca-Cola, American Express and Wells Fargo account for another $50 billion. If anyone should be rated by the S&P 500 Index, it's Warren. But this is too simplistic, conceptually, because his portfolio is overconcentrated in financials. Last time I looked, banks and American Express accounted for 40 percent of the portfolio.

Few money managers could get away with this level of concentration, over twice this sector's weighting in the S&P 500. Maybe Buffett should be measured by a 40 percent weighting in the KBW Bank Index, which was up 38 percent in 2013.

The Buffett symbolism is he's pretty much done picking stocks. Bought a slice of America and hopefully will live happily ever after.

My visceral conclusion is that the S&P 500 Index, alone, is no longer able to capture what's going on with equities, in the world or even domestically. This index is stodgy and conceptually should be easily beatable, but sadly it is not. Institutional clients should demand more of their money managers, and change performance measurement to embrace a percentage weighting in NASDAQ 100 or at the least the NASDAQ Composite Index. A 25 percent weighting seems appropriate, maybe more. If nothing else, this change, pressed by institutional clients, forces money managers to consider more aggressive overweighting or underweighting of sizable sectors in both indices, and to react faster to information at the margin.

Don't hold your breath.

SIXTEEN

The Enduring Rape of Shareholders

These managements need shaking up—they're horrendous. They take money from the peasants and then hire mercenaries (lawyers) to protect their castles, mainly by browbeating the peasants. So we attack the castle. Wait. I don't want to call shareholders "peasants"—don't put that in the article. Call them an "oppressed majority."

CARL ICAHN

*A*t least in financial markets, it's considered appropriate to submit to rape by management rather than protest and wrestle and wrangle with your aggressor. Activist investors take the other side, but need to own 10 percent to 15 percent of a target company's market capitalization to make any impression when calling for change. Ray Irani, headman at Occidental Petroleum, extracted over $500 million, backed by complacent boardroom friends. He was finally forced into retirement by activist shareholders who didn't control much stock but made a lot of noise in the press.

The two cases I'm treating herein—Gilead Sciences and Salesforce.com—are comparably egregious but deemed acceptable in different ways by analysts, money managers and individual investors. Market capitalization of Gilead has soared to over $150 billion, so it's beyond serious activist intervention. Moreover, management's "take," substantive over time, is within the realm of acceptability among public pharmaceutical companies. So far, the SEC ignores this issue.

Consider today's glamorously draped beauties. Start with Facebook, because you can rationalize current valuation. This is unlike Salesforce.com, which I sold on its revelatory yearend 2013 earnings release. Most tech analysts recommend Salesforce.com based purely on its revenue growth rate, pegged at 30 percent for the next few years. Twitter and Yelp rest far beyond my modeling powers.

Facebook sells under 20 times 2015's EBITDA ratio, even after its gutsy acquisition of WhatsApp for $19 billion (55 employees, no revenues to speak of), but headed towards a billion users on its Internet message network. Access is pegged at a buck, annually, a great service but as yet no prospective advertising revenues.

Facebook sells around 10 times 2015's projected revenues, which is considered a rock-bottom bargain ratio. Ahem! This holds water only if you grow revenues north of 30 percent. Post-2015, Facebook's momentum probably decelerates.

In March 2014, Salesforce.com dropped 6 percent overnight, even though management met its numbers, earlier dished out to analysts. This pernicious system of "management guidance" keeps The Street from going off the deep end on its projections. Sooner or later, if you passively accept management's guidance, they will bury you by failing to meet the consensus numbers that they created.

Tech analysts act like reporters at a presidential press conference, looking for nuances in gobbled-down reportage. If Salesforce.com had missed its quarterly revenue number by just 1 percent, all hell woulda broken loose, probably a 10 percent schmeiss for the stock. The surmise would be that management had lost control of its growth trajectory, and worse lay ahead. More often than not, momentum players would bang out at least half their position.

Salesforce.com's 37 percent revenue growth yielded next to nothing for its shareholders. Diluted non-GAAP earnings hit 7 cents a share in its fourth quarter 2013, but GAAP earnings were negative by 19 cents. Anytime a tech house's disparity is wide between GAAP and non-GAAP earnings, I look for share dilution. For this baby, it's enormous.

This is a near $40-billion market cap piece of paper. For the fiscal year ended January 2014, share count bulged some 33 million shares. At $60 a share, management and key employees received compensation of approximately $2 billion, over 5 percent of the company's market capitalization on minus zero adjusted earnings. Another slant—insiders received 40 percent of the company's projected revenues for 2014.

I've never seen a construct like this, but I haven't looked too zealously. The norm for technology is management and staff are awarded 10 percent to 15 percent of annual earnings. Even this ratio I consider overly generous. In Qualcomm's case, and others where the chief executive sets research and development priorities in a rapidly changing business, I'll accept this 15 percent payout construct.

Techies following Salesforce.com brushed me aside, pontificating that earnings, at least next several years, have nothing to do with the trajectory of the stock. The sole pivotal metric is revenue growth, which my house analyst pegs at 31 percent this year and 24 percent for 2015. If he misses by one percentage point, the stock surely tanks and I'd push him out the office window.

Optimistic projections of other metrics, like EBITDA and operating margins, if you accept them, put Salesforce.com at an EBITDA ratio for 2014 near 40 times.

Even if operating margins move from negative to positive 10 percent, earnings tot up to 47 cents a share. This is about 120 times, on a price-earnings ratio measurement. Let's assume they make $300 million this year; it's possible, but management likely awards itself another 30 million shares worth $2 billion or more.

Analysts tell me this is OK because management is attracting busloads of sales personnel with options grants. Eventually, they will harvest earnings. Maybe yes, maybe no. The only other large capitalization property that sells anywhere near Salesforce's premium is Adobe, which I throw up my hands as unanalyzable. They are at least close on an enterprise value to sales ratio two years out, approximately seven times. So what?

Isn't this too much ciphering to justify the valuation of a cloud software house? A fair question is: Which constituency is Salesforce's management running the company for? So far they are big winners in terms of asset accumulation in their stock, gratis. Shareholder dilution of 5 percent, annualized, holds constant, excessive for me to swallow. When does it end? When does management's "take" relate to some reasonable percentage of earnings, say 10 percent to 15 percent? "The answer, my friend…" Analysts jumped through their asses to rationalize this baby. Maybe they'll get away with it. I'll take my chances on Facebook, which I can model with some certitude in the firmament of Internet houses with position on the board.

The deep basic is Salesforce pays out 12 percent of revenues in stock compensation. Most tech houses' payout is 12 percent of earnings. Passive shareholders must accept equity dilution running at 5 percent per annum. Software houses when they're small use Salesforce's construct, but for a house running at a $5-billion revenue clip beginning to decelerate, the quandary is whether this isn't a Hail Mary pass from their 40-yard line.

Contrast all of this with Amazon, analogous in the sense of a big revenue generator with minimal reported earnings. Dilution from stock issuance runs under 1 percent. Amazon sits with $11 billion in liquidity and stock-based compensation relative to revenues running at 1.5 percent vs. Salesforce's 12 percent. I was around for the 1974 debacle in growth stocks and obviously the 2000 Internet bubble, spanning two generations of shelf life for tech analysts composing optimistic music sheets on software houses.

As for Salesforce.com, its "take" is an enormous toll on outside shareholders. Nobody seems to care. Analysts say "It's a software house. All we focus on is revenue growth trajectory for the next several years. This will determine its stock price and EBITDA to enterprise value multiplier." Insanity! Analyst groupthink usually ends badly. Next couple of years tell the story.

The statutory rape of shareholders by public companies' managements is awesome and continuous. But carefully manicured compensation guidelines in proxy statements apparently meet standards that preclude interference by the SEC. Pillage varies directly with the thickness of the proxy document itself. Shareholders rarely vote against "full package" largesse. Institutions look the other way just so long as the stock outperforms.

For anything I own in size, the annual proxy document is a must-read. I own over 400,000 shares of Gilead. Its 85-pager caused me considerable heartburn for its revelations of largesse to its headman and cohorts. First, consider Gilead's place in the sun. Market capitalization end of November 2014, over $150 billion, placed it 25th in the S&P 500 Index, below Walt Disney and above Comcast. As a stock, Gilead levitated some 90 percent—triple the index's gain for 2013—and added another 25 percent during 2014.

A $150-billion company on the Big Board attracts inevitable public scrutiny of all its documents filed with the SEC. They must walk the straight and narrow of acceptable conduct. In-house and external counsel vet proxy documents, abetted by consultants on executive compensation capable of devising overly complex structures whereby management gets its deserved rewards with approval by the board of directors rubber-stamped.

Outside board members normally stay passive, just so long as the consultant blesses the executive compensation package. Shareholders normally ignore and approve these constructs, rarely able to stymie management's gimmes.

To date, the SEC has not interfered in this realm with any declarations on what is or is not appropriate compensation. Neither did Attorney General Holder, who relentlessly extracted fines, penalties and restitution monies from banks ranging into tens of billions, each. These actions penalized shareholders, who saw book value on their investments in JPMorgan Chase, Bank of America and Citigroup eaten away by at least 10 percent. Management, individually, escaped fines, penalties and jail time. Jamie Dimon at Morgan still walks on water.

Median compensation packages for headmen at the hundred largest companies in the S&P 500 Index can range up to $20 million in salary, bonus and options. I don't have a problem with such packages if the company had a relatively good year compared with its peer group of competitors. Even a bonus at 150 percent of salary, I can live with. But when stock options and grants together dwarf the salary and bonus package, I turn crimson.

Gilead is a perfect example of excessive largesse to its handful of management participants. There is an invariable symmetry to its profile of rewards. The proxy statement points out on page one that total shareholder return for the year was 105 percent, second highest in its peer group. Further, that the three-year TSR compounded at 61 percent, highest in its compensation peer group. I was there, Charlie, but so what? Gilead's equity compensation embraces performance share awards as well as options.

I noted that John F. Cogan was appointed lead independent director in May 2013. Dr. Cogan is a senior fellow at the Hoover Institution, a conservative think tank patronized by far-right Republicans, unlikely to concern themselves with income distribution. The top 0.1 percent control a growing, alarming share of the country's wealth. Our middle class shows little growth in compensation and net worth since peak of cycle 2007.

The nitty-gritty on compensation starts on page 27 of Gilead's 2013 proxy document. Its compensation mix for Gilead's executive group is skewed towards equity awards that are over 200 percent of base salary and annual bonus opportunity. On page 34 it's noted that Gilead's CEO, John Martin, took home more than $90 million, making him one of the 10 highest-paid CEOs in the country. His five-year compensation exceeded $250 million—top man in the pharma sector. Generous options and stock grants fueled by marked equity appreciation in Gilead told the story.

There's no problem for me in the CEO's base salary upped 5 percent or even the annual bonus of 155 percent of his base. But outright equity awards are based on total shareholder returns and revenue performance for the company. For why? Revenue performance is only meaningful if profits keep pace.

Key drug patents expire for Gilead starting in 2017. Unless the reinvestment rate is very high, Gilead's earnings peak three years out. So management is rewarding itself, repeatedly, year after year, for patented drugs that have a definable, finite growth trajectory that surely ends. Future earnings rest precariously on a diving board. The problem I have with Gilead's performance-based awards up to 200 percent of base salary is they're tied to relatively low hurdle rates for annual corporate revenues. Gilead currently has a revenue run rate of $7 billion quarterly, up from the $2.7-billion year-ago quarter, thanks to the ramping of its hepatitis C drugs, Sovaldi and Harvoni.

In February 2013, target maximum revenue payout was set at $10.4 billion, a number management knew was easily reachable based on its prescription script run rate early in 2013. The compensation committee needed to set a hurdle rate of at least $20 billion for 2014 based on minimal revenues, expected at $5 billion quarterly. For the year, revenues exceeded $24 billion.

I looked in vain for the 2014 revenue target for bonus calculations. Dr. Martin's package for 2014 approximates 220,000 shares at $80, made up of options on 162,260 shares and 57,910 performance shares at $80. His underlying unexercised options, which appear to remain outstanding for 10 years from date of grant, tot up to 7.5 million shares with very low exercise prices. No problem there. He's a newly minted billionaire. I don't begrudge reasonable stock options issuance, but it does add up to a lot of money with the stock over par now. The lion's share of unexercised paper ranges from $18 to $24, currently worth over $500 million. Related to the share base of Gilead, Dr. Martin's eight-million option portfolio represents under 1 percent. The total for Gilead's corporate equity incentive plan is 76.7 million shares available. This is 6 percent of the current share base, a fair number, but Dr. Martin's share approximates 10 percent of this package, which seems excessive by 50 percent. In summary, by yearend he controls 11.6 million shares or approximately 1 percent of the total capitalization of Gilead, with minimal invested capital on his part.

There are more egregious examples in high technology, Salesforce.com, for example, where management and key employees garner huge options grants but GAAP earnings remain negative. Management and a coterie of executives received compensation of approximately $2 billion, over 5 percent of the company's capitalization in a foreshortened time period.

Stepping back from all this carping and ciphering, where I come out is corporate insiders and employees of growth companies should be limited to no more than 5 percent of annual earnings in the form of salaries, bonuses and stock options. I'm allergic to outright stock grants because there's no risk and rarely any clawback. In Gilead's case my 5 percent-of-earnings construct last year would have totted up to, say, $150 million, so maybe they aren't an exceptionally bad example. Big picture, the gap between management compensation and median income of employees widens and widens. Income inequality for the country looms as its most divisive issue, looking ahead.

Gilead is my example of a CEO's package bordering on excess, but still deemed acceptable by all concerned.

SEVENTEEN

General Motors:
Love Me, Love Me Not

*D*ecades ago, my wife and I took breakfast in the General Motors cafeteria on the second floor of the GM building at 59th Street and Fifth Avenue. One of those quietly delicious insider moves New Yorkers love to practice. Never use the Triborough Bridge, even when the toll-free Willis Avenue span is backed up. Don't call Sixth Avenue by its old new name, Avenue of the Americas. That's for tourists.

The GM building remains premium space. You pay plenty for the view of Central Park, $100 per square foot. From our 42nd floor office, the Wollman Rink looked like a postage stamp. Short-order cooks in the cafeteria whipped up eggs Benedict and toasted outsized corn muffins brushed with liquid butter. It was impossible to spend more than $1.07 for breakfast while you gazed out on Madison Avenue's uptown traffic revving up.

Years later, the cafeteria was abolished and FAO Schwarz leased the space. On Wall Street in the seventies, the prodigality of General Motors' management was an open secret. I'd rank it with Ross Johnson's "RJR Nabisco air force," the company's fleet of corporate jets. But, after you lose share-of-market points to Honda and Toyota, you notch in your belt. It took KKR's LBO to disburse Ross and his RJR fleet. No securities analyst ever, in print, referred to such mufti-pufti or to GM's cafeteria.

Over decades, GM frittered away tens of billions on ill-conceived factories that fulfilled management's compulsive need for vertical integration but had minimal marginal return on invested capital, probably negative. Same goes for IBM in the eighties.

GM is forever a value stock, but so what? It can sell below 10 times earnings when the market's at 20. Now reorganized, it pays dividends, but it's not Boeing, which sells at 20 times forward 12-month earnings because its return on invested capital is very high and it generates ample free cash flow. GM's problem is Honda, Toyota, et al.

I'm a little softhearted over General Motors' battle scars. Not that money managers are sentimental. We'd sell our mothers down the river for 25 basis points' performance. Consider that manufacturing employment in the U.S. over the past 20 years has declined from 25 percent of the workforce to 10 percent. The United Auto Workers, now defanged, recently lost an organizational vote at Volkswagen's plant in Chattanooga, Tennessee.

My wife chooses to drive Benzes so I have no say on the "Buy America" issue. The only GM model I ever lusted for was their 1962 red Caddy convertible with white sidewalls. They now go for six figures at antique car shows, along with the two-toned '52 Chevy I knew so well when priced at $2,000.

Early fifties, GM was the number one corporation in the country and the largest employer in the world. Revenues relative to GDP also made it top listed. My employment stats only go back to 1965 when GM's headcount was 665,000; it's now around 200,000.

I'm still intrigued by recovery possibilities for the automobile sector and specifically for GM. Consider the average age of vehicles on the road rose steadily from 8.8 years in 1999 to 10.8 years in 2011. We are talking about over 200 million U.S. vehicles.

The demand for "good" used cars (i.e., three to four years old) remains buoyant. This keeps new car prices firm, increasing the residual value for lessors. Higher residuals lead to enticing financing terms on three-year leases. Interest rates are so low that when you're watching baseball on TV you'll see a proliferation of new-car lease offers of $239 a month, even $199 a month. If you're gainfully employed, new wheels are within your reach.

As shown in *Figure 25 on page 170*, 10 of the top 15 compact car models rated by *Consumer Reports* in 2014 are foreign.

The history of GM is the *Rake's Progress* profile—from hubris and dominance ultimately to ward of the state needing a $50-billion bailout. GM's postwar market share peaked at 50 percent. When I was called up by the army in 1952, I landed in Fort Benning, Georgia, where the infantry officers' school prepared you for Korea. All of West Point's recent graduates who chose the infantry landed there, too. They drove down in two-toned 1952 Chevy four-door sedans and religiously read *Time* magazine, usually resting on the front seat.

GM then was deeply ingrained in the U.S. psyche. Its executives wore double-breasted sharkskin suits, snug around the hips, with wide lapels. Ford struggled

2014 RATINGS COMPACT CARS

● Excellent
◐ Very good
○ Good
◖ Fair
● Poor

✓ Recommended

Rec.	Rank	Make & model	Price as tested	In this issue	Overall road-test score 0 — 100 P | F | G | VG | E	Predicted reliability	Overall mpg
✓	1	**Subaru Impreza** Premium	$21,345		82	◐	27
	2	**Kia Forte** LX (1.8L)	19,570		81	new	28
✓	3	**Hyundai Elantra** SE (1.8L)	19,410		80	○	29
✓	4	**Subaru Impreza** Sport Premium (hatchback)	22,345		79	◐	26
✓	5	**Mazda 3i** Grand Touring (2.0L, manual, hatchback)	24,040	●	78	◐	32
✓	6	**Mazda 3i** Touring (2.0L)	21,740	●	78	◐	33
	7	**Ford Focus** SE Sedan SFE	21,650		77	●	31
	8	**Ford Focus** SE Hatch	22,185		74	●	28
	9	**Volkswagon Jetta** SE (1.8T)	22,610		73	new	30
✓	10	**Toyota Corolla** LE Plus	20,652		72	◐	32
	11	**Ford Focus** SE Sedan	20,280		71	●	28
✓	12	**Honda Civic** EX*	21,605		71	◐	29
	13	**Chevrolet Cruze** 1LT (1.4T)	20,530		70	◖	26
	14	**Dodge Dart** SE (2.0L)	20,680		64	●	27
	15	**Nissan Sentra** SV	20,570		64	○	29

*Powertrain has changed since last test.

Figure 25

Source: Consumer Reports

under family management and ownership before Sidney Weinberg of Goldman Sachs brought them public. Chrysler was an also-ran. Later, the U.S. Treasury bailed out Chrysler. They figured it was cheaper to keep Chrysler running than mail out unemployment checks to 100,000 furloughed employees. Under Lee Iacocca, Chrysler came back and in the early eighties the Treasury cashed in its warrants for a profit. Iacocca had pleaded for sterilization, but Uncle Sam was no Uncle Sucker, even then. I had bought Chrysler's preferred stock at Mike Milken's urging and cleaned up.

GM's market share started its long, downward slippery slope in the late sixties from 48 percent market share, falling to some 44 percent in the seventies and 40 percent in the eighties. It dropped alarmingly to 32 percent in the nineties and pretty much has bottomed out at 18 percent to 19 percent presently *(Figure 26, page 172)*.

Strategic mistakes turned ludicrous. Volkswagen got a toehold in the fifties and sixties and then Honda and Toyota barged in. There was an unspoken gentlemen's agreement between domestic automobile managements and the UAW. Wage hikes in the seventies ran at 7 percent to 8 percent and so did car prices.

The U.S. auto industry then turned into the engine of domestic inflation, running at 7 percent to 8 percent. Our country, too, waxed uncompetitive. Teamsters extracted premium wages for drivers of forklift trucks. The only person ever challenging Jimmy Hoffa was feisty Bobby Kennedy in the sixties.

Paul Volcker, our great Federal Reserve Board chairman, studied this construct and then single-handedly created a bone-chilling recession for the country. Interest rates on five-year FNMA debentures rose to 15 percent. Builders mailed Volcker two-by-fours in the form of crosses. Volcker tamed all the country's inflammatory excesses, hopefully forever. The Fed under Janet Yellen now prays for at least 2 percent inflation years ahead.

From its recent peak employment of 266,000 in 2007, GM has cut its rolls by 25 percent. Negotiations with its European unions over work practices, retirement benefits and the size of the workforce remain a running story. Wall Street looked on with skepticism that Euroland plants could be downsized or shuttered. But GM is shading European losses, down from $1.9 billion in 2012 to $1.4 billion in 2014, half restructuring costs. Meantime, the North American selling rate late '14 to early '15 waxes buoyant. Thank $2 gasoline.

There are positive offsets. GM, 20 years ago, formed joint ventures with Chinese automakers. It has a leading 13 percent market share there, with EBITDA running at $2.5 billion in a reasonably good year. Industry car production in China

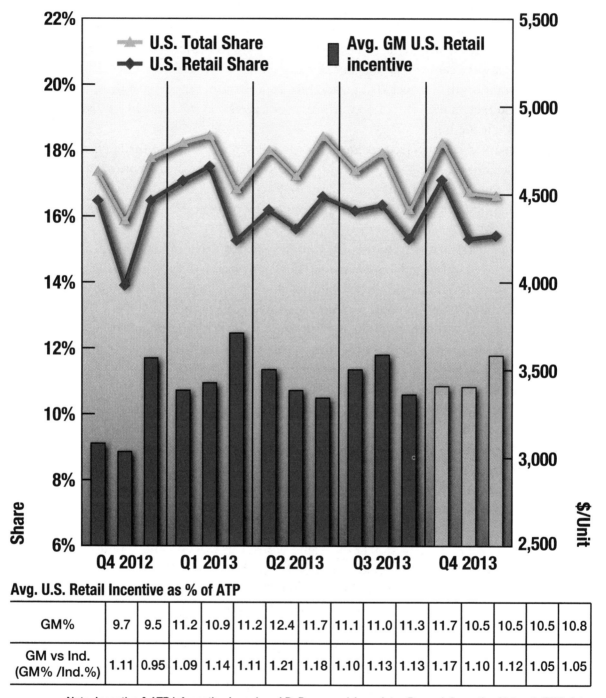

KEY GMNA PERFORMANCE INDICATORS

Avg. U.S. Retail Incentive as % of ATP

GM%	9.7	9.5	11.2	10.9	11.2	12.4	11.7	11.1	11.0	11.3	11.7	10.5	10.5	10.5	10.8
GM vs Ind. (GM% /Ind.%)	1.11	0.95	1.09	1.14	1.11	1.21	1.18	1.10	1.13	1.13	1.17	1.10	1.12	1.05	1.05

Note: Incentive & ATP information based on J.D. Power and Associates Power Information Network (PIN) data.

Figure 26

Source: General Motors' Quarterly Reports

approximates 19 million units, far above our 15.5-million run rate. A 30-million car year for China is in the cards within five to seven years. GM so far gets minimal credit for its gambit in China.

Market share in light and heavy-duty trucks is firm, along with heavy SUVs, but it's tough to gain incremental share in the U.S. When you read *Consumer Reports'* annual auto issue, Japanese and South Korean carmakers place very high in road tests and the incidence and cost of repairs, as well as gas mileage. In many model categories foreign makers take seven out of the top 10 places.

GM's pension fund is in a better place, partially rationalized after the company bought an annuity from Metropolitan Life. The take rate on GM's offer of pension buyouts is still in question. Meanwhile, I was unhappy to see GM cut its sector allocation to equities from 28 percent in 2009 to 14 percent in 2013. This was a bad call, considering the buoyancy of equity indices, particularly in 2013–'14. Debt securities comprise two-thirds of this asset base of $25 billion. Overall, pension liabilities trend lower, just $7 billion, halved during 2013.

I liked Dan Akerson, headman at GM, appointed to the board by the government in July '09. Akerson retired yearend 2013, joining the Carlyle Group's private equity board as vice-chairman. He was a tough, hands-on manager when he ran Nextel in the nineties. Just what GM needed, but he ignored the ignition-switch failures, a costly mess running into billions.

A minimal 15 million cars sold in North America is an average year. GM finally is a competitive operator able to keep up with the time compression for innovative model changes, fuel efficiency and quality engineering. As a stock, GM could range between $25 and $45, admittedly a wide sector, but I'm a bull on consumer confidence, low interest rates and gas pump pricing. I prefer GM to other deeply cyclical industrials, like U.S. Steel, Peabody Energy and even Caterpillar and Cummins. High-quality industrials sell north of 15 times earnings, too pricey for me, but in demand during 2013–'14 as a play on economic recovery.

General Motors is a global player, but North America accounts for nearly 90 percent of adjusted EBITDA. Recovery in the domestic selling rate for automobiles since the nadir in 2009 turned them around from a basket case clutching a $50-billion lifeline from the U.S. Treasury. GM's credit rating was restored to investment grade in 2013 and they declared a cash dividend of $1.20 a share. At yearend '14, redundant capital rested on their balance sheet, possibly $20 billion, net of debt. All this happened over four years of recovery. Management bumped up its dividend 20 percent to $1.44, making GM a respectable 4 percent yield piece of paper, higher than ExxonMobil et al.

The market's attitude towards GM is forever ambivalent. There are plenty of solid reasons for this love-hate attitude. The automobile business is a tough grind, with a dozen muscular competitors who field annually better and better cars, hold down prices and post gas stats north of 40 mpg. (I love my Prius made by Toyota.)

Just read the *Consumer Reports* spring '14 assessments. They rate dozens of Japanese, Korean and European carmakers highly. GM's Silverado heavy-duty truck was singled out, the new-model Cadillac and Chevrolet as well. But Ford's truck entry also is rated high, more aluminum with solid handling.

Roiling currents get expressed in North American and worldwide share-of-market stats. GM's global and North American numbers show stability but no apparent gain. They moved into China early on and are big in Brazil. But you can drop money in Europe. Worldwide market share holds around 11.5 percent, with North America at 17 percent.

Analysts follow these numbers with beady eyes. If GM ever gained market share, say 0.5 percent, the stock would elevate into a new zone of valuation. As it stands, GM sells as if it were a small-town corner delicatessen. We are talking about an enterprise value to EBITDA approximating three times. Ford sells closer to four times EBITDA.

Sooo, part of the GM story is about the possibility of closing this valuation gap in 2015. For 2014, GM is at 2.9 times and Ford is at 3.4 times. This is a valid investment concept that I subscribe to. When things get a touch better operationally for marginal companies, their stock gets a lot better. We've seen this in airlines, banks, insurance underwriters, coal and steel producers—anyone whose balance sheet is leveraged in a viciously cyclical business.

Contrast this three to four times EBITDA valuation with what goes on in the Internet and cloud computing sectors: Amazon, Twitter, Priceline.com, Salesforce.com and LinkedIn. EBITDA ratios hold in the mid-twenties or higher, and price-earnings ratios of 65 to 78 times abound. GM sells at eight times projected earnings for 2015, but nobody uses aggressive metrics for its evaluation because of their checkered history going back 50 years.

When I searched for whether any of today's feisty operators had cottoned on to GM, I did find Soros's fund with a $200-million position. George is a value player with big positions in Teva Pharmaceuticals, Herbalife and Halliburton—all somewhat controversial. GM is just 2 percent of his portfolio.

Latest negative surprise for GM was hiding problems with dated ignition switches. The switch turned off when jarred, causing vehicles to stall or lose power, disabling airbags, cutting off power steering and power brakes. All this goes back to its 2005 Chevy Cobalt, pre-bankruptcy, 2009 filing. Toyota recently agreed to a $1.2-billion federal criminal settlement for an improperly fitting floor mat. My guess is GM better reserve $5 billion for its tardy mea culpa.

I bought into GM early in 2013, at $24, before it turned obvious that a positive surprise was coming for North American car sales. The analyst consensus rested behind the numbers by a million units of production. Rightly, they all remained skeptical that GM could even hold market share. Car and truck models needed much refreshment. By the time everyone believed in a 15.5-million car year, the stock ticked in the mid-thirties.

In 2013, GM's global deliveries lifted from 9.3 to 9.7 million cars. Adjusted EBITDA for North America surged from $6.5 to $7.5 billion, with free cash flow of $3.7 billion. On my 2015 modeling, GM at $35 sells at 2.3 times enterprise value to EBITDA. I'm assuming a 16-million car year with easy financing and a strong consumer open-to-buy, but no heavy share buybacks. GM holds onto share of market.

Variables abound: used car market trends and new-model pricing, particularly for the Silverado heavy-duty truck vs. Ford's new entry. So far, so good. Buick, Cadillac and the Impala must encounter tough competition from Ford as well as Japanese offerings nearly uniformly top rated by *Consumer Reports*. If Toyota and Honda go for share of market by price cutting, GM's profit margins will flatten out at best. Last year, model-by-model pricing comparatively edged up, an important plus.

Early seventies, market share had already slipped into the low forties. I drove a stick shift Volkswagen "Bug," happy with its gas mileage. GM's lumbering station wagons then got maybe 10 miles to the gallon. You could watch the gas gauge sinking towards empty while you cruised on. (I'm not kidding.) When the Saudis tripled the price of oil from $4 a barrel to $12 in 1973, the handwriting was on the wall.

Since 2011, the average selling price for GM cars levitates, up 4 percent in 2013 and comparably in 2014. I see this metric as a pivotal variable for GM's competitive mettle. On a $150-billion revenue base, GM sells at 35 percent of revenue. Tech houses like Salesforce.com get pegged at 10 times revenues. Something has to give here, but before I bought the stock I'd give *Consumer Reports'* annual auto issue an intensive perusal. Year-to-date, December 2014, GM's a terrible laggard, down 15 percent while Facebook rose 37 percent and high-quality industrials like Union Pacific moved ahead 25 percent and Dow Chemical showed 20 percent.

Early 2014 music sheets from JPMorgan Chase, Morgan Stanley and Goldman Sachs almost uniformly projected GM at a near $50 piece of paper. Whistling in the dark? Analysts put earnings at four bucks, with a five-dollar bill coming in 2015. At $50 a share GM would be selling on parity with Ford's EBITDA to enterprise value. All this was possible but didn't pan out.

You're supposed to buy metal benders when their factories stand padlocked. Big money is made once they return to normal. Market capitalization of GM, December 2014, approximated $55 billion. This puts them among the top 100 market capitalizations in the S&P 500 Index.

GM's price chart traces a gigantic necklace. It went public, again, in December of 2010 at $33, fell below $20 and didn't reassert itself until the third quarter of 2012. At yearend 2013 it peaked at $41. Whether it makes another necklace over the coming three years is the open question. It surged to $36 on good fourth quarter 2014 numbers (*Figure 27*).

Considering GM coulda fallen off the screen in 2009, thank the resilient economy, consumer spending and low finance costs on new cars. GM's management should commission a life-sized bronze of Ben Bernanke and display it in their boardroom as a reminder that Uncle Sam waxed benevolent in their hour of deshabille.

When Chuck Wilson, GM's headman in 1953, was tapped by President Eisenhower for the Secretary of Defense post, he said at his hearings before the Armed Services Committee, "I thought what was good for the country was good for General Motors, and vice versa." Soon on, the press foreshortened this sentence to read "What's good for General Motors is good for the country." The abridged version touched off an uproar in liberal circles.

It's taken only 60 years and a government bailout to make this quip right as gold.

GENERAL MOTORS' VOLATILE 5-YEAR HISTORY

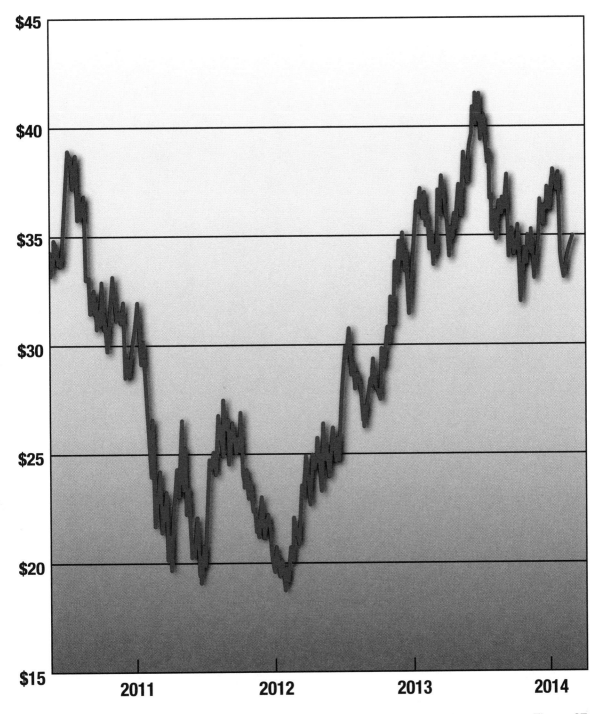

Figure 27
Source: Bloomberg

PART III

How Long Do the Good Times Last?

JEFF KOONS, *BALLOON DOG (ORANGE)*, 1994–2000

EIGHTEEN

Venezia:
My Beloved Leading Indicator

*E*ver since the early fifties, I've revisited Venice time and again. The Piazza San Marco adumbrates timelessness, but the sociology of its ambulatory tourists changes markedly, a leading indicator as to the health of Euroland if not the world. Summer of '14, the pizzas were delicious, along with fried zucchini and fresh sea bass in the alleyway bistros. But Venice was a step closer to Disneyland. Day-trippers jammed San Marco from the bagel barges that were allowed to cruise on the Grand Canal. At night, the piazza dozed forlornly empty.

I concentrated on the wines of the Alto Adige north of Verona, Jermann Pinot Grigio and the deeply honest Cabernet and Syrah blends of Tuscany. Quintarelli's great Amarone della Valpolicella, running into 200 euros for the 2002s, still ranged beyond my comfort zone.

Lemme take you back to the fifties in pre–air conditioned Venice. The small hotels off the Piazza San Marco let rooms for five bucks a day. These cubicles waxed so hot and humid in August that you stayed up half the night singing and drinking in the piazza, itself jammed with college students shouldering rucksacks, decades before wheeled baggage made the scene.

What I remember about Florian's, the outdoor café, is that its six-piece combo played Viennese waltzes and Italian ballads like "O Sole Mio." Young blond-bearded giants from wherever strode up to the bandstand, grabbed a microphone, belted out lyrics, and we'd all join in. That egalitarian ambiance is gone forever, but so what? "Tea for Two" resonates for octogenarians.

The problem today is kids with backpacks can't take a table at Florian's. What with cover charges, music imposts and pricey beer and cappuccino, a couple easily drops 100 euros over an hourly interlude. I saw this in the summer of '12 and made a mental note to short the euro at 1.45 to the dollar. Two years later, with the euro at 1.25, I began to make serious money. Peg it at $1.14 early February

'15. Nobody explained to my satisfaction why the dollar isn't near parity with the euro. In an existential investment world, simply, you are what you do, not what you think, say or write about. I'm adamant the euro is way overvalued in terms of purchasing power, while major financial risk pervades their bourses, both equities and bonds.

The euro should sink to dollar parity before 2016. If Euroland doesn't get its act together, the European Central Bank needs to inject maybe a trillion euros directly into banks and state treasuries in Spain, Greece and Italy. Otherwise, refinancing government debt at high interest rates adds to budget deficits and outstanding national debt. Players call this the death spiral. At the least, Euroland is mired in a GDP funk for years and years, maybe till the end of time. Call it 1 percent GDP momentum, even while its politicians won't get reelected on deficit financing infrastructure projects.

I denoted some misery in the melodies emanating from the combo at Florian's: The clarinetist blowing plaintive, melancholy tonalities; no Benny Goodman or Artie Shaw riffing with glissandos ranging over two octaves of pure melody. There was no lilt or *schlag* in Strauss's "Blue Danube." When darkness enveloped the piazza, few tables at Florian's or elsewhere had seaters. Tables were taken by fifty-ish couples, not groups of six, eight or 10. The animation of the 1950s had left. Then, four combos vied against each other, with few take-10 intervals of respite.

I read *The Great Gatsby* at 19, but I didn't quite penetrate to Fitzgerald's theme, which is: You never can relive the past, and it's too dangerous to try. Sixty years later, I got it in spades. Lucky for me, the money game is always about tomorrow, not yesterday's news. I've learned never to look back, gaining zilch from mistakes, which I instantaneously blot out, forever. Count your winners. It's like playing Go. Press your pieces across the board aggressively. I saw this in the Korean War as a young infantry commander, when the Chinese troops crossed the Yalu in arctic clothing, we in our field jackets and boots, frostbitten, wet and miserable.

America would've lost the war but for our superior communications infrastructure. When needed, I called in air strikes 300 yards from my company position. Man-for-man, Chinese and North Korean fighting men matched us in bravery and initiative. Without our deadly accurate artillery strikes they would've pushed us into the sea on the retreat from the Yalu to the southernmost port of Pusan. Was it 1952? Jeff Bezos reminds me of a Chinese general flooding the enemy lines with wave after wave of shock troops carrying bags of rice for provisions (low overhead).

Time your arrival in Venice for when the moonlight bathes the dome of Santa Maria della Salute. Lunch alfresco on the Campo Sant'Angelo at Acqua Pazza.

Alas, we were the only foursome in a sea of empty tables. The Pinot Grigio, Contest by Alois Lageder, was pure cucumbers and honeydew melon.

General Ulysses Grant certainly misspoke when he pontificated that Venice would be a great place if they only drained their canals. My vaporetto ticket for 72 hours' usage cost 36 euros. In the early sixties, I remember a 15-cent equivalent, and everyone gamed the system. Early fifties, the vaporetto was free. Am I remembering this right?

Italy's 10-year debt now trades to yield 5 percent, on parity with our BB corporates of five years' duration. I prefer our below-investment-grade goods, where there's the probability of an upgrade. As for Venice, its glory and hegemony radiated in the 15th century, when the *Canale Grande* teemed with anchored sailing vessels by the dozen, their holds filled with spices from the Orient.

Today, the *Queen Elizabeth* inches its way up the Grand Canal, laden with day tourists. This is the ultimate, incongruous insult, Venice as Disneyland.

Back home, the hostile tender surfaced for Allergan, a $50-billion deal pursued by Bill Ackman and Valeant Pharmaceuticals. I construed this as a leading indicator of deal activity finally moving into high gear. During the mid-eighties LBO insanity, deals accounted for at least 20 percent of the S&P 500 Index's upward trajectory. Label this market bullish, too. It's axiomatic that the guy who initiates a hostile tender rarely gets the company. Allergan arranged a friendly deal with Actavis at a higher price. Only a bear hug works when you tender with cash for the entire outstanding equity.

Looking at world bourses and ours, the best leading indicator is the Value Line Index. This is a straight arithmetic compilation of 1,650 stocks, many of whose names you and I wouldn't recognize, no less analyze. Nevertheless, Value Line makes new highs months before the S&P 500 Index and tops out months before it. When the S&P 500 broke through its W formation in the autumn of 2013, Value Line had already dwelled in new high ground for several months. When the market peaked in 2007, Value Line had been flashing yellow lights months before (*Figure 28, page 184*).

Hard to reason why, but institutional inertia supports IBM, ExxonMobil, Google, even Apple. Small- and mid-cap stocks forever wax volatile to change at the margin, react faster and plunge deeper or rebound faster. You may not like the composition of this index, but it's near infallible. The Russell 2,000 Index of small-capitalization stocks had declined 5 percent, while the S&P 500 Index rose 7 percent end of the third quarter 2014.

VALUE LINE INDEX 2000–2014

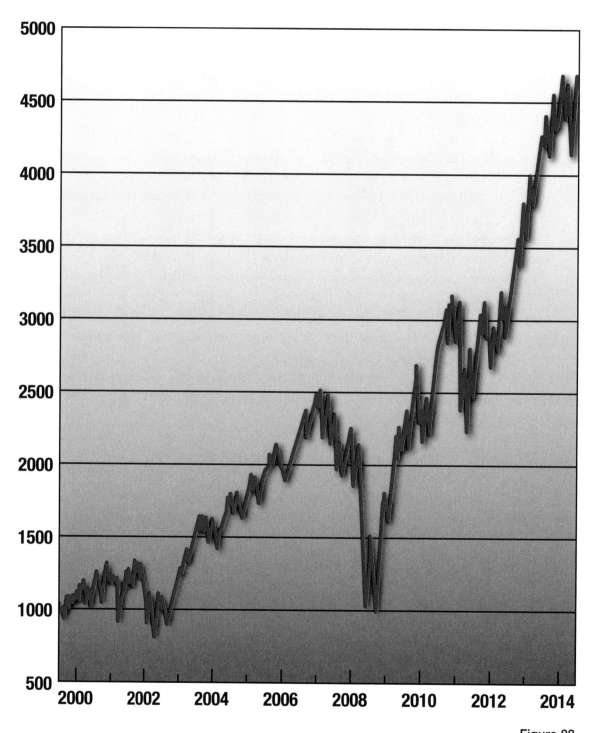

Figure 28
Source: Bloomberg

NINETEEN

The Big Board vs. Contemporary Art: Siamese Bubbles

Many see pictures without knowing what to look at
—BERNARD BERENSON
ITALIAN PAINTERS OF THE RENAISSANCE

*A*lan Greenspan once opined you only recognize bubbles after the fact. Said another way, nobody ever pinpoints when the music is ready to stop. I'm bullish on stocks and contemporary art. My assets are nearly evenly spread between both classes, so to hell with black swans, but I'm dealing in pricey markets during 2014. I never, ever, consider art an investment asset class. It's a luxury for the super-rich, whereas the Big Board endures as my life's blood. I spend easily 90 percent of my working hours doping out the market and major asset classes. Then I filter down into stock selection, trying to be early and standing alone.

Art today is neither a leading nor lagging indicator. This shooting star is a coincident indicator. Hundreds of newly minted billionaires in Russia, the U.S. and China, as well as oil sheiks in the Arab world, now yearn to erect museums of contemporary art (in their name) but lack inventory to cover their walls as yet. In a private transaction, a Paul Gauguin canvas changed hands near $300 million. The buyer was said to be based in Qatar, an oil-rich emirate with a museum filling up with trophy Western world art. The picture, *Nafea Faa Ipoipo,* was of two outdoors-seated nubile females, eyes darting askance. Open-to-buy starts with Warhols, Richters and Rothkos and then works down into my inventory category of Joan Mitchell, Hans Hofmann, Ed Ruscha, Georg Baselitz and Anselm Kiefer. What will Warhol and Lichtenstein be worth 50 years ahead? *¿Quién sabe?* The long-term history of art prices covering three centuries shows a viciously cyclical pattern, where one age's indulgences can turn nearly worthless decades later. Unsaleable goods.

The contemporary art market leaped far ahead of the stock market in 2013–'14, at least in terms of its frothiness. I'm no longer seeing music sheets on how reasonable equities remain based on the traditional academic valuation, except for the risk premium. The only reason the risk premium is so high is the risk-free rate of return sits near zero. This won't last forever, probably not even through 2015. Draw a trendline near 4 percent for money market rates over the entire postwar financial history. Comparable with equities, from the 2009 bottom in contemporary art prices, it took until late 2014 to forge into new high ground. The 2009–'10 decline was 48 percent.

Market pundits, few of whom projected a 1,650 S&P 500 Index by yearend 2013, fast-forwarded to 2014, justifying their new, improved 1,725 valuation extrapolation. I was there, projecting earnings growth of 6 percent in 2014 and a mid-teens price-earnings ratio, which got me to 1,800 in the index. By September 2014 the S&P 500 was pushing past 2,000. The art market felt more like a 25 times price-earnings ratio, historical bubble territory, but a lagging indicator. Art probably won't peak until financial markets head south by 10 percent (*Figure 29*).

Point to point, since the millennium, the S&P 500 returned to investors under 6 percent, compounded. However you compare this return, it stands as subpar. The market endured the tech bubble of 2000 and then the financial meltdown of 2008–'09. It traced a gigantic W formation but finally broke out late in 2013.

Over the past decade, if I had reversed working hours and spent 90 percent of my time doping out first-class contemporary and modern art works, I'd be dancing on Easy Street rather than singin' in the rain. I was sobbing over this to my friend Steve Mazoh, who deals in front-rank canvas output spanning the past 70 years. I'm talking about Warhol, Mondrian, Hans Hoffman, Ruscha, Lichtenstein, Rothko, Francis Bacon, Ellsworth Kelly, Cy Twombly, et al.

As the past decade showed an 800 percent increase in unit art sales, my take is that I should have been 10 times more active in the art market than stock jobbing. U.S. auction sales rose 20 percent during 2013 for postwar and contemporary art. The buoyancy continued during 2014. It's hard not to conclude that the art market is at least comparable in volatility with the Big Board. Secondly, unless the stock market remains buoyant, the inflation in art prices must flatten out.

Steve was saying that if he had held on, his inventory would be worth hundreds of millions. When an operator in the art world splurges, he'd normally buy 20 or 30 canvases of an artist's oeuvre, store 'em in a warehouse for 20 years and then dribble them singly into the auction market.

The difference between Steve and the Lauders, Eli Broad and François Pinault, who owns Christie's, is they hardly ever sell much. Rather, they build museums and

THE S&P 500 INDEX 2000–2014

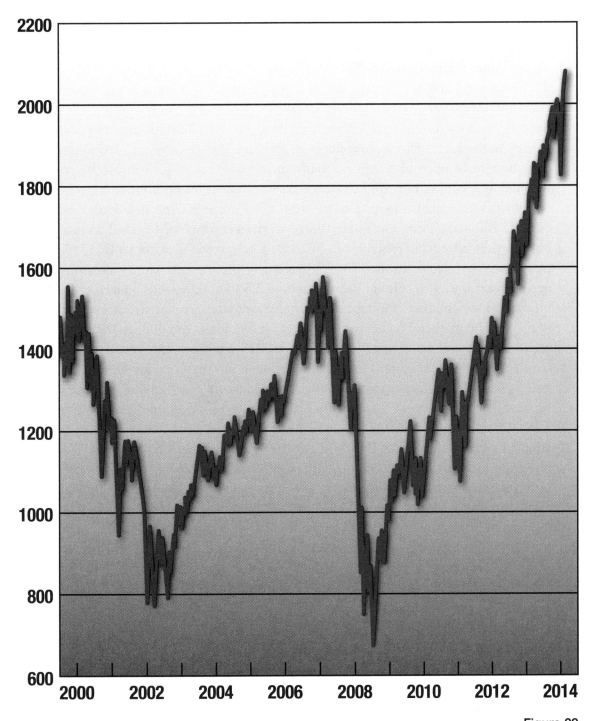

Figure 29
Source: Bloomberg

exhibit their collections, which can run into thousands of pieces. Collecting over a 50-year period, you'd be surprised how much inventory accumulates. Warren Buffett is a perfect example of a collector (of companies and stocks) who marries his goods for life but stays on the lookout for additions. Market capitalization of his Berkshire Hathaway exceeds $350 billion.

November 2014, Steve and I left Sotheby's and Christie's evening auctions of contemporary art empty-handed, wallets intact. Not that we didn't often raise our paddles, with enthusiasm and conviction. Alas! We were outbid, impetuously, by parties on the auction floor plus telephone bidders. Both houses on auction nights carry dozens of open phone lines, many manned by pretty girls in black dresses who belt out counterbids to the auctioneer standing at his podium.

Statistics I see that ring true come from the European Fine Art Foundation's (TEFAF) annual report. The international art market rose to €47.5 billion including antiques, advancing 8 percent in 2013, and then rose 7 percent to €51 billion. Domestically we've accounted for 39 percent of the market value, increasing 25 percent year over year. Online sales, maybe €2.5 billion. Serious collectors don't buy art on the Internet. Modern and contemporary art accounted for 46 percent of the auction market. We are just back to the level of sales in 2007. In the financial meltdown art volume dropped by a third to $28 billion, totally understandable. Contemporary art accounted for 48 percent of all fine art sales during 2014.

TEFAF's 155-page report categorized the world's billionaire population, because they are natural buyers of so-called iconic modern and contemporary work. Their count is 2,170 billionaires in the world, currently worth $6.5 trillion, almost half the valuation of the Big Board. The U.S. contains 24 percent of such ultra-high net worth honchos. I assume, as do many researchers, that this cohort budgets more than 10 percent of their net worth for art, jewelry, racehorses, yachts, jets and $100 million mansions. I can't prove it, but viscerally I expect more than half of these passion plays go for art.

If this $6.5 trillion cohort allocates at least 5 percent of their boodle to investments of passion, we are at $325 billion for expendables. Consider that Sotheby's and Christie's May and December auctions normally reach $500 million per session. Then bring in the wealth group of $100 million up to a billion bucks. These players add $1.3 trillion to the wealth pot, maybe $65 billion for Warhols and vintage Ferrari cars. We are up to almost $400 billion in open-to-buy, possibly per annum, in buoyant financial markets with real estate holding firm. This seems unsymmetrical with the dollar value of auction markets, probably an overestimate of open-to-buy.

Over the past decade, the contemporary art market left the Big Board in the dust. Its biggest growth spurt came between 2003 and 2007, with sales rising from €593 million to €3.5 billion in 2007. Afterwards, a lagging indicator on the downside in 2008–'09, its absolute decline in sales reached 60 percent. It's impossible to distinguish accurately the price decline in sales volume with actual declines in comparable works of art. My memory is prices declined some but not a lot. Sellers first withdrew consigned lots from auction houses. In 2013 the number of consignments grew 6 percent, to a record level. Some 80 lots made over €10 million each. Contemporary art comprised 40 percent of all auction sales, with Old Masters as a category just 10 percent. Modern art, 29 percent of the market, began to get my money with multiple purchases of Miró and Degas canvases.

I attend auctions to gauge depth of bidding, particularly on iconic pieces ranging to $50 million, as in Basquiat's 1982 pictures as well as Jackson Pollock's work. Even Philip Guston made $25 million. Lichtenstein's piece *Woman with Flowered Hat*, a cartoonlike canvas using a Picasso painting for its derivation, had three active bidders down to the wire and made over $50 million, with scattered applause at the conclusion.

Some $22 million went for Yves Klein's sculpture *Eponge Bleue Sans Titre*, a blue sponge on a stick. Gimme a break! My bourgeois sensitivities bled through. Gerhard Richter's *Domplatz, Mailand*, a photograph, made $37 million, with a Barnett Newman canvas hitting $43.8 million. Francis Bacon's *Study for a Portrait of P.L.*, estimated at $30 to $40 million, was passed at $28 million, the first bit of rationality experienced in the house.

Christie's Pollock lot, a standard drip on paper, *Number 19, 1948*, made $58.3 million. Pollock was selling his production then, happily realizing a thousand bucks per canvas from Peggy Guggenheim. You do the compounded annualized rate of gain. In 1950, with few shekels in my pocket, I bought prints for $50, my sane budget level. Sometimes, I'd buy a $300 painting and pay for it $30, monthly.

The going rate for iconic art, May and November 2013, and then in May and November '14, was bumped up from $25 million into the $40- to $50-million range. It likely presses higher until the next major worldwide recession takes down world bourses for a *lavage rapide* of 25 percent or more. Consider that the number of newly minted billionaires inexorably climbs by hundreds per annum, so don't hold your breath. Still, the Russian ruble was nearly cut in half in late 2014 and early 2015.

Sooner or later, a new crop of feisty honchos meets with and hires art advisors. Now that gold is passé and prime real estate pricey, where else do you go and have fun, make the society pages while decorating multiple homes? Big operators smugly house Jeff Koons's balloon dogs and Lichtenstein's canvases.

Unlike Eli Broad and the Lauders (serious collectors spanning several decades), the new guys with bags of money carry no institutional memory of the ebb and flow in art prices, nor do they possess any connoisseurship of an artist's development over his lifetime. Which were his best years, and why should one canvas rate a $10-million price tag and another $25 million? They're only comfortable bidding at auction against half a dozen of their contemporaries. One-on-one, working with dealers, makes them uneasy, because they don't contain the smarts or apperceptive mass, and could be taken to the cleaners.

Soooo...not only does a million bucks buy you next to nothing (Steve's quip), but secondary work, even $10 million down excludes you from this circle of buyers, embracing a regiment of deeply lined pockets operating in trophy art. Over $150 million, call it super–trophy art. Damn them all! They've ruined the market for us $5-million schlubs. Let them go buy Pebble Beach golf courses, The Plaza Hotel and the General Motors Building. If I'm wrong about risk-based equities as the preferred asset class for years to come, at least I can bang out my portfolio in 15 minutes. Even preferred real estate can take years to unload. As for the art market, if your canvases go out of fashion there are no bids.

Nobody knows whether today's $50 million Jeff Koons balloon dogs hold up for generations to come. Some art critics I know bend thumb and index finger into a big fat zero when I pose the question on future prices. And yet, I had plenty of opportunity to buy Basquiat's best work, from 1982, then at $2,500 apiece. But I didn't. Bids today close in on $50 million. The art world is filled with ironies and non sequiturs. Too much bad art is bought with $6-million price tags. Like de Kooning's squiggles on canvas done in his near senility. One man's graffiti becomes another man's prized canvas. Whenever my equity portfolio levitates 10 percent, whether I cash in or not, I normally reinvest the paper profits in contemporary art. Conceptually, I'm a fool, because all I'm doing is trading in a pile of liquid assets for canvases and bent metal that could turn into junk.

For handicapping the art market, my valuation yardstick is the 0.1 percent, richer than Midas, who often spend 1 percent of their net worth on a single work of art without blinking. Consider, a billionaire's open-to-buy for a single canvas or sculpture easily counts to $10 million. Our well-heeled mark doesn't care that his current squeeze sold at auction for $100,000 a decade ago. (You're late, fella.) Connoisseurship counts! (At least for some of us disciplined collectors.) For the $100 million Warhol, Francis Bacon or Giacometti *Walking Man* bronze, whittle down the players to a couple of dozen sporting net worth of $10 billion or more. They make up the pool of rabid telephonic bidders. Up yours, Steve Cohen!

If I'm on the money (why not?), connoisseurship in art contains a bigger payoff than riding super-growth stocks that sooner or later surely deconstruct. Apple, for example, dropped 40 percent from its high after its ascent from the thirties nine years ago. It ran around the clock 20 times. Fewer than 10 years ago I bought a Christopher Wool word piece for $250,000. One recently got knocked down for $26 million. I'm not bragging. I sold my Wool prematurely for $1 million. We're talking about hundredfold advances in art valuation. There're fewer Apple occurrences, but hundreds in the contemporary art world. No art index catches such pyrotechnics. Think Macy's Fourth of July fireworks under the Brooklyn Bridge, which surge for an hour or less, irrepressibly.

I discount the proliferation of academic art indices, particularly those that track auction prices year over year. These constructs don't capture the concentration of interest in specific subsectors and the rapid escalation of anointed American artists' production. It misses, too, instant markups and markdowns by a thousand legitimate dealers, worldwide.

What's comparable in the financial world is buying ragamuffins selling at option value, a buck or two per share. I've done this in the past with airlines, banks and insurance operators, all highly leveraged capital structures. But I bought Lehman three days before they filed for bankruptcy, a total write-off. Citigroup, US Airways and Geico come to mind. I've taken fliers on Sirius XM Radio, MGIC and a coal operator whose name I dare not mention, still a candidate for cardiac arrest if metallurgical coal prices fail to turn around in 2015. OK, it's Arch Coal, ticking at $1.03, early 2015.

Courage that you bring to the table counts when playing option value paper and controversial art. Assume nobody is as stupid as you, throwing money away, that you have no more than one chance in four of prevailing (calls for diversification). After buying a chancy piece, next day I write it down to zero so as never to feel burned and disappointed. Axiomatically, you find what's most difficult to pull the trigger on soars to the moon next 20 years—Basquiat, Rothko, Warhol, et al.

Low interest rates remain the granddaddy of all leading and coincident indicators for equities and art. Not only does easy money induce home buying and new car purchases, it also becomes the pivotal variable in capital spending, deal activity and art buying. Mid-decade, margin credit utilization on the Big Board is absent from the scene, unremarkably modest relative to the market's capitalization level.

When a bunch of hedge funds ganged up on Sotheby's with a market capitalization of $2.5 billion, I thought operators like Dan Loeb were off the mark. Art auction houses periodically endure viciously cyclical years, more volatile on the downside than Wall Street brokers, with less upside leverage during good years. Big consignees ask for and get the lion's share of commissions on iconic pieces put up for auction. Financial houses normally sell no higher than 10 times earnings. Sotheby's early 2015 tracked closer to 20 times forward 12-months profits. For why? There's irony and absurdity, maybe symmetry in auction houses attracting financial operators like Christie's owner, François Pinault. Gimme Morgan Stanley. Headmen at Sotheby's and Christie's tapped out even with record revenues for both houses during 2014.

Handicapping 2015, I see up to a 10 percent annualized gain for the S&P 500 Index, refusing to anticipate the death knell of rapidly escalating interest rates or inflation. The market can sell at a high-teens price-earnings ratio, even with earnings rising mid-single digits if corporate operating profit margins hang in. My call.

My feel for the contemporary art scene is rosier. Dozens of million-dollar canvases can make $5 million in under five years. Paintings going for $5 million can get knocked down at $10 million. A handful of pieces maybe reach $200 million or more, but net worth limitations of even the super-rich entail a self-imposed art budget ceiling now within sight. Hundreds of buyers with net worth of $100 million to $500 million buoy the market in the $1 million to $10 million category.

My favorite yardstick is 10 percent compounded doubles in seven years, the rosiest scenario I expect for contemporary art prices. This exceeds what I expect for the stock market, a more rational setting with more disciplined players, many in control of hundreds of billions, even trillions of invested capital, but still, other people's money. OPM money managers annually get judged by clients in percentage points. Billionaires don't even report particulars to their spouses.

I missed Twitter's ascendancy. Conceptually, I saw Twitter as the bedrock personal Internet communications medium, comparable with the advent of Polaroid's near-instant photos in 1949. My security analyst's discipline did get invoked. Twitter peaked at $74 early in 2014 and then corrected to under $40. The art world, swarming with hundreds of swinging dicks, billionaires, divorcées and heiresses, beckons for indulgence by the ever-passionate, who long to possess objects and don't count their money daily.

Ironically, the intellectual crux of money management is the image of minimalist art. There is a downgrading of talent, facility, virtuosity and technique. Conceptual power is be-all and end-all. How else do you rationalize Carl Icahn's play in Apple? He couldn't possibly know or model Apple's numbers any better than a $200,000-a-year young security analyst. Carl must think Apple is simply a cheap stock. All he needs to know. How do you compare it to Samsung, now selling at six times earnings? Microsoft is more conjectural, struggling to reinvent itself in cloud computing while its desktop franchise sinks slowly below the horizon. The next couple of years round out the Apple and Microsoft stories.

In the art market today, much of the action takes place in the modern and contemporary sectors. Supply isn't finite, because in all categories, spanning 500 years, supply exceeds authentication scrutiny. There may be dozens of counterfeit canvases extant attributed to Jackson Pollock, Modigliani, de Kooning, even Basquiat. There are name artists like Jeff Koons who operate cavernous workshops employing dozens of artisans and computer technicians who perform microtasks like layering paint on four-inch squares of a 10-foot canvas. Many sculptures are done in multiples of three to 10 impressions, but take years to complete.

The Koons pieces I own took almost two years for completion. One comes away with the feeling that Koons sets meticulous standards for work in process, the sole conceptualist. *Balloon Dog (Orange)* resonates, an immaculate, mirrorlike metallic surface. Metaphorically, it speaks to me of conspicuous consumption, in-your-face Pop art. Just what an oligarch thirsts to position on his front lawn.

Bernard Berenson, writing in *Italian Painters of the Renaissance*, said that "without art, visual, verbal and musical, our world would have remained a jungle." I'd substitute "economic growth" for "art." Avid collectors of Old Masters, early 20th century, had made their fortunes in oil, railroads, steel, retailing, even on Wall Street. Their names still resonate: John D. Rockefeller, Baron von Thyssen, the Rothschilds, Henry Huntington, Calouste Gulbenkian, Jules Bache, Benjamin Altman and Otto Kahn. I'd include Samuel Kress, J. P. Morgan, Henry Clay Frick, Joseph Widener, Andrew Mellon, of course, and Isabella Stewart Gardner.

This core group of feisty operators and collectors came to a couple of dozen. Many of these passionate, oldish robber barons dealt with Joseph Duveen, who relied on Berenson for authentication and critiques of the canvases under consideration. Currently,

JEFF KOONS, *BALLOON DOG (ORANGE)*, 1994–2000

there're a thousand "squillionaires" open-to-bid for name artists, instead of competition between the dozen or so collectors early in the 20th century. They sat, massaged by gallerists like Duveen who pushed his inventory of Bellini, Botticelli, Raphael, Rembrandt, Gainsborough, Watteau, Velázquez, Vermeer and Titian.

The British landed class, perennially short on liquidity, turned sporadic sellers. BB's tome on Renaissance art endures as the outstanding critical work in terms of taste making and aesthetic sensibilities starting with his essays from 1894 to 1907. In his posthumous list, Berenson downgraded many paintings he had personally recommended vociferously to Duveen's clientele. During the Great Depression, previously aggressive buyers saw their collections turn unmarketable, or at least badly marked down on sale.

At the onset of World War II, refugees from Hitler's onslaught let go of Rembrandts for $7,500, according to Gerald Reitlinger. His three-volume discourse, *The Economics of Taste*, is a must-read for serious collectors. The markdown of all markdowns took place in 1931 when the Soviets, short of dollars, depleted their Hermitage Museum of 21 masterpieces. The Russians earmarked the sale to Andrew Mellon, then Secretary of the Treasury, because they hoped for favorable conditions for the export of oil, lumber and cheap steel. (Nothing changed.)

From 1930 to 1931, Mellon leafed through the Hermitage's catalog and cherry-picked 21 pieces for $6.1 million (serious money at the time). This cache later formed the nucleus of the National Gallery of Art in Washington, DC. The museum was paid for by Mellon. FDR despised him, and in 1933 the Treasury sued Mellon for tax evasion. Mellon died before the case was decided in his favor. His collection of Italian Renaissance art adumbrates timelessly in Washington, DC.

Raphael's *The Alba Madonna*, bought by Mellon for $1,166,000, long stood as a record price for a single canvas. Mellon's entire collection was valued at $36 million. Today, I'd add at least two zeros. Always an astute banker, he inventoried a conservative loan portfolio, believing recurrent economic cycles in the U.S. were a given every five years. He saw industrialists as mainly foolish operators who created inventory and capital goods recessions by their periodic overspending. This was a good call that repeated itself into the sixties. The Hermitage's masterpieces dated back to the late eighteenth century collection of Catherine II, Catherine the Great. They included Rembrandts, Tiepolo, Watteau, Veronese, Poussin, many van Dycks, Raphael, Chardin, Rubens, Botticelli and Titian. Art dealer Knoedler & Co.'s main client, Andrew Mellon, outbid Gulbenkian for many of these pieces. In 2011, the Knoedler Gallery in New York, overnight, shut its doors, permanently. They were besieged by collectors for selling, among other pieces, fake Jackson Pollocks and de Koonings.

Back in Mike Milken's heyday, he could locate practically every individual or family with net worth of over $500 million. His count was several hundred back in the early eighties. The objective was to do business with every one of them. I remember him introducing me to Sam Walton, exiting his pickup truck in duck-hunting boots. Early on, Sam had given away to his wife and children major stakes in Wal-Mart. Alice Walton has ended up worth over $34 billion and turned into an active buyer of American art for her relatively new museum situated in Bentonville, Arkansas.

In the 2008–'09 financial meltdown, the S&P 500 Index was cut in half. The NASDAQ Internet bubble peak of 5,048 hasn't been regained, as of February 2015. Financial markets did snap back from the spring 2009 nadir. If the Big Board trades three to four billion shares daily, at a $50-a-share median, art transactions account for no more than a couple of hours' activity on the Big Board *(Figure 30, page 196)*.

When Lichtenstein's canvases were priced at $100,000 by Leo Castelli in the eighties, I asked to buy one and was told by Leo that there were 40 collectors ahead of me on his list. (I was late, late, too late.) Same goes in financial markets. Anyone can buy Apple at $450 or $600, but ask yourself why you weren't operating when Apple ticked in double digits.

What indices on art cannot capture is activity at the dealer level. Why should Larry Gagosian or Bill Acquavella reveal what he's getting for Picassos and Jeff Koons's work? Consider this exponential impact: An Andy Warhol or Richter goes for $50 million at auction. Next day, dealers and owners worldwide read the auction sales report and *tout de suite* mark up their inventory to reflect latest knocked-down auction lot prices. Dozens of pieces.

Spiraling can go on until a pricey lot fails to sell, is labeled as "burned" and cannot return to the market for years. Everyone's inventory then must be marked down in the interim. That's how cycles are made. It's like Google reporting a bad quarter overnight and opening next morning down 10 percent.

When I saw Munch's *Scream* made $120 million, I shook my head in disgust. The 0.1 percent set had transmogrified into decadent role models for a world enduring 24 percent unemployment among Europe's weak sisters. College graduates squirm, unable to make a dent in student loan debit balances while states like California up tuition far beyond a student's carrying capacity. Leon Black was the buyer of *The Scream*.

Let's diss telephone bidders who pay nine figures for auction lots. Giacometti's *Walking Man,* Picasso canvases and now Munch's *The Scream.* Sooner or later, buyer identity surfaces. The widow of Edmond Safra, who built a personal banking empire, and Alice Walton turned into active players along with Elaine Wynn, buyer of the Francis Bacon triptych for $142 million.

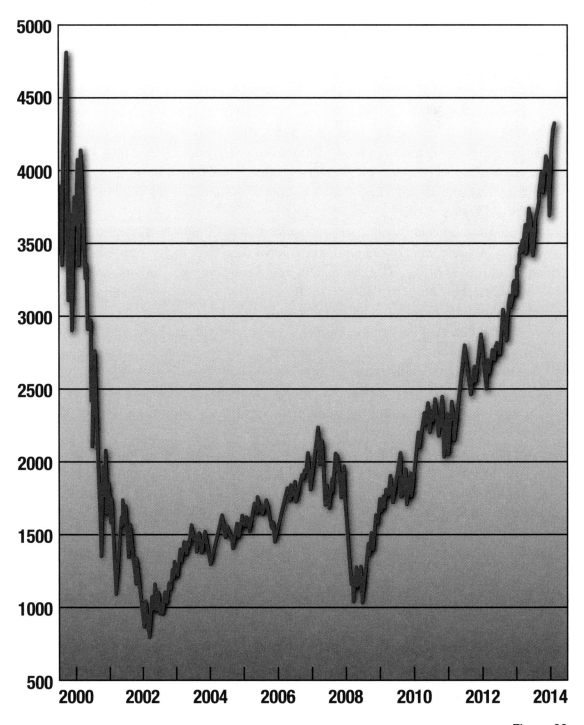

NASDAQ COMPOSITE 2000–2014

Figure 30

Source: Bloomberg

I'm waiting for contemporary art to top out and drop 50 percent, but it doesn't comply. Catalogs from Sotheby's and Christie's wax fatter, elaborately packaged and scholarly annotated, with eight pages of notes categorizing the work in question's derivation and historical context. If highly estimated, they'll give you an eight-page spread on your lot. You don't have to thumb through dozens of books on art criticism, biography and illustration. Sotheby's and Christie's researchers do it for you. Many pieces at auction are bought sight unseen, employing transparencies or images sent over the Internet to smartphones and iPads of prospective bidders.

For over 5 years, savers remain disenfranchised, averaging just 1.9 percent on 10-year Treasuries and little more than 3 percent on AAA corporates of five years' duration. Money market rates border zero to 25 basis points. No wonder art today is considered a repository of value, promising appreciation.

Price escalation in Italian Renaissance painting on the eve of 1929's Black Friday can be laid at the feet of Wall Street operators, too. A goodly dozen embraced Andrew Mellon, Jules Bache, Otto Kahn, Benjamin Altman, Solomon Guggenheim, Samuel Kress, Henry Frick, Joseph Widener and industrialists like Edsel Ford and Baron von Thyssen. J. P. Morgan belongs here, and later John Paul Getty. Similarly, the contemporary and modern art scene today is propelled by a comparable coterie of billionaires throwing their weight around at Sotheby's and Christie's night auctions.

Eli Broad and François Pinault are great collectors, fully engaged since the seventies. The arrivistes—Russian, Asian and Mideastern players—are trophy buyers of Warhol's Mao portraits, Jeff Koons's immaculately finished sheet steel tulips, Richter's squeegeed colored canvases and Mark Rothko's hazily-colored biomorphic cloudlike pieces.

Even in the eighties, if your fortune counted up to $250 million, you made the Forbes 400 list. Art in demand sold for $100,000. Gallerists who bought and inventoried work from their stable of artists over decades ended up seriously rich. I'm thinking of Anthony d'Offay, Ileana Sonnabend and Pierre Matisse. These dealers loved and coddled their stables, many artists receiving monthly stipends to keep them functional. They owned 'em for life—the Buffett approach. There is much to be said for connoisseurship and its second derivative—huge future returns.

I can't find any linkage between art prices and the S&P 500 Index these past 10 or even 50 years, not to say they won't be more closely attached going forward. Huge fortunes made in Silicon Valley, natural resources, retailing, hedge fund management, private equity investing and Internet startups like Google and Facebook, Twitter and Alibaba seem likely to remain intact if not appreciate during the next decade.

Sooner or later, many artists in demand crank out cookie-cutter work. The market wises up. Prices top out and then decline. The Sistine Chapel wasn't painted overnight and was never put up for sale. Many Warhols and Basquiats were finished in a couple of hours. Swish, swish, schlock, schlock went the brushes, and then out the door to foolish collectors. Same goes for much minimalist art.

Bernard Berenson, over a lifetime of connoisseurship, disdained German, American and English academics, just as I avoid market pundits. For Berenson, looking at a picture was always an emotional experience, a new discovery, and only then to be placed in the continuum of Italian Renaissance painting from Duccio, Masaccio and Giotto through Botticelli, Titian, Leonardo and Michelangelo. Over 70 years, Berenson built a library of 34,000 books but tells us not to waste much time reading about pictures instead of looking at them. A good rough test is whether you feel reconnected with life on viewing a canvas.

Strangely, BB barely warmed up to Impressionism, was neutral on Matisse but liked Degas. He lived long enough to see the blossoming of abstract expressionism in the early fifties but never paid it any attention. I can only imagine his revulsion against minimalist art, geometric abstraction, Op and the Pop art of Warhol and Lichtenstein. Nobody's perfect! According to Berenson we see much more with our mind than with our eye. I keep repeating this to myself as I parse analysts' spreadsheets and watch the tape zip by, a mindless sitcom.

I hate to bid at auction, where the buyer's premium is serious money. Whatever I missed over the past 30 years, I'll view in a museum. Most of my open-to-buy is earmarked for dealers, particularly those I trust who have bought and sold pieces for decades. The art dealer market is fragmented, but under 30,000 dealers account for 60 percent of market value sales. Over a lifetime of collecting, I've never dealt with more than a couple of dozen, mainly in New York and London.

For 2013, the auction market alone reached €4.9 billion for contemporary and modern works. Interestingly, the global art market 2013 approximated the $48 billion level of 2007. This sum is far below my conceptual projection of $400 billion open-to-buy. Anyone who doesn't believe financial markets and the art world function in tandem needs to explain why the high correlation. The contraction in art sales at auction during 2008–'09 amounted to 40 percent, a viciously cyclical pattern. The Chinese market flattened in 2013, while our S&P 500 Index rose 32 percent. China's stock market contracted through the first quarter of 2014, before it took off for a 40 percent run. There was much reneging by art auction buyers.

I remember many contemporary works—Joan Mitchell and Christopher Wool canvases, for example—sold around $100,000 as late as 1995 when offered in New York galleries. These works now can range over $10 million. Hundredfold appreciation decade over decade is unheard-of in the financial world unless you employ maximum leverage and operate in commodities markets and options—dangerous to your stability and staying power. Tap City beckons for high rollers.

Financial markets normally stand more rational and less pricey than modern and contemporary art offerings at auction, but not always. Short sellers circled around Twitter and cut it in half in a matter of months, early in 2014. You can short Sotheby's but not Warhols. When the circus comes to town you try to sell peanuts. Sotheby's and Christie's surely remain able facilitators, but carry huge overhead not so easily reduced during market contractions.

Collectors who bought quality work five years ago suddenly find themselves filthy rich, dozens worth hundreds of millions, at least on paper. Their open-to-buy subliminally expands materially. Bottom line, the upward price cycle for art waxes irrepressibly until suddenly the music stops. Explanations proliferate: The geopolitical situation in Europe and China is strained. Financial markets are freefalling because of the stupidity and greed of large banks. Even little Iceland's overleveraged banks roiled financial markets in 2008–'09. During the tech bubble in 2000, news surfaced on big collectors reneging on lot purchases of van Gogh, Warhol and 10-carat diamonds. History repeats itself. China is too tough to call.

Pundits then pull out of their files dusty charts that show long-term appreciation of art is less than that of bonds, under 4 percent per annum these past 300 years. News stories surface on commodity-tied billionaires washed down the tubes in Brazil and elsewhere because of leveraged debt service they can no longer meet. The price level of raw materials like steel, copper, oil and iron ore collapses 35 percent periodically to their cost of production. In 2014 this was the case for metallurgical coal and iron ore because of surplus inventories and overproduction. Volatility is a given (*Figure 31, page 200*).

Walter Energy, a major producer of metallurgical-grade coal, peaked at $141 a share in 2011, but early 2015 ticked under a buck. Acquisitions made top of cycle leveraged Walter's balance sheet to an extreme and precarious condition. Long-term debt of $2.8 billion stood near four times net equity, an even higher ratio for Peabody Energy. Arch Coal's debentures yield over 40 percent to maturity. Absent a sharp turnaround in met-coal prices, down from over $2,000 a ton to $1,300 in 2014, Walter and Arch could face insolvency within two years unless their bankers agree to carry them. In business and the art world, cycles overwhelm leveraged players and some get washed out (*Figure 32, page 201*).

WALTER ENERGY: FROM STARDOM TO THE DUMPS

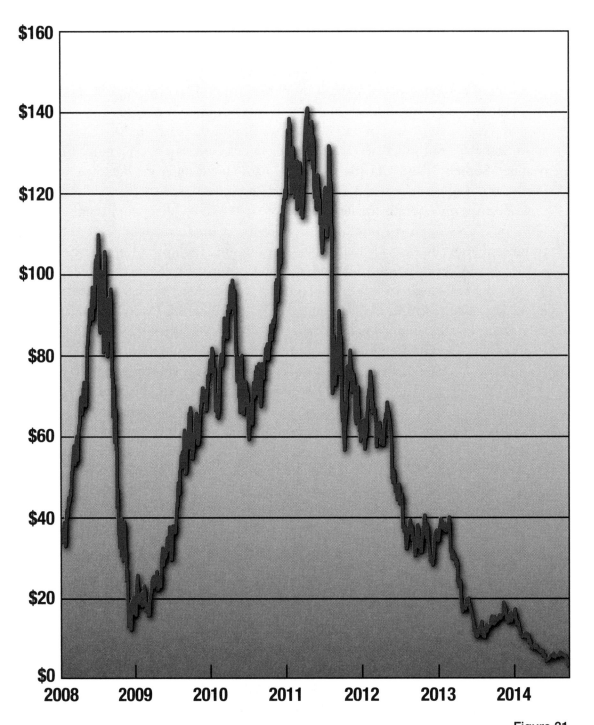

Figure 31
Source: Bloomberg

CONTEMPORARY ART — PRICE INDEX 2004–2014
Base €100 in 2004

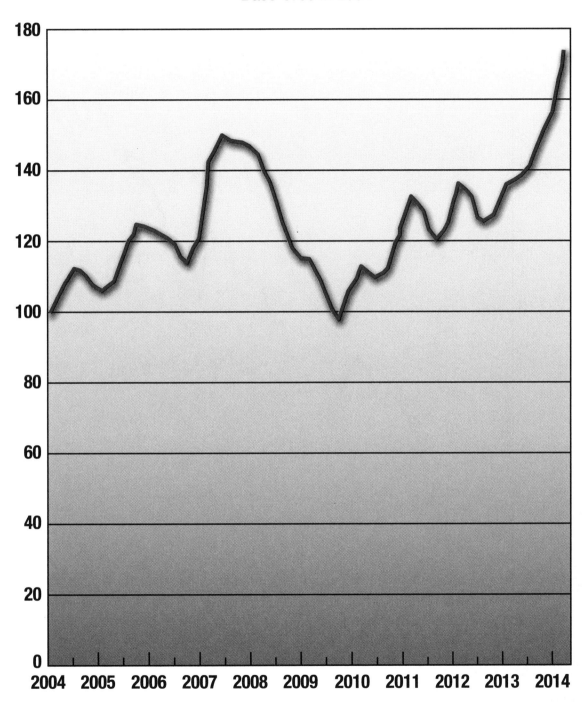

Figure 32

Source: Artprice.com

COMPARISON OF RETURNS, 1900–2012: EQUITIES WIN

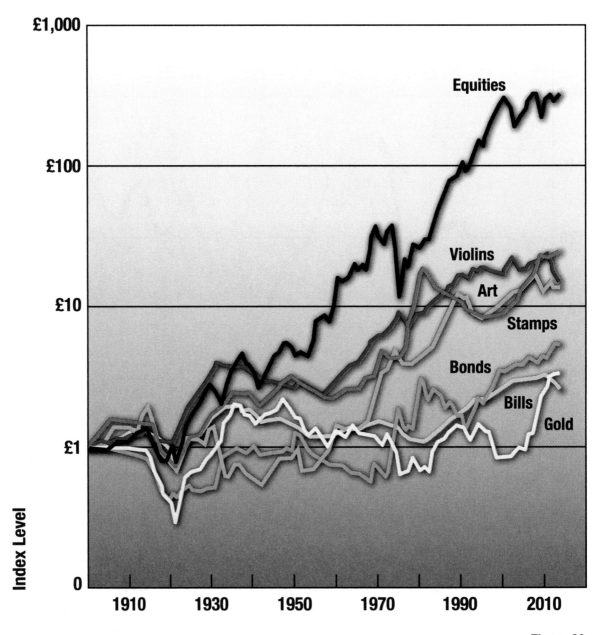

Figure 33

Notes: Figure 33 shows index values in real British pounds for various classes of emotional and financial assets. Each index is set equal to 1 at the beginning of 1900.

Sources: Goetzmann, Renneboog, and Spaenjers (2011) and Artprice.com for data on art; Dimson and Spaenjers (2011) and Stanley Gibbons for data on stamps; Graddy and Margolis (2011, 2013) for data on violins; Dimson, Marsh, and Staunton (2013) for data on equities, bonds, and bills; Global Financial Data and the World Gold Council for data on gold.

To sum up and compare real rates of return for emotional plays vs. financial assets since 1900, this chart is illuminating (*Figure 33*). It's an English database but is good for making final determinations on asset plays. Art comes between stamps and violins, but is outdistanced by equities nearly 150 percent. Note how gold underperforms even Treasury bills. Art and equities since 2000 both traced W-like formations, which were not topped until late 2014. Negative shocks to wealth were felt pretty equally since 2000. Art's real compounded return was 3.1 percent, compared with 7.1 percent for equities. Putting serious capital in art is betting against history unless you're early and smart, knowledgeable and don't seek to make money. Nobody fits all these qualifications, barring a few Swiss collectors dating back over a century.

TWENTY

Step Up! Buy and Hold
the Best of Everything

*When some proud Morgan Stanley father tells me how he bought
his 10-year-old a mint condition Mickey Mantle for $800 and it's now
worth $1,500, so he's got it in the safe deposit box, I figure the kid
is about to have his first investment lesson.*
BARTON BIGGS

I remember walking into Betty Parsons's gallery in 1954 when she was showing Mark Rothko. The canvases seemed suspended in air on the white walls, like colored clouds. They were tagged at $1,200 apiece. I loved Rothko then as much as now, but I had just returned from the Korean War, an unemployed English major in recessionary New York. My only club was the "twenty-five twenty" club: Veterans got $25 a week for 20 weeks maximum while unemployed.

"You can pay me a hundred a month over a year," Betty said. In those days nobody paid cash for art. You pleaded poverty and negotiated from there.

"They're beautiful, Betty, but I have to pass," I said. "The first thing I need to do is find someplace to live."

"You're making a big mistake," Betty said, piercing a ring of cigarette smoke.

I said they were gorgeous and took the elevator down to 57th Street. During the fifties there were maybe a hundred serious collectors of contemporary art in New York. They made the rounds on a Saturday morning and nodded to each other in the slow-rising elevators.

My wife is a leading indicator of risk-averse attitudes. She is uncanny at or close to market bottoms. After the market had declined 700 points in '87 she was thirsting for worldly goods, not paper stock certificates.

"When you lose money on paper," she was saying, "you have nothing to show for it. If you hold diamonds and a waterfront palace in Palm Beach and the market drops, you can still enjoy your life."

204

"That is totally erroneous," I said. "The value of precious metals, diamonds and real estate fluctuates as wildly as securities markets. Gold is off 20 percent since Black Monday. I don't know about Palm Beach. Trump turned his white elephant there into a country club."

"But diamonds always seem to come back. Look at the fuss they made over the Duchess of Windsor's baubles," she objected.

"That was a historic occasion. Sentimentality clouds everyone's sense of intrinsic value."

"Maybe," she said. "Look at all the great Art Deco pieces that have appreciated."

"Maybe so, but fundamentally sound stocks, like beautifully wrought Cartier pins and bracelets, bounce back, too," I said.

"It's not the same," she said. "If you've collected Cartier, Bulgari and Van Cleef & Arpels and they go down, you still enjoy wearing 'em."

"What you're saying is when IBM tanks you get heartburn and have nothing to wear."

"Something like that."

My mother rationalized all the stocks she bought and filed away. Mother owned many "Generals"—Electric, Motors, Foods—and lots of oils. The U.S.'s, too: Steel, Gypsum, whatever. As long as she didn't sell after they dropped, she didn't count her losses. Meanwhile, Boeing, Polaroid, IBM and Xerox were zooming to the moon. I found mildewed stock certificates of Royal Dutch Shell in her steamer trunk sitting in my garage. It was a tough press gathering back the accrued dividends long after her demise.

"So what are you saying?"

"There is an opportunity cost to everything," I said.

"Nothing you say will convince me," my wife said. "I want to feel and enjoy the goods around me when markets turn psychotic. They can't take that away from me."

After Jackie's simulated pearl necklace sold north of $200,000 to the Franklin Mint at Sotheby's, I scrambled up my library ladder and pulled out Guy de Maupassant's short stories and reread *The Necklace*. This is a fitting companion piece to the Mint's successful bid, I guess, tied to some mail order promotion.

In Maupassant's story, Mathilde, a vain housewife, borrows her rich friend's diamond necklace for a ball dress and loses it running for a cab on her way home. Frantic and proud, she slaves for 10 years, ruining her looks to pay for the replacement gems bought at usurious interest. In the end, she tells her story, only to be floored by the news that the borrowed necklace was paste. Maupassant's scalpel is cold and incisive. Covet false values and you'll pay dearly.

The Jackie sale, $34 million for household goods and keepsakes, tempted me to conclude we had started another cycle of trophy investing comparable with the mid-to-late eighties. It was then that the Japanese bought control of Rockefeller Center, later a bankruptcy. Donald Trump flexed his muscles and outbid everyone for the Plaza Hotel, the Pan Am Shuttle, the Castle Hotel and Casino in Atlantic City (bought from Hilton) and Mar-A-Lago, the 124-room white-elephant estate in Palm Beach previously owned by Marjorie Merriweather Post.

Impressionist and modern art made auction records between 1988 and 1989. At that time Walter Annenberg, a great collector of 20th-century art, reallocated some of his billions from his sale to Rupert Murdoch of *TV Guide*. The price was fancy, and Walter put much of it to work in a big block of Wells Fargo, which has done everything a stock should do over a 25-year span. Annenberg followed his friend Warren Buffett on this investment.

Heady prices for art and collectibles in the late eighties were a function of the liquidity in the junk bond market and Japanese speculation with appreciated yen. The Jackie auction was different. I didn't see Annenberg bidding for President Kennedy's golf clubs and cigar humidor. It was B-list wealth raising paddles at Sotheby's. The top 1 percent of the population indulged themselves just like they've been doing since the nineties. The disparity in wealth between guys in work boots and the B list of entertainment and media personae and Wall Street dot-comers didn't stop widening until 2001, and then took over again in 2003. There was no connoisseurship involved in buying John-John's Victorian high chair.

No collectibles market flourishes without well-heeled patrons, whether they be the white-haired Annenberg or the Beverly Hills crowd of Spielberg, Sly Stallone and Arnold Schwarzenegger (who bought JFK's golf clubs). The reciprocal is the middle class putting its spare change into the stock market, funding the Magellan Fund and its ilk. Fittingly, Alan Bond, the Australian operator who gobbled up van Gogh's *Irises*, choked on this $54-million canvas and his $40-million sailboat. He had to forgo over $5 million a year in interest on his capital. Later, Bond stood bankrupted and jailed in Australia.

In 1989, the art market failed to parse the connection between the peaking of prices for collectibles and the final bell for monetary liquidity. In New York it was the RJR Nabisco leveraged buyout of KKR which sopped up The Street's open-to-buy. Over in Tokyo, the recurrent bubble in real estate had stretched to the bursting point. Twenty-five years later they're still in the funk of deflation.

It was early on, lot 23, and John Marion, Sotheby's head auctioneer, his meaty face impassive rather than its normal ebullient sheen, sniffed the air and dropped his blade with dispatch, putting de Kooning into a deep sleep. Sotto voce, he said "Passed," meaning bought in, unsold, burned. It was the May '90 auction of contemporary art at Sotheby's.

"My God!" my wife Toni emoted. "It's a disaster. We're seeing history made tonight." (In the May 2014 contemporary art auctions, de Kooning canvases sped into overdrive, going for tens of millions.) There were so few scattered bids for lots that Marion speeded up his rpms and passed and passed and passed on four Cornell boxes. A smallish Pollock, not even 18 by 36 inches, with a reserve of $1.8 million, scratched its way to $950,000 for a pass. It took 20 years, but Cornell and Pollock now are coveted buys.

Media events like Liberace's pianos with candelabra and Duchess Wally's valuables and Marilyn Monroe's sheath dress exceeded estimated prices by a couple of hundred percent. My wife tells me I'm not a particularly romantic man, so I couldn't understand the celebrity of Liberace's ermine cloak, Noël Coward's Jamaican landscapes or Andy's Art-Deco sitting room. Ditto for Judy's ruby slippers from *The Wizard of Oz.*

I've asked around and pondered the economic significance, the symbolism of the Warhol comet, Jackie O and Marilyn. Nobody—art critics, collectors, economists or even the successful bidders—has a clue. In economic terms, the Jackie bubble was a coincident indicator, something that ticks the day you're looking at it—like 10-day automobile sales. Celebrity auctions, alas, are just high-spirited recreation for planeloads of arrivistes.

What Sotheby's doesn't tell you is that the history of art at auction is more treacherous than the Big Board and, over 50 to 100 years, much less rewarding. Moguls like Alan Bond, who bought *Irises* on leverage, were the perpetrators of the inflation in art, just as Cortés's cutthroats flooded Spain with liquidity in the form of gold. If we blame Mike Milken for all the eighties mufti-pufti on Wall Street, we might as well charge him with Warholmania. Milken, a packager of properties but never a collector, once glanced at a Plexiglas box of mine filled with Parisian street garbage of the sixties.

"This guy Arman packages junk, just like you, Mike," I said. "It falls into the New Realists school."

"One generation's junk becomes the next generation's art," Milken said, shaking his head.

"And vice versa, Mike," I said, nodding my head.

I don't buy Sotheby's argument that Old Masters and Impressionists are in short supply, forever. The Hunts thought they had a lock on the world's silver until everyone melted down his tea service for cold cash. Hundreds of van Goghs better than *Irises* sit in private foundations and museums in Switzerland and Holland. Why shouldn't trustees peel off a few pieces? It'll pay for all the dry dog food their German Shepherds consume after dutifully patrolling the museum corridors at night.

Warren Buffett's portfolio of American Express, Wells Fargo, Coca-Cola and ExxonMobil may underperform year over year, but decade over decade, any viable stock portfolio will put away Renoir, van Gogh and Jasper Johns. Buffett, not Trump or Steve Wynn, ends up as high man. Wynn bought Jeff Koons's *Popeye* sculpture at Sotheby's May '14 auction for $23 million, destined for one of his casinos. Gold still has few takers even as supply and demand finally have reached a point of equilibrium. Central banks could top out any rally with sales of a hundred pounds of inventory. Trump now is litigating to get his franchised name off two casinos in Atlantic City, Trump Plaza and Trump Taj Mahal.

When I was young and foolish, I stored half a dozen banjos in my closet against a rainy day, pawn shop fodder. Thirty years later, the world learned that Andy Warhol outdid us all as the professional squirrel. The final service for Andy Warhol did not take place at graveside. The auctioning of Andy's worldly goods at Sotheby's mushroomed into an ultimate happening, dwarfing anything concocted at the Factory. Andy had to be smiling down from his warehouse in the sky onto the great barn that is Sotheby's on 72nd Street and York Avenue. They gave him a memorial service fit for an Egyptian pharaoh, his goods laid out, tagged in methodical piles in auction rooms. Missing was Andy, wrapped up, mummified in bandages, his signature camera dangling from his neck.

I hit Sotheby's initial viewing on April 23, 1988, and it was like Bloomies on Christmas Eve. A jostling crowd spanned a couple of generations, with a sprinkling of Viennese accents. Pop art was collected avidly by the Germans and Swiss in the sixties, and dealers had come over to see what's on. Andy's lifelong passionate shopper complex helped his artistic development. Many of the folk themes in his collection foreshadowed the original *Campbell's Soup Cans*. Iconography of Coca-Cola signs adumbrated his huge *Dollar Sign* paintings. Aside from Picasso, few artists have made it into nine figures and more, as Andy did.

Andy was king of the flea markets. Maybe 300 watches, multiple services of dishes, silver cigarette cases from the forties by the dozen, French silver dressing-table sets and four-piece tea and coffee sets from the mid-twenties. If Andy saw a catchy shaped urinal in a rundown motel outside of Cleveland, he'd buy it for kicks.

Andy's general manager, Fred Hughes, now gone, gets credit for making Andy the only court painter of the 20th century. Everyone rode downtown to the

Factory for his portrait sitting. Andy would snap a couple of hundred black-and-white Polaroid shots in two hours, paste 'em on a wall and then single out the one he'd paint. First, female sitters had to submit themselves for makeup. Lipstick, eyes penciled black and skin whitened into a stark mask with grease paint. Fifty thousand bucks got you two square canvases, 40×40 inches. Andy spent no more than a few hours on the process. You made your appointment like you were going to the hair colorist or barber. Sinatra had a cold the day my beautiful wife sat for Andy, so she picked up a double session.

Fifty years from now, art scholars will draw the analogy between Warhol, portrait painter of 20th-century society (Judy, Liza, Jackie and Marilyn), and Velázquez, court painter of Spanish royalty in the 17th century. Cookie jars and wristwatches were just incidentals. Andy treated the world as one great flea market worth browsing through. He caught the essence of feminine sexiness with a Polaroid shot and transformed it into a mask accented with blackened eyes and red-hot lips. Cher, Liza, Madonna, they all learned from Andy.

David Rockefeller bought art in the sixties for his Chase Bank and was snickered at behind his back by his employees for hanging Abstract Expressionist work at One Chase Manhattan Plaza. At its peak, the collection was worth more than this asbestos-ridden corporate headquarters, close to a billion. The corporate sector, until the eighties, stuck to Currier and Ives prints and English hunting scenes of horses and hounds. Today, almost every major corporation has a contemporary art advisor on its staff, and even straitlaced IBM built a major gallery beneath its corporate headquarters in New York, but closed it down in its '93 downsizing.

Back in 1973, when Robert and Ethel Scull were in the midst of an ugly divorce, they auctioned part of their contemporary art collection, 50 pieces. The sale included big names in Pop art—Claes Oldenburg, Jasper Johns and Robert Rauschenberg. Sotheby's grossed $2.2 million, with many pieces selling under maximum estimates. It was a front-page story in the *New York Times*. Today, a Jasper Johns canvas ticks above $35 million, depending on its date of production. Rauschenberg picketed outside of Sotheby's, claiming artists should share in the appreciation of their works. This is a naïve position. I never found a painter who would guarantee me against loss or promise not to paint a dozen canvases like the one he just sold me.

The Sculls started a trend of imitators, compulsive collectors like the Saatchi brothers who buy and sell en masse works of newly emerging art movements they think have celebrity potential. Although the Sculls made 20 times on their money, 25 years later such a collection would gross north of $500 million. Art, like the stock market, has become a commodity. Connoisseurs and syndicates buy and sell sectors like program traders. At Sotheby's the auction prices ripple on the screen, denominated in yen, pounds, euros, even dollars.

If you think the stock market is rigged from time to time by the Boeskys of the world or by front-running program traders, the auction markets remain snake pits, fathomable only by worldly dealers and collectors of impeccable connoisseurship. It is axiomatic that bargains don't exist at Sotheby's or elsewhere. Reserve prices are pegged at the prevailing market level for important pieces. Dealers are keyed into the auction process and may bid up faltering prices to protect their inventory carry valuation. Even some collectors and institutions paint the tape, as we say on The Street, with wild bids. You do better negotiating for unsold pieces with Sotheby's after the auction is history.

What gives an evening auction a sense of theater is the youthful high spirits of the new class of Russian moguls, rock stars, Beverly Hills Rambos and dot-coms from Seattle who flex their muscles vocally or with numbered paddles. Sixty thousand viewers surveyed Warhol's goods. You needed only a couple of dozen crazies and corporate bidders seeking free publicity to bid up Andy's cookie jars, watches and marble-sized zircons. I bid on one piece, a four-foot construction by Arman. Its subject was Andy's amphetamines cascading out of their bottles. The low estimate was $8,000, but I dropped out in the mid-thirties.

When I told my wife how much I had bid, she stepped on my foot and yelled "Idiot!" I accepted my punishment sheepishly but vowed under my breath to get even at the late Aga Khan III jewelry auction. I would sit on her paddle. Auction houses are awash in diamonds and pearls spanning several decades if not a century of conspicuous consumption here and abroad. The Duchess Wally's baubles grossed $50 million.

When it comes to art, few tycoons find time to do it themselves. Decades ago, I asked Norton Simon why he collected world-class art and second-class companies. He told me he had less time to spend on art than on his corporate remakes. Today, art consultants and dealers build collections for those anointed with high nine-figure bankrolls. How is some Chinese manufacturer of radial tires or cellphones, who has slaved away for 40 years after Pax MacArthur, going to know what to pay for a Jackson Pollock drip canvas? For him, there is no loss of face paying a $10-million entry fee. Meanwhile, the serious American collector cries himself to sleep, moaning over the fact that our Pacific Rim competitors buy our goods with depreciated dollars.

Back in 1983, Marshall Cogan and Steve Swid, Wall Streeters of my generation, tried to buy Sotheby's when it was a publicly traded equity in London. Management at Sotheby's sought protection from the Monopolies and Mergers Commission there, claiming it would be a dark stain on Britain's heritage to allow two upstart New Yorkers to carry away such a prize. I sensed an undertone of Anglo anti-Semitism. Sotheby's had been exporting Britain's heritage for over 200 years in the form of wall hangings, furniture and fixtures, but this was overlooked by the commission and they sided with management. (Very few hostile deals win, anywhere.)

Swid and Cogan flew back to New York empty-handed. Shortly thereafter, Sotheby's sought out Adolph Alfred Taubman as its white knight, albeit he was American. A few telephone calls later, Taubman formed a congenial partnership with Henry Ford II, Max Fisher, Milton Petrie, Leslie Wexner, Ann Getty, et al. Taubman's group deaccessioned 24 percent of their holding, but Sotheby's didn't come cheap. Salomon priced her at seven times book value and at 15 times the previous year's fully diluted earnings. The stock tripled by 1989 and then got cut apart when the spring '90 auction prices tumbled some 30 percent. By 2000, Sotheby's and Christie's admitted they had conspired in setting commission rates. The settlement ran into hundreds of millions.

Swid and Cogan remained serious collectors of contemporary art. They wanted to own Sotheby's for its staff of cognoscenti who would advise them on building an encompassing collection. They claimed making money was secondary. Nobody, except me, believes them, then or now. For me, Sotheby's is a leading indicator of the world's confidence level or lack thereof. Like investing, the most difficult things to buy normally turn out most valuable, but it may take 10 or 20 years before the public market confirms your early picks.

Gerald Reitlinger in his *Economics of Taste* wrote about the drastic comeuppance of art after the Great Crash. Prices stayed dull until the Allied landing in Italy in September of 1943. Credit and liquidity were tight, with a feeling of guilt in buying fine art amid the ravages of war, when the peoples of the Western world tightened their belts. Even after the war, there was no sense of confidence in the future when national systems lay in ruins. The dull period for art lasted from 1939 until 1952. Postwar stocks didn't elevate until the early fifties, either. Investment managers awaiting a big recession completely missed the concept of pent-up consumer demand fueling GDP momentum. Stocks yielded more than bonds then. A phenomenon that resurfaced during 2014.

Post–Great Crash, millionaires stopped outbidding each other for art. In London during the 1931–'32 auctions only eight paintings exceeded 1,400 guineas, the lowest numbers since the 1870s. The top auction price was for Frans Hals's *Smuggler*.

It made £3,600. You could barely give away Sargent's work. Impressionist and Postimpressionist works at the 1939 auctions sold for petty cash. Van Gogh's *Olive Trees* had to be bought in at £4,000 at Sotheby's. Picasso's work went for maybe a hundred pounds, along with Rouault and Braque. This is comparable to 90 percent declines in dot-com paper like Amazon and Yahoo during 2001.

An exceptional Renoir fetched no more than £10,000. Modiglianis and Monets were dumped in private sales in the war-anxious year of 1940 for the equivalent of $2,000. As a frame of reference, Old Masters—Rembrandt, Velázquez and Botticelli—made between £11,000 and £13,000, which was what English horse-and-jockey canvases then fetched.

1959 Sale Prices at Sotheby's (in GBP)

Picasso	La belle Hollandaise (1905)	55,000
Van Gogh	Bridge at Asnières (bought in)	45,000
Cézanne	Portrait of Madame Cézanne	40,000
Braque	Woman with a Mandolin	36,000
Cézanne	Self-Portrait	32,000
Degas	Three Dancers Rehearsing	22,000
Renoir	Ambroise Vollard as a Bullfighter	22,000
Renoir	Dead Pheasant in the Snow	19,000
Renoir	Misia Sert (National Gallery)	16,000
Cézanne	L'Assiette bleue	17,000
Braque	Still Life	15,000
Toulouse-Lautrec	Return from the Shoot	15,000
Toulouse-Lautrec	Marcelle Lender	13,000
Monet	Le Bassin aux Nymphéas	13,000
Modigliani	Portrait of Beatrice Hastings	12,000

Source: *The Economics of Taste*

I liked Reitlinger's old-world phrasing: "Historians of the changes of taste should not allow a crystal ball to form any part of their library equipment." Reitlinger then plunged ahead in 1961 and forecast a return to pictorial realism, art becoming a vehicle of propaganda as practiced in the Marxist world. Recent prices for Pollock and Jasper Johns point-blank refute his hypothesis.

Sotheby's, by 1988, not to miss a turn, held its first auction in the Soviet Union, much of it semi-abstract work. Prices exceeded estimates by 200 percent. Reitlinger, in 1961, suggested art could move out of reach of the individual buyer: "A world without art shops or sales rooms is not impossible." Museums were destined to own everything down to the last glass paperweight. This was another bad call.

A couple of times a year I go on the road to see clients. I always learn something. One of my favorites in Seattle was telling me about his 25th class reunion at Yale. At dinner, he was seated next to William Buckley, and my client Ned was telling him how Bill was surely the class's most distinguished alumnus.

"No, no," Bill said. "See that big guy over there with the round face. He's the most successful of us all."

"But I don't know who he is," Ned said.

"It's Claes Oldenburg, the Pop artist," Buckley said. "Come on, I'll introduce you."

"So what did you do?" I asked.

"What could I do? I went over and said I didn't remember him but I wanted to get to know him. I told him I wanted to consider a piece of his work. He could air-express me anything representative, along with a catalog. I figured if he was the best, I should own something." Ned got a gigantic clothespin piece for his front lawn.

From all this emerges bedrock stuff. Step up, buy and hold the best of everything. Leave ragamuffins to garmentos. If I had put Antonio Stradivari in my closet and not a bunch of commodity-class banjos, I'd be outbidding David Geffen on the auction floor at York and 72nd. If less pictorial, the Dow Jones Index is not as pricey as a canvas of some model Renoir picked up in the Paris vegetable market and painted as if she were an earth goddess. Google and Apple are bedrock reality, and those rosy-buttocked females, some octogenarian's squeeze?

I miss the ethereal stock market we had in the late fifties and early sixties. Silicon transistors came of age, along with Syntex's birth control pills, Boeing's 707, Polaroid's fast film and RCA color television. Growth stocks sported real earnings, not non-GAAP EBITDA. Today, our market waxes manic-depressive. Art during the past decade acted like a growth stock at 50 times earnings. Banks now margin art as readily as Treasury bonds. Art and equities forever swing violently throughout history. Art prices won't peak until we experience major wealth destruction running into trillions.

TWENTY-ONE

How to Deal with Technology Bubbles

I'm amazed how money managers deal or fail to deal with reality, how they rationalize valuations and take action based on what they see and expect to unfold. I try to recognize my own fallibility, correct it and be right more times than not. Money management is a survival battle of many short-term decisions and a few long-term calls. You must do both relatively well to succeed. If you're a perfectionist, visit some grave site where nobody talks back and you no longer have to jump through rings of fire and be judged.

I've seen everything over the last 50 years. If you flanked two giant trash cans beside me, one marked "right" and the other "wrong," both would be nearly filled to the brim, but I cut stupidities short and let the right decisions sail on and on. If you're good, over time you develop something called apperceptive mass, the equivalent of battlefield presence. I learned that in the Korean War. You sense how to keep yourself out of trouble by anticipating what's out there against you and buckling down before all hell breaks loose.

I wrote much of this chapter mid-summer 2001 when NASDAQ was in tatters and the economy stalled out. Democrats and Republicans were at odds on how to revive the setting. Icons of the new Gilded Age had crumbled—Cisco Systems, Yahoo and Amazon. Alan Greenspan, seemingly a subconscious captive of Wall Street, cut the federal funds rate bimonthly. The Street had discarded its belief in a V-shaped economic recovery, tired of jumping the gun.

Nobody wanted as yet to deal with reality, that corporate earnings were crumbling. This 2001–'02 slowdown was more than an inventory correction. Capital spending, fueled by the telecommunications sector and the Internet, hit a wall and wouldn't recover for years. None of the dot-coms and only a handful of the mid-nineties telecommunications footprints were bankable. Their business plans couldn't convince underwriters that corporate cash flow would even cover interest

expense. Forget about building out networks. There were too many wireless operators and long-distance telephony properties out there fighting for market share and
new subscribers. Internet enablers like Exodus cringed in the shadows darkening
their headquarters. Some mighty capitalizations traded in single digits—Nortel
Networks, Lucent Technologies and JDS Uniphase. Others, who still sported liquid balance sheets—Corning, Cisco and EMC—sold in the mid-teens after hitting
par in mid-2000. Earnings were measured in pennies per share, no longer dollars.

The new Gilded Age started the day after we beat Saddam (the first time).
It lasted a decade but ended in disarray. NASDAQ down over 60 percent in
12 months. Amazon, Yahoo and Cisco crumbling between 80 percent and 90
percent. It wasn't just technology that bit the dust. Some proud blue chips had
bleached out. Procter & Gamble, McDonald's and Coca-Cola struggled to grow
their revenue lines, no longer category killers. Properties like Polaroid and Xerox
had evolved into serious credit risks.

By the summer of '01, the penalty for preannouncing quarterly numbers below
the analysts' consensus (management's guidance) had risen from 10 percent to 30
percent. Nowadays, in 2014, the haircut is 5 percent to 10 percent. Earnings warn-
ings from JDS Uniphase, Nokia and EMC, announced after 4:00 p.m., dropped
these properties 30 percent overnight. Few tech houses could grow revenues
sequentially, and operating margins now were impacted by pricing concessions.
Corning bragged about staying solvent. It had just written off $5 billion in plant
and inventories. These factories were less than a year old or partially constructed.

Earnings misses were as wide as a church door. Instead of 20-cent quarters,
managements reported pennies per share or deficits. If there were any believers
in the efficient-market theory left standing, the rapid wealth destruction in technology properties should have snuffed them out. One analyst finally got it right.
Management guidance was worth what it cost to splice into a corporate conference
call. It's understandable that Merrill Lynch couldn't manage its quarterly earnings
vs. the consensus, but even Merck had no reserves left to pump into its numbers—
too many drugs coming off patent and new blockbusters like Fosamax and Vioxx
were anniversarying strong numbers and flattening out.

Economists still debated whether the country would succumb to recession,
two negative GDP quarters. The Dow Industrials had settled down near 10,000
and the S&P 500 Index eased below 1,200. Market pundits picked up on historical comparisons of stagnation. The Dow had breached 10,000 early in 1999.
Valuation comparisons with the eighties and early nineties suggested that this
market with comparable interest rates on Treasuries, around 5.5 percent, could

stand 30 percent overvalued unless corporate earnings bounced back at least 10 percent in 2002.

The consensus on earnings for the S&P 500 had slid steadily since yearend 2000 from $60 a share for 2001 to $50. Nobody dared forecast a recovery of more than 10 percent for 2002. Even at 1,100 the market would be selling at 20 times next year's earnings projection. There have been so many additions and deletions to the Dow Industrials and S&P 500 over the years that historical comparisons are shaky. The most quantitatively based research house, Sanford C. Bernstein, pointed out that options issuance since the mid-nineties, along with aggressive actuarial assumptions on defined benefit pension plans, accounted for three percentage points of the 9 percent compound earnings growth over the previous five years.

With the massive write-offs for impaired goodwill, corporate restructuring and employee terminations, an accurate appraisal of earnings growth was certainly less than was reported using generally accepted accounting conventions. Microsoft, Cisco, Corning, Nortel and Intel had written off approximately $30 billion by the summer of '01, JDS Uniphase alone, $40 billion. The only way of rationalizing the valuation structure of the market late in '01 was to move further down the list of large capitalizations on the index. The median price-earnings ratio was low teens once you got past the 30 to 40 times forward earnings projections for Microsoft, General Electric, Cisco, Intel and Oracle.

After a breakfast meeting of the Democratic Leadership Council in Jon Tisch's Regency Hotel, I came out into the Park Avenue sunlight reflecting that the party had taken a fiscal stand more conservative than the Republicans'. Joe Lieberman had voted against the tax cut. Nobody wanted to touch the current surplus of Social Security and Medicare. You couldn't get elected pushing for major tax cuts. Both parties had their fingers crossed, hoping the economic cycle would bottom out before 2002, resigned to a 5 percent unemployment level. After all, unemployment was a lagging indicator—right? I was now resigned to a very slow recovery. I sold our oil drillers and bought more HMOs and tobacco stocks. The drillers melted away, but the HMOs rallied, their growth rates intact, valuation too cheap. The market for now was allergic to Philip Morris and Loews. They were last year's big movers. Few properties are repeaters.

I ran more numbers on tech's destruction. Capital spending for information technology is pretty much a four-year cycle because the hardware's depreciation cycle is four to five years. We rested in the first down year for capital spending, so at least another year of drought is in the cards. Tech stocks still sold on the assumption that 2002 would be a strong recovery year, that comparisons would turn easier by the first quarter of '02. This point of view was shaping up more 'n' more as a gut call with no backup. My memory of the Internet bubble of 2000–2001 was indelible. Carnage in the biggest capitalization names in the NASDAQ 100 had left many red faces among managements, analysts and money managers.

NASDAQ 100's Top 12
Yearend 2001 Capitalizations

Company Name	Yearend 2001 Market Value (billions)	% Change from 52-Week High
Microsoft	344	-20.7
Intel	186	-63.3
Cisco Systems	118	-76.9
Oracle	98	-62.1
Dell Computer	66	-53.2
Amgen	60	-53.2
Sun Microsystems	45	-78.2
Qualcomm	44	-45.2
WorldCom	41	-70.3
Comcast	38	-16.0
Ericsson	34	-81.2
Applied Materials	34	-54.7

When you move down the list to the Internet infrastructure providers, the wipeout was complete. High debt levels adumbrated coming restructurings and bankruptcies. Capital markets shut their doors on these properties early in 2001. Stocks like Akamai Technologies and Inktomi mid-2000 sold at 80 to 100 times revenues. Analysts used 10-year discounted cash flow models to justify recommendations. Exodus Communications at its peak sported a market capitalization approaching $35 billion. The stock later traded at $1.41 a share, or $800 million. This was predictable pure wealth destruction. Today, I disremember Exodus.

Exodus was no more than a string of regional computer server farms purveying capacity to Web-hosting customers. This property was widely owned by tech funds and institutions, strongly recommended by JPMorgan Chase. Its $35-billion market cap was equivalent to Alcan Aluminum or Dow Chemical. Because Exodus is not a household name its demise didn't make page one of the financial press.

Internet Infrastructure Deconstructs

Company Name	Yearend 2001 Market Value (millions)	% Change from 52-Week High
Akamai	929	93.8
Digital Island	281	93.0
Equinix	82	93.8
Exodus Communications	797	98.0
Inktomi	1,078	94.2
Loudcloud	152	71.4
Metromedia Fiber Network	853	96.8
StorageNetworks	1,016	93.6
Universal Access	363	90.9
WebEx Communications	1,046	57.1

Intel kicked off the nineties at 10 times earnings, perceived as a cyclical growth stock. By 1998, Intel sold at 30 times forward 12-months earnings and was accepted as a great growth story. Today, no longer. Cisco at its peak sold over $80, at 100 times projected earnings. In the eyes of perceptive money managers today, it is a capital goods supplier to an overbuilt telecommunications industry. Maybe it is worth 10 times earnings. Cisco wouldn't earn more than pennies per share in 2001. John Chambers, its headman, was as bewildered as the analysts who listened to his conference calls. Cisco had just written off $2.5 billion in inventory it had amassed over the past 12 months. Let's not blame Alan Greenspan for everything. This business cycle died of old age. There was too much mindless capital spending and the consumer stood loaned up to his eyeballs. Nobody wanted to buy banner advertising on Yahoo's website. The ads drew no response. The headman at Yahoo took early retirement. DoubleClick, the advertising purveyor to websites, had downsized. Its headman, Kevin O'Connor, told me he was shorting Yahoo. Why not? It was a good hedge against his becalmed property.

When all else fails, money managers, even analysts, resort to the metric of revenues to market capitalization. It's a legitimate way of playing the darkest-before-dawn scenario, when big-cap tech properties like Cisco have no earnings but tens of billions in revenues. Yahoo at its peak sold at over 100 times revenues. Even Amazon was way up there, but both had fallen off our radar screen of the 20 largest tech properties outstanding.

Ten Largest Technology Stocks: Price to Revenues (Yearend 2001)

	Market Cap (Billions)	Trailing 5-Yr Average Price/Sales	Trailing 3-Yr Average Price/Sales	Trailing Year Price/Sales	Forward Year Price/ Sales
Microsoft	$357	16.4	18.9	14.3	12.3
Intel	$206	7.4	8.8	6.8	7.8
IBM	$184	1.8	2.2	2.0	2.2
Cisco Systems	$141	14.1	17.7	5.8	7.5
Oracle	$97	9.0	11.5	9.0	8.1
Dell	$72	3.5	4.1	2.2	2.2
Texas Instruments	$61	4.9	6.9	5.7	7.5
Sun Microsystems	$55	4.3	6.1	3.2	3.3
Qualcomm	$51	8.2	12.1	19.5	19.8
Hewlett-Packard	$49	1.8	2.0	1.0	1.1

Late 2014, Cisco seemed cheap at 2.6 times revenues (it was historically at seven times revenues), but this is still a big absolute ratio for a company whose gross margins dropped from 62 percent to 51 percent. Once you believe that the price-to-revenues metric is fair, you analyze gross margins and then extrapolate revenue growth. For a tech stock to be considered cheap, it had to meet all these metrics. Because we believed capital spending for information technology would come back slowly in 2015, very few properties enticed us. Moving down to mid-sized properties, many were priced for perfection. Few managements had dealt with the necessity of scaling back fixed and variable overhead to balance a possible shortfall in new orders. There were no bargains, anywhere, excepting Hewlett-Packard, selling at nine times earnings with a free cash flow yield over 10 percent.

Currently, the median price-to-sales ratio for major Internet properties still rests in bubble territory. It approximates a nine-times multiple, even 7.5 times forward 12-months numbers. Practically overnight, Twitter was cut in half at midyear '14 but steadied at Facebook's 10-times-revenues metric. Amazon looks like a bargain at 1.3 times forward revenues, but Jeff Bezos brings next to nothing down to the bottom line. Wall Street's analysts have scribbled hundreds of pages on why Amazon is the next Wal-Mart, with comparable operating profit margins. I'm holding my breath.

Big Capitalization Technology Stocks: Price to Earnings (February 2015)

	Market Cap (Billions)	Trailing 5-Yr Average Price/Sales	Trailing 3-Yr Average Price/Sales	Trailing Year Price/Sales	Forward Year Price/ Sales
Microsoft	$349	3.5	3.8	3.8	3.7
Intel	$164	2.5	2.5	3.0	2.8
IBM	$156	2.0	2.0	1.7	1.8
Cisco Systems	$141	2.6	2.5	3.1	3.0
Oracle	$190	4.4	4.4	5.0	4.1
Texas Instruments	$58	3.3	3.4	4.6	4.4
Qualcomm	$111	5.4	5.4	4.3	4.2
Hewlett-Packard	$70	0.5	0.4	0.7	0.6

Average monthly price changes for the NASDAQ Composite Index ran above 11 percent during 2001, a high watermark for the index since its creation in 1971. The 2001 technology bubble stands as the fitting metaphor for the shabby decadence of Wall Street's so-called star analysts and their underwriting houses, who had hyped and flogged their wares, riding them down 80 percent to 90 percent before turning "neutral." Corporate managements' flimflam game was over, too. No longer could they manage the earnings consensus. Some, like Cisco and JDS Uniphase, even stopped issuing "guidance." Too much obsolete inventory rested uncrated in their warehouses. Corporate overhead, decimated by tens of thousands of engineers, still remained scaled for a revenue base at least double the size of what they were experiencing. Many of us sat silently on our motorcycles, crash helmets snugly buckled, waiting for the natural bottom. Technology, after all, is a cyclical growth business. Comeback! Comeback! Anyone? The valuation metrics, even after the carnage, rested on stilts. During the summer of '01, technology properties were priced for a major earnings recovery in '02. Without that, its big-cap names—Cisco, Intel, even Microsoft—would be schmeissed again.

There is a cogent takeaway for individual investors. Cisco's John Chambers was blindsided by the splurge in capital spending by his customers. He over-ordered inventories and extended credit to marginal industry players while his stock was selling at 80 times forward 12-months' earnings. Mid-2014 he was still downsizing, cutting employment by 6,000. An armchair observer could have turned down tech as overvalued looking at five-year comparisons of price-to-revenues metrics.

Anyone who pays more than two times the growth rate for anything is also looking for heartburn. Normally, I won't pay more than four times revenues for anything that walks. Facebook, at 10 times revenues, is my only luxury, but it sells at 20 times enterprise value, a metric that outweighs its revenue multiplier.

More than a decade after the bubble, tech houses like Intel, IBM, Cisco and Microsoft sell at subpar price-earnings ratios. The major exception is Internet properties. Overvaluation of the technology sector took 25 years to correct. It now sells on parity with the S&P 500 Index—actually, late 2014, at a slight discount.

Internet Properties:
Price to Revenues (February 2015)

	Market Cap ($billions)	Price/Revenues CY14	Price/Revenues Est. CY15
Google	365.4	7.0	6.0
Facebook	211.1	16.9	12.3
Amazon	175.5	2.0	1.7
Priceline	54.9	6.5	5.7
Yahoo	41.2	9.4	9.3
Salesforce.com	37.6	9.2	7.0
Twitter	30.1	21.5	12.8
LinkedIn	28.9	13.0	9.7
Netflix	27.0	4.9	4.0
Workaday	16.8	22.1	15.2
Yelp	4.0	10.7	7.1
Mean		11.2	8.3
Median		9.4	7.1

PART IV
The Muscle Flexors

GEORGE BELLOWS, *JACK DEMPSEY AND FIRPO*, 1924

TWENTY-TWO

The Milken Meteor Struck the Establishment

*M*y wife caught me rummaging through her lingerie drawer. I was eyeing the label on a yellow spandex-and-nylon wash 'n' wear brassiere made by Warner's, assembled in Mexico, with U.S. components. Years ago, it sold for $16.50 at upscale department stores.

"You're turning crazy on me in your old age?" Toni asked.

"No, no. I'm looking for a Playtex bra. I want to compare it with higher pricepoint goods. Where it's made, how it looks."

"I don't believe you," she said. "But you won't find Playtex goods in my drawer."

"Well, call the lingerie department at K-Mart and get me the info," I said.

K-Mart carried the line, starting at $9.90 and going into the high twenties. A couple of hundred million Playtex bras are made in the USA, but I don't know whether 100 million females over 12 years old read labels. Hand wash, no bleach. Line dry, no iron.

Past decades saw International Playtex recapitalized at least five times. It was acquired by Meshulam Riklis of Rapid-American. From there it went to Esmark, bought by Beatrice Companies in 1985. BCI Holdings acquired Beatrice in an LBO in 1984, and later Playtex became a stand-alone LBO by the same management that ran it for all the predecessor owners. I was trying to figure out whether I should buy their high yield paper. This was a long time ago.

In the dog days of the summer of '82, I remember Milken calling me on International Harvester Credit Corporation bonds. They traded at 30 cents on the dollar because the insurance companies wanted this tainted paper off their books. Harvester was in the midst of being downsized, if not bankrupted. Milken sent his research people out to the farm belt to count the tractors in the distributors' showrooms. Simple arithmetic suggested more than enough marked-down inventory to cover the bonds, which I construed as a C credit.

Milken did a similar asset coverage exercise on Chrysler Financial. Unless you do this kind of research—stay away. Milken's early success was as a researcher/trader in iffy workout paper. There are dozens of guys behind unmarked doors who still do this.

The junk market made Milken and a coterie of gutsy managements super-rich. When the paper improved in quality, issuers called it away from us. Passive investors who owned subordinated paper took entrepreneurial risk, sweated bullets and ended up with peanuts. As Carl Icahn leveled, "If you want a friend, buy a dog."

Forty years ago, Textron, Northwest Industries, Rapid-American, Loews, Gulf & Western and Teledyne raised billions in high yield paper for acquisitions of insurance underwriters and industrial properties. For years, credit agencies refused to rate some of these bonds because frugal managements wouldn't pay their asking fees. Larry Tisch emerged as an establishment industrialist controlling CNA Insurance, Lorillard and Diamond Offshore Drilling. He didn't overpay.

One generation's junk becomes the next generation's prime paper and vice versa. In the doggy days of '82, some $40 billion of investment-grade paper lapsed into the fallen-angel category. It included faded blue chips like Chrysler, International Harvester and Bethlehem Steel. Leverage didn't cause the demise of basic industrials in steel, farm equipment, autos and even nuclear utilities. Just shortsighted managements.

Old Wall Street then wasn't keen on raising money for entrepreneurial managers, many of them Jewish. Old-line investment banking houses concentrated on their blue-chip clients, like Texaco and Phillips Petroleum, who posted 4 percent rates of return on capital. Drexel looked elsewhere for its clientele. Texaco and Phillips later on still worked down their leverage on protective buybacks of equity caused by hostile takeover plays from Icahn and others. Wall Street's lawyers prescribed poison pills and golden parachutes to protect the castles.

The concept of 30 percent annualized rates of return, as executed by high metabolic overachievers like Carl Icahn, worked. It was adopted by unions and employee groups in buyout proposals like those by United Airlines pilots and the guys driving the UPS brown trucks. Credit Mike Milken for raising the consciousness of American businessmen.

It took Milken most of the eighties to bridge the gap between stock market quotes for companies and their real value in the business world. Remember Tobin's Q ratio? Currently, the Q ratio is over 250 percent so there ain't no asset value steals around. Milken lived by the Q, creating the distribution machinery at Drexel for high yield paper that got deals done for LBO operators, both hostile and friendly. Fearless entrepreneurs of the eighties tapped this market with great success, notably Rupert Murdoch, John Kluge and Ron Perelman (*Figure 34, page 228*).

Dozens of corporations have employed junk to recapitalize themselves, either going private or making self-tenders that have preserved their independence during hostile takeover fights. Establishment corporations like Gillette, Texaco, Phillips Petroleum and Unocal were saddled with billions in high yield debt after jousting with Carl Icahn, T. Boone Pickens, et al. Owens-Corning Fiberglas didn't make it when all the asbestos litigation hit their overleveraged balance sheet. American Express wrote off $180 million in asbestos-related high yield paper held in their annuity accounts.

The public, whether it knows it or not, is invested in "junk" despite its pejorative connotation. Many insurance underwriters have built their annuity business around a portfolio of high yield bonds. If you're offering investors a guaranteed rate of return of 5 percent and your portfolio yields 7 percent, the two-point spread becomes operating profits. Just so long as the junk paper doesn't default, you have a comfortable "spread" business.

The "high yield" market is defined as any loan below investment grade. If you lend your brother-in-law a thousand bucks, unsecured, that's a high yield loan, particularly if he's between jobs. There are only 800 companies in the country with investment-grade ratings. The ratings agencies, Moody's and Standard & Poor's, lag a year or two behind the realities. Deteriorating credits get downgraded and improving credits upgraded, in time. An AAA rating has nowhere to go but down, so Milken said. A single-B rating can improve if the underlying business thrives. You make money in junk bonds as an investor when interest rates decline or your underlying company thrives.

J.P. Morgan used low-grade paper, $225 million of 5 percent bonds, to buy U.S. Steel from Andrew Carnegie at the turn of the century. It became a high-grade credit and then sank back, until by summer of '82 the steel industry faced multiple bankruptcies. Buying steel paper debentures, preferreds and convertibles at the bottom of the recession was a gut industry play. As late as 1988, Bethlehem Steel was in arrears on its preferred dividends, subsequently restored. Timely investing locked in 20 percent annualized rates of return.

High yield specialists converse as abstrusely as a couple of brain surgeons in the operating room. There is a variety of paper designed for particular corporate purposes and earmarked for specific "players." This is what a conversation between my bond trader and me sounds like:

TOBIN'S Q RATIO 1900–2015
as of January 2015

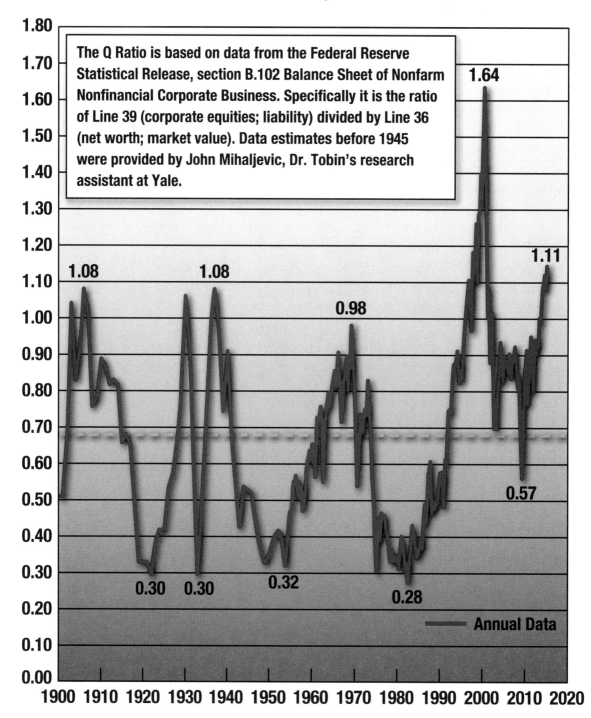

The Q Ratio is based on data from the Federal Reserve Statistical Release, section B.102 Balance Sheet of Nonfarm Nonfinancial Corporate Business. Specifically it is the ratio of Line 39 (corporate equities; liability) divided by Line 36 (net worth; market value). Data estimates before 1945 were provided by John Mihaljevic, Dr. Tobin's research assistant at Yale.

Figure 34
Source: Advisor Perspectives, Inc.

TRADER JIM: XYZ has a new issue coming next March. I like this double-B credit.

MTS: Give me the yield to first call and yield to maturity. Also the TED spread and the premium on new-issue double Bs to the market.

TRADER JIM: The yield to first call is 13.5 percent and the yield to maturity 14 percent. There is a new-issue premium of 50 basis points. It's non-callable for four years, but there's no protection in the indenture for releveraging. The TED spread is 70 basis points and widening.

Analytical terms can be technical. If you want to be a player, you'd better know what a MAD ratio is (the ratio of the market value of debt to the market value of debt plus equity). This ratio measures what percent of the total value of a company is debt. The lower your MAD, the better. An "adjusted MAD" allows for the volatility of a company's stock. MADs change like crazy and keep traders busy marking their paper up or down.

High yield bonds masquerade as bonds but are really equities. If the credit improves, it's called away from you. If it doesn't float, the bond collapses and you see a corporate reorganization. Your bond paper is exchanged for equity or, if it's low on the credit scale, warrants or zilch. Today, banks like Morgan carry up to 20 percent of their C&I portfolio in leveraged corporate loans, junk's equivalent. Institutional investors love this paper because yield is tied to LIBOR, thus protecting you from losses in a rising yield scenario. If a recession hits, you don't belong in this paper.

Milken dreamt early about insurance underwriters and banks firing trainloads of credit analysts and loan officers. Intermediaries would buy packages of mortgage and industrial paper instead of making risky real estate loans and bankrolling shoe-string oil-field operators. Their losses could be infinitesimal, not total. Lending institutions might become portfolio managers of securitized loans rather than initiators. This is what happened 20 years later. Milken could have precipitated a banking crisis in the late eighties comparable with 2008–'09.

Alfred Sloan got it wrong when he said, "The men who manage money, manage all." Almost a century later, the securitization of mortgages nearly destroyed our financial system, saved only by government intervention, almost a trillion bucks. The men who managed all were summarily escorted out the front door.

There is an unremarked but, for me, potent symbolism in junk paper. Much new issue paper generated each year is a product of high metabolic players. They are refinancing acquisitions, going private, indulging in hostile takeovers or friendly leveraged buyouts or building out huge footprints in telecommunications, media properties and energy plays. Their future is wrapped up in their deal. They can't get super-rich unless they make good on this paper. Managements owning 20 percent or more of the equity outperform custodial managers, meaningfully. Buying junk can be an adjunct to going with overachievers, sometimes losers. Let them work 12-hour days while you book the interest, sunning on the beach.

Mike Milken stood as the awesome starburst of the eighties, explainable only by what transpired in corporate America during the seventies: Soaring inflation, then spiraling interest rates plus a custodial management mindset were capitalism's fifth columns, not MM. By 1982, equity sold far below replacement cost, 70 percent, and even private market value.

The eighties were all about the harvesting of value by applying the leverage of synthetic equity, namely junk bonds. In the nineties the high yield market financed capital-hungry sectors like wireless telecommunications and Internet purveyors like Amazon. The default ratio was higher than in Milken's day, and yield disparities widened markedly in '99 and 2000. Not so curiously, during the deep recession of 2008–'09, junk defaults were light. This paper has outperformed all credit markets during 2013 and as of late 2014. A few years ago, Fannie Mae defaulted on its preferred stock while Continental Airlines debentures were redeemed at par.

Milken was never power hungry, but like a brilliant Jesuit he had an emotional commitment to being right. He was forever tuned in to the liabilities side of a corporation's balance sheet. At times, Mike would say everyone should be selling zero-coupon converts because it's a seller's market. If your equity sells at a multiple of book value, consider raising capital by selling equity, not buying-in your stock or making dilutive acquisitions. As an arbiter of who got financed at Drexel Burnham, Milken backed most of the winning teams. He was not only a great investment banker but an anointer of hungry entrepreneurs like Murdoch, Perelman, Nelson Peltz, Peter May and Riklis, too.

When critical issues of corporate governance bubbled over in the state courthouses, which almost invariably favored hometown boys, the SEC remained a silent bystander. Meantime, greenmailing, two-tiered tender offers, protective mergers, lockups and dilutive threats of poison pills were impacting capital markets and changing the face of capitalism. The SEC kept busy handcuffing printers, proofreaders and a handful of arbs that peeked at tender-offer documents on their eve of issuance. Ivan Boesky paraded himself as the guru of risk arbitrage, but he had no more than a momentary impact on financial markets.

The use of excess cash flow and even debt to shrink equity capitalizations is now common practice among even our biggest and most powerful corporations. Merck,

IBM, Coca-Cola and Philip Morris are much more sensitive to their shareholder constituencies. Before Milken, nobody was much interested in equity shrinks. Some of our biggest corporations kept in place overly ambitious capital spending programs and made disastrous acquisitions. Atlantic Richfield bought Anaconda, Burroughs took on Sperry, and Mobil choked on Montgomery Ward. Philip Morris's acquisition of Miller Brewing never earned its keep, nor did Prudential's top-of-the-cycle buyout of Bache.

Milken was a helluva lot more than the junk bond king. He was a sound diagnostician of our capital markets, their malfunctions and their moribund qualities, as witnessed in our banking and insurance systems' wobbly assets and in brain-dead corporate managers. Many forgot that the name of the game is a reasonable return on assets employed in their businesses. I'm an asset manager, but Milken understood how to construe the liabilities or debt side of the corporate balance sheet, make it sing and create entrepreneurial wealth.

The Drexel high yield bond department created its own franchise for repackaging the ownership of corporate America. Everyone forgets that most of the deals were user-friendly LBOs, management-led and entrepreneurially driven. Very few hostiles got off the ground; Ron Perelman's winning Revlon was the major exception. Pickens and Icahn failed to bag Texaco, Unical and Phillips.

The focus on one man's wealth and the late-eighties comet of junk bond proliferation is what you'd expect in the public's consciousness. The ingrained response is forever that of the street kid, face pressed against the restaurant window, goggle-eyed at the overflowing champagne goblets and mounds of caviar therein. The "nobody should be allowed to make that kind of money" argument is as flimsy as the radical-chic shanties erected on college greens by anti-apartheid teenagers. Simply, Milken and Drexel tore off the lion's share of Wall Street's underwriting business. Today, the powerhouse distributors running The Street's biggest printing presses are Goldman Sachs, JPMorgan Chase, Bank of America (Merrill Lynch) and Citigroup.

Both raiders and the raiders' prey meekly coughed up outrageous fees. Protecting the raided in several takeover battles was Drexel's gold mine, too. They fought me on my tender for Caesars World. Several corporate managements spent as much as 20 percent of their net worth defending themselves from beasts prowling around their watering holes. Much more than Milken and Drexel were involved. Philip Morris savaged Kraft, and Kohlberg Kravis Roberts dished out the RJR management-led buyout. Every major Wall Street house, led by Morgan Stanley, raised billions in private money pools for LBOs and bridge financing. They still do it. Banks like Citigroup and Wells Fargo quickened their earnings momentum by investing billions in loan syndicates for takeovers, hostile or otherwise. The Establishment simply played the fee-enrichment game.

Not to be left at the post, pension funds, particularly in the public sector, flocked to buyout operators as passive investors. States like Oregon put over half a billion to work and didn't much care if equity deals were friendly or not, just so long as their rate of return was exceptional. Private firms like Blackstone and Kohlberg Kravis Roberts have raised pools of capital in the tens of billions. Leveraged loan portfolios in major banks are outsized.

Milken's franchise was his seasoned network of junk bond buyers in the institutional sector, including me. I'm talking about insurance underwriters, savings and loans, mutual funds and privately owned money pools. All of us craved rates of return five percentage points above Treasury notes, and Drexel filled our orders. Like any powerful franchise, once you meet your fixed costs, incremental revenues are almost pure profit. It's true for soda water, ethical drugs, television syndication, recorded music, long-distance telephone networks and cellular radio. McCaw Cellular, a Milken-sponsored deal, sold out to American Telephone for $12.5 billion five years later.

Investment banking and underwriting is an event-driven business. Once deal flow proliferates, the staff and computers work around the clock packaging the deals. Whether the franchise belongs to one individual or his house affiliation is irrelevant. Drexel consented to one man making an unprecedented pot of money. If this contributed to Milken's sense of omnipotence, both he and Drexel were losers. Market share is everything, and there were several 800-pound gorillas like Merrill Lynch and Goldman Sachs who battled Drexel for every client.

Milken's ineradicable achievement was the creation of a new franchise in the country as to who is socially and financially acceptable to receive investment bank backing for controlling the ownership of even the top 100 corporate entities. The threat of private financial power forced a new mindset on professional managers, who now run their corporations in an entrepreneurial mode, shareholder friendly. It's what the past 25 years were all about, but it's still not enough. Management compensation remains a piggish scene. Starting with Apple and ExxonMobil—together over a trillion in market capitalization—corporations talk the talk about sharing earnings with their stakeholders, in dividends and share buybacks. Only tech houses get away with huge internal options giveaways, thereby diluting earnings meaningfully, as much as 5 percent per annum.

Decades ago, Texaco's management, with Icahn breathing down its neck, sold off low-yielding assets and pared its redundant staff. Today, outside directors are no longer rubber stamps. They fired their headmen at Citigroup, Bank of America, Merrill Lynch and AIG when mortgage backed securities portfolios blew up in 2008 along with other collateralized debt obligations. Mindless capital spending and acquisition programs must be justified with sharply penciled analysis or they are tabled, like Coca-Cola's quest for Quaker Oats. The Milken comet streaked across the sky, marking a turning point in the country's financial history—for the better, not that he was thinking about shareholders' rights.

The first time I met Mike was when he walked into my office, lugging in each hand a black lawyer's brief bag. I picked one up, and it must have weighed 30 pounds. Milken worked with a Jesuit's vision. Day after day, year after year, he stuck to his schemata of networking brainy people who were buyers and sellers of securities and corporate properties.

"Cuba is not Cuba anymore," Mike would say. "Cuba is Miami Beach, where all the smart Cubans work and live."

"You're going to get tendonitis of the wrists schlepping that crap around," I said.

The bags were filled with SEC filings and court decisions on defunct railroads, troubled utilities, shaky retailers, oil plays and farm equipment manufacturers with a lot of tractors languishing in their showrooms. These debentures and preferreds sold anywhere from 50 cents on the dollar down to a dime, with expected rates of return of 20 percent per annum and up. The investment concept was their implied high yield and hidden tangible asset coverage coupled with public perception that they were no good. Milken, 40 years ago, researched corporate reorganizations and analyzed the fallen angels of the corporate world. He traded this paper and got many professionals interested in his work. Mike made investors money. That's how relationships on Wall Street germinate.

The bankrupt Drexel Burnham wasn't domiciled at 60 Broad Street. It was found behind an unmarked door off Wilshire Boulevard, an old law office with pretentious but imitation French provincial furnishings, left there by the lawyers and sat on by Mike's noisy crew of traders and analysts of high yield securities. In the early eighties they wore jeans. The pinstripe suits came later. The bullpen resembled an Oriental bazaar. Each desk or work area contained its specialists hawking their wares—Grant's debentures, International Harvester Credit Corporation, Boston and Maine Railroad, Long Island Lighting preferreds and the hollowed carcasses of Dumbo banks, savings and loans, utilities, retailers and industrials.

Milken started his great run analyzing failures successfully and moved on to leveraging the brain power of his clients. For the guys with dreams who could show him a schema for realizing same, there was money available from capital markets. This is the biggest contribution Milken made: financing availability for the guys with brains. In the seventies, if you knocked on the merchant banking doors of Wall Street and asked for money, it was a polite but firm no. Capital was for Texaco, General Motors and Exxon (who didn't need it), and for Florida Power & Light and Con Edison (who soaked it up). They belonged to the corporate infrastructure. Here's big-picture stuff. One man successfully closed part of the gap between the market value of stocks on the Big Board and their private valuation, the control premium. Without takeovers, the S&P Index during the eighties would have returned less than Treasury bills. Academic studies, like Barrie Wigmore's of Goldman Sachs, suggest 30 percent of the eighties' appreciation gets laid at the feet of deals and buyouts.

First came Riklis, Saul Steinberg and Carl Lindner, the band of conglomerateurs who dated back to the sixties. They formed their companies with "Chinese paper," debentures with warrants. Most of them had less than arithmetic control of their public equity. Mike would finance them in going private and owning it all. Later, these operators would recycle their companies back to public status.

By the mid-eighties, Drexel changed the game by financing hostile takeovers. Icahn had just graduated from risk arbitrage, and Ron Perelman was a small businessman. T. Boone Pickens was chomping at the bit to buy cheap oil reserves for his Mesa Petroleum. The Bass brothers were greenmailing Texaco and red dogging Disney. Later, Merrill Lynch, First Boston, Morgan Stanley, Salomon, Goldman and Donaldson, Lufkin & Jenrette sported fully staffed high yield departments involved in the hostile takeover business. Drexel's clients became their clients.

Leverage, when it works, is magical. If you start with nothing, it takes a long time to make a billion unless you first borrow a billion. The only investor who has made it without leverage is Warren Buffett, who sits out in Omaha and occasionally buys or sells securities in big lots. It took Warren almost 30 years. Milken's Dirty Dozen wanted to do it in less, maybe six months.

An unrestrained optimism took hold of Milken when he dealt with numbers and people. If he believed in the applicant, the numbers were construed aggressively. All of a sudden Milken was projecting out five years, ciphering heady growth rates and ample cash flow coverages of embedded debt expense. The meritocracy of Wall Street is forever reserved in the form of higher price-earnings ratios and underwriting capacity for those who can deliver a growth story.

I have to confess. Years ago I had trouble spelling Icahn, putting the *h* before the *a*, but not anymore. When you personally buy a $4-billion tranche of Apple, somehow the spelling sticks in your consciousness. Even my widowed aunts, in their eighties, know the name. They don't have the attention span for the *Wall Street Journal* anymore, but they've heard the name Shakespeare, too. They don't read his stuff, either.

The world was never controlled from Bungalow 8 in the Beverly Hills Hotel, where Milken's Dirty Dozen would congregate after his Predators' Ball show. Their power was limited. There are world-class corporations like Boeing, General Electric and Halliburton that run their companies for all relevant constituencies—employees, management, customers, their place of domicile, even shareholders. No raider would dare go near them, although Pickens once made a feeble stab at Boeing and then scooted back into the bushes. (Boeing is huge free cash flow positive. I'm betting $15 a share by 2018.) Incidentally, GE was a raider, too: Management made an unsolicited bid for Honeywell and broke up their deal with United Technologies.

The Fortune 500 have been substituting capital for labor for decades. Ask the United Auto Workers. Only the service industries provide plentiful entry-level jobs. The Microsofts of the world increase research spending absolutely, year after year. Textile operators and aluminum can producers just concentrate on factory automation. Alcoa shut down 25 percent of its smelting capacity when the Russians flooded the London Metals Exchange with surplus aluminum ingot. They were the world's low-cost producer.

Milken's omnipotence was a myth. He never stood behind his paper like some Federal Reserve Board. For much of his goods there was no market when the cream curdled. The distribution system for junk bonds thrived without Milken. Nobody ponders what circumstances made it possible for Carl and Saul, Ron and Meshulam to succeed. Texaco, Unocal and Phillips Petroleum were underachievers, undermanaged. Shareholders dwelled in the cellar and had no constituency.

The SEC stood by, a casual observer, while greenmail, golden parachutes, lockups, poison pills and bastardized classes of common stock and preferreds proliferated under the aegis of Messrs. Flom and Lipton. The state courts played ball with their corporations of domicile. Meanwhile, the New York Stock Exchange worried about the profitability and solvency of its member firms. The people's capitalism came in second.

Our institutions failed us. This, for me, was the bottom line of the eighties. The coda for the decade was the imprisonment of Mike Milken. Was this another Don Giovanni, collared and hustled off to the inferno, unrepentant, defiant? After the curtain fell, the chorus chanted the Don's misdeeds and just punishment. I left our opera house admiring his rampaging through a moribund corporate establishment. Milken's biggest weakness was his color blindness and tolerance when it came to assessing characters like Boesky, Posner, et al.

We are talking about the former head Jesuit of corporate finance. Milken, the securities analysts' analyst, always scouting for value, sometimes perversely in problem-ridden companies. His scope blossomed to include problem-ridden countries—all of Latin America, even Russia. You could have made big bread at home, owning Disney et al after Black Monday, and again in the spring of 2009, but that makes you a passive investor.

Milken is no longer anti white-shoe America. John Kluge took Metromedia private courtesy of Milken and bought his way into a great cellular telephone franchise. Without Mike, MCI would have been crushed by Ma Bell and its Baby Bells. The price of long-distance telephoning has come down thanks to the new players. Milken believed in some oil operators, insurance underwriters and industrialists who disappointed investors. I, as a money manager, believed in many stocks that cost me some money, too. For professionals there are only batting averages.

In investment banking, you package a prospectus, put a price on a deal and sell it to the public. The due diligence is completed at a point in time, and then you go on to your next deal. Milken was probably the greatest optimist in the world about smart, educated, motivated people making their mark on the world's growth rate. He was no different than Steven Spielberg, packaging *Jurassic Park* fantasies that would grab the world. Today, Mike's unbiased think tank, the Milken Institute, is a respected contributor to the understanding of the pivotal economic variables and political forces that govern the future of the country. After contracting prostate cancer while incarcerated, Milken devoted serious money and much time to jump-starting medical research, with notable results, still ongoing. The other night I caught him in the Yankees' broadcast announcers' booth, talking about progress in beating prostate cancer. My kind of guy!

The crowning irony of the Drexel Burnham story is that they succumbed, themselves, to a mismatched balance sheet. Employed too much short-term debt to carry their inventory of long-duration junk bonds. When short-term rates spiked, their cost of carry skyrocketed. There was no liquidity in their high yield portfolio to offset this lethal mismatch. Too much leverage killed Drexel just like it destroyed Lehman a generation later.

TWENTY-THREE

The Paper War in Gaul
(My Biggest Mistake)

*I*t was Mike Milken of Drexel on the phone.

"Lights are flashing all over my board from the M&A Group."

"So?" I say to Mike.

"You asked for the unaskable."

"I want a seat on Caesars," I said.

"In the real world, you don't ask for a board seat. In the real world, you wait until they offer you one."

"What do you mean you don't ask for a seat? I own 13 percent of the company. Nobody on the board owns much more than a few thousand shares."

"The lawyers smell millions of dollars in fees. Flom, Skadden, Arps. They smell big fee money, protecting the company's flanks."

"But I'm friendly," I protest. "Henry's doing a great job. I just want to see what's going on from the inside."

"You can do that without going on the board. Gluck will talk to you. Any chairman of the board would do the same thing. How does he know you're going to stay friendly? The first time he does something you don't like, it becomes unfriendly. Henry has to deal with ten thousand employees who aren't sure anymore who's supposed to be running the company. Two years from now you have a fight with your wife and decide you want to run the company. What does Henry do then? You've got to understand that no management in the country is going to sit by and let you buy more than 10 percent of their company without a standstill agreement or some written assurance that you won't control them. Why should they let you buy 15 to 25 percent and do nothing? It's not the way the country works."

"I thought I was living in the free enterprise system, Mike. When a stock trades on the Big Board, you buy as much as you like, so long as you file timely SEC reports, whatever."

"Marty, nobody files an SEC report where they ask for a board seat. You don't do that. It's not friendly."

"I'm friendly."

"If you're friendly, you amend your SEC report and say that you've thought about it and don't want a board seat. That's friendly."

"I'm not going to do that."

"Then you're not friendly."

"I'm friendly, I'm friendly."

"What am I supposed to tell my merger-and-acquisition people?"

"I'm the friendliest guy in the world."

"I'm going to make believe we never had this conversation. You filed a 13D asking for a seat. Nobody does that. Icahn buys 40 percent of TWA and doesn't ask for a seat. That's a bear hug. Friendly people are invited on boards....You haven't been invited. Give 'em a bear hug or forget it."

"Mike...Mike...Listen to me. Would Henry prefer somebody really unfriendly owning four million shares? Icahn, Steinberg, Lindner, whoever?"

"You don't understand, Marty. Management sees you all the same way. There is no difference between you and Icahn—or anyone else. No management in this country is going to stand by and let you gobble up their stock. One day it's 15 percent, then it's 25 percent, and after that you want it all."

"I'm not Hitler, and I don't have enough money to buy it all."

"Why should they assume you're not Hitler?"

"Mike, we'll have another conversation."

"It's heading in the wrong direction," Mike said. "The lawyers smell money."

I heard some junk bond quotes in the background and hung up.

The message from Milken was clear. Caesars wasn't going anywhere. Later, Drexel negotiated a $10-million fee, payable whether Caesars steered clear of me or not. If not, Gluck had specified the fee was a liability of any new owner.

STOCKHOLDER: *My name is Dusty Kaplan. I have been a shareholder for many years and for all the years that I owned Caesars World it never seemed to move very much until Mr. Sosnoff attempted to buy it, and I'm glad he tried to buy it. Does this mean now that you are recapitalizing and he has no chance of buying it, and does this mean if we get our dividend and the stock then will become $8 a share? Is that it? Do you think that if we wish to buy some more that without Mr. Sosnoff there attempting to buy it again our stock will then appreciate? It didn't seem to until he came along and*

even though you had glowing reports about how much money you were making the
stock never budged. So, would you mind telling us whether it would be a good buy?...
We have to import Mr. Sosnoff from around the world to attempt to buy this....Even
though you send these fabulous reports to us, the shareholder has never really benefited
by, you know, the money that Caesars was earning up until the point that Mr. Sosnoff
arrived. So I've asked you a lot of questions, would you like to answer any of them?

"Congratulations," crackled Laurie Cohen of the *Wall Street Journal.* "There was
no leak."

"How'd you find out so fast, Laurie?" I asked. It was a late Sunday night in
March.

"Well, it's my night on and I saw the tender offer in the paper," she said. "We
get to see the first edition around 8:30."

Laurie specialized in takeover stories. I was warned by Peter Rosenthal, our
PR consultant, that she was tough and I had to talk nice or she would get back
at me by printing the hostile comments of analysts, competitors and corporate
management.

"Why'd you do it?" Laurie asked.

"You want the short answer or the long one, Laurie?"

"Gimme the short one," Laurie said. "I got a deadline."

"We saw a window in the money market with the prime rate at 7 percent. Also,
high yield bonds have backed off a hundred basis points. The financing package is
coming together and looking very reasonable right now."

"What else?"

"The company's doing very well. Caesars' earnings are accelerating beyond the
analyst consensus. If we didn't go for it now, the stock could run away."

"All right. Gimme your PR guy's number. I need access to your head lawyer
and to the bankers. Who's doing the financing?"

"PaineWebber," I said. "Chris Kahr is the lawyer."

"Who at PaineWebber?"

I gave her my two gladiators' phone extensions. Laurie knew them. When I met
her a few weeks later at my book party for *Silent Investor, Silent Loser*, this tough
cookie stood 4 foot 10 at 90 pounds. The power of the printed word, I thought,
hearing the *click clack* on the word processor.

I refused my head lawyer's limo late that night, a futile initial effort at frugality,
and taxied downtown to the printers. Financial printers like Sorg are busy Sunday
nights. Walking the corridors, I noted several conference rooms filled with lawyers,

Wall Streeters and corporation heavies. Each room housed a deal—an initial public offering, primary and secondary financings, a tender offer. Capitalism begins with a prospectus, I thought.

My guys had stacked piles of documents on the conference room table. Lawyers for the lead bank, Marine Midland, for PaineWebber, the underwriter, and mine, walked around in stocking feet. Empty soda cans and untouched tuna salad plates lay everywhere. It was for them D-day, and the adrenaline pumped. Two dozen lawyers, bankers and accountants had weighed, measured and screamed over every noun and verb in the tender offer document.

They all called him Henry, but I was the only one who knew Henry Gluck, chairman of the board of Caesars World. I had placed an urgent phone call and had reached him earlier in Las Vegas. He was three minutes from showtime. It was Caesars Palace's 20th anniversary, and there was a television spectacular with Henry sitting on the dais, a spotlight shining on the head table. Henry had to crawl off behind the stage to take the call. We both agreed our talk could wait until after the show. I wasn't about to rain on his party, but I knew by the time we talked a few hours later, he would have a dozen message notes.

"Henry, I swear to you I had no idea it was Caesars' anniversary. On my nine-year-old's head."

"I believe you, Marty. If you say it's so."

"Look. I hope we can make this a friendly deal," I said. "You guys are running the company just fine."

"Marty. We have to examine all our options. I don't know how we're going to come out on this."

"OK, let's talk again soon," I said. There was nowhere to go with this conversation.

"I always knew you were going to come for the company," Henry said. The tone was judgmental and he hung up.

Yes, I thought. You stonewalled me for a couple of years and wouldn't put me on the board. When I proposed a friendly leveraged buyout, you said you didn't want to saddle the company with debt. I remember you sketching new entrances and approaches, moving stairways for the Palace, a gaming floor expansion of the sportsbook sector. As Henry sketched on my yellow pad at that meeting 18 months ago, I sensed there was no way he would give an inch. I kept trying to get him to look at the computer printouts, the number-crunching language that showed clearly the feasibility of an LBO up to $25 a share. A hundred million becomes a billion in just five years. This is a good day's work. Henry had brushed aside the computer sheets, his booklet untouched, unriffled.

I, the spurned lover of money, faced a formidably methodical headman who loved position, absorbed in the campy grandiosity of the Palace. Power flowed through his fingertips as he sketched and talked about negotiating contracts with Diana Ross, turning down Sinatra—Frank was getting too old to sing reliably, too expensive—and how he embraced black fight promoters who would talk him out of his eyeteeth if he relaxed.

It was time for me to find an investment banker. The sociology of work in a first-tier Wall Street house says a lot about the country's values and focus. Assume feverishly good minds, impeccable academic credentials and the capacity to work a string of 15-hour days. Quantitative analysts massaging computers are slaves to the M&A deal makers. They are handpicked out of undergraduate schools in their early twenties and frequently work round the clock, spitting out fresh scenarios for all of us to contemplate. After a few years as drones, they are packed off to Harvard Business School and then return as junior members of the M&A group. They depart and come back with dollar signs in their eyes.

Senior members of a finely honed mergers and acquisitions group come in two varieties, early thirties and late forties. By the time you're 50, if not burned out, you are running your company or somebody else's in the corporate sector beyond Wall Street. My two fighter pilots from PaineWebber fit the mold: J.T. Atkins, thirtyish, black wavy hair, with a law degree, an MBA and a few years with Skadden Arps, the heavyweight law firm coveting Wall Street's business; Bob Hastings, greying on top, mild mannered and soft spoken. J.T., with icy eyes and a quick temper, wore the black hat. He was the deal breaker in all negotiations. Bob Hastings donned the white hat. He could always figure out an ingenious compromise that embraced millions of dollars, percentage and the rationing of power and control. When he could, Bob drove home to his wife on the Connecticut shore. J.T. reserved Friday evenings for a basketball game at his gym. He was to miss several during the next six months. Basketball made J.T. sweat. The fear of losing could make him stutter.

Nobody tells you about the emotional costs of a hostile deal. Toni and I had the ups and downs day after day. The random quality of several pre-deal events was a forerunner of the tensions that led to sleepless nights and days when your stomach ached dully, suppressing any longing for solid food. Later, when financing fees mounted into tens of millions as the construct of the capitalization changed, I felt like a punchy heavyweight, his purse cut up half a dozen ways.

In February, Caesars in Atlantic City had a big win at the baccarat tables: Some guy dropped $4 million. It meant that the company was all but assured of excellent numbers in its quarterly earnings report. Meanwhile, PaineWebber was having trouble putting together a banking syndicate for $500 million. J.T. was spending his days on the telephone, crossing off all the banks who didn't want to lead the syndicate but were interested in a participation. Finally, he was down to the last line, Marine Midland, and they committed to lead the syndicate and participate for $100 million. It had to go up to the board level for affirmative action. Until then, I was just a little boy with a ball, looking for someone to play with.

From yearend to tender offer in early March, the stock rose from $18 to $24. On a $35-million share capitalization I was staring at another $20 million a year in interest expense. As soon as the analysts caught on to the earnings report by mid-April, we might lose the tender window. Meanwhile, the junk bond market was in its post–Ivan Boesky rally phase. The spread between the junk and 10-year Treasury bonds had begun to close in favor of the junk. There were few new offerings. Mutual funds were promoting their high yield funds and the cash flow, which later dried up in June, was heavy in the opening months of 1987. It was an ideal time to pick a fight. I waited restlessly for the loan syndicate to jell.

It took Marine Midland a few weeks to put together the bank syndicate. A hundred or so bankers came to New York for our backgrounder presentation in the MM auditorium. The banks performed a few hours of due diligence. They made some calls to Las Vegas, Reno and Atlantic City and then signed on for the loan fees and profit participation. The feeling was that I really didn't want to own the company. I would be outbid and everyone would make easy fee money. The MM team, George, Ed and John, weren't so sure but did not discourage this point of view. It was an easier way to sell the deal.

J.T. and Bob Hastings revved their high yield bond department into gear. A dozen PaineWebber salesmen blanketed the country with calls to all the players. They were the same customers Drexel connected with. Fire and casualty underwriters like Saul Steinberg's Reliance, private money pools like the Belzbergs', mutual funds—T. Rowe Price and Fidelity—and corporations that had raised hundreds of millions in underwritings from Drexel and had become arbitrageurs of money. Through a nexus of commitment fees and profit participation, lenders were locking in an annualized rate of return of 17 percent. This kind of yield is not available anywhere else, and the deal, as they say, "went out the window." From Caesars Palace, J.T. brought back white sun visors for his high yield salesmen.

Because Caesars was a bet-the-family-jewels proposition, Toni sat in the strategy meetings with the lawyers, bankers and investment brokers. Within a few months she was well on her way towards financier status, although not quite conversant with the EBIT ratios and discounted cash flow multipliers that are crucial to pricing bids and estimating compound rates of return on your equity investment. This would come later, when Caesars began to outbid us and we had to counterpunch. On a clear summery evening in April, we sat alfresco on Columbus Avenue, washing down chiles rellenos with fruit-chocked sangria.

"Awesome," I said. "We raised a billion dollars practically overnight. Major institutions. All over the country. The system is fee driven. All this crap about hostile takeovers. Every major bank in the country wants a piece of the action. Insurance companies, mutual funds, corporate America. Everyone goes for the exceptional rate of return."

"This billion," Toni said. "It's making me a little nervous. Tell me again how we pay it off."

"Caesars pays it off from its cash flow. If earnings grow annually 5 to 7 percent the next five years, we pay off most of the bank loans."

"And if things go wrong?" Toni asked.

"Well, then we would try to refinance, sell some properties, cut back expenses, capital spending, whatever," I said.

"And if we lose all our money?" she asked.

"It's Lefrak City," I said.

"I can't take Queens and you're too old to go back to the Bronx," Toni said. "Promise me we'll be able to keep one house."

"Connecticut," I said.

"Where would we put four horses, four standard poodles and 40-foot corten steel sculptures?"

It wasn't that easy. If our tender offer was successful, I would have to eliminate over $50 million of margin indebtedness to Bear Stearns on my Caesars stock. Our chief counsel, Chris Kahr, inventoried our worldly goods. Before long, Chris knew our personal financial history better than I would ever care to know it. The art collection appraisal came in at twice cost, and Don Marron, chairman of PaineWebber, a distinguished collector of contemporary art, took it as collateral. MM accepted the three homes and everything else except the dogs and children. We were fully hocked. It depressed us to see it in our proxy solicitation, a public document. Bob Lenzner of the *Boston Globe*, an old friend, called: "Whadda ya mean you're hocking the villa in Nice? Where am I going to hang out?"

After working 72 hours straight, the lawyers had readied the documents that launched our tender offer. I had to delay an operation on my right hand until early April so I could sign my name. I signed and signed from 10:30 p.m. Sunday night to 1:00 a.m. Monday morning. Within days, we and they—Skadden Arps—had launched litigation in Florida, California, New Jersey, Nevada and Washington, DC. Skadden had shot a brief to the Federal Reserve Board challenging our financing as a violation of the board's margin requirements.

On our way to my initial deposition, I noted that the elevator swooshed up to the forties and stopped at four floors in succession. All Skadden.

"So how many lawyers does Skadden have?" I asked Rick Weinberg, my feisty litigator.

"They have about 800 including paralegals," Rick said.

"A Jewish law firm?" I asked.

"About half and half," Rick said. "I don't know everybody there."

The Skadden corridor stretched out to infinity. A succession of cubbyhole offices housed guys who talked, wrote and processed information like artillery officers zeroing in on a lush target of opportunity...me. My interrogator, Mr. Lerner, was relentlessly thorough. I saw he had two books I had written at his elbow, and they led to a line of questioning.

Q: Have you ever been arrested, Mr. Sosnoff?

A: Arrested? No.

Q: Never?

A: I don't think so.

Q: Isn't it a fact that during your youth you were arrested?

A: No. I was not arrested.

Q: Did you write a book?

A: I wrote a book.

Q: Memoirs?

A: Memoirs, yes.

Q: *Humble on Wall Street* is the name of that?

A: Yes.

Q: Isn't it a fact you described certain arrests in that book?

A: Arrest is an extreme term. I think I was collared.

Q: Were you arrested?

A: I was never arrested, booked. You will find no record of an arrest, either as a teenager, sub-teenager or as an infant.

Q: Were you detained?

A: Detained for a few hours, yes. There is a big difference between being detained and arrested. I must have been 10 years old.

Q: Is this your book?

A: Yes.

Q: Look at page 21, which described an arrest when you were 14 years old.

A: What part of the page is that, counselor?

Q: That is the second paragraph, beginning with "and" is the portion I am referring to. Actually, the second full paragraph: "Again, I was in trouble with the law, for trespassing, and they gave me a hard time at the station house."

A: Yes, I see that.

Q: Does that refresh your recollection as to whether you were arrested?

A: I was not arrested. I was detained.

Q: Look at page 22, Mr. Sosnoff. Isn't it a fact that immediately after this occurred, you went outside and said, and I quote, "I was arrested"?

A: I think I was using the English language improperly, counselor. I was not arrested. I was detained for a few hours.

Q: The book does say, on page 22, that you told someone you were "arrested," quote, unquote. Is that right?

A: The book says that.

Q: You wrote this book, did you not?

A: I also repeat that I was 14 years old and I used a word improperly.

Q: You were not 14 when you wrote the book, were you?

A: No.

MR. WEINBERG: He was reporting on something he said when he was 14.

Q: Was that the only instance when you were detained by police?

A: The only instance? As far as I know, yes.

Q: Did you ever try and bribe a cop?

A: Me?

Q: Yes, sir.

A: No.

Q: Look at page 20 of your book, Mr. Sosnoff. The first line of page 20 says, "When I was 12, I tried to bribe my first cop."

A: I was 12 years old, and I guess I was using the English language improperly, too.

Q: This doesn't quote anybody, does it? This was a statement you made in 1975 in your book. Is that correct?

A: That is correct.

Q: Is it your testimony under oath that you used the term improperly in your book?

A: Absolutely.

Q: Did you offer the policeman who "detained" you, to use your word, anything of value at the time?

A: Well, the book says I offered him a hot meal. That was quite presumptuous on my part at 12 years old.

Q: Were those the only two situations that you were ever detained by police?

A: As far as I remember, counsel, yes.

Q: Listen, I didn't write this book. Even younger, you had a bout with the law. Is that correct?

A: Tell me and refresh my memory.

Q: You don't recall it?

A: No.

Q: There is an indication on the first line of page 18 that you were first arrested when you were nine years old, Mr. Sosnoff.

A: Again, I think I used the term "arrested" in an extreme manner.

Q: Would it be fair to say you were detained in connection with a juvenile offense?

A: I think I was detained for maybe an hour or two until the Macy's Day Parade was finished. I would not term that an arrest.

Q: But you did term that an arrest, did you not?

Mr. Weinberg: You are asking him if the book referred to it as an arrest?

A: I think I was using poetic license in the book, counselor, for dramatic effect.

Q: How would you define arrest?

A: I would define that as a booking.

"Let's get off the record," I said. "It's getting silly. Let's take five."

Coming back from the men's room, I got lost in the maze of offices and corridors. I noted the kitchen going full blast with coffee beakers bubbling and cases of soda cans piled on the floor. Smoked tuna salad plates sat on the counter like great pats of cow dung. This monstrous squid, Skadden, with 20-foot tentacles, had engulfed me. The deposition had started at 1:00 p.m. and it was now 10:00 at night. Rick called time. They had had me long enough, he said.

"How many hours a week do you work, counselor?" I asked.

"Oh. I log between 90 and 100 hours," he said.

"Wait a minute," I said, counting on my fingers. "That's 14 hours a day, seven days a week. Don't you guys have wives, families? Don't you have hobbies and take vacations? It's a big world out there."

"You don't understand," said my pale-faced interrogator. "My work is my hobby. That's all I do."

Our adversary piled his notepads together and shuffled out. "This case is going to be decided on the paper exhibits anyway," he said. "I don't think I'll need Mr. Sosnoff again." He didn't.

Between our initial tender offer early in March and the expiration of our second amended offer in mid-June, Henry Gluck and I talked twice for about two minutes. The incentive to make the deal friendly would have saved us both tens of millions in interest payments annually if we could have agreed on a fair price. In a power struggle, money comes in second.

"I'm not sleeping too well. How about you, Henry?" I asked.

"My 85-year-old mother asked for your phone number. She wants to yell at you for making so much trouble for her son," Henry said.

"What can we do to make this friendly?" I asked. "You run the company, Henry. I just want to own a piece of it."

"We aren't through examining all our options," Henry said. "The board has to consider the well-being of all our shareholders, not just the biggest one."

"But your shareholders are arbitrageurs," I said. "PaineWebber tells me half the stock is in the hands of the arbs. Most of the institutional holders are long gone."

"You caused the change in the sociology of ownership," Henry said, "not us." The voice had begun to sound a little testy.

"Well, we have built in a lot of flexibility in our financing package." I started to sound threatening.

"Look, Marty. If you have a better offer, just put it on the table." Henry had turned up the volume on his speakerphone. "We're not going to respond to words."

"OK, Henry," I said. "I guess we'll have to put it somewhere the board can read about it. Let's talk again soon," I said and hung up. Then I called Drexel and talked with Joe Harch, their corporate finance man on the Caesars account.

"What can we do so everyone wins?" I asked Joe.

"You've got to understand, Marty, that you're the one who started all this," Joe said. "The guy who starts it generally doesn't get to own it. It's the way management reacts."

"So there's going to be a big fight?" I asked.

"Look. We know that anything we do has to make you happy, otherwise it won't work," Joe said.

"You have to know where I'm coming from. I'm only interested in a good rate of return on my money. Henry runs the company. I stay in the background."

"I hear you, Marty," Joe said. It was the last time I talked to Joe or Henry. I began to understand they would let me make a lot of money but I wouldn't get the company. Mike Milken bottom-lined it: "Caesars ain't going anywhere."

We raised our bid from $28 to $32. Caesars countered by declaring a cash dividend of $25 a share payable after the recapitalization of the company with approximately a billion dollars in debt. The stock traded actively on the board between $31 and $32. The two offers were competitive, with The Street leaning towards our higher all-cash package.

Bob Hastings and J.T. were my Rosencrantz and Guildenstern. I always saw them together, talked on the phone with both on the line and traveled with them. J.T., the short-fused lawyer, was feeling like we could win.

"The arbs now think we are for real. With the $32 bid for 92.4 percent of the company, they like us better and better. Caesars has a problem."

"Maybe Henry will sit down and talk now," Bob said. "Our high yield desk tells us Caesars has exhausted its short list of white knights." Caesars responded by raising their cash dividend from $25 a share to $26.25.

"It was typically Germanic, a methodical action by Henry, entirely predictable," I said. "Let's spend half an hour on the valuation of the stub equity, which is like a warrant. I want to understand that completely," I said. J.T. said they had run the numbers and were ready.

Several stub equities traded on the Big Board. Owens Corning, Holiday, FMC, Colt Industries. In most instances managements had saddled their companies with enormous debt to avoid takeovers. Money managers bought the stocks as leveraged speculations. For me it was ominous that the Holiday stub had doubled in a few months. Stubs were fashionable goods in a bubbly market.

J.T. tried to reassure me: "Our computer work suggests that the Caesars stub is worth $5.40. If you use a 35 percent discount rate on terminal earnings five years out, it presents values there. Look at the cash flow multiples of the group and their price-earnings ratios. I think we're in the ball game with our $32 offer."

"I don't like the way the Holiday stub trades up," I said. "Caesars is a better company. It could turn out to be the premium stub in the marketplace." Bob Hastings nodded his head.

When we were out in Las Vegas meeting with the gaming commissioners, who were telling us we'd better have a complete plan for management succession, the Caesars stub had its debut. My trader, Brian, called: "Goldman is making it 6¾ to 7. It's traded 700,000 shares and going on the board tomorrow. What should I do?" I told him to watch it. During a tender offer the principal can't buy or sell a share.

"How the hell did they get that stub listed so fast?" I asked Chris Kahr. "Go down to the New York Stock Exchange tomorrow and get the son of a bitch delisted. The Exchange has approved a piece of paper with incomplete financial disclosure, subject to regulatory approval in New Jersey and Nevada that is months away. It's outrageous they listed that piece of crap. There's a negative net worth of half a billion dollars."

The Caesars stub started to trade a million shares a day and moved above $8. Our $32 offer was fading fast and the NYSE held its ground. They didn't want to lose the volume to the over-the-counter market, and it was easier to keep track of the trading in the issue on the board. The SEC would not intervene, Chris told me.

The arbs were locking in profits, shorting the stub above $8 a share, which valued their total package above $34. These guys had bought millions of shares around $28 and had a time-weighted rate of return close to 100 percent in under three months. It had taken me three years to do as well. That the theoretical valuation of the stub was so tentative and they could do so well hurt. I began to feel like a number on a broker's ledger, again. We had begun to lose. Rosencrantz & Guildenstern hid silently in their offices, avoiding their prince.

With Caesars trading at $34, we had to decide if it was worth staying in the ball game. J.T. crunched some new scenarios at $45 a share where I gave up 30 percent of the company to shareholders. I would have the flexibility of buying in the stock at a later date or even selling part of my holdings. The projected compound rate of return for me by late May had edged below 40 percent a year. We had started at 60 percent in March. The deal was getting full for us, Caesars, for anybody, unless you were willing to project high-teens top-line revenue growth and above-average margins. The competitive forces in the gaming industry are too tough for such unbridled optimism.

Count up another $4 million to press ahead. I asked Hastings, the senior man, to confer with Don Marron to see if PaineWebber would share part of the expense by reducing their fees if we were successful. After many separate whispered conferences we reached agreement. Everyone wanted to go ahead and try to win.

Meanwhile, the banks and preferred shareholders agreed to the new construct for additional fees and profit sharing. Even if the Caesars stock moved up a few points if they sweetened their offer, I was so cut up by topping fees that I could make no more money.

I was enmeshed in the dialectics of winning, and the economics of the deal began to fade into my subconscious. Ed Fanning of Marine Midland, their senior man on the loan syndicate, looked at me with banker's eyes. From the beginning, Ed had assumed I was just playing a rich man's game. Everyone would make some fee money and the banks would never be called on to fund the loans. Ed saw something new: This guy might be for real. Loan commitments might actually be funded. Was the paper exercise about to turn into bricks and mortar?

We put a June 14 expiration date on our second amended tender offer at $35. By mid-May the Caesars stub traded actively at 8½. This action closed any gap between the two offers. Arbitrageurs would decide, thumbs up or down. There was little more give in the opposing packages. How much more pressure would Caesars' board of directors want to sustain in terms of leveraging the capitalization? I knew that the implied rate of return for me now had eroded to the deal-breaking point. Rosencrantz & Guildenstern glided back to their offices. It was wait-and-see time.

The focus shifted to outstanding litigation and to the proxy solicitors, Georgeson, who were counting noses among big block holders. It looked as if we had enough votes to adjourn Caesars' special meeting of shareholders on June 12 and postpone voting on the company's special dividend offer until after our tender offer closed. It added a tactical edge. My head lawyer, Chris, his left eye squinting involuntarily from lack of sleep, marked up our chance of winning to 50 percent, the high point on the chart.

The Caesars stock backed and filled around $34 as I got very busy interviewing ex-presidents of Caesars, the head of surveillance, accounting and auditing specialists, former gaming commissioners interested in high administrative jobs. The paper chase was turning into real-world stuff. Weekends were chewed up interviewing retired captains of police and FBI officers who knew all the scams playable on the casino floor and on the loading and unloading platforms for food and beverages. Entertainment directors could cheat you on the floral displays they rented, and some guys had even changed the weights on the Toledo scales in the money counting room.

I had a vision of tens of millions slipping through our fingers. I saw myself sleeping in the bowels of Caesars Palace until I knew every dark corner and corridor, while Toni worked Atlantic City and my Reno lawyer, Bud Hicks, reported to me from Lake Tahoe. Several paid consultants with high-level gaming experience coalesced into a shadow cabinet ready to step into the near daily meetings with teams of lawyers and investment bankers. The briefs and financial scenario numbers crunching was over. I was totally energized by the impending reality of owning Caesars.

On June 4, our litigators and Caesars' would argue their motions for preliminary injunctions in the United States District Court, Central District of California. Caesars attacked the incomplete disclosure of my personal finances and the construct of our preferred stock, which they claimed violated Federal Reserve Board margin requirements. Rick and Bob, our litigators, were confident on both points. There was no precedent for finding our preferred stock in violation, and we had submitted to the court my audited net worth statement. We had attacked Caesars' failure to disclose Drexel's financial projections, which were more negative than those they used in their initial shareholders proxy. Judge William Rea seemed unschooled and unsophisticated in matters of high finance, according to our litigators. Anything might happen.

Maybe both plaintiffs spoiled the judge's weekend. On June 8 Rea ruled against both our houses. Caesars would have to defer their shareholders meeting for 30 days and include Drexel's numbers. We would have to recommence our tender offer and comply with the board's margin requirements. My head counsel gave me the good news first and the bad news last. It sunk in like a kick to the scrotum.

A new tender would push us out to mid-July. Printing and advertising expenses would add another $200,000. Refiling with the SEC $186,000. (I was getting to know all the expense categories.) Preferred shareholders would want a further $1.2 million a month in standby fees. I saw myself staring at another $5 million in expenses, with about a 30 percent chance of winning.

Later, PaineWebber went through the motions of crunching more numbers with a new, non-exchangeable preferred stock. The high yield market faced $10 billion in new supply. Harcourt Brace Jovanovich was battling a hostile tender. Other LBO deals surfaced. Rosencrantz stuttered halfheartedly about a 16½ percent preferred, but I hardly heard him. Ed Fanning looked up at me with tender moose eyes. Enough was enough, they said. Chris, squinting, adrenaline running, hoped he would hear me say, "Fuck the money. Let's go ahead and play to win." The timetable was so tight, the appeal brief writers wouldn't shut down, and the litigators caucused strategy hour after hour.

Toni and I retreated to Connecticut. We agreed to offer up our decisions in

24 hours on Saturday night. Chris had reviewed page after page of percentage probabilities, actions, opposing courses of action, timetables, expenses—there was nothing more to talk about. My stomach processed it all. I had gotten a bellyful and couldn't eat.

"You go first," I said.

"No. No. You first," Toni said. "I don't want to influence you."

"Nothing can change the way I feel, but thanks. We would be crazy to go on. I don't have to own all of Caesars, after all."

"I agree," Toni said. "It has taken over our lives. Unless you want it more than anything else, I have a problem going on."

"We needed great investment bankers and great lawyers to win," I said. "I see two strategic errors. We never should have had an exchangeable preferred, and we should have had a stub equity from go."

"Maybe the judge wasn't as dumb as the lawyers made him out," Toni said. We were sitting together in an easy chair. "You had good lawyers and good investment bankers, but they didn't protect you."

"I blame myself for not thinking of a stub equity on the initial tender offer. It would have preserved our flexibility and we would never have had to go back to the banks and preferred shareholders. No additional expenses. As the deal price escalated we could have given out increasing percentages of the equity. It all could have been built into the deal."

The securities distribution machinery of the country had finally shut me down, I thought. Maybe it was a fluke, maybe not. A greedy New York Stock Exchange allowed the stub to trade. Judge Rea said fight it out in the marketplace. The banks, institutional investors and mergers-and-acquisitions people exacted their tolls. It was a highly structured ballet that had cost me $30 million to produce. By the time Caesars finished with its investment bankers, their all-in numbers would approach $60 million—a hefty chunk of the corporation's net worth. Deeper pockets help the house win. When we arrived in Nice a few days later, bronzed Jean-Claude, my closest friend, said: "*Bienvenue en France*, Martin. I never saw you looking worse."

The outer limits of what you can do in a capitalist system had to be respected. The financial history of the industry, its revenue growth, rate of return on equity and optimal capital structure supplied the framework for all earnings projections and interest coverage ratios. Without such coverage no investment banker could distribute debt securities and no banking syndicate would commit loan funds. We remained hostages to the numbers. Once the coverage of interest expense was reduced close to one, it ratcheted up costs to keep the financing in place.

Caesars was equally tied to its numbers. Drexel's computer printouts neatly matched ours. Caesars' board of directors finally would have blown the whistle on management's increasing the onetime cash dividend to shareholders. As the deal approached full economic value at $35 a share, once the lawyers had finished with their gladiating, the marketplace would vote its shares. If we were still in the ball game, would the arbitrageurs, who controlled the majority of shares, have voted for us or them? Would they have decided on the basis of whether one offer was worth 10 cents more or less? Maybe. The disenfranchisement of shareholders under Caesars' recap booked no interest.

For Henry and me it was a fight for ultimate power. The economics of the deal governed the outer limits and the expense logistics of the fight. Gluck had to be tossing in his sleep. I forced a recapitalization that saddled his company with onerous debt for years. Any grandiose future capital spending was squelched. There was little net free cash flow to build new palaces. Next door to the Palace, built 25 years ago, the Golden Nugget spent over $600 million for a new pleasure dome, the Mirage. In the nineties, Caesars faced head-to-head competition with a 21st-century facility. Who knows where the high rollers will play?

After a few days' sleep, Chris's eyes had lost their squint. We met in my office to discuss legal bills.

"Five law firms were working until we shut them down last weekend," he said.

"Right now we have outstanding litigation with Skadden. So what's the number?" I asked.

"It looks like two and a half million," Chris said. "I don't have everyone's time sheets yet. We would like a million now to cover direct expenses, the rest in a couple of weeks after the accounting."

It had taken just 10 weeks to fill a bookcase full of briefs, proxy statements and depositions.

"It's not a problem," I said, writing a check for a million dollars.

"There is something else, Martin," Chris said. "I want to discuss our bonus."

"Wait a minute, Chris," I said. "My God! We lost. Who ever heard of a bonus for losing?"

"You don't understand, Martin. I can't go back to my partners without a bonus."

"Explain that to me," I said.

"We had dozens of people working 16-hour days, seven days a week. You can't get people to put out that way without the thought of a bonus."

254 MASTER CLASS FOR INVESTORS

"So how much do you want?" I asked. My fingers were trilling rapidly on the round marble table.

"We think $500,000 is fair and reasonable. Some of my partners wanted a million. Obviously, it would have been more if we won."

"I can understand something for winning but for losing it's crazy," I said. "Maybe I should fire you guys and find another law firm."

"Skadden's bill to Caesars has to be enormous," Chris said softly. "We saved you money."

I never expected this conversation. We looked each other in the eyes for several seconds.

"You can have your money," I said. "If I weren't going to retain your law firm, you wouldn't get a cent." (Later, I changed my mind and decided a bonus for losing the way we lost was the ultimate absurdity.) My scarred gladiator left with a perfunctory handshake. He sensed I had had my fill of lawyering. These were the spoiled, middle-aged children who played intellectual grab-ass, sleeplessly, with the country's institutions. Their clients, the players, flexed their muscles and tried to win or at least not lose.

Win what? I thought, gazing at my video screen of the Big Board tape. Leverage and hubris getcha every time. The numbers, of course, streamed across in irrepressible high spirits. Six years later, Caesars ticked in the high thirties, not much more than its peak when we fought on the eve of Black Monday. Gluck had missed the proliferation of gaming on Indian reservations and riverboats, ceding those markets to Promus and a bunch of upstarts bankrolled by Wall Street.

I didn't return to Vegas for 10 years. Caesars World had changed hands a couple of times at higher prices than mine. It was sandwiched between Steve Wynn's Bellagio and Mirage. They cost billions to construct and were world-class hotels. The gaming floor at Caesars Palace now looked dowdy, tinselly, with its low-ceiling Christmas light pattern.

Wynn's cash flow was mighty, and he had outflanked this 1960ish facility with his Mirage only to be undone by Kirk Kerkorian's bear hug. My deal was five years premature. Common law in the federal courts had evolved sufficiently by then to favor buyers. Mid-nineties, Wall Street hailed proactive money managers like Michael Price as heroic gladiators. Nearly two decades later, Carl Icahn stood tall as a revered shareholder activist, his greenmailer moniker long forgotten. I was just a shadowy, controversial lone wolf, soon forgotten. The mistake was going outside my power game, which is focusing on properties that periodically take you to the moon or are misunderstood.

My biggest mistake was the premature timing of my unsolicited bid for Caesars World. The second-biggest mistake was not executing a proxy solicitation for a board seat, which I think could have succeeded. If I had waited five years, the New Jersey Casino Control Commission probably would have approved the construct of my deal. After all, they okayed Donald Trump, and he used more leverage than I proposed.

A lot more had changed after 10 years. The common law on corporate governance evolved to the level where federal courts turned more evenhanded towards prospective buyers. Shareholders no longer rubber-stamped poison pills, and institutions turned more proactive on issues of shareholder rights.

Today, money managers and institutional investors press managements for proactive results. They are lauded by the press. I was the first money manager to press a hostile takeover. My clients wagged their fingers at me and said it wasn't done. "Sell your stock if you're displeased," they said.

I would never take on a management in a regulated industry again. It's an additional layer of uncertainty. You never know how it plays out. I had owned my stock in Caesars for several years, but the regulators gave it no weight.

There are no situations where I'll ever hold a reportable position again. My goal is to spend as little time as possible with lawyers, investment bankers and accountants. Kirk Kerkorian tangling with General Motors was crazy. At 90, he shoulda been home, spending quality time with his grandchildren.

I took my company private over 10 years ago, overpaid for the property, but so far I'm living happily ever after.

TWENTY-FOUR

Donald Trump's Finite Name Recognition

One of my favorite women on the Côte d'Azur is a youngish auburn-haired lady married to a macho 70-year-old shopping center developer who pole-vaults out of bed at 5:45 for a snappy five-mile jog. "You gotta know where the fish swim," Rita was saying. It takes serious research—reading financial magazines and gossip sheets, then mapping out your plan of attack. You find friends who know your target's personality and interests. If he collects art, you'd better know which century and who the players are. If your guy does tennis, join his club and play with the women first, who later slip you into a mixed doubles game. If the son of a bitch goes in for scuba diving, you buy a wet suit, take lessons, hold your nose and plunge 60 feet with a knife strapped on your ankle, gripping your speargun.

Investing's no different, I thought. With a stainless steel heart, you hunt the earth for coveted properties to keep you in long-haired furs and bijous. "The Donald" qualifies herein. I never understood Trump's popularity rating when the Trump Tower opened. The *New York Times Magazine* published a longish puff piece extolling the richness of its accoutrements, the waterfall cascading down pink marble interiors. Hadn't Donald and Ivana's TLC touched every last gilded faucet in this impeccable monument, the world's best address bar none?

Seventy years ago, I lived in three rooms in the Bronx. The rental was pegged at $40 a month, bedrooms 9×12 feet, painted pink and blue. Standard ¾-inch gypsum wallboard boxed in our rabbit hutch. Its cheap, hollow, wood-veneer doors slam-banged shut from the slightest of drafts. Life's repetitious cyclicality gets even. Forty years after "getting out," I was living in approximately the same square footage, but at a better address than 964 Sherman Avenue.

"Donald, I look out at the tops of buildings. I am eye to eye with huge neon signs that say RCA and 666 and Newsweek and the time is 10:46 in 22-foot numerals."

"Marty, how many people can look out their windows and see the tops of such fantastic buildings?"

"Donald, the air-conditioning is too sophisticated. It cuts off because not enough people are living in the building."

"Marty, we are going to simulate a fully inhabited building so you can have your air-conditioning."

"Donald, I thank you. But what do I do for an elevator? You are always checking them out, so they never run. My wife used the construction elevator, and I haven't seen her for three days. She is being passed around among 200 hundred construction workers, Donald. The last I heard, they made her into a runner peddling football pools between the thirtieth and sixty-fifth floors."

"Marty, that's not funny. I will admit that a few nonunion workers sneak into the building from time to time, but the union boys would never do things like that, Marty."

"Donald, 40 minutes for hot water. Can you simulate fully occupied so the computer will be nice to me?"

"Marty, I already told you we have put you on red alert. And don't forget the party in the atrium."

The promoter's blitz was over, and I stared out at old 666. A police siren pierced the 59th-story aloofness. 666 Fifth Avenue was Tishman's place—by now probably fully depreciated by three consecutive owners at higher resale values, with few or no paid taxes to the city, state, and federal governments. In fact, the tax laws encourage accelerated depreciation on commercial real estate that never seems to depreciate at all. But my standard of living had depreciated greatly since the old Bronx days. I missed the smell of baked potatoes on every stair landing in the old walkup. From a working microwave oven there is only the electronic, odorless *beep...beep...beep*.

In 1983, Trump as a real estate operator topped out with his 56th Street condominium hyped so successfully to speculators, including me. Actually, Equitable Life was the controlling owner. He delivered apartments with minimal amenities—tiny closets, Pullman kitchens and low ceilings. Few lights were burning at Trump Tower, most apartments for trading, not living in, at that time.

Trump, who had a great talent for perceiving premium land parcels in New York early on, tried to leverage his real estate wins on Wall Street. Trump Tower and the Grand Hyatt Hotel were standouts, but their unleveraged equity interest, long since tapped, probably amounted to no more than $100 million. Back in the nineties, his three casinos stood borrowed up with no free equity. On more than $2 billion in debt, it looked to me that Trump had an annualized cash flow deficit of $150 million. The cash flow shortfalls, in turn, depreciated the "going concern" value of his properties. At the bottom of the cycle, it looked as if Trump was underwater, marked-to-market, by as much as half a billion dollars.

It took Wall Street until the end of 1990 to figure out that Trump was not to be taken too seriously. Yes, he had come out ahead greenmailing a frightened Bally management and had out-negotiated Merv Griffin, who ended up with James Crosby's obsolete Resorts Casino, a converted Holiday Inn dating back to the sixties, while Trump assumed control of the unfinished Taj Mahal property—and a year later Griffin defaulted on his junk bonds. Then Trump lost credibility as a financier (anyone with over $100 million) with his aborted bid for AMR (American Airlines). The October '89 bid of $120 a share was so tentative and vague that The Street laughed it off their screens. No financing source ever surfaced, and 11 days later it was withdrawn by Trump. He bragged to the press about enjoying Black Monday safe and sound in cash, the cat forever landing on his feet. Two years later, the cat was immobilized in wet cement after outbidding everyone for the Plaza Hotel and Eastern Air Lines' northeast corridor shuttle. His Taj Mahal bonds, six months after issuance by Merrill Lynch, traded under 50 cents on the dollar despite 14 percent coupon interest.

Trump, through his publicist, Howard Rubenstein, fed the press a daily dose of success stories. Not only was his fortune approaching the rarefied multibillion status of great entrepreneurs like Sam Walton, but everything he touched was destined for success. The old lady, the Plaza Hotel, would be resurrected in all its turn-of-the-century glory. Did Trump do more than scrape the black paint off the cast-iron lampposts?

The renamed Trump Shuttle proffered deluxe-class amenities—concierge services and fresh bagels with complimentary newspapers: the *Wall Street Journal*, *Financial Times*, whatever. USAir took it over in '92, and Delta Air Lines owned the Pan Am Shuttle. Down in Atlantic City, the Trump casinos would outbid Caesars for the championship fights and the Sinatras of the world. Trump bragged publicly that the spring opening of the Taj would stimulate business for his Trump Castle and Trump Plaza casinos. Television spots heralded the Taj as the Eighth Wonder of the World, a relatively modest claim coming from Trump.

Actually, Trump was doing all the right things with his properties. It was his financial construct of excessive leverage that was the problem. He was competing with a wobbly Pan Am for market share, but he couldn't get much above 50 percent. Trump thought his name was good for 10 more market share points. The Plaza was getting $350 a night for its rooms, but $25 million in cash flow didn't cover the interest on a $400-million investment.

The junk bond credit analysts finally sensed Trump's casino properties were too overleveraged, with cash flow peaking. Nobody as yet had a construct of declining revenues for Atlantic City casinos or parsed out a revenue shortfall of 15 percent for the Plaza and Castle properties. By the summer of '90 it was obvious that the Taj was siphoning off traffic from Trump's older properties. His bankers coughed up the cash to cover bond interest and debt amortization while looking for equity partners. It looked as if the shortfall was at least $50 million, annualized on properties that were fully borrowed up. Not even Barron Hilton, who had been denied a gaming license by the New Jersey gaming commission, seemed anxious to buy his way back in and repurchase the Castle that Trump bought from him in '85. More than 20 years later, Trump was litigating to get his name expunged from the Trump Plaza and Taj. Atlantic City stood moribund. Never a destination resort, more a weekend hangout outclassed by regional competition. Summer of '14, a wave of bankruptcies cascaded like dominos.

Back when Trump's hands-on relationship with Marla was beginning to affect his business, casino operators in Atlantic City worried that tourists would stay away. Vincent Roppatte was helicoptered down to Atlantic City to dress and coif Marla for her Diane Sawyer interview on prime time. Vincent fussed for six hours, lightening Marla's hair and picking out her jewelry accessories.

I remember the spring 1990 debut of the Taj Mahal drew good but not spectacular crowds. This monstrous T-shaped barn did shoulder burdensome fixed costs. Trump's equity in the Taj was a skinny $75 million, against $675 million in 14 percent debentures. Even with a gross win of $1.2 million a day, the Taj would run a cash flow deficit of $30 million a year for several years.

When I asked the corporate finance men at Merrill Lynch why they allowed Trump a nine-to-one debt-equity construct, they sheepishly said, "We looked on it as a real estate deal. Trump's name meant a lot to us." Out in Las Vegas, Steve Wynn of Golden Nugget had brought in his Mirage casino, a comparably ambitious project, but his leverage was closer to three to one. Similarly, the best operator in the business, Bill Bennett of Circus Circus, opened his Excalibur destination resort on the Las Vegas Strip, paying for it out of cash flow from sister casino properties. Later, Wynn lost his property to Kirk Kerkorian in an all-cash bear hug.

Trump's major strategic error, aside from overleveraging, was the assumption that his name would not only put the Taj on the map but the overflow crowd would hit the doors at the Plaza and Castle. By the summer of '90 their numbers had trailed off and Trump was forced to cut back the head count at the Taj by hundreds of employees just months after opening. Its revenue stream was running over a million daily, but short of expectations. Trump's accord with his lead banks—Chase, Citicorp, Manufacturers Hanover and Bankers Trust—ceded them operating control. Adnan Khashoggi's gas-guzzling yacht was put on the market, too, and Donald was reduced to a living allowance of $500,000 monthly. The press focused on Donald's allowance, not his loss of business acumen.

As early as the June '90 quarter, banks like Manny Hanny were writing off hundreds of millions in Trump loans. In lending Trump some $2 billion they had missed critical loan coverage criteria. Not only were Trump's casinos fully borrowed up to their estimated equity valuation, but extrapolating even a modest decline in operating revenues at his casinos would trigger cash flow deficits in the tens of millions plus comparable amounts for debt amortization on his public bonds. In turn, these deficits would lower the perceived asset values of his casinos. The Castle was leveraged with $372 million in debt and just $22 million in apparent equity. Japanese trophy buyers were active in Las Vegas but avoided Atlantic City, which still had skimpy convention center amenities and no world-class air terminal.

Trump's bankers held loan paper with inadequate asset coverage, the cardinal no-no in banking. Under the moderately negative economic scenario of 1991, Forbes had trouble figuring out his net worth. His bankers couldn't afford to pull the plug on his life-support system. They kept him alive for a couple more years and hoped asset values turned up enough to cover most of their outstanding loans. On the cover page of the Merrill Lynch prospectus for the Taj Mahal bond offering was a telltale sentence: "The net proceeds could be applied including funding interest on the bonds for 15 months from the dates of issuance." When a promoter is borrowing money to pay interest, in this instance over $100 million—run away, fast.

Marvin Roffman, the lone securities analyst who had the audacity to challenge Trump's Taj Mahal optimism as premature, was muzzled and then fired by his employer, Janney Montgomery Scott. This was a regional brokerage house owned by Penn Mutual Life Insurance Company. Trump complained and threatened to sue unless Roffman was terminated. Roffman countered with a suit against Trump for interfering with his employment. Roffman first apologized to Trump for his report but slept on it and then rescinded his apologetic missile. Later, Roffman won his case.

Within six months, Merrill Lynch's clients had dropped half their capital on their Taj bond play. Among the losers were some of the insurance annuity underwriters, like First Capital Holdings, swimming in impaired bond paper, controlled by Shearson/American Express. The paper loss on its equity was approaching $100 million. A year later, the insurance regulators took 'em over.

What does all this mean? The man with a long yacht and a gift for gab applied a real estate construct to almost all his operating properties and came up short on projected numbers. Put it within the context of our overleveraged banks in 2008–'09, the periodic topping out of collectibles like contemporary art and antique cars, and the steady erosion in the price of gold. Add in the flattening out of resale prices for homes throughout the country. Nobody got a free ride on hard assets between 1988 and '93, and this was repeated in 2007–'10.

In the mid-sixties, when Howard Hughes's agents toured Las Vegas on a buying binge for casinos and raw land, the going price for a hotel-casino on the Strip was $20 million. The locals grabbed Howard's Hughes Tool and TWA underwriting money. They knew how hard it was to grind out positive cash flow, year after year. Owners of the Las Vegas Hospital realized more profit selling it to Bobby Goldsamt of American Medicorp than on their casinos. Irwin Molasky and his partners reinvested their capital, building La Costa outside of San Diego. There was just enough cash left to finish the massive, teak lobby doors on opening night. Golf course home sites were moving slowly.

Unlike in Trump's case, the New Jersey Casino Control Commission denied my application to buy Caesars World, albeit I showed them a less leveraged construct. Four years later, it looked as if they had done me a backhanded favor. To this day, marginal gaming properties are known as "grind joints." Periodically, Caesars gets recapitalized by new owners employing too much debt leverage almost 30 years later.

Mar-A-Lago, the white elephant in Palm Beach, was bought by Trump in '85, at the same time he purchased the Castle casino from Hilton. It was built by Marjorie Merriweather Post, the Post Toasties heiress, before the flight patterns from the Palm Beach airport oozed incessant jet-engine pollution over the property, comparable with Citi Field, which abuts LaGuardia. Maybe Trump's purchase of the Eastern Air Lines shuttle was a reflexive reaction to such self-inflicted torture. The compulsive pick of Mar-A-Lago I leave out there with all the other trophies, but I give him credit for a tasteful remake into a country club with a spacious poolside setting. The tall boy with big eyes wanted his name perpetually up in lights. Happily, nearly everything in the world is available at a price, and Trump dipped in. Currently Mar-A-Lago thrives on one benefit night after another. Palm Beach loves to dress up at night. Trump initiated a $100-million lawsuit, early 2015, against the City of Palm Beach, claiming overhead aircraft were damaging this property's physical integrity.

In the spring of '93 Trump petitioned the Palm Beach town council for permission to convert Mar-A-Lago into a "world class" country club. "We want to make sure it's preserved forever," he said. Consequently, Merrill Lynch essayed a new offering of $325 million in mortgage notes for Trump Plaza that repeated the strategic deficiency of its initial bond offering for the Taj.

Twenty years later, Trump is thriving, but I'm disinterested in the details. My only wonder is how long he survived a mountain of debt on his name brand. A nice smile and P. T. Barnum's patter took him a long way—net worth estimated by Forbes around $7 billion.

TWENTY-FIVE

Decoding Buffett, Tisch and Contrasting Activists

A bet on ever-rising U.S. prosperity is very close to a sure thing.
WARREN BUFFETT

*H*ow to rate Buffett's prowess as a money manager today? Well, first you look at the composition of his $100-billion-plus portfolio. Nearly 50 percent dwells in financials, so this part should be measured against the Keefe, Bruyette & Woods large bank stock index. The remainder clearly falls in the domain of the S&P 500. For measuring Buffett, give him a 50/50 ratio of the S&P 500 Index and a financial sector index of choice.

Money managers controlling serious sums should be rated on an evenly melded ratio of 50 percent S&P 500 and 50 percent NASDAQ 100. There's no excuse to have missed the recovery in Apple. (Go, Carl!) All thinking operators shoulda owned from go properties like Google, Amazon, Facebook and Gilead and played the snapback in Microsoft. Even in the NASDAQ Composite, the top five names comprise 25 percent of the index, including Facebook. This is the raw reality of our volatile investment universe.

By rating managers 50 percent NASDAQ Composite or even the more extreme NASDAQ 100, you'd force them to take a stand on critical investment issues like whether the Internet continues to grow apace, capturing a bigger slice of the advertising dollar. So far, it's happening. In the NASDAQ Composite, technology comprises 43 percent of the index and consumer services 20 percent. Financials carry just 7 percent weighting.

Buffett doesn't want to play in this game, but so far he's missed much of the market's dynamism. Maybe he awaits in his crash helmet the next financial meltdown. During 2008–'09 he handled himself as a master macro player, pumping blood into Goldman Sachs, and later Bank of America et al, exacting an enormous toll in levied interest rates and equity participation, with warrants recently harvested. On Bank of America alone, his paper profit on warrants approximates $6 billion. All this in a couple of years!

No longer rate Buffett as a stock picker, because a goodly portion of Berkshire's $117-billion portfolio is sterilized goods. The danger in Berkshire Hathaway as an investment is it may sell at a discount to asset value before long, even if Warren sticks around 10 more years. For 2013, BRK rose 32 percent, at least keeping pace with the S&P 500 Index. But the Keefe, Bruyette & Woods bank index, BKX, gained 38 percent. For 2014, BRK advanced 26 percent, nearly double the S&P 500 Index.

Part of a money manager's job is to wrestle with sizable new faces going public. Take Alibaba, almost a $250-billion valuation. Google, a 2014 non-performer, rests below Berkshire in the S&P 500. Facebook, with a market cap over $200 billion, is number 14, right below Chevron. Berkshire is hard on the heels of ExxonMobil, a $400-billion property in business nearly forever.

Google went public nearly a decade ago and has risen over 1,300 percent. My point is: If you can analyze Comcast and DirecTV, you can deal with Google, which still sells under 20 times projected earnings power. Go, Google!

A fair question to put to Buffett is, what does he see in stodgy, tired blue chips like Exxon and IBM? Exxon is finding it difficult to replenish oil reserves, while it costs twice as much capital to do so vs. five years ago. With exploration and development of oil reserves taking the lion's share of cash flow, there's less 'n' less capital available for acquisitions and buybacks.

IBM is doing right to get out of hardware and build software capabilities in cloud computing and storage. But it's late. Amazon now is number one and even Microsoft a distant second. Meanwhile, it's difficult growing IBM's services business at more than a 5 percent annualized clip with price competition for large, long-term contracts so contentious. ExxonMobil and IBM went negative in 2014 with the market ahead 14 percent.

Before I cite more carping negatives, I'll step back for a wide-angle snapshot of Berkshire, showing the truly awesome enormity of Buffett's achievement. Warren has built Berkshire's shareholders equity to $224.5 billion. And there's $42 billion in liquidity on the balance sheet, so he's still a work in progress.

While Wall Street belched black blood during 2008–'09, Buffett got busy shoring up some of its players' balance sheets. The price demanded was stiff—high yielding debentures, many with sizable kickers in warrants not far out of the money then, subsequently redeemed, but in the money.

- $4.4 billion Wrigley 11.45 percent subordinated notes

- $5.0 billion Goldman Sachs 10 percent preferred stock plus warrants on 43.47 million shares
- $3 billion General Electric 10 percent preferred stock plus warrants on 134.8 million shares
- $3 billion Dow Chemical 8½ percent convertible preferred stock
- $5 billion Bank of America 6 percent preferred stock

The best deal ever came Buffett's way in 2011. Bank of America, transitioning to a new headman worried about outstanding litigation settlements overwhelming its balance sheet, granted Berkshire options on 700 million shares at $5 billion, worth $12 billion by yearend 2014. I bought B of A's preferred stock in the dark days of 2009 at $5 a share, but took ultimate risk. Ticks at $25 a share now, at its call price, and yields 6 percent. Buffett took some market risk but doubled his capital in two years. His warrants don't expire until 2021, September. Prospectively, we are talking at least another $5 billion–plus probable gain.

Without sufficient history to rate the couple of young money managers Buffett has surrounded himself with, I discount whether they'll ever have full or even sizable control of Berkshire's open-to-buy for new positions or sales governance on older established property.

When Buffett purchased the remaining outstanding stock in the Burlington Northern Railroad, I understood the opening gambit of his grand design. Why not sop up Berkshire's tens of billions in open-to-buy with established GDP-type properties? In short, these holdings would form his legacy once he's gone. Railroads and energy properties, even IBM and Wal-Mart, won't entail huge financial risk and will surely grow along with the country.

Maybe yes, maybe no. After all, the Pennsylvania Railroad and New York Central fell into receivership in the early sixties. IBM, pre–Gerstner's arrival, was headed for the manure pit. Currently, JCPenney and Sears fight for survival. Absent astute management that's balance-sheet sensitive, anything can happen. In the sixties, IBM's Tom Watson bet his company on the 360 computer introduction. IBM won primacy against feeble competition like Burroughs and Sperry Rand.

I don't buy Buffett's excuse that he eschews technology as unanalyzable. After all, he owns old technology, as in IBM, a non-performer. I see nothing but trouble for old tech, including Oracle and Intel, who must reinvent themselves fast or erode into also-rans. Facebook sells under 20 times 2015's EBITDA to enterprise value, and is analyzable. I can understand Buffett's reluctance to consider properties like Twitter, even Baidu and Priceline.com, on a valuation basis, but not

Facebook and Apple, even Alibaba.

For rating Buffett, give him a 60/40 ratio of the S&P 500 and a financial sector index of his choice. The deep basic is whether this is too conservative for such a world-class investor. Absolutely not! I, too, hold 20 percent of my stock market money in financials, namely big banks like Citigroup and Bank of America. They are great hedges against escalating money market rates lurking in the bushes. But I owned weighted positions in Facebook and Alibaba, not to mention Gilead. I rate myself against the NASDAQ 100 index, which includes all these names, barring banks. For 2014, NASDAQ 100 performed 50 percent better than the S&P 500. Energy stocks don't make this listing.

All in, when Buffett invested $20 billion in five properties, he demanded outlandish high yields with equity kickers that turned money good. By contrast, currently, BB corporate credits carry maybe 5.5 percent coupons with no equity kickers, just duration risk. You want Buffett managing your money throughout a bear market. Amazon could be cut in half then, along with Facebook and Salesforce.com, or at least all go down twice the market's slide. Meanwhile, ExxonMobil could erode slowly.

New issue convertibles during 2014 yielded under 2 percent, with a 40 percent premium over market. Many high yield managers do salivate for more paper, which of course gets absurdly, richly priced. Berkshire's H. J. Heinz acquisition came in 2013, some $12.25 billion with a joint partner, 3G Capital. Berkshire holds $8 billion in a 9 percent preferred stock. Yearend 2014, preferred stocks, mainly below-investment-grade financials, yielded 6 percent. Alibaba sold long-duration debentures at a small premium over U.S. Treasuries.

Berkshire's operating businesses can be characterized as bread-and-butter enterprises. Investors shouldn't just think of Geico and the reinsurance properties. Pretax earnings at the BNSF Railway are almost as large. Insurance accounts for one-third of total operating earnings. I put a price-earnings ratio of 12 times earnings on the combined properties, somewhat below the S&P 500's multiplier. Investment income for the insurance properties ran pretty flat, past three years, and this line dwarfs underwriting profits. BNSF, as large an earnings factor as insurance, was suffering a flat year in 2014. Management blamed it on the weather. But Union Pacific and Canadian Pacific showed high-teens growth.

I'm bothered by Buffett's final morphing into his staid money management construct, saddling himself with underperforming big capitalization properties like ExxonMobil, IBM and Wal-Mart. Coca-Cola, his big long-term winner, rose just 7 percent in 2013, and underperformed during 2014. This is forgivable because its low cost tax basis makes it prohibitive to bang out. Why reduce the federal deficit single-handedly? Incidentally, the U.S. deficit now runs at a livable 3 percent, probably headed lower in a better economic setting. For 2014, only nine of the top 25 largest capitalizations outperformed the market. General Electric, Google, Chevron, ExxonMobil, Verizon and AT&T dwelled in negative territory. Parse 2013 performance of the S&P 500 Index and you find sizable disparity among the top 50 names. Properties like Apple, Facebook, Microsoft, Intel, Merck and Gilead Sciences were huge winners.

In summary, owning Berkshire stock today, you own a slice of America through its operating entities and equity portfolio. There's balance sheet strength, over $40 billion in excess capital available for a couple of big deals. Never discount Buffett's capacity as an investor of last resort, during hard times like 2008–'09. Bank of America's giveaway should go down in history, with many blushing red faces in their boardroom.

There was an eerie symbolism embedded in Warren Buffett's 2013 annual report for Berkshire Hathaway. First off, this was a fat 136-pager, inclusive of the chairman's copyrighted 24-page letter. His no-nonsense discussion, the world and word according to Warren, eschews the bland phraseology of, say, ExxonMobil's 10-K: "ExxonMobil was incorporated in the State of New Jersey in 1882" (John D's Standard Oil of New Jersey).

Buffett wants you to read him, retaining ghostwriters in the past to liven his wordage, but the flow is breezy and he's solid on metaphors, at intervals self-deprecating. This is novel in the world of corporate rotundity unless your net worth runs over $25 billion. Catch this: "I must confess that their investments outperformed mine. (Charlie Munger says I should add 'by a lot!') If such humiliating comparisons continue, I'll have no choice but to cease talking about them."

Don't own Berkshire Hathaway for Buffett's portfolio management prowess. That's history. But 50 years ago, even 60 years ago, when Wall Street's research capacity dwelt in its most primitive state, comparable with the 1920s, Buffett was busy doing fieldwork and management sit-downs. During the twenties, you needed to know who was doing what to whom in the backseat of the Ford. Without inside information you floundered, clueless and helpless.

Buffett (and a handful of others) studied specific industry and corporate pivotal variables to muster discounted cash flow models, using a company's projected growth trajectory. Stocks sold at 10 times earnings in the late fifties. Technology hardly existed. No computers, just adding machines. We all used slide rules for our numbers work, plotted on semi-logarithmic sheets of paper. Bell Laboratories first licensed the transistor in 1958.

I didn't come across Buffett until the early sixties, when American Express had just introduced its green card. Why couldn't American Express gain primacy in their credit card venture, putting away Diners Club? I was friendly with the AmEx money managers who handled the company's float, and they confirmed this hypothesis. Buffett was there, too, and still owns American Express, 50 years later. I worked for a rich operator then, Jack Kaplan, but he banged out our AXP position for a short-term trading profit. Staying power counts in the investment world, and nobody's better at it than Warren. I wish I wore his iron pants.

Later, when Geico almost landed in receivership because of too-aggressive premium rate discounting, I bought a big block of stock from Goldman Sachs for two bucks, after confirming with Pennsylvania's insurance commissioner that he would give Geico some running room to restructure. Within a year, I sold out my position for $8. Buffett held on and in 1990 tendered for all remaining shares in public hands.

When I pulled a dozen 13F filings of large hedge funds and other private capital pools, I saw something I didn't expect. Namely, many of these operators unconsciously imitate the Buffett of 50 years ago, beating the bushes for inefficiently priced stocks, undervalued and underresearched. Many holdings are small- to mid-capitalization properties. Unlike Buffett, Carl Icahn, for example, is a porcupine, swishing his tail, an unfriendly, contentious shareholder, no passive cheerleader.

The financial press labels such operators "activists," but they're closer to the bothersome greenmailers of the seventies and eighties. Carl Icahn, earlier an arbitrageur, then was labeled as such, but he's too rich to be designated so dismissively today. His $5-billion position in Apple, however, carries no weight in their boardroom. Apple, with a $700-billion market capitalization, is too hefty to bully. A pure gut play on Icahn's part, a luxury he can well afford, but he can't possibly know any more than a busload of security analysts taking down notes at quarterly informationals. The remainder of his ragamuffins leave me agnostic, at best, particularly his energy holdings. Transocean was a 3 percent position, dismembered by the market, down 60 percent as oil futures dropped 40 percent in a matter of months. Icahn kicked it out.

ICAHN ASSOCIATES
TOP 10 HOLDINGS
AS OF SEPTEMBER 30, 2014

Security	Weighting	Market Value ($ billions)
Icahn Enterprises	33.7%	11.3
Apple	15.8%	5.3
CVR Energy	9.4%	3.2
eBay	7.7%	2.6
Federal-Mogul	5.3%	1.8
Chesapeake Energy	4.5%	1.5
Hertz Global	2.9%	1.0
Nuance Communications	2.8%	0.9
American Railcar	2.6%	0.9
Hologic	2.4%	0.8
Total	**87.3%**	**29.3**

Icahn's portfolio is concentrated in difficult-to-analyze properties. Leaving aside the Icahn Enterprises holding, nine properties account for over 50 percent of assets. Aside from Apple, you won't find these stocks among the top 100 names in the S&P 500 Index. I don't have the courage or inclination to tackle Herbalife. I assume Carl banged out his Transocean, an oil rig operator, before it dropped over 50 percent.

As a money manager and go-for-control, stir-'em-up operator, Icahn is as gutsy as it gets. Comparing Buffett's top 10 with Icahn's, you see a different dynamic. Buffett has grown into stock concentration largely through market appreciation. Even so, holding 50 percent of your portfolio in financials is a construct only Buffett gets away with. My partners would throw me out the window if I tried that. His four top holdings comprise 61 percent of invested capital, but they are big capitalization, definable properties.

BERKSHIRE HATHAWAY
TOP 10 HOLDINGS
AS OF SEPTEMBER 30, 2014

Security	Weighting	Market Value ($ billions)
Wells Fargo	22.3%	24.0
Coca-Cola	15.80%	17.0
American Express	12.3%	12.3
IBM	12.4%	12.4
Wal-Mart	1.3%	4.6
Procter & Gamble	4.1%	4.1
ExxonMobil	3.6%	3.9
U.S. Bancorp	3.1%	3.1
DaVita HealthCare	2.5%	2.7
DirecTV	2.4%	2.6
Total	**82.8%**	**86.8**

Turning to Third Point's portfolio, you see comparable concentration in its top 10, over 56 percent of assets. Most names are more recognizable—Dow Chemical, Alibaba. Some are controversial but not so abstruse in terms of pivotal analytic variables. These include T-Mobile and Sotheby's, an "activist" holding. At 20 times earnings power, Sotheby's looks overpriced to me. Art at auction is more cyclical a venue than the Big Board and looked extended after the heady November 2014 auctions. Third Point's big short in Herbalife doesn't show up here, only "long" holdings.

For 2013, Berkshire's book value rose only 18 percent, vs. 32 percent for the S&P 500 Index, a huge disparity (I'd be out of business). Equities alone rose low teens. Actually, BRK underperformed its benchmark in four of the last five years. I'd definitely be running just my own money at that juncture. During 2014, several holdings underperformed, particularly Coca-Cola, IBM, ExxonMobil and Wal-Mart.

During the financial meltdown (2008–'09) Buffett emerged as the investment banker of last resort. Since then, Berkshire has acquired, mainly for cash, major properties like the Burlington Northern and spent $18 billion, purchasing all of NV Energy (a utility) and a major part of H. J. Heinz, where Berkshire is the financing partner, holding $8 billion in a preferred stock with a 9 percent coupon. (I scrounge for preferreds yielding 6.5 percent.)

THIRD POINT
TOP 10 HOLDINGS
AS OF SEPTEMBER 30, 2014

Security	Weighting	Market Value ($ billions)
Dow Chemical	13.8%	1.1
Ally Financial	11.6%	1.0
Actavis	8.3%	0.7
Alibaba	7.6%	0.6
eBay	3.0%	0.3
Sotheby's	2.9%	0.3
Dollar General	2.9%	0.3
Liberty Global	2.6%	0.2
Anheuser-Busch InBev Sensata Technologies Holding	2.6%	0.2
Total	**57.9%**	**5.0**

During the darkest days of the 2009 recession, Buffett purchased the BNSF Railway, his biggest deal ever. I've owned Union Pacific and Canadian Pacific Railway, where operating earnings growth exceeds the BNSF's, but these rails weren't for sale to outsiders. Believe Buffett when he says he's investing for the next hundred years. His focus is building stable operating earnings.

Larry Tisch was one of my favorite Wall Streeters and, like Buffett, a confirmed value player going back to the 1970s. Unlike Buffett, Larry was also a short seller. In the late nineties, with the market selling over 20 times earnings, Larry shorted S&P futures but was too early and dropped a bunch of money for Loews, which he and his brother, Preston, controlled. It's now run by Jimmy Tisch, Larry's son, who, with his father, thirsted to buy oil tankers for scrap metal value when the oil majors shed them.

Larry read annual reports and 10Ks for recreation while the rest of us took Stephen King to the beach. Like a hawk hunting for mice, he'd swoop down and short The Street's myopia. He, too, avoided technology as outside his power zone. Tisch redlined any stock selling above 15 times earnings as extravagantly priced.

He and Buffett were stubborn in their core beliefs, ever patient with investments and bridge games. Buffett claims he is wedded to his core holdings, but take that with a grain of salt because of his tax basis. Tisch was more pragmatic. Everything is for sale at a price, as in CBS. Tisch's time span at times was one or two market cycles. Buffett's stretches longer just so long as he likes the basic economics of the business and management's ability to make its mark. When Gillette faltered, Buffett led the boardroom in terminating its headman, Mike Hawley.

The public's perception of the two men is 180 degrees apart and faulty because of its oversimplification. Buffett is venerated as the genius among geniuses. Larry was perceived more as a dealer in distressed properties, less proactive and capable of making big mistakes. Both men had tons of free cash flow at their fingertips and controlled sizable insurance company investment portfolios. Berkshire's properties Geico and General Reinsurance are first-class underwriters. Loews' CNA Financial was an also-ran casualty property that finally has been rationalized. The initial investments by both men, Buffett in Geico and Tisch in CNA, were made at rock-bottom prices when these properties bled from underwriting losses. They stepped up to the plate and hit a 3-and-0 pitch, bases loaded, out of the ballpark.

Tisch operated in relatively quiet obscurity. His public profile centered around huge grants to New York University, where he was chairman of the board and instrumental in raising NYU to a more prestigious standing. Yes, NYU's investment portfolio stayed in bonds for 10 years after Black Monday, but so what? The institution, step by step, created a great law school and an MBA program as good as Harvard's in the financial and international sectors. Tisch's performing arts school, particularly in film study, is as good as it gets. Buffett as yet seems too engrossed in business to put his personal stamp on academia.

The only one in recent financial history who approached Buffett in public veneration was Edwin Land, headman at Polaroid for decades. The annual meeting at Polaroid in its heady days (the breakthrough in instant color photography and, later, the inexpensive Swinger camera) attracted thousands of investors who made fortunes, dating back to 1948 when Polaroid's introductory instant camera, weighing a couple of pounds, bulkier than a milk bottle, made its debut. Golf carts ferried everyone around the Polaroid campus and then Land presided in a show-and-tell session where new products were unveiled. Steve Jobs imitated Land's camera presentations when he introduced the first iPhone. Edwin Land was a testy man, feared by his employees and stubborn to the point of shortsightedness. The Japanese developed lightweight 35mm cameras and Kodak pushed photo finishing to a two-hour process. Polaroid's research priorities floundered on X-ray technology and other still waters. The rest is financial history.

The irony for Larry Tisch, who led an exemplary life, whom I viewed as a role model, is that he was perceived in the press as a coldhearted mogul. The greater irony is that his sound investment ideology got him in this pickle and there was nobody to take him out of it. This is not Saul Steinberg, who enriched himself at shareholder expense, flew around in a converted Boeing 727 and stuck to an outrageous cash dividend policy, with a personal bonus and a salary scale far beyond the industry norm. The Tisch brothers worked for peanuts, frugal to the point of idiosyncrasy. Any corporate executive who owns a good piece of outstanding equity and takes options is a pig. Tisch took nothing. Buffett pays himself a hundred thousand and doesn't like options for himself, nor does he grant his executives any. Do a good job and the payoff is cash. I never saw a research report from Wall Street that commented on good character as a prerequisite for a stock recommendation. It's on my checklist, and I'm sure it's on Buffett's, too.

To test my intensity I surround myself with fortyish investment analysts and money managers. I'm interested not only in what new stories they come up with but the quality, the incisiveness of their thinking on specific industries and stocks. Is it superficial or exhaustive? Do they make the right conclusions from the facts? Nobody's perfect, but over time you're evaluated, like batters, on percentage points of performance. Late in 2000 our technology task force, including me, missed every inflection point in all the subsectors of tech—semiconductors, optical systems and computers. The carnage in Apple, JDS Uniphase, Corning Glass, Altera and Advanced Micro Devices set us back. What saved us was our gross underweighting in tech and our heavy concentration elsewhere in health care and financial services. Nobody ever said managing money isn't a humbling experience.

Buffett and Tisch were nearly one-man shows. Joe Rosenberg, a very sound investment man, worked for me over 35 years ago, then joined Tisch. Buffett can bounce ideas off Charlie Munger, his long-tenured partner. Both men could operate alone in a small room with a yellow pad and a telephone, maybe a stock screen, Bloomberg, and a trader monitoring the bond market and news ticker.

We can learn a lot about money management as it's practiced today from Buffett's underperformance during recent years and Tisch's periodic underperformance. Buffett is more of a portfolio manager than Tisch was in terms of coverage of investments relative to the breadth of the S&P 500 Index. He cites his performance relative to the index in shareholder reports, annually, over 50 years. If you have a great record, you report cumulatively. When the numbers are spotty, you just deal with the previous year. Curiously, Loews' annual reports were bland, murky and difficult to decipher, whether in a good year or a bad year. Buffett uses his annual as a bully pulpit for patting the heads of his executives covering a bevy of consumer-related businesses. But his operating companies, until recently, had little relevance to investment results.

Larry Tisch never talked much publicly about Loews. The numbers were the numbers. Parse the annual and CNA's convention statement to the insurance commissioner. "Figure it out for yourself" is the unstated message. The tenacity of both men is unassailable, except one says too much and the other just said yes or no. Breakfasting with Larry at his Regency Hotel, I found him personable, voluble, opinionated and candid—on any subject, including Loews. Right after Black Monday he turned silent, and a year later I learned he was then a big buyer.

I look on Buffett today as sort of a portfolio manager of a Focus 20 fund, ex–tech plays. Tisch was more the test-the-market player, aggressive in bonds and making strategic asset plays like the $500 million investment in new oil tankers that he cut with the South Korean shipyards when they were starving to keep their yards humming in '99. The buys in Lorillard, CNA Financial and Diamond Offshore Drilling were pure value plays.

Tisch and Buffett may fall under the "value player" classification, but they were miles apart in style and substance. Buffett's special competence was singling out, early on, great managements with near primacy in their industry. Hopefully, there was plenty of cash flow to buy back stock. Coca-Cola did this for 10 years. Tisch never operated this way. As Jimmy Tisch said to me years ago, "I stood on the deck of this tanker that was a couple of hundred yards long and thought to myself, 'You get all this for $5 million?'" Big oil was selling its tankers for scrap value at the bottom of the cycle in the late eighties. This is a junk peddler's investor psyche that I admire but pass up. I like to walk down Fifth Avenue holding hands with my pretty wife in her summer dress, hoping she doesn't make me stop at Tiffany's.

Many of NASDAQ's pretty girls got too expensive by late 2000, but the nineties were one helluva stroll for technology and for growth stocks as a category. Rates of return for growth and value players started to diverge in '98 and continued to do so until later in 2000. Before '98, both growth and value came out in the same place, measured over 25 years. That's worth an asterisk somewhere in your subconscious. They ran neck 'n' neck during 2014, too.

Buffett's awesome 50-year record is captured in the Bernstein graph on growth stock persistency, decade over decade. No more than 10 percent of growth stocks span more than one decade; perhaps 5 percent hold their primacy over 20 years. What happened to Buffett the past few years is that the failure rate mostly came in stable revenue growers like Coca-Cola (*Figure 35*).

SHARE OF COMPANIES PERSISTING IN
THE BERNSTEIN GROWTH-STOCK UNIVERSE

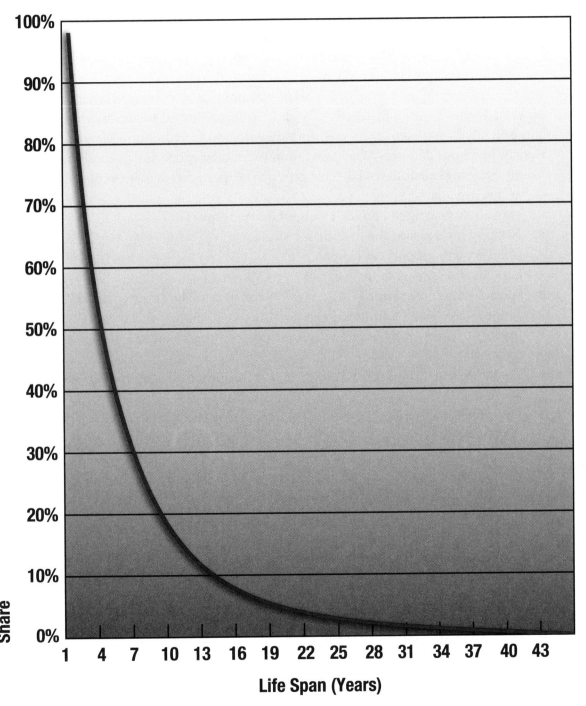

Figure 35

Source: Bernstein Research

A decade ago, Kirk Kerkorian, older than Tisch, had emerged as the more aggressive and successful value operator. He took out Steve Wynn's Mirage with a bear hug after Wynn turned off Wall Street with overspending on new properties—the Bellagio in Las Vegas and Beau Rivage in Biloxi.

The takeaway here is that nobody has a monopoly on brains. Coca-Cola isn't going anywhere. Buffett should have checked out and paid his taxes. Tisch's timing on shorting an overvalued market was premature by two years. Pausing on their virtues is more instructive. Both men were shrewd judges of character and executive competence. As investors they demonstrated enormous patience, were omnivorous digesters of facts and monitored their properties dispassionately. These fearless gladiators risked their reputations periodically with multibillion-dollar investments.

From all this emerges a bunch of disputable precepts:
- Nothing is forever in the investment world.
- There's no monopoly on brains.
- Growth stocks sport finite lives of five to 10 years.
- Special situation investing is the "in" place to be. The frontier beckons, so adopt a "Go West" attitude.
- Institutional investors aren't rating money managers within a task-fulfilling construct.
- The NASDAQ 100 is the best index to measure yourself against as an aggressive player.
- Discipline! Twitter and that feisty electric car maker Tesla may kill you on valuation alone.
- Burnish your image too protractedly and you'll invite my carping criticism.
- Understand macros. Politics leads economics ever since the Egyptian pharaohs. The Russians tried to bury Disneyland, but they failed. Khrushchev's GDP couldn't keep pace with U.S. defense expenditures, so we buried them and then they imploded.
- Go-for-control or ego investing (Sotheby's) is a luxury few can afford.
- Learn to stand alone. If you rub shoulders within the consensus, look out below.

If you find time to read financial statements, start with the annual corporate proxy statement. You'll see how managements compensate themselves. You may not like it. Years ago, the SEC forced public corporations to include five-year graphs showing stock performance relative to the S&P 500 and a peer group comparison.

Berkshire Hathaway underperformed the S&P over five years, before snapping back in 2014.

After you finish with the proxy statement, throw away the annual report and get the annual 10-K filing with the SEC. It's more informative and detailed, without the PR fluff of the annual report. Entrepreneurial managers produce annuals that exude confidence, individuality and plain talk, not bankerese. Buffett talks the talk but brushes off the details. His $100-billion equity portfolio is dismissed with a few sentences. Nobody's perfect.

Ivan Boesky, with his "greed is good" speech, was on the right track, except he executed with a suitcase of money, not brains. Known disaffectionately as "The Undertaker" because he paraded around The Street in a three-piece black suit with a gold chain draped on his vest, Boesky was talking about motivation and intensity. If you're not prepared to work like an animal, stand alone and parse all the facts, and make decisions that are controversial and less than obvious, even wildly abstract, buy an index fund.

TWENTY-SIX

My World Is Combustible, Changeable, but Manageable

*O*n my spread in the Hudson Valley, red-winged blackbirds and robins came back a week early, spring 2014, and met a six-inch snowfall. Nobody's timing is perfect, but so what? I thought of all of this while walking among the crosses and intermittent Stars of David in the American Cemetery overlooking Omaha Beach in Normandy. My second visit, tears flowed again. It was our country's finest hour. I regretted being too young for D-day.

I fought in the Korean War, at the end, as an airborne infantry company commander. Over the arctic winter of '52 I felt my country had failed us. Truman's cutback of defense appropriations dictated that we fought in combat boots and field jackets and nearly froze. Near the war's end, the quartermaster finally issued to the troops parkas and Mickey Mouse thermal boots. Eisenhower, in his 1952 presidential campaign, proclaimed he would go to Korea and end the war. That's all he had to do to win the election. A cease-fire was signed in August 1953. Fortunately for Truman, television was in its infancy, so the public had no idea of the Administration's shortcomings towards its troops in the field.

On Wall Street over 60 years ago, everyone wore grey flannel suits, white oxford shirts and fedoras. The Street was a small village outfitted by Brooks Brothers. I arrived as a junior analyst, then impeccably mentored by Bob Stovall and others to whom I am eternally grateful and indebted.

In the snappy downdraft of 1969–'70, when secondary stocks turned to dust, a prominent Park Avenue psychoanalyst dropped in to discuss his portfolio with me. Streetwise and clubby, he couldn't wait to tell me about all the "taxpayers" he owned on downtown Broadway that were clocking fat rentals. His equity portfolio told another story. My visitor whipped out a brown paper bag from his inside jacket pocket and showed me the list, scribbled in pencil, with dates of acquisition.

The doctor's portfolio consisted of all the doggy-eared picks of previous cycles.

For the sixties, there stood Four Seasons Nursing Homes, Parvin-Dohrmann and Vendo. Anaconda Copper Mining, U.S. Steel and American Motors were his undiscarded ragamuffin dreams from the fifties.

"You're an incurable collector," I said. "All these dogs shoulda been banged out long ago. If you want me to run your money, remember I'm not a shoemaker who repairs old goods. Everything goes. We start fresh."

The doctor barked back at me, "You guys are all the same. All you want to do is turn me over for the commissions."

"All I want to do is drag you into the twentieth century," I said. "You're a captive of your past." I thought if I used his jargon, I'd make my point.

The doctor sprang up from his swivel chair, snatched his paper bag out of my hand and dashed out, tight as a bull's ass. I called after him, "What you have is an emotional commitment to being right. If you don't sell, you're never wrong. Get yourself some help. The only perfection is six feet under."

I've learned to take my own advice and look on myself as a builder of a gigantic mosaic that is never finished. There are always stones to implant and others to pull out. That's money management. If you stop to admire your construct, it's the beginning of the end. When you lose your nerve and freeze, it's surely curtains.

The money management game can be compared to a Super Bowl extravaganza, even a soccer match. The roar of the crowd, whistles and trumpets blaring—the daily noise level has no meaning. During 60 minutes of closely matched football, the marginal differences are turnovers and injuries. Even the 1990 World Cup final between Germany and Argentina was decided by a penalty kick in favor of Germany, 1 to 0.

In money management, mistakes are costly, forcing you to turn over losers and reposition your portfolio, as dangerous as a fumble. *The solitary investor must ask himself if he should play in a market that the white shoes don't think twice about destabilizing.* The individual investor should be able to parse his mutual fund's semiannual report or his self-made portfolio and at least come to the conclusion that his ship is seaworthy and the captain isn't risking destruction to set a new world record on the Atlantic crossing. When the *Titanic* hit its iceberg, women and children scrambled into the lifeboats. Middle-aged guys in dinner jackets sang hymns as the deck sloped away from them. On Wall Street, it's forever every man hit the exit solo. Let the president appoint a commission after we're safe on the putting green.

Economists term the assumption that nothing changes as the naïve forecast, but that's what we had from the FRB throughout 2014. They were visibly jittery about overstaying their easy-money construct but craved more confirmation of a reaccelerating economic setting, specifically in housing and employment. Early February 2015, a strong employment report touched off a huge rally in bank stocks, the market ready to discount, finally, a step up in money market rates by midyear.

I thought of all this as I watched my home-based white swan pair molt into vicious fighters. On my pond, they drove off an intruding swan couple—biting, wing flapping and hissing hysterically. Bucolic serenity is a myth best left to Impressionist painters like Monet, I mused. My pets were a great metaphor for the Big Board, waxing ugly and then serene.

JAN ASSELIJN, *THE THREATENED SWAN*, 1650
Collection Rijksmuseum

The artist claims he witnessed this mother swan in a show of protest against an inquisitive dog encroaching upon her nest.

Invariably, when the market flirts with new high ground, Death Doctors surface and spout "The good times can't possibly last." Nouriel Roubini, along with a bunch of market letter writers, traders and gold bugs (somewhat eviscerated), expected the sequester syndrome to crunch GDP in 2012. For 2014, many bears played the China card, but China's GDP still grew irrepressibly at over 7 percent per annum. For 2013, nobody dared publish a forecast that the S&P 500 Index would take out old highs of 2000 and 2007, but the W formation in place for 13 years ended with a burst during December's animal spirits of 2013. Yearend punditry, as in Byron Wien, called for a correction of up to 10 percent, but by midyear '14 the market flirted with 2,000, up nearly 10 percent.

Lemme compare this bull market with others, going back to the nadir, 1982, when Volcker viciously snatched away our punch bowl. From 1983 to Black Monday, late in 1987, the market gathered speculative momentum. The system went LBO crazy and price-earnings ratios levitated to 20 times earnings. LBO money then cost over 8 percent, with preferred stocks issued at 12 percent or more, twice current rates. Debt interest coverage typically was skimpy, no more than two to one. The U.S. Treasury considered disallowing interest expense on deals, but was talked out of its position by Wall Street's honchos. Otherwise, Black Monday woulda blotted out the sun.

In the seventies and eighties, the market dealt with Dr. Doom (Henry Kaufman) as well as Dr. Death (Al Wojnilower). Henry was a senior partner at Salomon Brothers and Al, house economist at First Boston. Henry perennially feared irrepressible inflation and sky-high interest rates. Al usually found our economic system on the verge of dysfunctionality, but never opined, wisely, on the stock market's course. Neither did Henry, an old, old friend.

Bond traders at Solly and First Boston normally ignored their resident gurus, but both economists, widely respected, were fearless stand-aloners, outside their brethren's consensus. Kaufman annually published Solly's widely read report on supply and demand for funds, bedrock research for projecting interest rates over the next 12 months.

I'll grant you the world is combustible. The S&P 500 Index flirted with 1,900 Easter of 2014, while market letter writers chanted about triple tops and necklace formations, even sombreros. Market letter writers, scribbling on their little lady's ironing board, periodically spout that margin credit is dangerously high, but it ain't. It's around $350 billion, two days' trading on the Big Board. Interest on margin credit is next to nothing, an easy cross to bear. Why more investors and traders didn't arbitrage credit against BB bonds yielding near 6 percent mystifies me. This remains a great "carry" trade since 2009, and unlikely to unwind before 2016, unless the Fed turns antsy.

Our FRB prays daily for inflation, something I never expected to see in my lifetime. Lest we forget: Paul Volcker pressed money market rates up to 15 percent to purge the country of rabid inflationary biases, forged by the UAW and the Teamsters. But the Fed always wins. It has more money and power than you or me. Today the UAW and Teamsters snore away like defanged tigers.

Academic economists like Roubini, with lucrative consulting businesses on the side, expected consumers to tap out during 2014. Did they weigh the surge in family net worth, now back above its pre-meltdown peak? Consumers, finally, are ready to take on debt for big-ticket purchases at low interest rates. Just what Ben Bernanke wanted to see, and now Janet Yellen talks the talk. Our automakers prosper, with annualized car sales approaching 17 million.

Here's my mantra: The Fed wants to be your best friend. Market valuation is fair. The consumer can spend more and save less. Home construction and turnover soon show buoyancy, with escalating prices. Capital goods spending recovers and Detroit sells more cars, maybe as high as 17 million in North America for 2015. *Consumer Reports* endorsed GM's new-model Cadillac and Silverado pickup truck. (My feisty Toyota Prius gets 45 miles to the gallon with a quiet and smooth ride.) The FRB wins its game of reflation. Their ball. Reminds me of when I used to play tic-tac-toe against a glass-encased chicken in Chinatown. The bird got first move, so I couldn't ever win. She was rewarded with seeds, while I was out a quarter. One helluva chicken!

The unfathomable Westminster Dog Show is an apt metaphor for the market. Many big favorites laid an egg at the 136th Westminster Kennel Club Dog Show in 2012. I'm sure we can all hum old standards like "Stars Fell on Alabama," "Moonlight in Vermont," even "April in Paris" and "A Nightingale Sang in Berkeley Square," but many top winning dogs when they fail to make the cut fade into oblivion in their breed, or lose to lesser winning animals in the seven group rings. Stars did not shine in the rings for many exhibitors, with the exception of the Pekingese—very typy, number 2 All Breed dog in 2011—who took Best in Show.

Upsets for us at the show ran comparable with the market intermittently trashing Google, Amazon and Apple. At Westminster you encountered cutting, humbling lessons, reminders that beauty rests in the eyes of the beholder, the judge. The market surely is the Great Humbler, too. Nobody, for long, fully escapes successive cycles. Buffett has underperformed for the last five years. Even countries turn dysfunctional. Check out this chart on Greek 10-year bonds, which sold to yield 40 percent in 2011 after the government had fessed up to misstating its federal deficit—over 12 percent, not the 6 percent reported. Truly, a black swan event, unforecastable.

Financial markets rightly feared Greece would withdraw from the European Union, go off the euro and return to the drachma, thereby defaulting on all euro obligations. Actually, their politicians soldiered on. In the spring of 2014, their 4¾ percent five-year bond underwriting was wildly oversubscribed. Yet unemployment for high school graduates in Greece still runs at over 20 percent. They're lucky to find part-time work. Greece's bonds, rated B–, yield slightly more than our BB corporates. I'd rather buy American (*Figure 36*).

I did omit one major variable in dog showmanship. Contenders normally amass record points at shows where they avoid other contenders. Only judges, dog handlers, owners and your competitors know this. Westminster is the show of shows. Everyone needs to compete against serious contenders he can no longer avoid confronting. Thus, the "upsets."

GREECE 10-YEAR BOND ROLLER COASTER

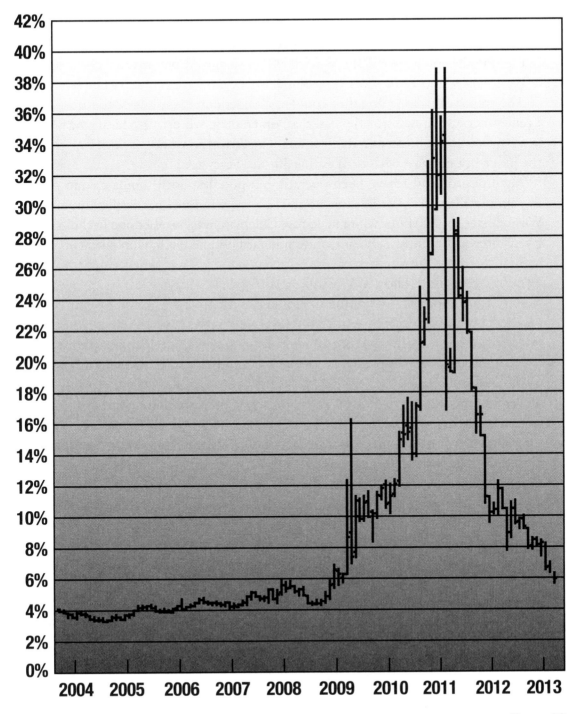

Figure 36

Source: Investing.com

Although 150-pounders like deerhounds sometimes win, the Garden crowd normally goes for showy 12-pounders like Norfolk and Norwich terriers. And yet, one great campaigner, the smooth-haired fox terrier, placed third in his terrier group. Stump, a Sussex terrier, came out of retirement to win it all in 2009. The number-one dog in the country for 2011, a black cocker spaniel, didn't make an impression at Westminster in February 2012.

The arena yearns for a dog they could easily encounter strolling in Central Park. I remember one showy crowd pleaser, a Pomeranian, who strutted into the "Best in Show" ring like he owned the Garden. The crowd went hog-wild. How could the judge not put that toy up? Was this 30-plus years ago?

My little lady and I have been operating in poodles, both standards and toys, for almost 30 years. We've done our share of winning, naturally, but never Westminster. In 2004 our white male toy, Coleman, was number one in the country, all breeds. Recently, Ally, our white standard poodle bitch, won over 100 Best in Shows and was the number-one non-sporting dog in the country. In 2014, Ally went Reserve Best in Show at Westminster!! Finally!

Rebecca Mason, my wife's mentor, going back to 1976, at one point commanded a breeding stock inventory of 106 poodles. We never reached that level, but I remember my wife working all night feeding newly whelped puppies, 11 of them, with tubes and supplements. Sometimes, mothers produce little or no milk for ravenous offspring.

Periodically, we reached out for new breed stock to stamp temperament, size, and tail set, whatever you feel you need to typify the breed standard. Lemme tick off a bunch of breed points for poodles: tail set, topline, feet, soundness, placement of ear leathers, under jaw, color of eyes (dark and almond-shaped), layback of shoulder, expression and temperament.

Reasons for top winning dogs losing at the big show can be multidimensional, but exhibitors like us understand and accept that an overwhelming winning record is not always coupled with universal acceptance. No dog ever meets all points of its breed standard and can be marked down by a judge who favors just the breed characteristics that your animal is short on. For every stock you own, you can find five analysts positive but few thumbs down. Right?

Starting in 1988, the market saw fewer black swans paddling around. Yes, the Russians almost defaulted on their Treasury bills and the Fed zigged with tightened credit in 1994 when they shoulda zagged. That policy mistake was soon corrected. Later, the market in 2000 had to wrestle with the Internet fiasco, when stocks were rated on clicks and inflated ways of new subscriber counting for cellular telephony. This was Wall Street's shabbiest interlude of pure decadence and stupid ciphering. Corporate finance honchos dictated what analysts must write about in specific underwritings. The Street had lost its way and precipitated the rather mild 2001 recession. Henry Blodget, Merrill Lynch's feisty Internet analyst then, now runs an Internet news service backed by Jeff Bezos. Blodget gets to opine daily, but the SEC has banned him permanently from working on Wall Street because of irresponsible bullish research reports and recommendations.

After 9/11, the housing boom took over and mortgage credit excesses nearly destroyed our financial system in 2008–'09. But they didn't. The Fed and U.S. Treasury stepped in; even Republicans went along with TARP to save AIG, General Motors and Citigroup, now legitimate revivals. Lehman Brothers, alas, was forced to bite the dust. Rarely remarked upon, even to this day, is how valuation was overstretched in 2007, near 20 times earnings. Corporate profit margins soared above trend. We don't have this construct currently. The market sells near 16 times earnings and corporations stand flooded with liquidity. Low cost of borrowing and stable wages could stick around for years and bolster profits.

Today's sobered valuation of most broad-based tech houses is best expressed in this chart on Microsoft. It didn't keep pace with the market and badly underperformed NASDAQ over five years before showing late foot in 2014 (*Figure 37, page 286*).

Corporate profit margins today are high, but not excessively so, and inflation ain't around the corner, either, except for Knicks tickets and the Metropolitan Opera House, which has an attendance problem now with average orchestra seats at $195. Commodities like oil, copper and iron ore remain in a surplus condition. Both metallurgical and steam coal spot prices stick in the dumps despite serious cutbacks in production worldwide. Gold bugs no longer deride stock pickers and bond traders.

So 9/11 was truly a black swan event that has taken over a decade to run its course. The country's fiscal deficit now looks no more than 3 percent of GDP. This is a very respectable number, historically speaking, and could work lower in coming years as tax receipts rise from individuals and corporations.

I don't buy Robert Shiller's academic pronouncements on market valuation. Shiller goes back a decade and averages real earnings to calculate the S&P 500's price-earnings ratio. This is the old rearview mirror construct. The market is a discounting machine on what the future brings. Based on minimal interest rates and the low ratio of employment costs to revenues, corporate earnings at least for a couple of years remain growable, as is GDP. Shiller is right that the market over 13 years posted a meager 2.4 percent in real growth. I'm betting this changes.

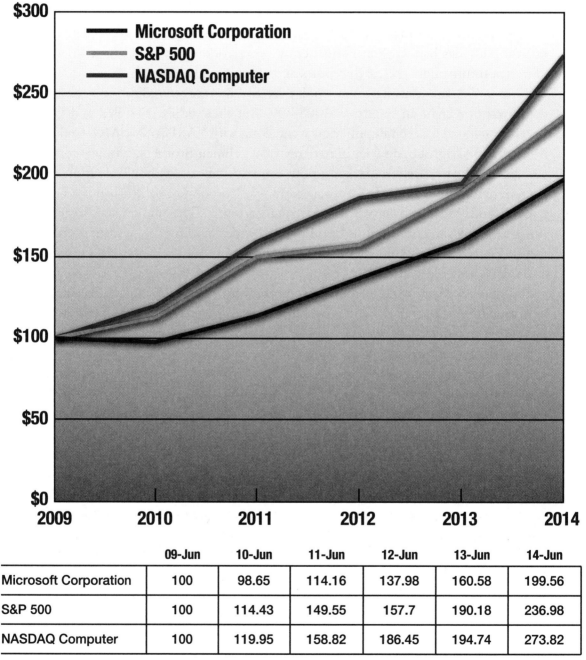

MICROSOFT'S 5-YEAR UNDERPERFORMANCE*
Among Microsoft Corporation, the S&P 500 Index and the NASDAQ Computer Index

	09-Jun	10-Jun	11-Jun	12-Jun	13-Jun	14-Jun
Microsoft Corporation	100	98.65	114.16	137.98	160.58	199.56
S&P 500	100	114.43	149.55	157.7	190.18	236.98
NASDAQ Computer	100	119.95	158.82	186.45	194.74	273.82

* $100 invested on 6/30/09 in stock or index, including reinvestment of dividends.

Figure 37

Source: Microsoft's 2014 Annual Report

The 2013 advance was 32 percent, the fifth-best market year over the past 50. Forklift truck jockeys no longer commanded much more than 10 bucks an hour. Jeff Bezos at Amazon took a strike in Germany over this issue. Look behind snappy 24-point headlines, written by copy editors with shiny pants. Does irrational exuberance radiate or rational discounting prevail? Forge your own working hypothesis on the years to come. Don't believe any economist unless he shows you his latest tax returns.

To paraphrase Warren Buffett: The past 238 years were pretty good for our country, but there is an elusive side to investing. You can't always solve for x using mathematical axioms. One of George Washington's horses, Blueskin, was rubbed down with white paste before our leader rode into town, his impeccable image artfully enhanced. This action is comparable with comparing GAAP earnings with non-GAAP numbers. There can be too wide a disparity. Technology investors need to make up their own minds which one is reality and which false ciphering. For a while, Twitter got away with paying out to its key employees 50 percent of its revenues in stock. Annualized share dilution ran at 8 percent. Nobody cared and then Twitter was cut in half *tout de suite*.

When Jerry Goodman ("Adam Smith"), an old, old buddy now gone, was interviewing Alan Greenspan decades ago, he asked Alan if what he did was "fun." Greenspan probably never had to field such a question, and he seemed nonplussed. Jerry, forever devilish and insouciant with bigwigs, had blindsided the oracle. He responded, "Well, not exactly" and moved on to more weighty pronouncements where he was at home. Central bankers don't talk like stand-up comics who, themselves, can be filled with wisdom. I find their seriousness almost laughable, the bankers whose pronouncements sound more like the blind man and the elephant, particularly in Japan and Euroland.

Chances are the Fed is going to be wrong, again, and miss the inflection point. I may have to eat these words, because the world surely is combustible. I see an accelerating economy mid-decade, led by the consumer. Deal activity, meanwhile, is a welcome tonic for the market. In this construct, fed funds rise sooner, but not enough to queer the bond crowd or top out the S&P 500.

Well into my SS years, I long for simplicity in my investment schemata. Thin files make me richer, when I go against the grain. Thick files adumbrate long-winded rationalizations for holding on to disappointing investments. I've learned to dump them and soldier on. The worst self-punishment is holding on to a property that has little chance of ever coming back. Let's face it: You never shoulda bought the dog.

Our neighbor John Madden once told me that in the Super Bowl, turnovers and injuries dictate the outcome. Think about XLIX. At Westminster, where over 2,000 dogs compete, there is an x factor unlike any other in national or regional dog shows: There are 10,000 spectators at Westminster who may not be an intimate part of the dog world. They're unaware of breed points that normally determine a dog's quality standing, but the crowd has lungs to express its choice. As for Westminster, wait till you see the secret weapon we bring out in 2015, a white toy poodle bitch with great presence. She moves like the wind. Steve Jobs once said to a colleague, "The journey is its own reward."

I'm sure Bill Gates and Steve Jobs never dwelled obsessively on how much money they'd amass during their lifetime of intensive concentration and productivity. The same goes for money managers, but we are measured every single day at 4:00 p.m. to the last decimal point, just like dogs. When I buy a stock or overconcentrate in a sector, I expect what I've done is good for the next five years. Apple, for example, traded in the thirties a decade ago. Overconcentration in financials hurt me one year but bore fruit in 2012, 2013 but not 2014. My framework is "the worst is over" for banks despite almost continuous headline risk. Nobody ever remembers yesterday's headlines, anyway.

I expected the U.S. Treasury would make money on their General Motors position but they sold prematurely, a political decision, and lost $11 billion. For stocks that are intrinsically valued, when operating results turn a little better, they soar. Does anyone remember Citigroup and Ford at a buck a share early 2009?

What happened to the country was, big sectors of the economy wound down to the level where they could easily rebound meaningfully. This embraced construction, capital goods and automobile demand. Most economists missed this phenomenon, but they've learned to forecast and re-forecast and thus catch up with events. Investors need to sensitize themselves more to intrinsically valued properties like GM, Apple, Google, even Microsoft, maybe JPMorgan Chase. Certainly Boeing, even Gilead Sciences.

Around the dinner table with friends, I'm invariably probed on how long the good times will last. Normally, I turn this question back. "Tell me why they can't last," I counter. "Every central bank in the world has endorsed an easy-money stance. Until we see wage inflation, stay the course. Nobody's goin' to bury Disney World!" I have no use for naysayers who stake out the "all is not well" territory of the natural bear. Did Roubini catch the inflection point of the market's bottom in early 2009 when bank stocks sold for a song? Absolutely not. Did Robert Shiller, so bearish on housing, catch the turn in prices and activity? I don't think so (*Figure 38*).

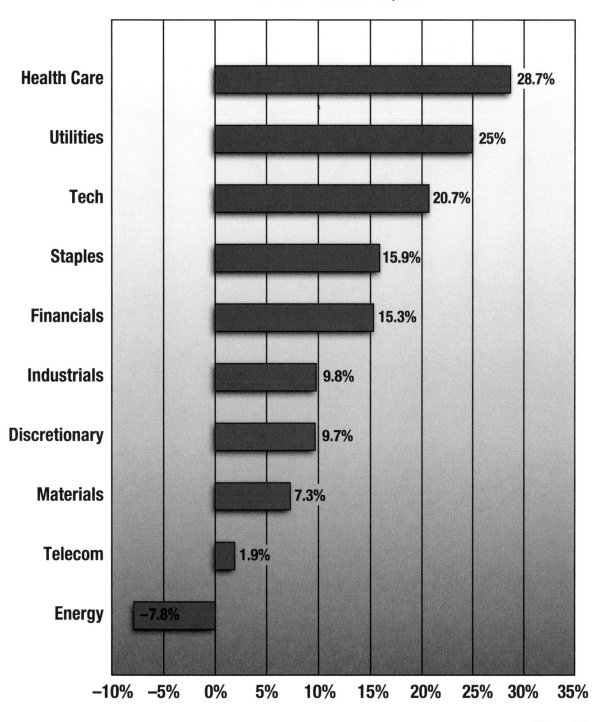

S&P 500 SECTOR RETURNS 2014
as of December 31, 2014

Health Care — 28.7%
Utilities — 25%
Tech — 20.7%
Staples — 15.9%
Financials — 15.3%
Industrials — 9.8%
Discretionary — 9.7%
Materials — 7.3%
Telecom — 1.9%
Energy — −7.8%

■ S&P 500 YTD Return

Figure 38
Source: FactSet

Disparate rates of return during 2014 for major sectors of the market determined how big capitalization money managers performed. Negative results for financials, energy and industrials surprised me, but buoyant technology and health care sectors made my year.

TWENTY-SEVEN

How to Compound
Inherited Wealth and Sleep Soundly

First, a brief history of financial markets:
- Stocks do better than bonds over a 25- to 50-year time span.
- Volatility of fixed income investments can equal that of equities in both directions.
- The market (S&P 500 Index) can sell at book value, sometimes two times book. Yields can range from 1 percent up to 5 to 6 percent at the bottom of a cycle.
- Thirty-year Treasuries, currently yielding 2.7 percent, in 1982 during FRB tightening yielded 15 percent. Five-year paper, too.
- Inflation now, imperceptible, under 1 percent, rose to 8 percent, early eighties. It made our country uncompetitive, as in General Motors.
- Dollar depreciation or appreciation can range between minus 25 percent and plus 25 percent.
- Deep-seated financial risk lurks in almost every type of asset. Banks capitalized at $200 billion can self-destruct with bad loans. AIG needed a government package of $180 billion to remain solvent.
- Municipalities, even countries, can bankrupt themselves. Consider Greece and Venezuela in 2015. Brazil, Iceland and Thailand were world destabilizing forces through their overleveraged banks even though their GDPs were miniscule. Chicago, Detroit, Sacramento, possibly New Jersey currently and New York City some 20 years ago saw the wolf at the door.
- Puerto Rico now hovers near basket case status.

From all this flux flows bedrock investment principles:
- Don't own muni paper rated below AA. To mitigate interest rate risk keep

291

bond duration averaging under 10 years.

- Be prepared to hold fixed income investments to maturity. Don't put more than 10 percent of assets in below investment grade corporates or in preferred stocks. Almost all preferred stocks are issued by financial corporations like banks and insurance underwriters. At the bottom of the financial meltdown in 2009, Bank of America's preferred sold at $5, sinking from its $25 par value. Citigroup's common stock bottomed at one buck before its 1-for-10 reverse split. Citi may not see its 2007 high, $560 adjusted, for the next 50 years, if then.
- You need a specialist investment manager for high yield securities. They'd need to log a risk adjusted return way above investment grade bonds as well as stocks.
- Don't retain an investment advisor for stock market participation. Buy an index fund from a reputable house like Fidelity Investments or Vanguard. Make sure their fees, all-in, hold under 20 basis points per annum. Your mindset must be to hold index funds through a full cycle—as long as five, 10, even 20 years. Don't trade in and out, the sure way to serfdom and self-loathing.
- Fix on a ratio of half equities, half bonds. In a historically low interest rate environment (today), hold maturities no longer than five years. If your tax rate is relatively high, municipals afford a better after-tax return than corporates and Treasuries.

March 2015, the stock market yielded under 2 percent and sold at 16 times forward 12-months' earnings projections. With 30-year Treasuries yielding 2.7 percent, 10-year paper at 2.1 percent and minimal inflation, stock market valuation remains within historical norms. In a low interest rate setting, markets levitate in tandem with earnings power, approximately 5 percent to 7 percent, annually, but not a given.

Fixed income investments currently aren't competitive with equity markets. The S&P 500 Index, weighted primarily by large capitalization companies—Apple over $700 billion and ExxonMobil near $400 billion—is the standard of measurement appropriate for passive but serious investors taking a long-term stance on their invested capital.

Remember, NASDAQ 100 is for speculators. Don't get involved in whether growth stocks or value paper is preferable. In the long run both come out neck 'n' neck. Investing offshore is laden with extra variables. Not just geopolitical risk but sizable currency exposure. Foreign accounting standards remain less rigorous

than ours.
- I don't invest in a property where I've concluded management is not socially responsible or its headman's character is impeachable.
- As Warren Buffett has written, you don't want to bet against America over 230 years going back to George Washington's presidency. No short selling or naked options writing necessary. You'll screw up your head and at best break even.
- Never wax emotional about what you own nor live in the past. Consider icons like IBM, Polaroid, Eastman Kodak and Xerox are either gone or much diminished, decade over decade. Remember you're just a number on a broker's ledger.

The average life of a growth stock rarely lasts over five years, and only a handful a decade or more. Your image of a corporation's viability and competitive mettle is probably 5 to 10 years out of date. They don't know you own their stock and love it passionately for its product offerings.

Disregard how I manage my own money. I've big blocks of capital in high yield debentures and preferred stocks. My muni portfolio is single A rated paper. I'm overconcentrated in a dozen stocks. They are researchable, understandable, liquid and aggressively managed. Leverage is usable for me because today it's cheap to borrow at 70 basis points. In short, I arbitrage money.

Mine is a super volatile group of stocks. They trade actively, millions of shares, daily. I can bang out all my investments while drinking a cup of java.

You won't rate money management status working at it 15 minutes, weekly. If you want to manage money like I do, concentrate 60 hours a week, get yourself an MBA and lease a Bloomberg console. Cream puffs don't get rich.

Deviate from these precepts, like the Commendatore in *Don Giovanni*, I'll come back in a shroud and intone dolorously, *repente!...repente!* The Don came to a very bad demise, engulfed in flames and dragged off to Hell like an inside trader.

TWENTY-EIGHT

My Bedrock Portfolio

PIET MONDRIAN,
Composition with Red, Blue and Grey, 1927
Private Collection

*T*his Mondrian canvas made £15.2 million at Sotheby's June '14 London auction. Financial markets keep me young and draw 90 percent of my attention span. The smell of the grease paint, the roar of the crowd. But $300 million for a Gauguin canvas catches my attention. Am I in the right business?

In the twenties, Mondrian lived off commissions for watercolors of flowers comparable with his early representational canvases. Then his abstract work turned ultra-minimal. In this piece he reduced the visual elements to five black lines on a white ground with just two small colored blocks. Later, Mondrian tested the force of painting colors against each other, boiled down to black against white. By 1930, his focus turned to just lines, some in color.

Poor Mondrian lived hand-to-mouth well into his sixties. Friends, including Hans Arp, once organized a lottery for his benefit in 1930. The painter received 300 francs from 25 subscribers. Architects like Philip Johnson were drawn to Mondrian's work because they, too, dealt with vibrant black lines. As late as 1941, a few years before his demise, working in New York, his canvases sold for as little as $400.

What determines a great money manager is extreme sensitivity to that fine line separating extreme order from total anarchy, meticulous control from disaster. When Ireland imploded in 2008 from mindless overbuilding of middle-class homes, thousands of horses were turned loose by their owners to starve and die in the very harsh winter, victims of home buyers' remorse. Knowing how much the Irish love horses, I construed this news as a bottom-of-cycle confirmation—for better or worse.

We live in a dangerously systemized world where you can be destroyed by the openness of life itself. I'm always trying to restore form in a messy universe. In 2009, if Bank of America survived, its preferred stock selling at $5, I reasoned, would be worth par or $25 a share before long. It actually edged above par in 2014. Near yearend '14, with oil futures in a free fall, the cost of credit default swaps on Russian and Venezuelan debt spiked, both potentially black swan events, but I wasn't ready to cut back my portfolio.

I don't measure personal performance against the S&P 500 Index, the common yardstick. First, I measure portfolio content against a Piet Mondrian abstract painting of the 1920s. Even the early landscape works celebrated some inherent sense of tragedy in nature, which he later eliminated in his abstract work as he moved towards giving up matter. "I construct lines and combinations of color on a flat picture frame with the aim of deliberately depicting a general sense of beauty...I abstract everything until I come to the essence of things. I believe this can be achieved through horizontal and vertical lines constructed in a conscious but non-calculating way and guided by a large degree of instruction, and reduced to a rhythm and harmony. There is nothing vague about this. It is only vague to a trivial person looking at nature."

This was Mondrian's personal interpretation of reality, not visible reality like the Cubists and Fauvists, but a cosmic reality. "One has to change natural appearance so that nature can be seen in a more pure (cosmic) manner." On the eve of World War I, when Mondrian was on holiday in the Netherlands, he was trapped there when hostilities broke out in August. His work then turned more intensive, a simplification of color, form and line as well as an unsentimental handling of paint.

All this reminded me of what I do as a prosaic money manager. Boiled down, I'm a manufacturer of money. If a failure, then I'm a destroyer of capital and should be terminated with extreme prejudice, or at least face voluntary retirement. I see myself dancing in a syncopated style through all the market's sectors and big-cap names like Apple, Google, Microsoft, Facebook, Gilead Sciences, Alibaba and Schlumberger. But there's a more apt metaphor than dancing. I see myself as a trapeze artist back-flipping high above the ground looking to grip the trapeze floating into my path.

Watch me singing and floating on their heads. Apple, I love you because you're misunderstood. You, too, Gilead. As for you, Schlumberger, you're one polite play on deepwater drilling, but it's too early. Just like Mondrian, I'm liberating myself from consensus figuration, including all sector lines other than horizontal and vertical. It doesn't matter if I'm wrong, just so long as I busy myself construing the future.

Mondrian possessed the best characteristics of a great money manager. First off, he had a theme, call it a vision, of reducing the world to its essentials. Then he executed the theme in his real world of canvas and paint. Those of us who thirst after mammon push buttons on our phones and place orders for stocks and bonds. Unless there's conviction that we are implementing a grand design, we are destined to fail. If our grand design is wrong, wimpish in execution, or the world changes suddenly and unexpectedly, we must change.

I assume anyone who invests seeks an above-average return on capital, but maybe not always so. For some, playing the market is like playing the ponies, a mindless distraction. For my brother-in-law, all his capital rests in short-term paper. He doesn't care that T-bills carry a negative rate of return adjusted for inflation or that some of us soared to the moon with Apple. He aims to sleep secure that his money is safe and available when called for. He's right—in his own way. I'm at the other end of the spectrum, craving the moon, taking as little risk as possible while retaining absolute liquidity. I can bang out my portfolio in 15 minutes, if necessary.

My decisions, hopefully, are research based, not dreamland. I speculate from facts and how I think they'll play out. Big-picture macro conclusions normally differ from those of the Federal Reserve Board, Wall Street's pundits, security analysts and other money managers. If I find myself within the consensus on financial markets for more than a day, I panic and try to figure out where I went astray.

The advent of jet aircraft, early sixties, afforded me a player's stake in the business. My hostile tender offer for Caesars World, coming on the eve of Black Monday, set me back a decade, but so what? Our journey is near its end, from my newspaper selling days in front of Yankee Stadium, then the 9/11 comeuppance following the Internet bubble, and the 2008–mid-2009 meltdown of our financial system. Tested. My sense of bedrock valuation conflicted with 1982's dire conflagration of 15 percent interest rates. So I bought. Today, regulators and investors finally are overly sensitized to the buildup in private sector lending, forever the tinderbox leading to loan defaults. Ironically, leverage has turned into a dirty word—except for individual players like me who borrow at 70 basis points. I arbitrage high yield bonds, master limited partnerships and equities. So far, so good.

My call on interest rates is moderate for longer in a GDP environment of at least normalized growth, probably more. The market is efficiently priced, but playable. Just be in viable sectors with the right horses between your thighs. Mondrian's late canvases show us how much you can paint yourself out of the picture and still make a deep impression. This is a great metaphor for investing. *Never wax emotional about what you own.* Stocks aren't your friends or enemies. Love your dog but hate ISIS. We are numbers on the ledgers of the brokerage houses we trade through, nothing more. Faceless!

In the interest of full disclosure I'm listing herein major holdings in my portfolio March 2015. I hope to gallop ahead for the next five years, but *quién sabe?* For 2014, I posted 15 percent, after a 52 percent gain for 2013. Gilead's correction at yearend cost me five percentage points, alone. My enormous overweighting in energy is solely pipeline infrastructure plays located in the Southwest and Midwest. MLPs also key off interest rates and growth in payout capacity. Many yield 4.5 percent or better. If interest rates escalated rapidly, I'd suffer. These positions were opened in 2009, when the group sold to yield 9 percent, valued under 10 times EBITDA. Many doubled and tripled but still rest fairly valued.

If my portfolio is hypercompressed, consider that Pershing Square Capital Management held 80 percent of its boodle in three stocks—Allergan, Canadian Pacific Railway and Air Products & Chemicals. All big winners. Our clients carry just 3 percent positions in Allergan and Canadian Pacific, the best management in railroads. This is a huge winner for Pershing that had nothing to do with deal dynamics. Pershing got there early and stayed the course. Its capital gain on Allergan, some $2.5 billion, was more than a double. Probably, half of the 80 percent concentration is from market appreciation. I've a huge 36 percent position in Gilead Sciences, but 75 percent is from its stock trajectory past two years. If you're puzzled by my 160 percent invested percentage, consider that I margin my account for 70 basis points interest. As long as you're right, it's known as arbitraging capital.

Martin Sosnoff Revocable Trust (March 2015)

Summary of Investments

	Percent of portfolio
Corporate bonds	8%
Municipal bonds	17%
Preferred stock	16%
Common stock	160%

Industrials	Percent of Portfolio
Boeing	6%
General Motors	3%
Delta Air Lines	9%
Total Industrials	18%

Health Care	Percent of portfolio
Actavis	14%
Biogen Idec	9%
Endo International	4%
Gilead Sciences	36%
Total Health Care	63%

Financials	Percent of portfolio
Bank of America	7%
Citigroup	10%
Total Financials	17%

Information Technology	Percent of portfolio
Apple	6%
Cisco Systems	6%
Micron Technology	6%
Facebook	6%
Total Technology	24%

Energy	Percent of portfolio
Energy Transfer Equity	10%
Enterprise Products Partners	8%
Regency Energy Partners	8%
Plains All American Pipeline	4%
Williams Partners	8%
Total Energy	38%

With serious capital in energy-related paper, it's a fair question—"Do they carry this guy out on a stretcher?" Consider: Nobody in the OPEC or non-OPEC world has forecasted accurately the price of a barrel of oil for more than six months straight. Professionals work within broad ranges. Years ago, the State of California tried to forecast the price of electric generation capacity, assuming a surplus and low quotes for natural gas. They sold power short and thereby raised their cost of electricity in the state by over $10 billion. Many economists as well as the greens and politicians shared blame for such insanity. (Who remembers this?)

Leon Hess probably enjoyed his holding in the New York Jets a helluva lot more than being married to Amerada Hess for 40 years. Return on capital got so low in the nineties for "big oil" that megamergers like Exxon and Mobil made sense. Exxon got bored just buying back their own stock, year after year. This still goes on, but now it's called "creating shareholder value." Does anybody but me remember when oil was $4 a barrel in the seventies, and even the mid-eighties when it was at $10 a barrel, and again at $10 in 1999? Exploration budgets flattened out, but a year later oil snapped back to $30 a barrel. Summer of 2014 we moved from well over par, tracking down below $50 yearend (*Figure 39, page 300*).

Oil futures dropped as low as $19 in November 2001, then spiked at $140 a barrel mid-2008. In retrospect, why oil ticked at $140 as the country lapsed into its financial funk and deep recession is beyond me. There's no such thing as an average or trendline price for oil. Note the drop from $110 in mid-2011 to $80 some 12 months later. I can't remember why! A more miserable contraction took place second half of '14. Rig operators like Transocean got diced into thirds. The U.S. Energy Information Administration's summer of '14 forecast for U.S. crude oil was $95. Months later their revised projection was for oil to average $77.75 during 2015. Supply, they noted, was rising three times as much as demand, some three million barrels. Come on, fellas, this didn't happen overnight! By early January '15, Brent futures ticked around $45.

I cotton more to matzoh farfel than I do to oil. Assume somewhere between $50 and $75 a barrel could be the going price for oil next year or two. This reduces pipeline rates of return but doesn't destroy the investment case. I don't need Bernie Baruch telling me to sell down to the sleeping level. If I have to, I'll execute same. It won't be the first time I proved wrong-footed, tossed my goods into a dumpster and started fresh. I believe natural gas, not coal, is the boiler fuel for the country's utilities, looking ahead 10 years. Kinder Morgan, for example, is a major natural gas pipeline owner-operator with rising throughput.

THE ROLLER COASTER IN OIL FUTURES
2000–2014

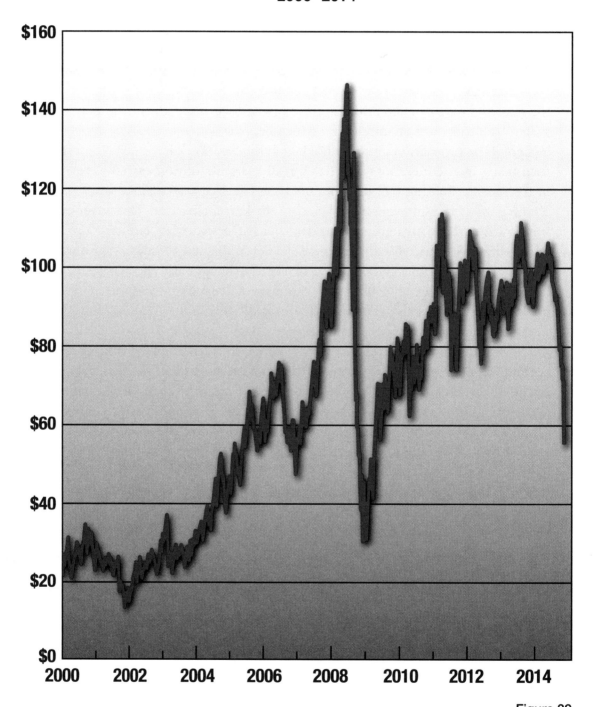

Figure 39
Source: Bloomberg

The initial MLP investments made in '09 played on interest rates, but became the means of passing capital to my children while I avoided ordinary income taxes. Their correction at yearend '14 was understandable, but dividend payouts stand mainly intact. I've started buying more on big down days. This is either benign fortitude or sheer insanity.

Mondrian lived hand-to-mouth into his sixties. Last two paintings, *Broadway Boogie Woogie* and *Victory Boogie Woogie*, seemed exercises in destruction through repetition. There is no geometric identity, just color and rhythm. In the end game, Mondrian won by destroying form, if not painting itself. He called it "shredding the useless clothing of the world." *Victory Boogie Woogie* rested on his easel after nine months' work, unfinished, when Mondrian was ambulanced to Murray Hill Hospital with pneumonia and expired on February 1, 1944.

My pet name for the Big Board is "The Great Humbler." Nobody maxes the macro picture for more than a couple of quarters, running. Stock picking? We're talking about batting averages. Ted Williams hit .406 one season. Nobody since is a challenger. Who extrapolated Brent oil futures below $50 a barrel?

I remember Williams expounding that you can fit 24 baseballs over home plate worth swinging at. Everything else, take for a ball. Never have I owned more than 24 stocks. A dozen feels right. How else outperform? Just months before its fall, 24 analysts out of 32 labeled Schlumberger "Outperform." If you scroll down the top 25 names in the S&P 500 Index, normally, no more than one in three are standouts. For every Apple there's a losing Google. Iconic names of the past like IBM, ExxonMobil and JPMorgan Chase lag badly. Major bank stocks shed 10 percent on their yearend '14 financial reports.

For every Facebook there's a Twitter. General Motors drove south last year, but Canadian Pacific Railway was hot stuff until oil futures collapsed. Mark it down 20 percent. Gilead Sciences quadrupled over two years, then corrected 15 percent practically overnight when Express Scripts chose AbbVie over Gilead for its price-competitive hepatitis C drug of record.

Punditry isn't worth two cents. Interest rates and inflation softened rather than quickened during 2014, early '15. Operating profit margins for major corporations held firm rather than softening. The euro wanes while the dollar waxes. Coming off a great year in 2013, the market still turned in double-digit numbers for 2014. Few of us expected such largesse. Weighting sectors, practically everyone missed the 28 percent rise in electric utilities. Nobody forecasted the collapse in oil prices from $115 a barrel to $50. Most professionals coalesced around par for 2015. The reciprocal of declining oil quotes is airline stocks. A few analysts banged the table, but money managers with long memories of airline bankruptcies passed on this concept of rationalization for a leveraged industry. The collapse in industrial commodities like coal, steel, iron ore, copper and nickel went much further south than expected. Coal properties like Arch Coal and Walter Energy sell at their option value, near a buck a share. Their debentures sell to yield 40 percent or more.

The biggest miss of all, domestically, was and still is the course of long maturity Treasuries and the shape of the yield curve. It wasn't supposed to flatten during 2014 and ease further in 2015. Bank net interest margins mid-2014 were to levitate, but they didn't. I still borrow money tied to LIBOR—at 70 basis points. Arbitraging cheap funds against high yield bonds, thought a dead man's hand, proved a big winner along with muni paper and preferred stocks.

So-called smart money departed these fixed income sectors, but where do they go for yield? The answer is junk. Last year, my high yield portfolio kept pace with equities, and I didn't spend more than 30 minutes thinking about it. I expended dozens of intensive hours doping out Internet properties like Amazon, Google, Facebook and Alibaba, with nothing to show for it but heartburn.

Here are the big upsets I see coming; positive and negative:

- Oil ranges between $50 and $70 a barrel for a couple of years. Worldwide production rises at a 1.5 million barrel per day clip. The Saudis hang tough. Yields and intrinsic value keep international producers from a free fall.
- Interest rates remain flattish. Bank stock earnings stick underleveraged for net interest margins. Loan losses surface for them in Greece and Venezuela. Analysts no longer believe major banks can earn more than 10 percent on tangible capital. The stocks, again, could underperform.
- Deal activity surprises everyone—on the upside. Staid properties like Dow Chemical and DuPont realign their businesses. The health care sector explodes, with maybe a half dozen $50-billion deals comparable with Allergan put into play. Old pharma companies, as in Merck, Eli Lilly and Johnson & Johnson, leverage comfortable capital structures to make deals that count accretive to earnings in year two. The S&P 500 benefits by 5 percent in 2015 because of deals, alone.
- Low-multiple technology properties outperform many high flyers. I'm talking about Micron Technology and Hewlett-Packard, but not IBM and Intel. Money managers tire of playing the greater fool game. Stocks like Salesforce. com, Amazon, Twitter and others selling at huge multiples of revenues and EBITDA show no late foot.

Some issues I refuse to forecast: When Euroland turns around; China's GDP growth rate next couple of years; when Japan emerges from its funk and whether Greece leaves the European monetary union. No idea which Internet property excels, but I'm betting on Alibaba. So far, I'm wrong.

None of these variables should seriously impact our financial markets, but the noise level stays high and staccato. U.S. fiscal condition hasn't been so strong in decades in terms of tax receipts, comfortable debt service and the size of our deficit relative to GDP, maybe as low as 2 percent in 2015.

Our economy, like China's, proves self-generating, with the consumer carrying GDP to a 4 percent growth rate. We don't even need capex and housing kicking in. Why doesn't Obama seize these talking points? The Big Board outperforms the Morgan Stanley World Index. Only valuation keeps us from elevating more. BB bonds run neck 'n' neck with the S&P 500 Index, but Treasuries barely earn their coupon, a measly 2.5 percent for 30-year paper.

I inventory stocks where the analyst and money manager community is seriously but legitimately divided. These "lady or tiger" stocks embrace Boeing, Gilead, Biogen Idec, Alibaba, Micron, even Apple, Microsoft and Delta Air Lines.

Money management stands forever as the reciprocal to Mondrian painting himself out of the picture. Simply, you are forever what you do, not what you think about or don't fully execute. And they'll measure you in decimal points, exactly. Like *Victory Boogie Woogie*, money management sticks forever as an unfinished work in process.

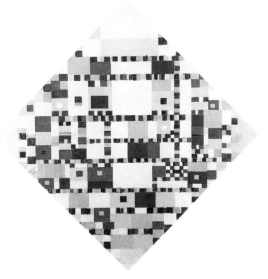

PIET MONDRIAN, *VICTORY BOOGIE WOOGIE (UNFINISHED)*, 1942–1944
Collection of Gemeentemuseum, The Hague

APPENDIX

Lifetime List of Great Operators

Retailing	Company	Yearend 2014 Market Valuation (in billions)
Sam Walton	Wal-Mart	$273
Ray Kroc	McDonald's	$93
Bernard Marcus, Arthur Blank	Home Depot	$130
Leslie Wexner	L Brands	Privatized
Phil Knight	Nike	$85
Howard Schultz	Starbucks	$60
Industrials		
J. Irwin Miller	Cummins	$26
Marcel & Conrad Schlumberger	Schlumberger	$111
Elon Musk	Tesla Motors	$25
Charles & David Koch	Koch Industries	Est. $80
Technology		
Joe Wilson	Haloid-Xerox	$14
Steve Jobs	Apple	$680
Tom Watson, Sr.	IBM	$163
Bill Gates	Microsoft	$396
Gordon Moore	Intel	$180
Larry Ellison	Oracle	$186
Paul Jacobs, Sr.	Qualcomm	$124
John Chambers	Cisco Systems	$142
Internet Purveyors		
Jack Ma	Alibaba	$250
Mark Zuckerberg	Facebook	$200
Larry Page & Sergey Brin	Google	$360
Jeff Bezos	Amazon	$146

Financial Services	Company	Yearend 2014 Market Valuation (in billions
Warren Buffett	Berkshire Hathaway	$368
The Sandlers	Golden West Financial	Privatized
Sam Zell	Equity Office Properties	$17
Larry Tisch	Loews	$17
Charles Schwab	Charles Schwab	$35
Michael Bloomberg	Bloomberg	Est. $35
Carl Icahn	Investments	Est. $28
Michael Milken	Investments	Est. $2.5
Media Entertainment		
Ralph & Brian Roberts	Comcast	$147
Walt Disney	Walt Disney	$158
Steve Wynn	Wynn Resorts	$22
Sheldon Adelson	Las Vegas Sands	$60
John Malone	Liberty Media	$32
Rupert Murdoch	21st Century Fox	$80
Bill Paley	CBS	$35
Ted Turner	Turner Broadcasting	Sold
Health Care		
Alejandro Zaffaroni	Syntex	Sold

Few industrialists make my list. Even fewer oilmen. Integrated oil operators are mainly custodial managers. No new John D. Rockefellers, creating Standard Oil. Carnegie, Guggenheim, even Vanderbilt and Jay Gould were turn-of-the-19th-century phenomenons who rolled up railroads, steel and copper producers. They, along with the Rosenwalds of Sears, Roebuck, created the blue chips for the first half of the 20th century. IBM came later with its 360 computer. Excepting Wells Fargo and JPMorgan Chase, our biggest bank, Citigroup, declined 97 percent by November 2008 and had to be bailed out because it carried $2 trillion in assets on its balance sheet. Lehman Brothers, much smaller, was allowed to fail. Both Citi and Lehman were leveraged at the top almost 100 to 1 in terms of equity. ¡Nunca más!

Larry Tisch's comments to me on Wall Street turned prophetic. "There are 200 guys in the Garment Center smarter than headmen at big banks and brokerage houses. The only difference is the garmentos can't get the leverage The Street commands." Modestly leveraged insurance underwriters like MetLife and Allstate easily made it through 2008–'09, pretty much intact. AIG, which had foolishly guaranteed a trillion in credit default swaps, needed over a $100 billion transfusion to survive the deluge. Hank Greenberg, its old maximum leader, turned loose a flurry of litigation against the government, but so far to no avail.

I've dropped Edwin Land of Polaroid into purgatory because he couldn't survive technological change in photo imaging. His was a great run, late forties to mid-sixties, the number-one growth stock for over a decade. Syntex, first out with a birth control pill, couldn't build on their culture-changing phenomenon, either, but the stock made me rich, along with Haloid-Xerox, Hertz and Time Inc., late fifties, early sixties. My many runners-up include David Geffen, Eli Broad, Steven Spielberg, Bill McGowan, even Jeff Koons, Craig McCaw and Charlie Ergen of Dish, Steve Roth of Vornado and Leon Hess.

INDEX

Page numbers in *italics* refer to figures and illustrations.

About the Author

Martin Sosnoff is chief investment officer and CEO of Atalanta Sosnoff Capital, LLC, managing approximately $6 billion in assets. His career on Wall Street spans over fifty years. He has authored two books on the money management business, *Humble on Wall Street* and *Silent Investor, Silent Loser,* and has been an active columnist through the years, presently writing a weekly blog on Forbes.com. Martin and his wife, Toni, divide their time between upstate New York, NYC and Florida. Inclusive in their lives are their children, grandchildren, eight poodles and three competing dressage horses.